Hindu Law and Legal Theory

The International Library of Essays in Law and Legal Theory
Series Editor: Tom D. Campbell

Schools

Natural Law, Vols I & II *John Finnis*
Justice *Thomas Morawetz*
Law and Economics, Vols I & II *Jules Coleman and Jeffrey Lange*
Critical Legal Studies *James Boyle*
Marxian Legal Theory *Csaba Varga*
Legal Reasoning, Vols I & II *Aulis Aarnio and D. Neil MacCormick*
Legal Positivism *Mario Jori*
American Legal Theory *Robert Samuel Summers*
Postmodernism and Law *Dennis Patterson*
Law in History, Vols I & II *David Sugarman*
Law and Language *Fred Schauer*
Sociological Theories of Law *Kahei Rokumoto*
Rights *Carlos Nino*
Law and Psychology *Martin Lyon Levine*
Feminist Legal Theory, Vols I & II *Frances Olsen*
Law and Society *Roger Cotterrell*
Contemporary Criminological Theory *Francis T. Cullen and Velmer S. Burton Jr.*

Areas

Criminal Law *Thomas Morawetz*
Tort Law *Ernest J. Weinrib*
Contract Law, Vols I & II *Larry Alexander*
Anti-Discrimination Law *Christopher McCrudden*
Consumer Law *Iain Ramsay*
International Law *Martti Koskenniemi*
Property Law, Vols I & II *Elizabeth Mensch and Alan Freeman*
Constitutional Law *Mark V. Tushnet*
Procedure *D.J. Galligan*
Evidence and Proof *William Twining and Alex Stein*
Company Law *Sally Wheeler*
Privacy, Vols I & II *Raymond Wacks*
Lawyers' Ethics *David J. Luban*
Administrative Law *D.J. Galligan*
Child Law *Harry D. Krause*
Family Law, Vols I & II *Harry D. Krause*
Welfare Law *Peter Robson*
Medicine and the Law *Bernard M. Dickens*
Commercial Law *Ross Cranston*
Environmental Law *Michael C. Blumm*
Conflict of Laws *Richard Fentiman*
Law and Religion *Wojciech Sadurski*
Human Rights Law *Philip Alston*
European Community Law, Vols I & II *Francis Snyder*
Tax Law, Vols I & II *Patricia D. White*
Media Law *Eric Barendt*
Labour Law *David L. Gregory*
Alternative Dispute Resolution *Michael D.A. Freeman*

Legal Cultures

Comparative Legal Cultures *Csaba Varga*
Law and Anthropology *Peter Sack*
Hindu Law and Legal Theory *Ved Nanda*
Islamic Law and Legal Theory *Ian Edge*
Chinese Law and Legal Theory *Michael Palmer*
Russian Legal Theory *W. Butler*
Common Law *Michael Arnheim*
Japanese Law and Legal Theory *Koichiro Fujikura*
Law and Development *Anthony Carty*
Jewish Law and Legal Theory *Martin P. Golding*
Legal Education *Martin Lyon Levine*
Civil Law *Ralf Rogowski*
African Law and Legal Theory *Gordon Woodman and Akintunde Obilade*

Future Volume
Cumulative index

Hindu Law and Legal Theory

Edited by

Ved P. Nanda

Evans University Professor and Director
International Legal Studies Program
University of Denver

and

Surya Prakash Sinha

Professor Emeritus
Pace University School of Law
Associate, Columbia University Seminar on Peace

NEW YORK UNIVERSITY PRESS
REFERENCE COLLECTION

First published in the USA in 1996 by
NEW YORK UNIVERSITY PRESS
Washington Square
New York NY 10003

Library of Congress Cataloging-in-Publication Data
Hindu law & legal theory / edited by Ved P. Nanda and Surya Prakash Sinha.
p. cm. – (International library of essays in law and legal theory. Legal cultures ; 12)
ISBN 0-8147-5772-3
1. Hindu law. 2. Dharma. I. Nanda, Ved P. II. Sinha, S. Prakash. III. Series.
KNS122.H56 1997
349'.54–dc20
[345.4] 96-43414
CIP

;ontents

PART III MODERN HINDU LAW

Acknowledgements

The editors and publishers wish to thank the following for permission to use copyright material.

American Association for the Comparative Study of Law for the essays: Harrop A. Freeman (1959), 'An Introduction to Hindu Jurisprudence', *American Journal of Comparative Law*, **8**, pp. 29–43; J. Duncan M. Derrett (1958), 'Statutory Amendments of the Personal Law of Hindus Since Indian Independence', *American Journal of Comparative Law*, **7**, pp. 380–93.

Boston College Third World Law Journal for the essay: Gita Gopal (1993), 'Gender and Economic Inequality in India: The Legal Connection', *Boston College Third World Law Journal*, **13**, pp. 63–86.

Hastings Law Journal for the essay: Ludo Rocher (1978), 'Hindu Conceptions of Law', *Hastings Law Journal*, **29**, pp. 1283–305.

The International and Comparative Law Quarterly for the essays: Günther-Dietz Sontheimer (1964), 'Recent Developments in Hindu Law', *International and Comparative Law Quarterly Supplement*, **8**, pp. 32–45. Copyright © International and Comparative Law Quarterly. This article is reproduced from 1964, I.C.L.Q., 8, pp. 32–45, with permission from the publishers, The British Institute of International and Comparative Law, 17 Russell Square, London WC1B 5DR; Alan Gledhill (1954), 'The Influence of Common Law and Equity on Hindu Law Since 1800', *International and Comparative Law Quarterly*, **3**, pp. 576–603. Copyright © International and Comparative Law Quarterly. This article is reproduced from 1954, I.C.L.Q., 3, pp. 576–603 with permission from the publishers, The British Institute of International and Comparative Law, 17 Russell Square, London WC1B 5DR.

Journal of Family Law for the essay: Ram Singh (1966), 'Matrimonial Property Law Among Hindus', *Journal of Family Law*, **6**, pp. 129–55.

Law and Society Association for the essay: Ludo Rocher (1968–69), '"Lawyers" in Classical Hindu Law', *Law and Society Review*, **3**, pp. 383–402. Reprinted by permission of the Law and Society Association.

Ved P. Nanda (1960), 'Marriage and Divorce in India: Conflicting Laws', *Northwestern University Law Review*, **55**, pp. 624–34, 645–7. Copyright © 1960 Ved P. Nanda.

Surya Prakash Sinha (1995), 'Non-Universality of Law', *Archiv Für Rechts und Sozial-philosophie*, **81**, pp. 200–205. Copyright © 1995 by Surya Prakash Sinha.

Sweet & Maxwell Limited for the essay: S.G. Vesey-FitzGerald (1923), 'The Place of Hindu Law in Comparative Jurisprudence', *Law Quarterly Review*, **39**, pp. 357–71.

Albrecht Wezler (1982), 'Manu's Omniscience: On the Interpretation of *Manusmrti* II, 7', in *Indology and Law: Studies in Honor of Professor J. Duncan M. Derrett* (eds), Günther-Dietz Sontheimer and Parmeswara Kota Aithal, Wiesbaden: Franz Steiner Verlag, pp. 79–105. Copyright © 1982 Albrecht Wezler.

Every effort has been made to trace all the copyright holders but if any have been inadvertently overlooked, the publishers will be pleased to make the necessary arrangement at the first opportunity.

Series Preface

The International Library of Law and Legal Theory is designed to provide important research materials in an accessible form. Each volume contains essays of central theoretical importance in its subject area. The series as a whole makes available an extensive range of valuable material which will be of considerable interest to those involved in the research, teaching and study of law.

The series has been divided into three sections. The Schools section is intended to represent the main distinctive approaches and topics of special concern to groups of scholars. The Areas section takes in the main branches of law with an emphasis on essays which present analytical and theoretical insights of broad application. The section on Legal Cultures makes available the distinctive legal theories of different legal traditions and takes up topics of general comparative and developmental concern.

I have been delighted and impressed by the way in which the editors of the individual volumes have set about the difficult task of selecting, ordering and presenting essays from the immense quantity of academic legal writing published in journals throughout the world. Editors were asked to pick out those essays from law, philosophy and social science journals which they consider to be fundamental for the understanding of law, as seen from the perspective of a particular approach or sphere of legal interest. This is not an easy task and many difficult decisions have had to be made in order to ensure that a representative sample of the best journal essays available takes account of the scope of each topic or school.

I should like to express my thanks to all the volume editors for their willing participation and scholarly judgement. The interest and enthusiasm which the project has generated is well illustrated by the fact that an original projection of 12 volumes drawn up in 1989 has now become a list of some 60 volumes. I must also acknowledge the vision, persistence and constant cheerfulness of John Irwin and the marvellous work done by Mrs Margaret O'Reilly and Sonia Hubbard.

TOM D. CAMPBELL
Series Editor
The Faculty of Law
The Australian National University

Introduction

I

'e reject the notion held generally in Western legal thought for over 2000 years that law something universal. A consequence of that thought has been to identify in various ocieties symptoms that respond to the notions of law and call them law. There has even een a tendency to gauge civilized achievement on the basis of these symptoms and to ank societies using that scale under which Western societies excel in civilized attainment, s, for example, was done by Henry Sumner Maine[1] or even H.L.A. Hart[2].

The history of various civilizations, their anthropology and their philosophy, however, ell us that civilizations have developed different concepts as their fundamental principles f social organization. Law is only one such principle, which, in Western civilization, is erived from the Greek concept of *nomos*. The Chinese civilization has its *li*. African ocieties have their own particular patterns. And the Hindu civilization has its *dharma*, hose meaning is broader than law alone.

Fundamental to the formation of these principles in the various civilizations has been eir respective cosmologies, that is to say, their views of the relationship between man nd his universe. The *nomos* cosmology, in which order is imposed from outside, has roduced an abstract way of thinking and speculating about the laws of nature. This has enerated the potential for man-made law. The creation of law is attributed to a law-giver. he validity of the precepts depends upon the authoritative statement, promulgated publicly, bout those precepts. The precepts are furthered through specific commands. Consequently, e need arises to establish and justify rights and duties to delineate and effectuate the law.

The cosmology underlying *li* generated the idea of order wherein ways of conduct regulate an's worldly existence in harmony with nature, thereby obviating the need for commands manating from an outside source. This produces a general and all-pervasive way of life. *i* becomes the social obligation directed towards the harmonious state of the world. The alidity of *li* precepts does not depend upon their authoritative statement promulgated ublicly. Instead of following an abstract way of thinking about laws of nature, *li* is made oncrete in socially-created *wu lan* relationships. Individual rights are not contemplated, or the concomitant of the antagonistic behaviour of claiming those rights is excluded by e concept of seeking an all-embracing harmony within all human relations. The important sk becomes the discovery of obligation, not the justification of laws and of rights and uties under those laws. The internal coherence of this duty-bound way of life cannot be ound through an institutionalization of rights.

The *dharma* cosmology produced the conception of order-that-exists, as contrasted with e *nomos* idea of divine agencies creating the universe and gods issuing commands for overnance, from which came the idea in the West of earthly rulers giving law in society. he order in *dharma* is pre-ordained. *Dharma* produces in man a conviction of duty to omply with this pre-existing order of *rta*. Consequently, *dharma* has produced authoritative texts to teach man his duty to support the *dharmic* state of the world. Instead of proceeding along the basis of specific commands, *dharma* – like *li* and unlike *nomos* – produces a general and all-pervasive way of life as an organizational principle of existence. Attribution of precepts to a law-giver, therefore, has no place here, although *dharma*, as distinguished from *li*, does have sacred literature of eternal validity, namely the *sruti* literature of the *Vedas*, *Brahamanas*, *Aranyakas* and *Upanishads*. The Hindu *dharmasastras*, or treatises on *dharma*, have as their task to show man his duty and to guide him in close adherence to *sruti*, not the articulation and distribution of individual rights. In the internal coherence of these duty-bound ways, the important task becomes the discovery of that obligation and awareness of its hidden sources.[3]

Thus, to reiterate, law is only one of the several fundamental principles of social organization produced by various civilizations in their own particular historicity. And although *vidhi* is the official Hindi translation for law under the constitution of India, the Sanskrit word to express both religion and law has been *dharma*. It is not appropriate to reduce *dharma* to law, for *dharma* does not equal law but is broader than law, and Hindu law is a part of *dharma*.

II

Next, then, the question arises how we are to comprehend the development that has been called Hindu law. There are at least four different settings in which the term 'Hindu law' has been used: (1) as a synonym for *dharma*; (2) as the precepts of behaviour found in the literature of the *Vedas*, *Dharmasutras* and *Dharmasastras*, and elaborated in various commentaries; (3) as part of the indigenous custom given effect by the British rulers; and (4) as the personal law of the Hindus given effect by the courts, both in the British period and in the post-independence era.

Hindu Law as a Synonym for Dharma

Although law does not equal *dharma*, the terms have been used as synonyms. The root of the word *dharma* – *dhar* – connotes the act of maintaining, keeping, preserving, holding. In *Mahabharata*, Bhishma explains the meaning and scope of *dharma*: 'It is most difficult to define *Dharma*. *Dharma* has been explained to be that which helps the upliftment of living beings. Therefore, that which ensures welfare of [living beings] is surely *Dharma*. The learned *rishis* have declared [that] that which sustains is *Dharma*.'[4]

The concept of *dharma* may be hard to define, but it guides the way in which one ought to and does act; it is the way in which the cosmos is maintained.[5] As Justice Ramajois explains, *dharma* is that which 'sustains and ensures progress and welfare of all in this world'.[6] *Dharma* guides all the activities of every individual and, as Professor Rocher states:

> [*D*]*harma* is the way in which every constituent element of the cosmos contributes its share to maintaining the overall balance. Each element has its own *dharma*, its *svadharma*. As long as each element of the cosmos performs its specific *svadharma*, the overall balance does not suffer. As soon as an element, however, deviates from its own *dharma*, that is, commits *adharma*, the balance is disturbed.[7]

As Professor Rocher further explains:

> The *dharma* ordains when the individual shall awaken, how that person shall divide the day, and when the person shall retire at night. The *dharma* rules a person's diet, quantitatively and qualitatively. The *dharma*, of course, regulates the human's relationship to the supernatural powers, and prescribes the rituals and ceremonies by which these relations shall be sustained; it therefore deals with the Hindu's religion. *Dharma* also governs the individual's relations with fellow people; it rules social contacts, many aspects of which belong to the field of law. To put it differently, Hindu law is, together with every other aspect of a Hindu's activities, part of Hindu *dharma*. Hindu rules of law are to be found in the *dharmasastras*, but these texts also contain a variety of other rules which have little or nothing in common with law.[8]

As to the sources of *dharma*, *Manusmriti* states: '*Veda* is the first source of *dharma*. The expression by the Seers (*Smritikaras*), handed down from generation to generation by memory, the virtuous conduct of those who are well versed in the *Vedas*, and lastly, what is agreeable to the good conscience, are the other sources.'[9]

Hindu Law as Precepts of Behaviour Found in the Literature

The oldest source of Hindu law is *Sruti* (that which is heard), which is believed to be of divine inspiration, revealed by a number of privileged sages, and heard and handed down verbally from generation to generation. *Sruti* consists of the four *Vedas* – *Rig Veda*, *Yajur Veda*, *Sama Veda* and *Atharva Veda* – and six auxiliary works called *Vedangas*, and generally also extends to the *Aranyakas* and *Upanishads*. The *Vedas* and the *Dharma* are generally treated as synonymous.

Sruti addresses primarily religious issues. None of its provisions directly pertains to law or the legal system, although several contain enumerated positive (*Vidhis*) or negative (*Nishedhas*) ideals or injunctions regarding social life, such as: (1) 'Tell the truth', (2) 'Never tell untruth', (3) 'Never hurt anyone', and (4) 'Follow *Dharma*'.[10] These injunctions lie at the foundation of the *Smriti* laws. To illustrate,

> [T]here are provisions in the *Smritis* for punishing plaintiff, defendant and witnesses, for giving false evidence, which have their source in the first two *Vidhis*. There are provisions declaring that acts causing injury to human beings and even to animals as offences and penalties are prescribed, the basis of which is the third *Vidhi*. The *Smritis* declare that a conduct censored by *Dharma* (law) alone gives a cause of action before a court, and the law on contract provides that a contract contrary to *Dharma* (law) is void and unenforceable. This can be traced to the fourth [Follow *Dharma*] *Vidhi*.[11]

Smriti (that which is remembered) is often translated as 'tradition' in order to distinguish it from *Sruti* or 'revelation'. The *Smriti* literature is also known as the *Dharmasastras*, a term used for both *Dharmasutras* and *Dharmasastras*, which collectively constitute the primary sources of classical Hindu *Dharma*. The former are in the form of *sutras* or aphorisms, while the latter are in the form of *slokas* or verses. Of the three classes of *sutras*, only the *Dharmasutras* address questions of civil and criminal law, thus constituting the foundation of the Hindu legal system; the other two primarily regulate rituals related to the stages of life, especially that of *grahashthya* or householder.

The *Dharmasastras* or Legal Institutes show a developed legal and judicial system. They were a codification of the legal principles contained in the *Vedas* and *Dharmasutras*, and also those in usage and practice in society, for the *Smritis* provided for *sadachara* – usage, custom, practices and good conduct – to be one of the sources of law.[12] They also provided for the constitution, composition and gradations of courts of law, qualification of judges and their appointment, and procedural law. To illustrate, *Manusmriti*, one of the most important *smritis*, prescribes rules of procedure as it enumerates 18 *vivadapadas* (paths or areas of dispute), these being:

> (1) non-payment of debts [,] ... (2) deposit and pledge, (3) sale without ownership, (4) concerns among partners, and (5) resumption of gifts, (6) [n] on-payment of wages, (7) non-performance of agreements, (8) rescission of sale and purchase, (9) disputes between the owner [of cattle] and his servants, (10) [d] isputes regarding boundaries, (11) assault, (12) defamation, (13) theft, (14) robbery and violence, (15) adultery, (16) [d] uties of man and wife, (17) partition [of inheritance], (18) gambling and betting.[13]

In a later period, rules of interpretation of laws (*mimamsa*) were developed in order to elaborate upon the *Vedas*, *Dharmasutras* and *Smritis*. Various *Nibhandas* or commentaries and digests on the *Smritis*, written by eminent jurists, contributed to a further growth of Hindu law. The commentators clarified the ambiguous and occasionally conflicting rules contained in the *Smritis* and recommended the adoption of those which they thought reasonable. They addressed themselves to questions of the substantive law (*Vivada*), the procedural law (*Vyavahara*) and the administrative law (*Niti*).

Among other sources of Hindu law are the two epics, *Ramayana* and *Mahabharata*, and *Kautalyas's Arthasastra*, an important treatise on statecraft written between 322 B.C. and 300 B.C. by Chanakya, who was the prime minister of King Chandragupta Maurya.

The Indigenous Custom and Personal Law of Hindus

Starting in 1772, the British rulers decided that Hindus should be governed by their own laws in several areas of private law.[14] Thus, *Dharmasastras* began to be used in the courts to resolve disputes among Hindus that related generally to issues pertaining to family law, property, succession and religious usage. By the end of the century, courts started using the Sanskrit texts as statutes. However, several areas of the law were codified on the British model, such as the Indian Penal Code in 1860, the Criminal Procedure Code in 1898, the Indian Evidence Act in 1872 and the Code of Civil Procedure in 1908. In certain areas, such as torts, English law was transplanted through judicial decisions. The applicable law was 'subject to modification by custom, which varied from time to time, place to place, family to family, and caste to caste. ...'[15]

Since the British judges were not conversant either with the Sanskrit language or with Hindu religious traditions and usages, the pandits (Hindu law officers of the court who were sworn to give their opinion according to the *sastras*) were appointed to research and interpret the applicable laws. As Professor Rocher points out:

> [T] he judges introduced a few changes of their own. They arbitrarily separated law from religion. The commentaries were, relatively speaking, the least ambiguous sources of law, therefore the

judges reversed the traditional hierarchy, and stated that the wording of the commentary overrules that of the *dharmasastra*, and the latter that of the Vedas. They gradually avoided consulting and reinterpreting the translations of Sanskrit texts by making Hindu law into a regular case law, invoking precedent and *stare decisis*. When the Hindu lawbooks appeared to be unacceptable, they overruled them on the grounds of justice, equity, and good conscience.[16]

Serious efforts were undertaken to codify Hindu private law during the period preceding the independence of India in 1947, but these bore no fruit as there was no consensus on the underlying basic principles. However, modifications in Hindu law have proceeded through legislation which began as far back as 1850 with the adoption of The Caste Disabilities Removal Act. This abrogated the provisions of Hindu law which deprived persons from their right of inheritance on loss of caste. These modifications by the British authorities pertained primarily to matters of marriage, property and inheritance. Following Independence and the coming into force of the Constitution of India on 26 January 1950, Hindu law continued to be the personal law governing Hindus for such matters as inheritance, succession, marriage, gifts and partition, though it has been further modified by the following: the 1954 Special Marriage Act, the 1956 Hindu Marriage Act (amended further by the Hindu Marriage Amendment Act (1976)), the 1956 Hindu Succession Act, the 1956 Hindu Minority and Guardianship Act and the 1956 Hindu Adoption and Maintenance Act. Meanwhile, the Constitution's provision that 'The State shall endeavour to secure for the citizens a uniform civil code throughout the territory of India'[17] has yet to be realized.

III

Ancient Hindu law is so rich and varied that it was difficult to choose a small number of essays for inclusion in the limited space of this book. The conceptual design of the volume, however, helped us immensely in the selection process. In Part I, we have chosen three papers which introduce the reader to the basics of understanding Hindu law and legal theory. In Part II, seven studies address various aspects of ancient Hindu law and legal theory, ranging from Hindu Jurisprudence, Manu's omniscience, verses of *Nirnaya* (decisions) in *Vyasasmriti*, and human rights, to 'lawyers' in classical Hindu law and matrimonial property law among Hindus. Part III is a collection of six essays which provide a glimpse of some of the recent developments in Hindu law, such as the reception of common law and equity and pertinent legislative modifications. The focus here is on marriage, divorce, property and gender issues.

The selections obviously reflect our subjectivities. In our decisions, however, we have been guided by three objectives: (1) to provide the reader with a comprehensive yet manageable view of the seemingly unfathomable reservoir of literature on ancient Hindu law and legal theory; (2) to acquaint the reader with a sampling of the literature available in British and American law journals; and (3) to sketch a few recent developments to illustrate the nature and scope of changes that Hindu law is currently undergoing in its evolution from the ancient to the modern.

IV

As already mentioned, the first three chapters constituting Part I help the reader understand Hindu law and legal theory. In the first chapter, Professor Ludo Rocher, a Sanskrit scholar, explains Hindu conceptions of law. Specifically, he describes how classical Hinduism understood *dharma* and law, what the sources of law were, how *dharamsastras* provided a framework for the Hindu legal and judicial system, and the role of commentaries and custom in Hindu law as practised in the Indian middle ages.

Next, Professor David A. Funk observes that Hindu jurisprudence 'justifies special rules limiting the political power of the king (rajadharma) and legitimizes his duty to preserve all types of *dharma* by punishments (danda). Thus this jurisprudence limits the absolute power of the king on the one hand through rajadharma, and on the other hand legitimizes obedience to proper positive legal acts of the state, especially punishments' (p. 28).

Professor Funk excerpts ten traditional works of Hindu jurisprudence, noting that there are questions concerning their authorship, translation and chronology. To illustrate:

> Hindu authors apparently were more interested in the reception and influence of their work, rather than getting 'credit' for writing it. Hence they usually do not indicate the historical time at which they wrote. This must be inferred usually from the contents of the manuscript. Often, therefore, the basic documents in which these ideas are expressed can only be attributed to a range of years, and scholarly opinion often differs concerning their earlier and later limits (p. 31).

The works excerpted are those attributed to: Gautama, Baudhayana, Apastamba, Vasishtha, Vishnu, Kautilya, Manu, the Mahabharata, Yajnavalkya and Narada. He notes that the general principles expounded by the Hindu legal philosophers

> were bound to be applied somewhat differently in different kingdoms, in practice. The extent to which a particular principle of Hindu jurisprudence was put into practice in various places may affect its importance in world intellectual history; but these historic facts do not add to, or detract from, its status as a basic principle of Hindu jurisprudence (p. 70).

In the concluding chapter in Part I, Professor Sinha's focus is upon the particular historicity of the Indian way of life. He shows that the fundamentals of it were already achieved in ancient India and that those 'fundamental principles abide to this day' (p. 76). Professor Sinha also reviews the Muslim period (8th century to 18th century) and the British period (post-18th century), and concludes that

> about eighty percent of the Indians live in villages and continue to conduct their lives through traditional institutions, traditions, and beliefs. Even in urban centers, where the changes are most evident, there has been a peculiarly Indian blend of Western ways with the Indian traditions in which the fundamental principle of *dharma*, the institution of joint family, the social organization of castes, and other traditions and customs are very much alive and practiced (p. 78).

Part II, comprising seven essays on selected aspects of ancient Hindu law, opens with two chapters which introduce the reader to Hindu jurisprudence. Professor Harrop Freeman presents a survey of Hindu jurisprudential theory; he discusses the development of Hindu legal institutions and examines schools of jurisprudence in ancient India. Next, he analyses ncient Hindu thought regarding the nature of the state and the king, punishment and rocedure, and the meaning of law and the rule of law. Conveying a sense of the rich-ess, diversity and growth of Hindu jurisprudence and its similarity to Anglo-American urisprudence, he concludes as follows:

> Though India is evolving many original rules of her own, it need not be assumed that her appetite for imported legal principles is exhausted. She will doubtless pick and choose among the systems with which her citizens become acquainted. India has always shown a tolerance and hospitality for other cultures, even those forced upon her. Hardly a writer facing Indian jurisprudence but remarks on this (p. 94).

In Chapter 5, Judge S.G. Vesey-FitzGerald compares Hindu and Roman jurisprudence. His specific areas of comparison are the caste system; the village community, which he says ıas retained 'stubborn vitality ... against which despotism and anarchy beat alike in vain' p. 100); and family law, including adoption, inheritance, marriage, the position of women nd guardianship. He concludes that 'the Roman and the Hindu families spring from the ame source, and were both clothed with a religious sanction ...' (p. 107).

He also discusses the contribution of the Hindu system in other branches of law, such s the origin of contract and its relation to conveyance, or suretyship and deposit. He pecifically refers to Narada's saying:

> I.(i)43: 'A claimant may arrest his adversary until the arrival of the summons, if the latter tries to evade the claim he is about to prefer or does not refute his charge.'
> I.(i)6: 'In a lawsuit made by wager, the loser has to pay the wager made by himself and a fine to the king' (p. 111).

Chapters 6 and 8 address specific *smriti* literature. In Chapter 7, Ludo Rocher discusses whether, in the ancient Hindu texts, a person representing a party to a lawsuit corresponds o the advocates or attorneys of modern India. Of the final two chapters in Part II, one liscusses matrimonial property law among Hindus and the other Hinduism and human ights.

In Chapter 6, Professor Albrecht Wezler's interpretation of *Manusmriti's* verse, 'What-ver law has been ordained for any (person) by Manu, that has been fully declared in the Veda: for that (sage was) omniscient',[18] is aimed at clarifying what is meant by Manu's mniscience. The following question is posed by Professor Wezler: 'Is it more probable hat the assumed author of the Manusmṛiti in the course of time "has become omniscient", r that he, albeit originally conceived of as "omniscient", has later been denied this xtraordinary quality'? (p. 117).

The issue may appear to be purely technical in nature, but Professor Wezler observes hat: 'A study of the indigenous Indian ideas about its alleged author is likely to yield esults that are most instructive, i.e. [,] from which one may learn much about Indian ulture in general and the tradition of Dharmasastra in particular ...' (p. 114). Professor Wezler studies the verse closely in a contextual setting and discusses glosses by two of nany commentators, Medhatithi and Kulluka. He concludes that the doctrine 'according to which Manu, or the Manus, and other sages were the first persons who by virtue of an xtraordinary cognitive faculty ... peculiar to them learned language which prior to them existed only in the form of God's intention' (pp. 135–6), is the one 'that adequately explains the origin of the conception of Manu's and the other sages' omniscience and renders it fully intelligible. For, to know God's intention as regards words implies the knowledge of all the *designata* too, i.e. of everything that has the character of being (*bhavarupa*)' (p. 136).

Heramba Sastri studies *Vyasasmriti's* verses relating to decision making or *vyavaharanirnaya* in Chapter 8. Decisions, according to these verses, are of eight types

> (i.e. may be arrived at through any of the eight means), such as – three recognized modes of proof (document ... possession ... and witness); circumstantial evidence (*hetu*); established usage or convention (*carita*); oath or ordeal; royal order and declaration of the truth of the claim (p. 166).

Sastri analyses works contained in several *smritis*, including those attributed to Narada, Yajnavalkya, Brhaspati and Katyayana and to Kautilya's *Arthasastra*, related to these eight types of decision and concludes that,

> in adjustment with the four varieties of *nirnaya* of Bhraspati (1.18), the eight types of *nirnaya* propounded by Vyasa (verse 1) may be explained to be practically of four types, of course with the addition of a new one, namely, *hetu* [circumstantial evidence]. ... *Hetu* ... is an additional one, but on this point it may be stated that this has been recognized by all the writers on law in some form or other (p. 203).

In Chapter 7, Professor Rocher explores legal procedures in ancient Hindu law that safeguarded litigants through the services of a class of experts. He begins with a 1777 translation of *Vivada rnavasetu*. In it, a section entitled 'Of appointing a *vakeel* (attorney)' reads, in part:

> If the plaintiff or defendant have any excuse for not attending the court, or for not pleading their own cause, or, on any other account, excuse themselves, they shall, at their own option, appoint a person as their *vakeel*; if the *vakeel* gains the suit, his principal also gains; if the *vakeel* is cast, his principal is cast also (p. 141).

Professor Rocher refers to many modern authorities whose opinions confuse rather than clarify the subject. He examines the works of Narada, Katyayana and Vyasa, as well as the *Arthasastra*, and concludes that, at the time of the *Dharmasutras*, there were no specialists on *dharmasastra* and hence no specialists on law. At a later time, however, as the texts on *dharma* began to depart from the Vedic schools, there could have been such specialists. He observes that

> as the amount of textual material increased, we may assume that certain experts, without detaching themselves completely from other aspects of *dharmasastra* and from Hindu learning generally, accumulated a very specialized knowledge of one aspect of *dharma* ... in modern terminology, law. ... The impression which we gather from the texts is that, even in cases where the representative was chosen because of his special competence on legal matters, and, a fortiori, in all other cases, the necessary condition for a person to represent a party was the existence, between the former and the latter, of a certain form of close personal relationship (pp. 157–8).

In his study of matrimonial property law among Hindus in Chapter 9, Professor Ram Singh observes that '[s]ince the dawn of early civilization women in India have enjoyed an elevated position so far as their proprietary rights are concerned' (p. 209). Acknowledging that the legal history of India shows that Indian women have enjoyed unique independence with regard to their property rights, he explains: 'The whole range of property of a married woman known as "Stridhan", whose intricacy has lured a large number of jurists to deal with its subtleties, indicates where the systems of "Separate Property" and "Community Property" seem to be intertwined' (p. 211).

Professor Singh examines the Vedic literature on *Stridhana*, referring to Katyayana's *smriti* which treats the subject in a detailed fashion in 27 verses. He also alludes to Manu and then discusses the changes brought about under British rule and through post-Independence legislation, concluding that '[t]he Hindu community today needs a redefined, objective, and egalitarian approach to the problem through the legislative process' (p. 235).

In the final essay in Part II, Professor Ved Nanda studies Hinduism and human rights. He describes Hinduism and its pertinent major tenets, including its firm belief in universal brotherhood, articulated in its tenet 'Vasudhaiv Kutumbkum' (all humanity is one family). He points to Hinduism's belief in the oneness of all religions and its advocacy of universal tolerance. In the light of these principles, Professor Nanda shows that Hinduism is fully compatible with the International Bill of Human Rights – the Universal Declaration of Human Rights, the International Covenant on Civil and Political Rights and its Optional Protocol, and the International Covenant on Economic, Social and Cultural Rights.

Professor Nanda specifically addresses some features of Hinduism which critics consider to be at odds with the modern concept of human rights, such as the caste system, untouchability and the status of women. He also discusses slavery and the place of humanitarian law in ancient India. He concludes that Hinduism and the modern development of international human rights reflect similar views and are both aimed at promoting human dignity.

Part III, comprising six papers, examines certain modern developments in Hindu law. In Chapter 11, Professor Günther-Dietz Sontheimer considers various statutes and their implications; namely, the 1955 Hindu Marriage Act, the 1956 Hindu Succession Act, the 1956 Hindu Adoption and Maintenance Act, and the 1956 Hindu Minority and Guardianship Act. He finds the study of ancient Hindu law to be important in this context, for 'a systematic and unbiased study of the *dharmasastra* can reveal for instance that nowhere in the world has more thought been devoted to the philosophical concept of Property and its legal implications than in India' (p. 251).

Professor Sontheimer concludes that '[t]he achievement of providing a simple unified legal system for a society with widely different customs and laws, *e.g.*, succession laws which stretch from patriliny to pure matriliny, is indeed unique in the history of codification' (p. 264). However, he calls for further legislation to clarify ambiguities and flaws in these Acts which he believes the judiciary alone may not be able to resolve.

Professor J. Duncan M. Derrett also analyses these Acts in Chapter 12, entitled 'Statutory Amendments of the Personal Laws of Hindus Since Indian Independence'. He observes that some strangely archaic features still remain in the Hindu personal law. For instance, '[a]doption is not possible if the adopter already has a son, or a grandson by a son, or, if a girl is to be adopted, has a daughter or even a son's daughter. The state cannot take property as *ultimus heres* until an infinite number of degrees of kindred is exhausted' (p. 277). He also draws attention to 'an interesting reliance on foreign legal experience [as] [n]umerous rules have been introduced from English law' ... (p. 277).

Next, Professor Alan Gledhill studies the influence of common law and equity on Hindu law since 1800. He suggests that 'the development of the Hindu law in the courts was conditioned by an approach to its problems which [he] would describe as Anglo-Indian' (p. 282). Tracing the history of the use of common law and equity in many areas such as marriage, adoption, inheritance, estates, religious and charitable endowments and caste questions, he concludes that '[f]rom the standpoint of the legal practitioner, despite the recognition of schools of Hindu law, a large measure of uniformity has been achieved and the Hindu law has become largely a matter of case-law' (p. 306).

Of the remaining three chapters, one discusses marriage and divorce in India, while the other two address gender issues. Professor Ved Nanda discusses marriage under old and new Hindu law, noting a fundamental distinction between the Hindu system and others in that the former 'considers marriage not as a contract but as a sacrament. ... The Hindu ideal of marriage is that it is a holy union for the performance of religious duties' (p. 310). He analyses the 1955 Hindu Marriage Act which amends and codifies the law relating to marriage. He predicts that the laws of marriage and divorce in India are likely to resist unification for a considerable period of time and cautions that '[a] hasty action on the part of the legislature is not in the interest of the society. Until the time is really right for codification and unification, personal laws should be left alone, with minor changes wherever deemed necessary' (p. 320).

The last two chapters, one by Professor Ateeque Khan and the other by Dr Gita Gopal, are concerned with women's property rights. Professor Khan examines the extent to which the statutory rules of inheritance, succession through survivorship and partition are in conformity with India's twin constitutional objectives of equality and socio-economic justice. Dr Gopal examines women's property rights upon marriage, divorce and death, including women's ability to own agricultural land. She concludes that

> [t]he primary task remains to amend all legislative provisions that institutionalize economic distributions based on gender differences and those that increase a woman's economic dependency. Such legislative reforms must be accomplished in a sensitive manner. ... Examination of women's status in the family and society is incomplete without the discussion of problems in a holistic manner.

Dr Gopal believes that

> [e]qual access to productive resources will provide women with an enabling environment in which they can break down gender-based traditional barriers that currently seem impenetrable. ... Women will be taken seriously only when they have these economic rights (p. 354).

V

Hindu law has never been static. Progressing through various stages of evolution in the last three or four millennia, it has adapted itself to changing circumstances and needs. Although various schools of Hindu law have developed over the ages, a great deal of uniformity exists at the present time. Much of Hindu law today is judicially created and has the usual imprint of case law.

In order to understand Hindu legal theory, we need to understand *dharma*. In order to understand *dharma*, we need to reject the generally-presumed notion that law, in the Western philosophical sense, is a universal phenomenon that is merely manifested variously in different parts of the world.

What is characteristic of Hindu law in our opinion is a conceptual system of two layers. Its fundamental layer is of *dharma* whose internal coherence is provided by a system of *karma*, or duty, and not by a system of rights, as in law. The result is that, at this level, the important task becomes not the institutionalization of rights and responsibilities, as in 'law', but the discovery of one's duty to act in adherence to that which maintains, sustains, preserves or holds (that is, *dharma*) and the comprehending of the hidden sources of that duty. Upon this fundamental layer, we have the reception of Western-style institutions of law and techniques of administering it. This composite is what we might call Hindu law. Most Indians conduct their lives pursuing the values of *dharma* through traditional institutions and beliefs, significantly assisted by the techniques of law received more recently from the West.

Notes

1 See H.S. Maine (1861), *Ancient Laws*: (Pollock ed. 1963), (Morgan ed. 1965); H.S. Maine (1966), *Lectures on the Early History of Institutions* (7th ed.).
2 See H.L.A. Hart (1961, 1967), *The Concept of Law*.
3 R. May (1985), *Law and Society East and West: Dharma, Li, and Nomos*; S.P. Sinha (1989), *What is Law?*; S.P. Sinha (1993), *Jurisprudence: Legal Philosophy in a Nutshell*; S.P. Sinha (1996), *Legal Polycentricity and International Law*; S.P. Sinha (1989), 'Why Has It Not Been Possible to Define Law?', *Archiv fur Rechts-und Sozialphilosophie*, **1**; S.P. Sinha (1995), 'Non-Universality of Law', *Archiv fur Rechts-und Sozialphilosophie*, **81** at 185.
4 Cited in M. Ramajois (1984), *Legal and Constitutional History of India*, 3.
5 See generally Ludo Rocher (1978), 'Hindu Conceptions of Law', reprinted here as Chapter 1; see pp. 4–9.
6 Ramajois, *supra* note 4, at 4.
7 Rocher, *supra* note 5, at 5.
8 *Id*.
9 *Manusmriti* II, 6.
10 Cited in Ramajois, *supra* note 4, at 20.
11 *Id*.
12 *Manusmriti*, II, 6.
13 Rocher, *supra* note 5, at 15.
14 See *id*. at 24–25.
15 Alan Gledhill (1954), 'The Influence of Common Law and Equity on Hindu Law Since 1800', reprinted here as Chapter 13; see p. 280.
16 *Id*.
17 Indian Constitution, art. 44 (1950).
18 *Manusmriti* II, 7.

Part I
Bases for Understanding Hindu Law and Legal Theory

[1]

Hindu Conceptions of Law

By Ludo Rocher*

ANY DISCUSSION of Hindu conceptions of law has to start with the basic observation that nowhere in the Hindu tradition is there a term to express the concept of law, neither in the sense of *ius* nor in that of *lex*. Not until the arrival of the colonial powers was the concept of law used on the subcontinent, by Europeans and through the medium of European languages. It was not until 1772, the year in which it was decided that, "in all suits regarding inheritance, marriage, caste, and other religious usages or institutions,"[1] the Hindus should be governed by their own laws, that an effort was made to study and translate the Sanskrit books in which the Hindu laws were codified. These books happen to be the *dharmaśāstras,* treatises on *dharma.* Hence, the equation established by the Western editors and translators of these books was *dharma śāstra* equals lawbook, code, or Institute. They also established the equation: dharma equals law.[2]

To be sure, Indians have followed this well-established practice.[3] When it comes to expressing the concept of law in modern India through the medium of modern Indian languages, however, different

---

* Professor of Sanskrit; Chairman, Department of South Asia Regional Studies, University of Pennsylvania. Doctor of Laws 1950, Ph.D. 1952, Ghent (Belgium). Corresponding member, Belgian Royal Academy of Overseas Sciences, 1964-; Fellow, Asiatic Society of Bengal, 1971-. Editor and translator of Sanskrit legal treatises. Author, *Bibliographie du droit hindou ancien* (1965) and other books and monographs on Hindu law and Indology.

1. Plan for the Administration of Justice Extracted from the Proceedings of the Committee of Circuit (Cossimbascar) 15 August, 1772. (B. K. Acharyya, Codification in British India, Calcutta 1914, p.153).

2. *E.g.*, Institutes of Hindu Law, or the Ordinances of Manu (W. Jones trans. 1794); The Institutes of Manu (G. C. Haughton ed., trans. 1825); Lois de Manou (A.L. Deslongchamps ed., trans. 1830-33); Yājñavalkyas Gesetzbuch (A. F. Stenzler ed., trans. 1849); The Ordinances of Manu (A.C. Burnell trans. 1884); The Laws of Manu (G. Bühler trans. 1886); The Code of Manu (J. Jolly ed. 1887).

3. *See, e.g.*, G. Jha, The Laws of Manu. Jha began publishing this translation in 1920.

terms are used. For instance, recent dictionaries of India's official language, Hindi, normally give two terms for law, one borrowed from the Arabic-Persian (Muslim) tradition, *kānūn,* and one from the Sanskrit (Hindu) tradition, *vidhi.* In addition, when the Indian Constitution was translated into Hindi, *vidhi*[4] became the official translation for law, both in the text of the Constitution and in the English-Hindi wordlist published along with it by the Government of India.

The reason why modern Indian languages looked for different terms to express law may, at least in part, have been due to the fact that, in the meanwhile, they had all accepted *dharma* as the Indian equivalent for another concept imported from the West—religion. It is not quite clear when and by whom *dharma* was first used in the restricted sense of religion. One thing is sure, however, it represents a conscious effort to find, for a category that had no equivalent in India, a word from the Indian vocabulary which, even though it was not perfectly identical, came at least closer than any other available term.

Dharma and Law

After the above introductory remarks, this Article will now attempt to interpret the data as they emerge from the Hindu tradition. The pivot of the entire system is *dharma,* which is neither religion nor law, and yet crucial for the topic of this Article—the Hindu conceptions of law. *Dharma* has been rightly described as "one of those Sanskrit words that defy all attempts at an exact rendering in English or any other tongue."[5] It is therefore essential to approach it from within the Hindu tradition, and describe how classical Hinduism itself understood it.

Dharma[6] is a noun formed with the suffix °*ma*[7] from a root *dhar* or *dhṛ*. The root expresses actions such as to hold, bear, carry, main-

4. *Vidhi* is a traditional term, meaning "injunction," referring to those sections of the Vedas that contain actual rules rather than other sections that are merely explanatory.

5. 1 P.V. Kane, History of Dharmasastra 1 (rev. ed. Poona 1968) [hereinafter cited as Kane). Kane's monumental work, in five volumes, is the principal sourcebook on *dharma* and law. Volume 3, addressing Hindu law, appeared in 1946.

6. For studies on *dharma,* see Rocher, *Bibliographie du droit hindou ancien* in Introduction bibliographique À l'histoire du droit et a l'ethnologie juridique (J. Gilissen ed., Brussels 1965); L. Sternbach, Bibliography on dharma and artha in Ancient and Mediaeval India (Wiesbaden 1973).

7. Compare *-men* in Latin *carmen, -ma* in Greek *rheuma.*

tain, preserve, keep. Hence, *dharma* is the way in which, or the means by which, one holds, bears, carries, or maintains, and, in accordance with semantic development common in Sanskrit, it means not only the *way* of doing these things, but also *the* way of doing them. *Dharma*, then, is the way in which one ought to hold, bear, carry, or maintain. On a cosmic level, *dharma* is the way in which one maintains everything, the way in which the cosmos or the balance in the cosmos, is maintained. At the micro level, *dharma* is the way in which every constituent element of the cosmos contributes its share to maintaining the overall balance. Each element has its own *dharma*, its *svadharma*. As long as each element of the cosmos performs its specific *svadharma*, the overall balance does not suffer. As soon as an element, however, deviates from its own *dharma*, that is, commits *adharma*, the balance is disturbed.

Theoreticians of *dharma* will, of course, insist on the fact that every cosmic element has its *svadharma*. The sun is supposed to rise in the morning and to set at night; water—the rains—has to arrive at a set time of the year and disappear at another set time. In practice, however, Hindus have primarily paid attention to the *dharma* of human beings. Each individual human being has a *svadharma*, which is determined essentially by two factors: belonging to one of the four stages of life (*āśrama*); and belonging to one of the four social classes (*varṇa*). From these two factors comes the expression, *varṇāśramadharma*.

For a better understanding of the Hindu conception of law, one characteristic of the human *dharma* deserves to be pointed out above all. A person's *dharma* regulates all activities, whatever their nature. The *dharma* ordains when the individual shall awaken, how that person shall divide the day, and when the person shall retire at night. The *dharma* rules a person's diet, quantitatively and qualitatively. The *dharma*, of course, regulates the human's relationship to the supernatural powers, and prescribes the rituals and ceremonies by which these relations shall be sustained; it therefore deals with the Hindu's religion. *Dharma* also governs the individual's relations with fellow people; it rules social contacts, many aspects of which belong to the field of law. To put it differently, Hindu law is, together with every other aspect of a Hindu's activities, part of Hindu *dharma*. Hindu rules of law are to be found in the *dharmaśāstras*, but these texts also contain a variety of other rules which have little or nothing in common with law.

A first important consequence of the concept of *dharma* is that, in Hinduism, law, religion, and all other topics dealt with in the *dharmaśāstras* are inextricably intertwined. All attempts to disentangle the various categories and to label particular concepts or institutions as essentially religious or essentially legal, are bound to force upon them categorizations which are foreign to the Hindu way of thinking.

An example is the implication, in classical Hinduism, of committing what Western society would call a crime: killing a human being; more specifically, killing a member of the highest class, a Brahmin. Not to complicate the description, this examination shall restrict itself to quoting from a single text, the *dharmaśāstra* attributed to Manu.[8] First,[9] killing a Brahmin is ranked among the four great sins, *mahāpātaka*. Subsequently,[10] punishment for great sins is said to be corporal punishment: in the specific case of killing a Brahmin,[11] the brand of a headless corpse on the offender's forehead. This rule is followed by a number of social implications:

> Excluded from all fellowship at meals, excluded from all sacrifices, excluded from instruction and from matrimonial alliances, abject and excluded from all religious duties, let them wander over (this) earth.
>
> Such (persons) who have been branded with (indelible) marks must be cast off by their paternal and maternal relations, and receive neither compassion nor a salutation; that is the teaching of Manu.[12]

The text continues that corporal punishment[13] may be replaced by the highest fine, if the killer at the same time performs a variety—too long to enumerate here—of intricate penances described in great detail elsewhere in the text.[14] Manu then[15] makes the usual distinction between the case in which the crime was committed by a Brahmin and

---

8. 25 THE SACRED BOOKS OF THE EAST (F.M. Muller ed., G. Bühler trans. 1886) [hereinafter cited as MANU]. For editions and translations of the texts, see bibliographies cited in note 6, *supra*.

9. MANU, *supra* note 8, at 9.235.

10. *Id.* at 9.236.

11. *Id.* at 9.237.

12. *Id.* at 9.238-239.

13. *Id.* at 9.240.

14. *Id.* at 11.73-87, 90.

15. *E.g.*, at 9.241-42.

by someone belonging to a lower class; the former has to be less severely punished than the latter. Finally, in another chapter, the text describes the fate of the killer of a Brahmin in the next rebirth: "The slayer of a Brahmana enters the womb of a dog, a pig, an ass, a camel, a cow, a goat, a sheep, a deer, a bird, a Caṇḍāla, and a Pukkasa."[16]

In short, killing a Brahmin was a transgression of *dharma*, with all the consequences thereof. The transgression implies a criminal element requiring puishment by the king, an element of sin to be expiated by performing penances, and an element of exclusion from one's usual social circles. It is also to be noted that the Hindu penal code is strongly influenced by the caste system. For the same offense a member of a lower class is more severely punished than one of a higher class (a Brahmin is totally exempt from any kind of corporal punishment), with the correlative provision that, for the same offense, punishment is higher or lower depending on whether the victim is of a higher or lower class. Also, Hindu crime extends beyond this life, and is linked to the theory of rebirth.

The extent to which private law was interwoven with other categories cannot be better illustrated than by referring to some of the difficulties which the British judges were to experience when they were called upon to apply the *dharma* texts as legal codes in the Anglo-Hindu law courts. They soon came to the conclusion: "All those old text-books and commentaries are apt to mingle religious and moral considerations, not being positive laws, with rules intended for positive laws."[17] No matter how much they were concerned not to interfere with the religious beliefs of the Hindus—a concern that is expressed over and again in the law reports—they decided that "the Courts are to enforce only rules of positive law and not religious or moral precepts."[18]

One of the simplest applications of this position concerns the validity of adoption. The Sanskrit texts clearly require that, for an adoption to be valid , a particular ritual, called *dattahoma*, has to be performed. The question arose, whether or not the *dattahoma* was a legal prerequisite for adoption, the legal character of which was, of course, never doubted. The dilemma was described as follows:

16. *Id.* at 12.55.
17. Rao Balwant Singh v. Rani Kishori, 25 I.A. 54, 69 (1898).
18. S.V. Gupte, Hindu Law in British India 49 (2d ed. Bombay 1947).

> In certain circumstances the point might be the subject of a prolonged and very conflicting argument, as the authorities, ancient and modern, are not in accord on the point as to whether this is a legal as well as a religious requisite. There is a danger, on the one hand, of not paying due respect to those religious rites which are observed and followed among large classes of Indian belief, while, on the other hand, the danger must also be avoided of carrying these, except when the law is clear, into the legal sphere, so as to affect or impair personal or patrimonial rights.[19]

The result was that, in Anglo-Hindu courts, the legal act, adoption, was separated from the religious act, *dattahoma*, and that the former was held valid without the latter.[20]

Another, more complex, example involves both adoption and inheritance. The *dharma* texts forbid adoption of an only son. Vasiṣṭha,[21] for instance, allows the father to give, sell, or abandon his son, but adds the proviso, "let him not give or receive (in adoption) an only son."[22] In a case that was to become very influential, the Privy Council reiterated their view that one should not "take for strict law precepts which are meant to appeal to the moral sense,"[23] and decided that the adoption of an only son is not null and void under the Hindu law.

Although the *dharma* texts rarely exhibit justification for their statements, the rationale of Vasiṣṭha's rule is clear. The text is obviously concerned about the fate of the natural father who becomes deprived of his only son. The son is, of course, the natural heir of his father. At the same time, however, he is much more than that; he frees his father "from his debt to the Manes,"[24] and, after the father's death, he is the only person capable of performing the ritual, called *śrāddha*, which is required for the father to join the ranks of his ancestors. This example not only explains why an only son should not be the object of an adoption; it also shows that what we call inheritance in Hinduism involves far more than the legal rights to an estate.

---

19. Bal Gangadhar Tilak v. Shrinivas Pandit, 42 I.A. 135, 148-49, (1915).

20. MAYNE'S TREATISE ON HINDU LAW AND USAGE 238-39 (11th ed. N. Chandrasekhara Aiyar, Madras 1950).

21. VASIṢṬHA 15.2, in 14 THE SACRED BOOKS OF THE EAST (F.M. Muller ed., G. Bühler trans. 1882) [hereinafter cited as VASIṢṬHA].

22. *Id.* at 15.3.

23. 26 I.A. 113, 136 (1899).

24. MANU, *supra* note 8, at 9.106; VASIṢṬHA, *supra* note 21, at 11.48.

The Privy Council became acutely aware of the scope of Hindu inheritance when they were faced with a murderer claiming the estate of his victim. The Council stated:

> Before this Board it has been contended that the matter is governed by Hindu Law, and that the Hindu Law makes no provision disqualifying a murderer from succeeding to the estate of his victim, and therefore it must be taken that according to this law he can succeed.[25]

It was seen earlier that the Hindu *dharma* does not condone murder. On the contrary, it is both a crime and a sin. The problem confronting the Privy Council lies elsewhere: who are, according to the *dharma*, those who are disqualified from succeeding to an estate, and, more importantly, what is the underlying justification? Manu has the following enumeration: "Eunuchs and outcasts, (persons) born blind or deaf, the insane, idiots and the dumb, as well as those deficient in any organ (of action or sensation), receive no share."[26] Murderers are not among them. Those listed in the text as "incompetent to receive a share" are individuals who are unable to administer it, and, also, to perform for the deceased the necessary funeral rites. In this case, the Privy Council decided to overrule Hindu law: "The alternative is between the Hindu law being as above stated or being for this purpose non-existent, and in that case the High Court have rightly decided that the principle of equity, justice and good conscience exclude the murderer."[27]

Sources of Law

Another consequence of the Hindu concept of *dharma* is that law shares its basic features with religion and all other categories treated in the *dharmaśāstras*. To illustrate this point this Article will first present a brief description of these texts, and then it will examine the characteristics of their contents generally and their legal materials in particular.

---

25. Kenchava v. Girimallappa Channappa, 51 I.A. 368, 372-73 (1924).

26. MANU, *supra* note 8, at 9.201.

27. Section 25 of the Hindu Succession Act, 1956, states: "A person who commits murder or abets the commission of murder shall be disqualified from inheriting the property of the person murdered, or any other property in furtherance of the succession to which he or she committed or abetted the commission of the murder."

The source materials for our knowledge of classical Hindu *dharma* are primarily the *dharmasūtras* and *dharmaśāstras*. Although the latter term is also used collectively for both kinds of texts, the principal difference is that the *sūtras* are older, and composed in the succinct and often enigmatic prose style used in many other branches of Hindu learning (such as *Yogasūtras, Vedāntasūtras*, and *Pānini's* grammatical *sūtras*). The most important *dharmasūtras* are those attributed to Gautama, Apastamba, Vasiṣṭha, and Baudhāyana.[28] They may have been composed between 600 and 300 B.C.[29]

The more recent *dharmaśāstras* are in verse, in the typical thirty-two syllable distichs called *śloka* or *anustbh,* which are characteristic not only of the Sanskrit epics but also of learned treatises in many fields such as medicine and architecture.[30]

Closely related to the *dharmaśāstras* are the epics and the Purāṇas. Long passages from these texts are devoted to various aspects of *dharma,* including legal topics. In fact, many verses and passages are more or less identical with verses and passages in the *dharmaśāstras.* The question of which text, in such cases, is the borrower, and which the one borrowed from, is one that is bound to tempt Western, or Western-trained, philologists. For the present purposes, the solution of these problems is less important than the fact that the same legal materials that occur in the *dharmaśāstras,* are also found in epic and bardic literature. The later commentators were to quote from the epics and the Purāṇas, perhaps not as often as from the *dharmaśāstras,* but definitely giving all those sources the same legal authority.

28. Apastamba and Gautama, in 2 The Sacred Books of the East (F.M. Muller ed., G. Bühler trans. 1879); Vasiṣṭha and Baudhayana, in 14 The Sacred Books of the East (F.M. Muller ed., G. Bühler trans. 1882).

29. The dates of these texts are, like the dates of most Sanskrit texts, highly uncertain. *See* 3 Kane, *supra* note 5, at xvii.

30. The most important texts of this category are attributed to Manu (200 B.C. - A.D. 100), Yạjṇavalkya (A.D. 100-300), Viṣṇu (A.D. 100-300) Narāda (A.D. 100-400), Bṛhaspati (A.D. 300-500), and Kạtyayaṇa (A.D. 400-600). There also are numerous minor metrical *dharmasastras,* some of which have been preserved, often in larger collections, whereas others are known only from quotations in later commentarial literature. Dates are from 3 Kane, *supra* note 5, at xvii-xviii. *See* Manu, *supra* note 8; Visnu in 7 The Sacred Books of the East, (F.M. Muller ed., J. Jolly trans.); Nārada and Bṛhaspati in 33 The Sacred Books of the East (J. Jolly trans. 1889); Kātyāyana (Kane ed. & trans. Poona n.d.); Yājñavalkya (A.F. Stenzler trans., Berlin 1849).

The beginning of this century saw the discovery, in South India, of a manuscript of a text which had been known only through a few indirect references. The title of the book is *Arthaśāstra*,[31] and it is attributed to an author variously called Kautilya or Kautalya, and other names, who may have been the minister of Candragupta, the famous Maurya emperor in the third century B.C. This book exhibits a large amount of legal materials, and, especially, provides a totally new, detailed account of Hindu administrative law. Indic scholars have rarely been as excited as they were by the discovery of Kauṭilya's *Arthaśāstra*, and in a short period of time a vast scholarly literature on Hindu society and law developed, based on Kauṭilya, using the newly discovered book as their principle source, it being considered superior to the well known *dharmaśāstras* and allied texts. This author shall place the *Arthaśāstras*, as a source of law, in its correct perspective later in this Article.

Vedic Basis of Hindu Law

The *dharma* literature does not exist in a vacuum, according to the Hindu tradition. On the contrary, it has a well-determined place within a larger literary framework, with important consequences for the Hindu conception of law. First, the *dharmasūtras* each belong directly to one of the branches of the Vedas. Together with other sūtras, such as the *śrautasūtras*, which regulate the most elaborate ritual, the *gṛhyasūtras*, which describe the more modest house ritual, and the *śulbasūtras*, which are devoted to the correct construction of the sacrificial altar, the *dharmasūtras* form the class of *kalpasūtras*. One such *kalpasūtra* exists in each branch of the Vedas. Within each branch the *sūtras* attach themselves to the earlier *āraṇyaka*, via the *āraṇyaka* to the *brāhmaṇa*, and ultimately, to the basic *saṃhitā*. Thus, the *dharmasūtra* attributed to Vasiṣṭha belongs to the Rigveda, that of Gautama to the Sāmaveda, and those of Āpastamba and Baudhāyana to the Taittirīya branch of the Black Yajurveda.

The way in which the versified *dharmaśāstras* are related to Vedic literature is less clear. An idea, first proposed by Max Müller,[32] and

31. The text was first translated into English by R. Shamasastry in 1923, then into German—with abundant annotations—by J.J. Meyer, in DAS ALTINDISCHE BUCH VOM WELT- UND STAATSLEBEN (Leipzig 1926), and, most recently, into English by R.P. Kangle (Bombay 1965).

32. A HISTORY OF ANCIENT SANSKRIT LITERATURE (London 1859).

further elaborated by Bühler[33] in the introduction to his translation of Manu, was that the *dharmaśāstras* are versified recasts of earlier and lost prose *dharmasūtras*. In this way the *śāstras,* too, belong to specific branches of the Vedas. The *dharmaśāstra* attributed to Manu would then belong to the Maitrāyaṇīya branch of the Black Yajurveda, and that attributed to Kātyāyana to the Vājasaneyi branch of the White Yajurveda.

According to a different theory, the *dharmaśāstras* came into being at a time when Hinduism was threatened nearly simultaneously by Buddhism and Jainism.[34] To react successfully against these threats it was felt necessary to eliminate the differences between schools and couch the texts in a more popular and more easily accessible form. The result was that the historical, vertical sequence of *saṃhitā, brāhmaṇa, āraṇyaka, sūtras,* within each branch of the Vedas was replaced with a horizontal cross sequence, each of which specialized in one particular topic across school boundaries, *in casu*: *dharma.*

The important point here is that all the texts on *dharma* derive more or less directly from the Veda. The standard phrase is *vedo dharmasya mūlam* (the root of the *dharma* is the Veda.) Veda and *dharma* are, in many ways, synonymous. This premise has important consequences for the nature of the rules on *dharma* and, hence, for the Hindu conception of law. The Veda was not created by men. It has been revealed by a number of privileged sages who subsequently transmitted it to mankind. The Revelation, (*śruti*) *stricto sensu,* comprehends only the *saṃhitās* and *brāhmaṇas,* and most often extends to the *āraṇyakas,* and *upaniṣads.* The various *sūtras,* including the *dharmasūtras* and *dharmaśāstras,* technically belong to a less direct type of revelation, *smriti,* often translated as "tradition" to distinguish it from revelation. The epics and Purāṇas also belong to this category. This distinction, however, is unimportant for present purposes. The main point to be remembered is that the Veda, and therefore the *dharma,* and, for that reason, law, are, for the orthodox Hindu, perfect, complete, eternal, and, above all, not to be altered through human intervention.

33. *See* Introduction to MANU, *supra* note 8.

34. This theory was, as far as the author knows, first formulated in P. vom Bradtke, *Ueber das Manavagrhya,* 38 ZEITSCHRIFT DER DEUTSCHEN MORGENLÄNDISCHEN Gesellschaft 417-77 (1882).

Comprehensiveness of Hindu *Dharma* and Law

In reality, the situation is far more complex than the above portrays. Even though the useful *Dharmakośa* "Encyclopaedia of Dharma,"[35] under most headings, starts its quotations with the extracts from the Vedas, and notwithstanding assertions that the Veda provides information of "considerable importance" on *dharma*,[36] even a casual observer will notice that there are hardly any rules of *dharma* and even less rules of law in the *śruti*.

The extent to which *dharma* has a Vedic basis may be illustrated with the following example. Yājñavalkya[37] lays down as one of the qualifications required of an acceptable bride the necessity for her to have a brother. Indeed, the Rigveda points, at least twice, to the low reputation of a woman who has no brother; she is tempted to deviate from the right path because she is unable to acquire a regular husband. In addition, Vasiṣṭha indicates the reason why such a woman is unacceptable as a bride: "[a] maiden who has no brothers comes back to the male ancestors (of her own family); returning she becomes their son."[38] The text even adds that this fact "is declared in the Veda."[39] From the above example comes the orthodox conclusion that the rules of Yājñavalkya and Vasiṣṭha have a Vedic basis, and that the passages from the Rigveda are illustrations of their rules in Vedic times.

Elsewhere, at a much higher intellectual level, the tradition does recognize that the *dharma*, taught by the Veda, is far from complete. Primarily the highly sophisticated Mīmāṃsā, has developed a number of fictions to account for the situation. Some of these fictions are extremely technical and scholastic.[40] Basically, they all say that the Veda is indeed complete, but that it has only partly been revealed to the humans in this world.

35. L.S. Joshi ed. It lists, solely in Sanskrit, all the ancient texts, together with extracts from commentaries, relative to specific topics of *dharma*. The legal section is in three volumes (Wai 1937-1941).

36. *See generally* P.V. Kane, Vedic Basis of Hindu Law (Dharwar 1936).

37. Yājñavalkya 1.52-53.

38. Vasiṣṭha, *supra* note 21, at 17.16.

39. *Id.*

40. *See generally* C. Sankararama Sastri, Fictions in the Development of the Hindu Law Texts (Madras 1926).

More important for present purposes than the number of rules of law contained in the Vedas is the fact that the earlier *dharmasūtras* also remain very sketchy and that they hardly pay any attention to the legal aspects of *dharma*. Two different historical explanations have been proposed. Either the legal rules had not yet been formulated at the time when the *sūtras* were composed, or the compilers of these texts felt that legal prescriptions, even though they did exist, were not important enough to be included in a more exhaustive fashion.

As time goes on, more and more legal rules appear in the texts, far more in the *dharmaśāstras* than in the *sūtras*. Besides the *dharmas* of the four *āśramas* and the four *varṇas* generally, more prominence is now given to the *dharma* of one special individual of the kṣatriya caste, namely, the king. Under the heading *rājadharma* (the king's *dharma*), to which Manu, for instance, devotes three full chapters, out of twelve, is found assembled a collection of prescriptions which are essentially of a legal nature. This is not to say that law now becomes more separated from religion and the rest; it only means that those aspects of *dharma* in which western civilization's category of law plays a more prominent role are joined together around the central figure of the king.

Here, as elsewhere, the texts approach the subject etymologically, that is, the king is called *rājā* because his highest *dharma* is to make his subjects happy (*rañjayati*). Once again, his duties are looked upon as a contribution to maintaining the overall equilibrium. His is the responsibility to maintain the balance between the individuals in his kingdom. He shall protect the weak against the attacks of the strong, lest the latter devour the former like fish in water. The molested party in a dispute (*vivāda*) shall have recourse directly to the king, who sits as judge in a regular legal procedure.

At the most developed stage of the texts, this principle leads to detailed regulations on the composition of a court of law, presided over by the king and assisted by a varying number of Brahmins "who are experts on dharma." This description of the court is followed by a fourfold treatment of the proceedings. The qualifications, or lack of them, of the plaintiff and the written plaint are followed by equally elaborate discussions of the defendant and his plea. The third section analyzes the various types of evidence, and goes into detail on witnesses, written evidence, possession, oaths, and ordeals. The final section deals, much more briefly, with the verdict, but hardly alludes to its implementation.

In most texts the rules of procedure are set forth on the occasion of the treatment of the first *vivādapada*, literally path or area of dispute. The *vivādapadas* are invariably eighteen in number. Manu enumerates them as follows:

> Of those (titles) the first is non-payment of debts, (then follow), (2) deposit and pledge, (3) sale without ownership, (4) concerns among partners, and (5) resumption of gifts, (6) [n]on-payment of wages, (7) non-performance of agreements, (8) rescission of sale and purchase, (9) disputes between the owner (of cattle) and his servants, (10) [d]isputes regarding boundaries, (11) assault, (12) defamation, (13) theft, (14) robbery and violence, (15) adultery, (16) [d]uties of man and wife, (17) partition (of inheritance), (18) gambling and betting.[41]

Rather than discussing the validity of this division of substantive law, it is important, for a proper evaluation of the system, to keep in mind that the number eighteen appears in numerous subdivisions in India.[42] This probably means that whoever conceived the idea of eighteen *vivādapadas* had the number eighteen in mind first, and only later tried to provide eighteen titles. It also explains a later development which first appears in Nārada. The eighteenfold subdivision is not abandoned but the eighteenth title becomes "Miscellaneous," which allows authors to insert there any materials which do not find a place in any of the other seventeen chapters.

One final remark in connection with the theory that the Veda and Vedic *dharma* are comprehensive is in order. However lengthy and detailed the later *dharmaśāstras* become in their treatment of law, a number of serious lacunae remain.[43] A recent and carefully produced publication[44] convinced this author more than ever before how little is known about the Hindu laws of taxation in general, and of the laws of specific times and specific places in particular. It would be equally difficult to draw a clear picture of the laws governing land

---

41. MANU, *supra* note 8, at 8.4-7.

42. For example, the MAHĀBHĀRATA has eighteen books, the BHAGAVADGĪTĀ has eighteen chapters, and there are eighteen PURANAS.

43. These missing links were one of the reasons why the British, when they decided to apply the Sanskrit texts as the law of the land, abandoned the older *dharmaśāstras* in favor of the later and far more voluminous commentaries.

44. D. N. Jha, REVENUE SYSTEM IN POST-MAURYA AND GUPTA TIMES (Calcutta 1967). *See also* Book Review, 13 INDO-IRANIAN J. 287-89 (1972).

ownership and land tenure in classical India. The texts occasionally refer to these topics but, for some unstated reason, they fail to go into the same kind of details they provide for other and, from a Western point of view, less important subjects.

Unchangeability of Hindu *Dharma* and Law

The claim of the tradition that *dharma,* including Hindu law, is uniform and unchanging is even more complex. To be sure, the texts display a rare and fascinating uniformity, given the fact that they have been composed over a period of at least ten centuries and in various parts of the vast Indian subcontinent. There are, however, considerable differences, so much so that one might be inclined to speak of real contradictions.

It is tempting, in cases where one text differs from another, to explain the deviations as local or temporal variations—each text reflective of the situation in the part of India or the historical period in which it was composed. This is no longer an adequate explanation, however, when it is noticed that on various occassions, one and the same text exhibits more than one solution for the same legal question. Thus, Manu's chapter on inheritance begins with the rule: "After the death of the father and the mother, the brothers, being assembled, may divide among themselves in equal shares the paternal (and the maternal) estate . . . ."[45] The rule, however, immediately following, unmistakably states the principle of primogeniture: "(Or) the eldest alone may take the whole paternal estate, the others shall live under him just as (they lived) under their father."[46] Another rule speaks of different shares for the sons: "The additional share (deducted) for the eldest shall be one-twentieth (of the estate) and the best of all chattels, for the middlemost half of that, but for the youngest one-fourth."

Another well known and often discussed example concerns Manu's attitude toward *niyoga* (levirate). The text first states: "On failure of issue (by her husband) a woman who has been author-

45. MANU, *supra* note 8, at 9.104.

46. *Id.* at 9.105. The "(Or)" in Bühler's translation is not present in the Sanskrit text. Also his "may divide" and "may take" might equally have been meant to mean "shall divide" and "shall take;" they translate the same optative forms of the verbs as "shall live" later in the second stanza.

ised, may obtain, (in the) proper (manner described), the desired offspring by (cohabitation with) a brother-in-law or (with some other) Sapinda (of the husband)."[47] The text goes on to discuss whether one or two sons should be begotten, insists that the brother-in-law and the widow should behave even as a father and a daughter-in-law, and lays down the penalty for not doing so. The text then continues without any transition: "By twice-born men a widow must not be appointed to (cohabit with) any other (than her husband); for they who appoint (her) to another (man), will violate the eternal law."[48] It devotes another four stanzas[49] to the stern repudiation of the institution of *niyoga.*

In addition to offering different solutions for the same problem, the texts explicitly allow specific types of variations. On several occasions, after a particular topic of *dharma* has been expounded, supplementary rules are introduced to be applicable only in cases of *āpad,* which is usually translated as times of distress. The word is never, however, clearly defined. It may, obviously, refer to general calamities, such as floods or droughts, but it definitely also refers to distress involving one or a few individuals. For instance, the texts lay down strict rules on the specific occupations for each social group (*varṇa*), but these are invariably followed by exceptions, as in Manu: "[W]hen a Brahmin cannot live by his own activities as explained earlier, he may live by the duties of a Kṣatriya . . . ."[50] If he cannot subsist as a Kṣatriya, he may live as a Vaiśya.[51] These are clearly cases of individual *āpad,* which must have been numerous. An individual's *dharma,* and the law that is applicable, depends to a large extent on his caste. The theory of *āpad,* therefore, must be viewed as an indication that the authors of the *dharma* texts did recognize, to a degree, legal variation and adaptation of the law to differing circumstances.

The theory that *dharma* is eternal (*sanātana*) and unchanging had to be adapted to yet another concept that was very popular in Hinduism. The Hindus, even as the ancient Greeks, and many other civilizations, believe in the succession of four *yugas* (world ages), from the best to the worst. The present time is the Kaliyuga, which

47. *Id.* at 9.59.
48. *Id.* at 9.64.
49. *Id.* at 9.65-68.
50. *Id.* at 10.81.
51. *Id.* at 10.82.

corresponds to the Iron Age. *Dharma* was perfect in the first age, but it diminished by one fourth in each successive age, with the result that in the Kali age, *dharma* stands on one leg only.[52] Consequently a number of practices described in the *dharma* texts have been labeled *Kalivarjyas*, "practices to be avoided in the Kali age."[53] For instance, later *dharmaśāstras* have used this criterion to account for earlier contradictory statements on *niyoga*: levirate was a common practice in earlier ages, but it should be avoided in the Kaliyuga.

Hinduism believes, first, in the gradual deterioration within each *yuga*, and, second, in the eternal return, with interruptions, of the four ages. The logical conclusion, therefore, is that, for the orthodox Hindu, *dharma* and law are, in fact, subject to continuous change.

Finally, it should be pointed out that the Sanskrit texts themselves recognize unwritten sources of *dharma*. One important source, which often figures in enumerations together with *śruti* and *smṛti*, is variously called *sadācāra* (practices of the good) or *siṣṭācara* (practices of the learned). Irrespective of the lengthy scholastic disquisitions which these terms have provoked at a later stage, it is clear that, by introducing this type of unwritten and vaguely defined source of law, the texts wanted to give recognition to a number of practices which they themselves did not explicitly codify. Even more significant is the recognition by the texts, *expressis verbis*, of a wide variety of more specific customs as sources of *dharma*. As early as Gautama's *Dharmasūtra*, the king, when sitting as judge, is supposed to supplement the *dharma* contained in the *śruti* and *smṛti* with the laws (*dharma*) of specific groups. Thus, it has been stated:

> The laws of countries, castes, and families, which are not opposed to the (sacred) records, (have) also authority.
>
> Cultivators, traders, herdsmen, money-lenders, and artisans (have authority to lay down rules) for their respective classes.
>
> Having heard the (state of) affairs from those who (in each class) have authority (to speak he shall give) the legal decision.[54]

Similar rules are repeated throughout *dharmaśāstra* literature. Some texts go even further and provide for separate courts of law, which seem to be considered lower than the royal court, but at the

52. Sanskrit uses the same term for "one quarter" and "a foot, a leg."
53. B. Bhattacharya, The Kalivarjyas (Calcutta 1943).
54. Gautama 11.20-22.

same time are supposed to judge members of a group according to rules of law current within that group. For instance, Bṛhaspati states: "For persons roaming the forest, a court should be held in the forest; for warriors, in the camp; and for merchants, in the caravan."[55]

Nowhere in the texts have these specialized laws been described, nor is there any indication of their magnitude or contents. The sole requirement, already mentioned by Gautama and reiterated several times in later texts, is that they not be opposed to the Veda and Vedic *dharma*.

Dharmaśāstra v. Legal Practice

Occasional glimpses into the existence of uncodified and unknown sources of law in Hinduism naturally lead to a basic question: To what extent were the written texts on *dharma* true sources of law? Do the texts actually allow an evaluation of the real attitude of Hindus toward law?

Answers to these questions vary considerably. At one end of the spectrum there are evaluations such as this: "There can be no doubt that the smriti rules were concerned with the practical administration of the law."[56] At the other end, however, there is the opinion most forcefully expressed thus: "It is a profound error to regard the Smritis as complete codes of law or as getting all their 'rules' rigidly enforced by the political authorities of their times."[57] According to the same author, "Hindu Law was in the main never more than a pious wish of its metaphysically-minded, ceremonial-ridden priestly promulgators, and but seldom a stern reality."[58]

There have been attempts to demonstrate that the *dharma* texts were indeed put to practical use in classical India, and that they do reflect the law of the land. This author refers to an article published under the title: "The Harmonizing of Law With the Requirements of Economic Conditions According to the Ancient *Dharmaśāstras*."[59]

55. Bṛhaspati 1.25.

56. Mayne's Treatise on Hindu Law and Usage 2 (11th ed. Madras 1950).

57. Govinda Das, *The Real Character of Hindu Law, Introduction* to edition of Vyavaharabālambhaṭṭi 8 (Banaras 1914).

58. *Id.* at 16.

59. L. Sternbach, 23 Annals of the Bhandarkar Oriental Research Institute, 528-43 (1942).

One example mentioned in this article concerns the rate of interest. All *dharmaśāstras* agree on the normal rate of interest, fifteen percent. If the debtor, however, undertakes a long and, by implication, dangerous voyage, the interest is raised to 120%, and in case of a voyage overseas, to 200%. Although the texts reflect a logical adaptation of the rate of interest to risk, the very fact that this adaptation is identical throughout the literature proves that the system as such was considered more important than local or temporal differences.[60]

A more elaborate and far-reaching attempt to show the practical use of the *dharma* compares the legal systems as they emerge from the *dharmaśāstras* of Manu and Yājñavalkya, and concludes that they reflect two very different economic and social situations. Manu represents the Hindu nation of the Brāhmaṇic empire (150 B.C.); Yājñavalkya echoes the prosperous and liberal Sātavāhana empire (A.D. 150).[61] A detailed analysis of these arguments would lead this Article too far. This discussion shall therefore restrict itself to one example, to point out the danger of the tendency to apply modern concepts to the ancient Hindu lawbooks.

Manu distinguishes three levels of fines: the highest (1000 *paṇas*), the middlemost (500), and the lowest (250). These fines are just one of numerous instances throughout Hindu technical literature where quantitative categories are divided into three, each one following being half as large as the preceding one. Yājñavalkya follows the same system, yet his figures are different: 1080, 540, 270. The difference is attributed to a devaluation of the *pana* in the time separating both texts. In reality, Yājñavalkya's sole innovation—and a good one from the traditional point of view—is that he replaced Manu's round figure of 1000 by 1080, a variant on the basic number eighteen which has been met earlier in this study.

The above example probably allows, better than many others, an understanding of the true nature of the Hindu lawbooks. On the one hand, and most fundamental, there is the system. From the texts that have been preserved one can, to a certain extent, follow the

60. Even Sternbach acknowledged that "from the point of view of law, the Indian law-system can be discussed only as a static and not as a dynamic law, although there is no doubt that the Indian law, like all other laws, has its gradual development." *Id.* at 528.

61. *See generally* K.P. JAYASWAL, MANU AND YĀJÑAVALKYA, A COMPARISON AND A CONTRAST (Calcutta 1930).

development and formation of a number of specific systems. Once a system has been established, however, it is never again altered or abandoned. One example of the static nature of a system is the subdivision of substantive law. Once the basic scheme of eighteen titles is introduced, no later text deviates from it. Another example is that of the three degrees of fines. This author looks upon the compilers of the *dharmaśāstras* primarily as pandits, who worked with a set of data which they tried—very hard, as they ought to—to arrange within a number of acceptable systems. Some of them, totally unknown to us, succeeded in elaborating such systems. From then onward, these systems remained unchanged. This stability is the remarkable element in Sanskrit technical literature, and it is not restricted to law and *dharmaśāstra*.

On the other hand, there is the equally typical tendency of the Indian pandit to enrich, sophisticate, and beautify the work of his predecessors. This tendency explains why the later *dharmaśāstras* are far more detailed than the earlier ones. It explains why Nārada —more correctly, the pandit who piled the *Nāradadharmaśāstra*—further subdivided the eighteen titles of law into one hundred and thirty-two subtitles. It also explains why Yājñavalkya replaced Manu's highest fine of 1000 *paṇas* by 1080.

Many of the legal prescriptions in the *dharmaśāstras* must be more or less literal renditions of the mass of floating versified maxims which were current in India from very early times and in many fields. When the *dharmasūtras* are described as the older type of texts, it is sometimes forgotten that many of these *sūtras*, the literary style of the time, incorporate sections of existing maxims in *śloka* meter, the style of the later *dharmaśāstras*. It is these maxims which were collected, ordered according to subject matter, elaborated into systems, and enriched with an ever growing number of details in the texts. The fact that two or more maxims provided two or more different solutions for the same problem was no obstacle to their being included in the same texts. An example would be Manu's differing rules on the succession of an estate. It is possible that the differing maxims reflected different local usages. Too modern a view of local usages in ancient India, however, overlooks that these usages were definitely not the usages of North, South, East, or any other province of India. They may, from the beginning, have coexisted within small geographic areas. On the other hand, once they were formulated as maxims, they must, together with numerous other maxims, have started on their intriguing and inexplicable voyage across the width and breadth of the subcontinent.

Next to nothing is known about actual legal practice in ancient India. The texts on *dharma,* as they exist today, edited, published, and easily accessible in bookshops and libraries, were certainly not the most wide-spread sources of law. It must be logically accepted that those Brahmins who knew the texts must have tried also to enforce them, at least to a certain extent, whenever they were called on for advice. It is also logical to accept that, in such cases, the ancient Indian kings and minor executives would not normally and intentionally transgress rules of *dharma,* an attitude which would not only harm them in this existence but also in later incarnations.

More important than the texts were the legal maxims referred to earlier. These maxims, not necessarily in Sanskrit, and perhaps merely via illustrative parables, were much better known, as they are today. To the extent to which the maxims were applied to settle disputes, Hindu *dharma* was indeed a source of law. Finally, there must have been the whole spectrum of customs, the existence of which is, as we have seen, confirmed by the texts. Numerous disputes must have been solved in very definite and constant ways for the sole reason that they had been solved in these ways from time immemorial.[62]

Conclusion: Later Developments

Until now this Article has concentrated on the classical period of Hinduism, the time of the *dharmasūtras* and *dharmaśāstras.* To conclude, a few remarks on later developments are in order. Even though some of the less important *dharmaśāstras* may have been composed at a much later period, by about the eighth century A.D., possibly a little earlier or later, a new period sets in in the history of Hindu *dharma.* From that time onward the entire literature which has been discussed so far becomes, for about ten centuries, the object

62. In a letter dated 1714, Father Bouchet, S.J., reported at length on the legal system of the Hindus as he observed it. He said that they did not have written laws, but they did have a number of well established maxims, some of which Father Bouchet treated in detail. Also, he stated they had a wide array of customs and usages, unwritten but transmitted from parent to child, from which they would under no circumstance deviate. Bouchet assured his readers that, against all expectations, the system worked and justice prevailed. Bouchet's description may very well apply to most situations in ancient India.

of numerous and endless commentaries. A strict distinction is now made between, on the one hand, the *smṛti* which obtains absolute authority, and, on the other hand, its interpretation by the commentators which is subject to continuous discussion, innovation, and improvement. Two types of commentaries should be distinguished: (1) the commentaries *stricto sensu* that explain one particular text, *sūtra* after *sūtra*, or *śloka* after *śloka*, comparing them with select passages from other *dharmaśāstras* as they proceed; and (2) the *nibandhas,* often translated as digests, which treat one subject after another, quoting and commenting on ancient texts irrespective of their original contexts.

Opinions again vary on the role that the legal sections of the commentaries and digests played as sources of law. Most modern scholars, Western first, Indian later, believe that the commentators used the ancient texts actually to codify the laws of their respective provinces. The most recent study of classical Hindu law[63] even equates the transition from *śāstra* to commentary with the passage "from *dharma* to law."[64]

This author has consistently defended a very different interpretation of the commentarial period of *dharma* literature. The commentaries *stricto sensu* do not in any way attach greater importance to the legal sections of the ancient texts than they do to any other section of the *dharma,* nor do they treat them in any different way. The commentarial technique is identical throughout. In the digests there are now separate sections on *vivāda,* substantive law, *vyavahāra,* either procedure or procedure and substantive law, and *nīti,* administrative law. Once again, however, these legal sections are not more important nor are they in any way different from the many other sections which, together with them, make up the *nibandha.* The basic misunderstanding of these texts, and a total loss of historical perspective, came about during the colonial period, when the legal sections of the commentaries and digests were edited, translated into English, and used as lawbooks, whereas all other sections were left to be studied by historians of religion or totally neglected.

In this author's opinion the Hindu attitude toward law in these Indian Middle Ages was not different from what it had been in more

63. R. Lingat, Les sources du droit dans le système traditionnel de l'Inde (J.D.M. Derrett trans. 1973).

64. *Id.* at 143.

ancient times. In principle, the *śāstra* was still the theoretical source of law. In practice, maxims and customs were paramount. There was one difference, though. In many parts of India where the Moghul Empire was strong, Muslim law took over from Hindu law, also for Hindus. Some of this author's recent research seems to indicate that in certain areas Hindu law had, for all practical purposes, disappeared at the time when the colonial powers appeared on the scene.

As indicated at the beginning of this Article, in 1772 the British, under the impulse of Governor General Warren Hastings, decided that, in a number of areas of private law, Hindus should be governed by their own laws. The answer to the question where these laws might be found, was predictable: the *śāstra.* The British interpreted this answer literally and elevated, for the first time in Indian history, the *dharmaśāstras* qua texts to the rank of lawbooks. British judges were given the task of applying laws in the courts, the extent of which they did not know, the language of which they were unable to read, and the general background of which they could not understand. For several years, pandits were appointed to the courts to research the laws governing each case. Dissatisfaction with the system and distrust of the pandits led Sir William Jones to study Sanskrit and translate Manu's *dharmaśāstra.* The need to have a complete code of Hindu law led to the compilation, by hired pandits, of new digests, which were subsequently translated into English. The vagueness of these codes in turn created the concept of schools of Hindu law based on the premise, wrong in this author's opinion, that the medieval digests codified the laws of different provinces of India, and that they could be used as such. In short, a slowly growing number of legal sections of commentaries and digests were translated into English, and the British judges applied them, as well as they could, even against occasional odds. For instance, when a party or a lawyer presented the judge with a Sanskrit text which had not yet been translated, it should not therefore be less authoritative. Inevitably, the judges introduced a few changes of their own. They arbitrarily separated law from religion. The commentaries were, relatively speaking, the least ambiguous sources of law, therefore the judges reversed the traditional hierarchy, and stated that the wording of the commentary overrules that of the *dharmaśāstra,* and the latter that of the Vedas. They gradually avoided consulting and reinterpreting the translations of Sanskrit texts by making Hindu law into a regular case law, invoking precedent and stare decisis. When the

Hindu lawbooks appeared to be unacceptable, they overruled them on the grounds of justice, equity, and good conscience.

This description would be irrelevant for the study of Hindu conceptions of law, were it not that the Hindu judges, Hindu attorneys, and the Hindu public at large fully accepted this well-intended but perfectly hybrid system of law created by the British. They accepted it before independence, and they continued to live by it after 1947.

In the meanwhile, a number of basically Western codes had been introduced: the Penal Code (1860); the Indian Evidence Act (1872); the Criminal Procedure Code (1898); and the Code of Civil Procedure (1908). For more than a century, in the field of private law, several legislative Acts overruled and abrogated more and more provisions of classical Hindu law. In the years before independence, a serious effort was made to codify Hindu private law. The "Hindu Code Bill," however, never became law, in view of the lack of agreement, even among Indians, on the basic principles upon which private laws applicable to all Hindus should be built. The Indian Constitution was even more ambitious: "The State shall endeavour to secure for the citizens a uniform civil code throughout the territory of India."[65] Today, nearly three decades later, there is no evidence to show that this ideal will be realized in the near future.

65. INDIAN CONSTITUTION, art. 44 (1950).

[2]

TRADITIONAL ORTHODOX HINDU JURISPRUDENCE: JUSTIFYING DHARMA AND DANDA

DAVID A. FUNK†

By Law they came to truth, the Law's observers, bright by their birth, and pure, and sanctifying.[1]

Traditional Hindu jurisprudence deals with the relatively consistent philosophy of law expounded in the ancient and medieval Indian Sanskrit literature, until greatly increased Western influence in the 1700's and the "Indian Renaissance" of the 1800's.[2] The general principles of this philosophy of law

---

† Professor of Law, Indiana University School of Law—Indianapolis; A.B., The College of Wooster, 1949; J.D., Case Western Reserve University, 1951; M.A., Political Theory, The Ohio State University, 1968; LL. M., Case Western Reserve University, 1972; LL. M., Columbia University, 1973. The author has taught jurisprudence at the Indiana University School of Law—Indianapolis since 1973. He compiled ORIENTAL JURISPRUDENCE: SUPPLEMENTARY READINGS FROM THE NEAR AND FAR EAST (temp. xerox ed. 1974), 211 pp., which has been distributed *inter alia* to 17 law libraries. This article is the first of five chapters describing successively traditional Hindu, Chinese, Japanese, Jewish and Islamic jurisprudence. These chapters are to be republished as a book on Oriental jurisprudence, along with (1) an introduction arguing for inclusion of these subjects in jurisprudence courses to supplement and contrast with ancient Greek and Roman, and medieval scholastic, discussions of natural law and (2) a conclusion drawing cross-cultural comparisons. The author has been using his temporary readings to do this since 1974, to create comparative jurisprudence and provide a world perspective to what previously has been treated here as a Western civilization subject.

For recent similar attempts to do this in West Germany, *see, e.g.*: R. MAY, FRIEDEN UND DIE AUFGABE DES RECHTS (1978); 1 STUDIEN ZU NICHTEUROPÄISCHEN RECHTSTHEORIN: BEITRÄGE ZU INDISCHEM RECHTSDENKEN (T. Viehweg & R. May eds. 1979); 2 *id.*: BEITRÄGE ZU ISLAMISCHEN RECHTSDENKEN (R. May ed. 1985); and R. MAY, LAW AND SOCIETY, EAST AND WEST (1985).

The author assumes sole and full responsibility for the opinions expressed in this article, and the completeness, accuracy and form of the text and notes in all respects, though tildes replace macrons and many pronunciation symbols have been omitted from Sanskrit words.

1. R. GRIFFITH, THE HYMNS OF THE RIGVEDA (3d ed. 1920-26) VII.56, "To Maruts" verse 12, repr. in A SOURCE BOOK IN INDIAN PHILOSOPHY 29 (S. Radhakrishnan & Moore eds. 1957). These hymns probably were current in 1400 B.C. "somewhat in the arrangement in which we have them at the present time." *Id.* at 3-4.

2. *See generally* D. BROWN, THE WHITE UMBRELLA 79-86 (1953).

may be found in the ten classical Sanskrit works probably written before 600 A.D., which are discussed in Part B below. Orthodox Hindu jurisprudence, however, does not include the special approaches to law developed by the Jains and Buddhists from the 500's B.C., and by the Sikhs after the 1500's A.D.

A. *Orthodox Hindu Jurisprudence: A Composite Statement*

The primary problem for traditional orthodox Hindu jurisprudence is to explain the existence of rules of dharma and justify obedience to them. Dharma supports and sustains the individual through the vicissitudes of life, as well as the state and the community, and even the world and universe. This jurisprudence justifies special rules limiting the political power of the king (rajadharma) and legitimizes his duty to preserve all types of dharma by punishments (danda). Thus this jurisprudence limits the absolute power of the king on one hand through rajadharma, and on the other hand legitimizes obedience to proper positive legal acts of the state, especially punishments.

In general Hindu jurisprudence treats dharma as true Divine, cosmic law with special rules applicable to four basic castes (varnas) and, within each caste, to four stages of life (âśramas). The four basic castes consist of: (1) the priestly class (brâhmins); (2) rulers and others who use force (ksatriyas), with special emphasis on the king (raja); (3) farmers and merchants (vaiśyas); and (4) laborers (śûdras). The first three are twice born (dvijas) because they are "born again" when initiated into knowledge of the basic scriptures, the Vedas. Ideally the life of each (male) person in each basic caste progresses through four life stages: (1) the student (brahmacârin); (2) the householder (grhastha); (3) the ascetic (sannyâsa); and perhaps finally (4) the forest dweller (vânaprastha) unincumbered by worldly goods. This social structure and set of life stages also determines the basic division of labor in the ancient Indian economy.

Each person in each caste and each stage of life in this highly stratified society may be seeking, at any particular time, one or more of four life goals: (1) dharma; (2) wealth or success with respect to other practical aims (artha); (3) sensual pleasure (kâma); and finally, especially among later thinkers, release from all worldly concerns (moksha). General rules of dharma sometimes must defer to special customs of an Aryan locality, family, or guild, though custom cannot modify the most basic rules of dharma.[3] The wisest and most virtuous members of a community (the śishtas) have special authority to formulate these customs.[4]

The world has passed through four basic epochs (yugas), namely, the krita, tretā, dvāpara and kali age-cycles, each somewhat more degenerate than the last, so that the dharma of each epoch (yugadharma) may vary somewhat from that of other ages. Also, rules applicable to normal times within an epoch may be replaced by special rules (āpaddharma) during special periods of distress. This set of basic philosophical principles produces a traditional legal system (Hindu law) of considerable complexity, and a correspondingly complex jurisprudence justifying it.

The connection of Hindu law with the cosmos and the gods might lead one to suppose that it would be considered a universal standard applicable to non-Aryan as well as Aryan peoples. Ironically that apparently is not the case. Hindu law is a personal law and governs the relationships of Hindus with foreigners (mlecchas) in Aryan territories (in general they should be avoided), as well as the conduct of Hindus wherever they may be. Also, Hindu jurisprudence often is phrased in general terms. Hindu law, however, apparently does not apply to foreigners in foreign territories. Hence Hindu jurisprudence justifies obedience only to a particular legal system by particular people and, in the final analysis, does not purport to be a universal jurisprudence.

This complex Hindu legal system is to be administered by the king of each separate Aryan kingdom and his ministers, in cooperation with the priests who know dharma. The king is to choose a personal priestly advisor (purohita), and several priests of good character are to advise the king on disputed questions in the application of the rules.[5]

Hindu law and jurisprudence are derived from a complex, somewhat polytheistic religion,[6] more properly called "heno-

---

3. *See, e.g.*, III P. Kane, History of Dharmaśāstra 856-84 (2d ed. 1973).

4. *See, e.g.*, *id.* at 825-27.

5. *See, e.g.*, U. Ghoshal, A History of Indian Political Ideas 60 (1959 repr. 1966).

6. For a brief general description of Hinduism, *see, e.g.*, J. Kitigawa, Religions of the East 99-154 (1960).

theism," in which the god focused on at the moment is treated as the only god, without denying the existence of other gods.[7] Brahmā is the creator god and may be assimilated to Brāhman, the impersonal world soul, but Prajāpati is chief of the gods.

Ultimately dharma is derived from assumed Divine revelations (śruti) which were recorded in the four Vedas (signifying wisdom) between 1500 and 800 B.C. Human authors writing between 600 and 100 B.C. in aphorisms (sūtras), and writing books of "things remembered" (smrtis) later interpreted the revelations and molded them into a legal science of dharma (dharmaśāstra). Human authors cannot alter the Divine revelations, though some of them may be assumed to have been lost especially when found only in smrti works. Also, an assembly of priests who are living in accordance with their dharma, can use logic and reason to interpret the Divine revelations. A vast Sanskrit literature of "things remembered," commentaries, treatises and digests subsequently developed a complex system of detailed legal rules building on the foregoing fundamental jurisprudential premises.

Those portions of this legal literature which deal with the special dharma of the king (rajadharma) and the science (dandanīti) of his administration of punishments (danda) are especially apt to provide additional justifications for promoting and maintaining this code of behavior. At least in the present (kali) epoch, fear of punishment is necessary to assure that most people will perform their duties. If the king did not punish violations appropriately, the four basic castes would become mixed, ownership and marriage would disappear, chaos would reign, sacrifices necessary to propitiate the gods would not be made, the rains would not come, and mankind would be miserable.

If each person performs his or her duties properly, according to the doctrine of karma he or she may be reborn into successively higher castes and eventually achieve release (moksha) from the endless cycle of rebirth, and finally eternal bliss. On the other hand, if a person fails to perform his or her duties, he or she may be reborn into a lower caste and thus be farther from the goal of release from worldly cares and eternal

7. *Id.* at 106 and A SOURCE BOOK IN INDIAN PHILOSOPHY, *supra* note 1 at 4.

bliss. These doctrines apply to the king as well, so that he, too, is rewarded for performing his duties properly, and punished for failure to do so. Also, if the people are righteous, the king wins a share of their spiritual merits; but if they are sinful, the king is charged with a share of their sin. In extreme cases, violent and non-violent resistance, even to the point of tyrannicide, are justifiable when an evil king fails to protect the persons and property of his subjects adequately, so that they must live in extreme fear and want. Finally the king should provide especially for weak, poor and aged subjects, as a father would for his children, and serve as a moral model for his subjects.

B. *Ten Traditional Hindu Jurisprudence Works Excerpted*

Special problems of dating and authorship plague the literature in which this philosophy of law is expressed. Often the true author of a work has attributed it to an earlier real or perhaps mythical person, presumably to gain a larger audience and wider acceptance of his work. Many of the older works apparently were the composite work of many hands, sometimes poorly harmonized, so that it is often impossible now to say which anonymous authors wrote which portions of our version of the work. Different Sanskrit manuscripts of the same work often differ from each other, presumably due to copying errors, editorial changes or additions, and sometimes losses of portions of a manuscript. English translations differ in quality from the early days of British rule to more recent translations by contemporary Sanskrit scholars using better texts. Finally even the best of the modern translations from the best critical editions of the Sanskrit texts may be criticized by other scholars who would have rendered particular phrases differently. Hindu authors apparently were more interested in the reception and influence of their work, rather than getting "credit" for writing it. Hence they usually do not indicate the historical time at which they wrote. This must be inferred usually from the contents of the manuscript. Often, therefore, the basic documents in which these ideas are expressed can only be attributed to a range of years, and scholarly opinion often differs concerning their earlier and later limits.

With these caveats concerning authorship, translation and chronology, this essay will deal with each of ten major surviving works of Hindu jurisprudence, under their traditional names, in apparent historical order. In doing so, it will rely primarily on two attempts to assign dates to these works: those of Dr. U. N. Ghoshal[8] and especially those of Pandurang Vaman Kane.[9]

The English translations used here may not be the best available anywhere, but they are the best available to this author and sufficiently accurate, it is hoped, for these authors, whoever they may be, to convey their principal jurisprudential ideas to us in their own words, but through English translation.

In general the jurisprudential excerpts in Part B will be presented in the order in which they appear in the works as we now have them without rearrangement, though extracted from entire works which deal with many other legal and nonlegal matters. Sometimes the arrangement used by these authors is not very systematic by our standards, but the excerpts should fit into the systematic composite statement of orthodox Hindu jurisprudence set forth in Part A above.

Transliteration of Sanskrit into English is not uniform, and quotations preserve the transliteration system of the particular translation used. Hence the same Sanskrit word may be spelled several different ways below, depending on whether it appears in a direct quotation or is paraphrased by the author of this essay. Also, words in parentheses in direct quotations have been added by the English translator to clarify the meaning of an elliptical text. Words in brackets in direct quotations, on the other hand, have been added by the author of this essay to further elucidate the meaning of these laconic jurisprudential texts.

1. Gautama

The first readily available Hindu work which deals extensively with jurisprudence is that attributed to Gautama. It was written between 600 and 300 B.C., and is the oldest extant example of a dharmasūtra,[10] i.e., a work on dharma written in aphorisms (sūtras) rather than in the metrical verses

8. U. Ghoshal, *supra* note 5 at xxi-xxii.
9. I (Pt. II) P. Kane, History of Dharmaśāstra i-xliv (rev. ed. 1975).
10. *Id.* at ii & I (Part I) P. Kane, History of Dharmaśāstra 29 (rev. ed. 1968).

(ślokas) used later. Gautama is a generic name[11] and the present, rather unsystematic text may be somewhat corrupt.[12] Nevertheless, the following excerpts indicate its basic jurisprudential point of view.

Gautama held that "[t]he Veda is the source of the sacred law, [a]nd [the sacred law also includes] the tradition and practice of those who know the (Veda)."[13]

He views men of the present (kali) epoch as weak compared to those of earlier times.[14]

The four stages of life are those of the student, householder, ascetic and the hermit in the woods,[15] but the householder is said to be the source of the others, "because the others do not produce offspring."[16] A student who follows the rules of dharma previously set forth "gains the heaven of Brahman, and (of him it is said that) he has subdued his organs (of sense and action)."[17] "[T]hese (restrictions imposed on students must also be observed by men) of other (orders, provided they are) not opposed (to their particular duties)."[18]

Dharma has an exalted role in this scheme of possible life goals.

> Wealth, relations, occupation, birth, learning and age must be honoured; (but) each later named (quality) is more important (than the preceding ones).
>
> But sacred learning is more important than all (other good qualities),
>
> Because that is the root of the sacred law,
>
> And because the Veda (expressly declares it).[19]

Special standards apply in special times of distress. "(In times of distress it is permissible) to offer sacrifices[,] for (men of) all (castes), to teach (them), and to accept (presents

---

11. *Id.* at 23. The author of Gautama should not be confused with Gautama Buddha, the founder of Buddhism, who lived during the 500's B.C.

12. *Id.* at 32. The present discussion relies on *Gautama, Institutes of the Sacred Law*, translated by Georg Bühler, in THE SACRED LAWS OF THE ÂRYAS, PT. I, ÂPASTAMBA AND GAUTAMA in 2 THE SACRED BOOKS OF THE EAST 173-310 (F. Max Müller ed. 1879 repr. 1969).

13. *Id.* at 175.

14. *Id.*

15. *Id.* at 192.

16. *Id.* at 193.

17. *Id.*

18. *Id.*

19. *Id.* at 210-11.

from them)."[20] "On failure of the (occupations lawful for a Brâhmana) he may live by the occupations of a Kshatriya" and "[o]n failure of those, he may live by the occupations of a Vaisya."[21] "[I]f no (other course is) possible (a Brâhmana) may support himself in any way except by (following the occupations) of a Sûdra. Some (permit) even this in case his life is in danger. But to mix with that (caste) and forbidden food must be avoided (even in times of distress)."[22] "If his life is threatened, even a Brâhmana may use arms" and "(In times of distress) a Kshatriya (may follow) the occupations of a Vaisya."

Dharma is intimately connected with the natural order.

> A king and a Brâhmana, deeply versed in the Vedas, these two, uphold the moral order in the world.
>
> On them depends the existence of the fourfold human race, of internally conscious beings, of those which move on feet and wings, and of those which creep,
>
> (As well as) the protection of offspring, the prevention of the confusion (of the castes and) the sacred law.[23]

The king (raja) has a special role in the scheme of things. "The king is master of all, with the exception of Brâhmanas."[24] "He shall be impartial towards his subjects [a]nd shall do (what is) good for them."[25] "He shall protect the castes and orders in accordance with justice; [a]nd those who leave (the path of) duty, he shall lead back (to it). For it is declared (in the Veda) that he obtains a share of the spiritual merit (gained by his subjects)."[26]

The king, however, does not rule alone. He "shall select as his domestic priest (purohita) a Brâhmana who is learned (in the Vedas) . . . of a virtuous disposition, who lives righteously and who is austere."[27] "For it is declared (in the Veda): 'Kshatriyas who are assisted by Brâhmanas, prosper

---

20. *Id.* at 211-12. In ordinary times these activities are reserved for brâhmins. *Id.* at 212 n. 4.

21. *Id.* at 212.

22. *Id.* at 213.

23. *Id.* at 214-15.

24. *Id.* at 234.

25. *Id.* at 235.

26. *Id.*

27. *Id.*

and do not fall into distress.' "[28]

Dharma, custom and reason all enter into the administration of law. The administration of justice of the king

> (shall be regulated by) the Veda, the Institutes of the Sacred Law, the Angas [the six auxilliary branches of learning], and the Purâna [ancient lore].
>
> The laws of countries, castes, and families which are not opposed to the (sacred) records, (have) also authority.
>
> Cultivators, traders, herdsmen, money-lenders, and artisans (have authority to law down rules) for their respective classes.
>
> Having learned the (state of) affairs from those who (in each class) have authority (to speak he shall give) the legal decision.
>
> Reasoning is a means for arriving at the truth.
>
> Coming to a conclusion through that, he shall decide properly.
>
> If (the evidence) is conflicting, he shall learn (the truth) from (Brâhmanas) who are well versed in the threefold sacred lore, and give his decision (accordingly).
>
> For, (if he acts) thus, blessings will attend him (in this world and the next).[29]

The king "shall restrain those who do not restrain themselves."[30]

Divine rewards and retribution acting through the doctrine of rebirth (karma) "enforces" the rules of dharma.

> (Men of) the (several) castes and orders who always live according to their duty enjoy after death the rewards of their works, and by virtue of a remnant of their (merit) they are born again in excellent countries, castes, and families, (endowed) with beauty, long life, learning in the Vedas, (virtuous) conduct, wealth, happiness, and wisdom.
>
> Those who act in a contrary manner perish, being born again in various (evil conditions).
>
> The advice of the spiritual teacher and the punishment (inflicted by the king) guard them.[31]

This process also applies to the king. "If the sacred law is violated and the (king) does not do (his duty), he commits

28. *Id.* at 236.
29. *Id.* at 237-38.
30. *Id.* at 238.
31. *Id.*

sin."[32]

Special legal institutions may interpret and apply the rules of dharma.

> In cases for which no rule has been given, (that course) must be followed of which at least ten (Brâhmanas), who are well instructed, skilled in reasoning, and free from covetousness, approve.[33]

In conclusion, Guatama observes that "[h]e who knows the sacred law obtains heavenly bliss, more than (other) righteous men, on account of his knowledge of, and his adherence to it. Thus the sacred law (has been explained)."[34]

2. Baudhãyana

The work attributed to Baudhãyana probably was written between 600 B.C. and 300 B.C., but after Gautama and before the other dharmasûtras discussed below.[35] The complete text apparently has not survived,[36] is somewhat disjointed and not very concise.[37] Nevertheless its legal philosophy is generally consistent with that of Gautama.[38]

Baudhãyana identifies the sources of law, as follows:

> The sacred law is taught in each Veda. . . .
>
> (The sacred law), taught in the Tradition (Smriti, stands) second.
>
> The practice of the Sishtas (stands) third. . . .
>
> '(Those are called) Sishtas who, in accordance with the sacred law, have studied the Veda together with its appendages, know how to draw inferences from that, (and) are able to adduce proofs perceptible by the senses from the revealed texts.'
>
> On failure of them, an assembly consisting at least of ten members (shall decide disputed points of law).[39]

Baudhãyana makes a rather extreme claim for the au-

---

32. *Id.* at 274.
33. *Id.* at 310.
34. *Id.*
35. I (Pt. I) P. KANE, *supra* note 10 at 49 & 51.
36. *Id.* at 38 & 42.
37. *Id.* at 44.
38. The present discussion relies on BAUDHÂYANA, translated by Georg Bühler, in SACRED LAWS OF THE ARYÂS, PT. II, VAŚISHTHA AND BAUDHÂYANA in 14 THE SACRED BOOKS OF THE EAST 141-336 (F. Max Müller ed. 1882 repr. 1969).
39. *Id.* at 143-44.

thority of brâhmins in interpreting law. " 'What Brâhmanas, riding in the chariot of the law (and) wielding the sword of the Veda, propound even in jest, that is declared to be the highest law.' "[40] This, however, is modified by a more sober view: " 'Many thousands (of Brâhmanas) cannot form a (legal) assembly (for declaring the sacred law), if they have not fulfilled their sacred duties, are unacquainted with the Veda, and subsist only by the name of their caste.' "[41]

Some special rules apply only in the north of India and other special rules apply only in the south.[42] Baudhâyana explains this anomaly as follows:

> He who follows (these practices) in any other country than where they prevail, commits sin.
>
> For each (of these customs) the rule of the country should be (considered) the authority.[43]

Baudhâyana explains the divine origin and basic duties of the basic caste structure which dharma is to maintain, as follows:

> Brahman, forsooth, placed its majesty in the Brâhmanas, together with (the duties and privileges of) studying, teaching, sacrificing for themselves, sacrificing for others, liberality, and accepting (gifts), for the protection of the Vedas;
>
> In the Kshatriyas (it placed) strength, together with (the duties and privileges of) studying, sacrificing, liberality, (using) weapons, and protecting the treasure (and the life of) created beings, for the growth of good government;
>
> In the Vaisyas (it placed the power of work), together with (the duties of) studying, sacrificing, liberality, cultivating (the soil), trading, and tending cattle, for the growth of (productive) labour.
>
> On the Sûdras (it imposed the duty of) serving the three higher (castes).
>
> For (the Veda states), "they [the śûdras] were created from the feet (of Brahman)."[44]

The king is to "protect (his) subjects, receiving as his pay

40. *Id.* at 145.
41. *Id.* at 146.
42. *Id.*
43. *Id.* at 147.
44. *Id.* at 199. Note that the neuter pronoun here avoids any problem concerning the gender of the god, Brahman.

a sixth part (of their incomes [taxes] or spiritual merit),"[45] "choose a domestic priest (who shall be) foremost in all (transactions)"[46] and "act according to his instructions."[47]

Finally, the king has a personal stake in correct interpretation and application of the law.

> Of injustice (in decisions) one quarter falls on the party in the cause, one quarter on his witnesses, one quarter on all the judges, and one quarter on the king.
>
> But where he who deserves condemnation is condemned, the king is guiltless and the judges free from blame; the guilt falls on the offender (alone).[48]

3. Âpastamba

The work attributed to Âpastamba probably was written between 450 and 350 B.C. and after Gautama and Baudhâyana.[49] The author apparently had before him the dharmasûtra of Gautama.[50] He also utilized Jaimini's Mîmâmsâ principles of Vedic interpretation, which distinguish between seen and unseen motives: where an act is motivated by a worldly motive, such as pleasure, it cannot be assumed to be based on dharma.[51] The style of Âpastamba is more concise than that of Baudhâyana[52] but his legal philosophy generally reflects the basic principles of orthodox Hindu jurisprudence.[53] Âpastamba purports to

> declare the acts productive of merit which form part of the customs of daily life, as they have been settled by the agreement (of those who know the law).
>
> The authority (for these duties) is the agreement of those who know the law,
>
> And (the authorities for the latter are) the Vedas alone.

---

45. *Id.*
46. *Id.* at 200.
47. *Id.*
48. *Id.* at 203.
49. I (Part I) P. KANE, *supra* note 10 at 70.
50. *Id.* at 62.
51. *Id.* at 63-64. On Mîmâmsâ, *see generally* III P. KANE, *supra* note 3 at 838-55, and A SOURCE BOOK IN INDIAN PHILOSOPHY, *supra* note 1 at 486-505.
52. I (Pt. I) P. KANE, *supra* note 10 at 59.
53. The present discussion relies on ÂPASTAMBA, APHORISMS ON THE SACRED LAW OF THE HINDUS, translated by Georg Bühler, in THE SACRED LAWS OF THE ÂRYAS, PT. I, ÂPASTAMBA AND GAUTAMA in 2 THE SACRED BOOKS OF THE EAST 1-171 (F. Max Müller ed. 1879 repr. 1969).

(There are) four castes — Brâhmanas, Kshatriyas, Vaisyas, and Sûdras.

Amongst these, each preceding (caste) is superior by birth to the one following.. . . [A]nd (their) works are productive of rewards (in this world and the next).[54]

Neglect of the Vedas and "[c]onstant commission of (other) sins" *inter alia* causes a man to lose his caste.[55]

Each person is enjoined to live by his dharma, and warned of the consequences if he does not.

Despising all that which in this world is called an object (of the senses) a wise man shall strive after the (knowledge of the Âtman [the self, the universal soul]. . . . Therefore follow thou also this good road that leads to welfare (salvation), and not the one that leads into misfortune (rebirths).[56]. . . [R]egulation of one's conduct according to that of the Âryas, peacefulness and contentedness; — these (good qualities) have been settled by the agreement (of the wise) for all (the four) orders; he who, according to the precepts of the sacred law, practices these, enters the universal soul.[57]

In successive births men of the lower castes are born in the next higher one, if they have fulfilled their duties.

In successive births men of the higher castes are born in the next lower one, if they neglect their duties.[58]

The king, after having investigated a case carefully, may punish those who have gone astray, and "[a] king who acts thus, gains both (this and the next world)."[59]

Duties vary somewhat during the various stages of life.

There are four orders, viz., the order of householders, the order of students, the order of ascetics, and the order of hermits in the woods.

If he lives in all these four according to the rules (of the law), without allowing himself to be disturbed (by anything), he will obtain salvation.[60]

Finally,

---

54. *Id.* at 1-2.
55. *Id.* at 74.
56. *Id.* at 76.
57. *Id.* at 78.
58. *Id.* at 126.
59. *Id.* at 125.
60. *Id.* at 153.

[i]t is difficult to learn the sacred law from (the letter of) the Vedas (only); but by following the indications [below] it is easily accomplished.

The indications for these (doubtful cases are), "He shall regulate his course of action according to the conduct which is unanimously recognized in all countries by men of the three twice-born castes, who have been properly obedient (to their teachers), who are aged, of subdued senses, neither given to avarice, nor hypocrites. Acting thus he will gain both worlds [here and hereafter]."

Some declare, that the remaining duties (which have not been taught here) must be learnt from women and men of all castes.[61]

4. Vaśishtha

The work attributed to Vaśishtha, or Vasistha, probably was written between 300 B.C. and 100 B.C., but after the dharmasūtras of Gautama, Āpastamba and Baudhāyana.[62] It is a somewhat eclectic and derivative work, drawing on these three previous authors, as well as an earlier version of Manu[63] whose work will be discussed in section 7 below. Nevertheless some excerpts restating the leading jurisprudential ideas contained in these three previous Hindu classics may help clarify their overall point of view.[64]

Right living produces earthly and heavenly rewards.

He who knows and follows the (sacred law is called) a righteous man.

He becomes most worthy of praise in this world and after death gains heaven.

The sacred law has been settled by the revealed texts and by the tradition (of the sages).

On failure of (rules given in) these (two sources) the practice of the Sishtas (has) authority.

But [only] he whose heart is free from desire (is called) a Sishta.

(Acts sanctioned by) the sacred law (are those) for which

---

61. *Id.* at 171. Few other Hindu authors would agree with the unnamed sources of Āpastamba on this final point.

62. I (Pt. I) P. Kane, *supra* note 10 at 105.

63. *Id.* at 96-97 & 106.

64. The present discussion relied on *Vasishtha*, translated by Georg Bühler, in Sacred Laws of the Aryās, Pt. II, Vaśishtha and Baudhāyana in 14 The Sacred Books of the East 1-140 (F. Max Müller ed. 1882 repr. 1969).

no (worldly) cause is perceptible.[65]

Local customs may modify general rules of dharma.

> Acts productive of spiritual merit, and customs which (are approved of) in that country [the country of the Âryas — Âryâvarta], must be everywhere acknowledged (as authoritative);
> But not different ones, (i.e. those) of (countries where) laws opposed (to those of Âryâvarta prevail).[66]
> Manu has declared that the (peculiar) laws of countries, castes, and families (may be followed) in the absence of (rules of) the revealed texts.[67]

The familiar stages of life are enumerated.

> There are four orders.
> Viz. (that of) the student, (that of) the householder, (that of) the hermit, and (that of) the ascetic.[68]

Finally, the king has special duties to maintain the social order.

> The particular duty of a king is to protect (all) beings; by fulfilling it (he obtains) success (in this world and in the next).
> Let the king, paying attention to all the laws of countries, (subdivisions of) castes (gâti) and families, make the four castes (varna) fulfill their (respective) particular duties.
> Let him punish those who stray from (the path of duty).[69]

5. Vishnu

Vishnu is a relatively minor sun god in the Vedas who became the subject of almost monotheistic worship by a major Hindu sect which believes in salvation and release from the cycle of rebirths through loving faith.[70] The dharmasûtra work written as though it were a revelation of Vishnu,[71] is the only one of this type extant.[72] In its present form, it borrows heav-

---

65. *Id.* at 1.
66. *Id.* at 2.
67. *Id.* at 4.
68. *Id.* at 40.
69. *Id.* at 96.
70. *See, e.g.*, Braden, *Hinduism, Vishnu & Vishnuism, Vaisnavism*, respectively, in ENCYCLOPEDIA OF RELIGION 337-39, 814 & 815 (V. Ferm ed. 1945).
71. The present discussion relies on THE INSTITUTES OF VISHNU, translated by Julius Jolly, 7 THE SACRED BOOKS OF THE EAST (F. Max Müller ed. 1880 repr. 1970), 302 pp. *See, e.g.*, *id.* at 1-12.
72. I (Pt. I) P. KANE, *supra* note 10 at 115 & 117.

ily from Manu (discussed in section 7 below), Yãjñavalkya (discussed in section 9 below), and other authors.[73] Apparently it was later recast by some devotee of Vishnu.[74] The original version, which was mostly in prose sũtras, must have been written between 300 B.C. and 100 A.D., but the present expanded text, including verses (ślokas) often at the ends of chapters, must date from about 400 to 600 A.D.[75]

This book grows out of a conversation. When his consort (Lakshmî) asks the god Vishnu how she is to maintain herself upon the earth, Vishnu answers that "[t]hose who practice the duties ordained for each caste and for each order, and who act up strictly to the holy law, will sustain" the earth.[76] When she asks Vishnu to "[c]ommunicate to me the eternal laws of the castes and of the orders,"[77] Vishnu replies:

> Brâhmanas, Kshatriyas, Vaisyas, and Sûdras are the four castes.
>
> The first three of these are (called) twice-born. . . .
>
> Their duties are:
>
> For a Brâhmana, to teach (the Veda);
>
> For a Kshatriya, constant practice in arms;
>
> For a Vaisya, the tending of cattle;
>
> For a Sûdra, to serve the twice-born; . . .
>
> For a Kshatriya, to protect the world (and receive due reward, in [the] form of taxes); . . .
>
> In times of distress, each caste may follow the occupation of that next (below) to it in rank.[78]

The king has special duties, for which he receives special rewards. These duties of the king are:

> To protect his people,
>
> And to keep the four castes and the four orders in the practice of their several duties.[79]
>
> A sixth part both of the virtuous deeds and of the iniquitous acts committed by his subjects goes to the king.[80]
>
> Let him show honour to the righteous;

73. *Id.* at 116-18.
74. *Id.* at 124.
75. *Id.* at 125-26.
76. The Institutes of Vishnu, *supra* note 71 at 8.
77. *Id.*
78. *Id.* at 12-13.
79. *Id.* at 13-14.
80. *Id.* at 16.

> And let him punish the unrighteous.[81]

Legal institutions must be established and administered by the king in accordance with the sacred law. For example, he must appoint a domestic priest (purohita) conversant *inter alia* with the Vedas, epics, and the institutes of sacred law; his ministers must be "pure, free from covetousness, attentive and able"; and he must

> try causes himself, accompanied by well-instructed Brâhmanas.
>
> Or let him entrust a Brâmana with the judicial business.
>
> Let the king appoint as judges men of good families . . . who are eager in keeping religious vows, impartial towards friend and foe, and not likely to be corrupted by litigants . . . .[82]

Finally,

> [t]hose among the twice-born who will act according to (the precepts promulgated in) this excellent law-code, which has been proclaimed by the god himself, shall obtain a most excellent abode in heaven.
>
> It purifies from sin, it is auspicious, it leads to heaven, procures long life, knowledge (of the four objects of human pursuit) and renown, and increases wealth and prosperity.[83]

6. Kautilya

The work attributed to Kautilya was written sometime between 325 B.C. and 200 A.D.[84] It probably was composed mainly by a person named Cãnakya or Kautilya, who was a minister of Candragupta Maurry, who ruled an empire in northern India from 321 B.C. to 297 B.C. Therefore this work probably was composed between 320 B.C. and 300 B.C.[85] It is the earliest surviving work of arthaśâstra,[86] i.e. a work expounding the science of successfully achieving material well-being or wealth.[87]

---

81. *Id.* at 17.
82. *Id.* at 20-21.
83. *Id.* at 301.
84. I (Pt. II) P. KANE, *supra* note 9 at x. *Cf.* I (Pt. I) P. KANE, *supra* note 10 at 209 & 215.
85. *Id.* at 215. *See also id.* at 233.
86. *Id.* at 158.
87. *Id.* at 151 & 188. *See also id.* at 152.

It is primarily a Machiavellian book, emphasizing artha over dharma[88] and assuming that the end justifies the means.[89] For that reason it was an unpopular work even in ancient India.[90] In the process of expounding its rather cynical science of worldly success, however, even this practical treatise repeats some of the more lofty principles which justify the social order, the rules of dharma which sustain it, and specific duties of the king beyond the acquisition and consolidation of power.[91]

Kautilya restates the standard doctrine justifying dharma as follows:

> [t]he observance of one's own duty leads one to *svarga* [heaven] and infinite bliss. When it is violated, the world will come to an end owing to confusion of castes and duties.
>
> Hence the king shall never allow people to swerve from their duties; for whoever upholds his own duty, ever adhering to the customs of the Āryas, and following the rules of caste and divisions of religious life, will surely be happy both here and hereafter. For the world, when maintained in accordance with injunctions of the three Vedas, will surely progress, but never perish.[92]

Well-being and progress, in turn, depend on danda, the law of punishment or science of government.[93]

> . . . [P]unishment, when awarded with due consideration, makes the people devoted to righteousness and to works productive of wealth and enjoyment; . . .
>
> But when the law of punishment is kept in abeyance, it gives rise to such disorder as is implied in the proverb of fishes (A great fish swallows a small one); for in the absence of a magistrate the strong will swallow the weak; but under his protection the weak resist the strong.

---

88. *Id.* at 213 & 228.

89. *Id.* at 174 & 231.

90. *Id.* at 174 & 231.

91. The present discussion relies on KAUTILYA, ARTHA-ŚĀSTRA (R. Shamasastry transl. 2d ed. 1923) repr. in part in A SOURCE BOOK IN INDIAN PHILOSOPHY, *supra* note 1 at 193-223.

92. *Id.* at 198. Sometimes the Veda or Vedas is spoken of as a single unit, presumably then of all four Vedas. At other times, the first three Vedas are distinguished from the fourth. The three Vedas are the (1) Rig-Veda of hymns, (2) Yajur-Veda of rituals, and (3) Sama-Veda of more hymns, but omitting the fourth, Artharva-Veda, of magical spells.

93. *Id.*

> This people, consisting of four castes and four orders of religious life, when governed by the king with his sceptre [of danda], will keep to their respective paths, ever devotedly adhering to their respective duties and occupations.[94]

The sciences of logic, the three Vedas [including dharmaśâstra], and commerce "are dependent for their well-being on the science of government [arthaśâstra]" and "wealth, and wealth alone, is important, inasmuch as charity and desire depend upon wealth for their realisation."[95] The king is "a visible dispenser of punishments and rewards; [and] whoever disregards kings shall be visited with divine punishments."[96]

The king wields considerable power, but under the special restraints of rajadharma.

> . . . In virtue of his power to uphold the observance of the respective duties of the four castes and of the four divisions of religious life, and in virtue of his power to guard against the violation of the *dharmas*, the king is the fountain of justice.
>
> Sacred law, evidence, history, and edicts of kings are the four legs of Law. Of these four in order, the later is superior to the one previously named. . . .
>
> As the duty of the king consists in protecting his subjects with justice, its observance leads him to heaven. He who does not protect his people or upsets the social order wields his royal sceptre in vain.
>
> It is power, and power alone which, only when exercised by the king with impartiality and in proportion to guilt, either over his son or his enemy, [that] maintains both this world and the next.[97]

Sacred law generally prevails in adjudication, "[b]ut whenever sacred law is in conflict with rational law, then reason shall be held authoritative; for there the original text on which the sacred law has been based is not available."[98] Machiavellianism emerges from time to time, however, as in the following: "[t]he king in the interests of righteousness may inflict punishment in secret on those courtiers or confederacy of chiefs who are dangerous to the safety of the kingdom and

94. *Id.* at 199.
95. *Id.*
96. *Id.* at 201.
97. *Id.* at 202-03.
98. *Id.* at 203.

who cannot be put down in open daylight."[99]

In conclusion,

> [t]he subsistence of mankind is termed *artha*, wealth; the earth which contains mankind is termed *artha*, wealth; that science which treats of the means of acquiring and maintaining the earth is the *Arthaśāstra, Science of Polity*. . . .
>
> Thus, this *Śāstra*, . . . is composed as a guide to acquire this and the other world.
>
> In the light of this *Sāstra* one can not only set foot on righteous, economical, and aesthetical acts and maintain them, but also put down unrighteous, uneconomical, and displeasing acts.[100]

Divine "review" of kingly acts here seems more muted, and worldly success by any means seems more justified.

7. Manu

The dharmaśāstra work attributed to Manu, often referred to as the Manusmrti, probably was written in its present form between 200 B.C. and 200 A.D.[101] An anonymous author, perhaps Bhrgu,[102] wrote in the name of Manu, an ancient Hindu sage and mythical lawgiver and the father of the human race,[103] from which we get our word "man" or mankind. Despite some claims to the contrary, the Manusmrti probably was *not* a metrical rendition of an earlier dharmasūtra work attributed to Manu;[104] however, it apparently did combine two prior works on dharmaśāstra and arthaśāstra, respectively.[105] Regardless of its antecedents, in its extant form it became the most influential single statement of Hindu law and jurisprudence, both in India and Southeast Asia.[106]

At the outset, the great are said to have asked Manu "to declare to us precisely and in due order the sacred laws of each of the (four chief) castes (varna) and of the intermediate

99. *Id.* at 204.
100. *Id.* at 223.
101. I (Pt. I) P. KANE, *supra* note 10 at 344.
102. *Id.*
103. *Id.* at 307.
104. *Id.* at 143-49.
105. *Id.* at 311 & 344-45.
106. *Id.* at 345-46. The present discussion relies on THE LAWS OF MANU, translated by Georg Bühler, 25 THE SACRED BOOKS OF THE EAST (F. Max Müller ed. 1886 repr. 1969), 620 pp.

ones."[107] Manu replies that "for the sake of the prosperity of the world, he [the Lord, the divine self-existent] caused the Brâhmana, the Kshatriya, the Vaisya, and the Sûdra to proceed [respectively] from his mouth, his arms, his thighs, and his feet."[108] Manu describes the four ages of history and the successive decline of dharma in each:

> In the Krita age Dharma is four-footed and entire, and (so is) Truth; nor does any gain accrue to men by unrighteousness.
>
> In the other (three ages), by reason of unjust gains (âgama), Dharma is deprived successively of one foot, and through (the prevalence of) theft, falsehood, and fraud the merit (gained by men) is diminished by one fourth (in each). . . .
>
> One set of duties (is prescribed) for men in the Krita age, different ones in the Tretâ and in the Dvâpara, and (again) another (set) in the Kali, in proportion as those ages decrease in length.[109]

Different duties of the four basic castes are specified as follows:

> . . . in order to protect this universe He, the most resplendent one, assigned separate (duties and) occupations to those who sprang [respectively] from his mouth, arms, thighs, and feet.
>
> To Brâhmanas he assigned teaching and studying (the Veda), sacrificing for their own benefit and for others, [and] giving and accepting (of alms).
>
> The Kshatriya he commanded to protect the people, to bestow gifts, to offer sacrifices, to study (the Veda), and to abstain from attaching himself to sensual pleasures;
>
> The Vaisya [he commanded] to tend cattle, to bestow gifts, to offer sacrifices, to study (the Veda), to trade, to lend money, and to cultivate land.
>
> One occupation only the lord prescribed to the Sûdra, to serve meekly even these (other) three castes.[110]

Motives for right actions make a difference. "To act solely from a desire for rewards is not laudable," yet "[h]e who persists in discharging these (prescribed duties) in the right manner, reaches the deathless state and even in this (life) obtains (the fulfillment of) all the desires that he may have

107. *Id.* at 1.
108. *Id.* at 13-14.
109. *Id.* at 23-24.
110. *Id.* at 24.

conceived."[111]

Sources of law are listed in order of precedence. "The whole Veda is the (first) source of the sacred law, next the tradition and the virtuous conduct of those who know the (Veda further), also the customs of holy men, and (finally) self-satisfaction."[112] "But when two sacred texts (Sruti) are conflicting, both are held to be the law; for both are pronounced by the wise (to be) valid law."[113] "The custom handed down in regular succession (since time immemorial) among the (four chief) castes (varna) and the mixed (races) of that country, is called the conduct of virtuous men."[114]

Excessive pursuit of pleasure may vitiate right action. "Neither (the study of) the Vedas, nor liberality, nor any (self-imposed) restraint, nor austerities, ever procure the attainment (of rewards) to a man whose heart is contaminated (by sensuality)."[115]

Each person should "always slowly accumulate spiritual merit, in order (that it may be his) companion (after death)" for "(That companion) speedily conducts the man who is devoted to duty and effaces his sins by austerities, to the next world, radiant and clothed with an ethereal body."[116]

The four traditional stages of life are enumerated.

> The student, the householder, the hermit, and the ascetic, these (constitute) four separate orders, which all spring from (the order of) householders.
>
> But all (or) even (any of) these orders, assumed successively in accordance with the Institutes (of the sacred law), lead the Brâhmana who acts by the preceding (rules) to the highest state.
>
> And in accordance with the precepts of the Veda and of the Smriti, the householder is declared to be superior to [i.e. more distinguished than] all of them; for he supports the other three.[117]

Kings play an important role in this social system, and are deified. Kings "must duly protect this whole (world),"

111. *Id.* at 30-31.
112. *Id.* at 31.
113. *Id.* at 31-32.
114. *Id.* at 32.
115. *Id.* at 48.
116. *Id.* at 166-67.
117. *Id.* at 214-15.

"[f]or when these creatures, being without a king, through fear dispersed in all directions, the Lord created a king for the protection of this whole [creation] . . . ."[118] "Even an infant king must not be despised . . .; for he is a great deity in human form."[119] "[H]e assumes by turns many (different) shapes for the complete attainment of justice."[120]

Punishment is important in maintaining dharma and the natural order.

> For the (king's) sake the Lord formerly created his own son, Punishment [danda], the protector of all creatures, (an incarnation of) the law, formed of Brahman's glory.
>
> Through fear of him all created beings . . . swerve not from their duties.[121]
>
> Punishment alone governs all created beings, punishment alone protects them, punishment watches over them while they sleep; the wise declare punishment (to be identical with) the law.
>
> If (punishment) is properly inflicted after (due) consideration, it makes all people happy; but inflicted without consideration, it destroys everything.
>
> If the king did not, without tiring, inflict punishment on those worthy to be punished, the stronger would roast the weaker, like fish on a spit; . . . [O]wnership would not remain with any one, the lower ones would (usurp the place of) the higher ones.
>
> The whole world is kept in order by punishment, for a guiltless man is hard to find; through fear of punishment the whole world yields the enjoyments (which it owes). . . .[122]

The caste system, too, depends on punishment.

> All castes (varna) would be corrupted (by intermixture), all barriers would be broken through, and all men would rage (against each other) in consequence of mistakes with respect to punishment.[123]

The king administers punishment, but subject to special conditions. "By him who is pure (and) faithful to his promise,

118. *Id.* at 216.
119. *Id.* at 217.
120. *Id.*
121. *Id.* at 218.
122. *Id.* at 219.
123. *Id.* at 219-20.

who acts according to the Institutes (of the sacred law), who has good assistants and is wise, punishment can be (justly) inflicted."[124] "The king has been created (to be) the protector of the castes (varna) and orders, who, all according to their rank, discharge their several duties."[125]

As usual, customs (consistent with the Vedas) must be followed. "(A king) who knows the sacred law, must inquire into the laws of castes (gâti), of districts, of guilds, and of families, and (thus) settle the peculiar law of each."[126] "What may have been practised by the virtuous, by such twice-born men as are devoted to the law, that he [the king] shall establish as law, if it be not opposed to the (customs of) countries, families, and castes (gâti)."[127]

The eventual fate of the king depends on his properly discharging his earthly duties. "A king who punishes those who do not deserve it, and punishes not those who deserve it, brings great infamy on himself and (after death) sinks into hell."[128] "In consequence of his taking what ought not to be taken, or of his refusing what ought to be received, a king will be accused of weakness and perish in this (world) and after death."[129] "A king who (duly) protects (his subjects) receives from each and all the sixth part of their spiritual merit; if he does not protect them, the sixth part of their demerit also (will fall on him)."[130]

Proper punishment may even absolve the guilt of the wrongdoer. "[M]en who have committed crimes and have been punished by the king, go to heaven, being pure like those who performed meritorious deeds."[131]

Special rules apply in times of distress. Thus, "[t]wice-born men may take up arms when (they are) hindered (in the fulfillment of) their duties, when destruction (threatens) the twice-born castes (varna) in (evil) times."[132]

Special rewards await the good king. "A king who thus brings to a conclusion all the legal business enumerated above,

124. *Id.* at 221.
125. *Id.*
126. *Id.* at 260.
127. *Id.* at 261-62.
128. *Id.* at 276.
129. *Id.* at 285.
130. *Id.* at 307.
131. *Id.* at 309.
132. *Id.* at 314.

and removes all sin, reaches the highest state (of bliss)."[133] "[K]ings, solely intent on guarding their subjects, reach heaven."[134]

Even the śûdras are rewarded for doing their duty. "(A Sûdra who is) pure, the servant of his betters, gentle in his speech, and free from pride, and always seeks a refuge with Brâhmanas, attains (in his next life) a higher caste."[135]

The four basic castes are identified in the traditional fashion. "The Brâhmana, the Kshatriya, and the Vaisya castes (varna) are the twice-born ones, but the fourth, the Sûdra, has one birth only; there is no fifth (caste)."[136]

Each class must live by its own duties. "It is better (to discharge) one's own (appointed) duty incompletely than to perform completely that of another; for he who lives according to the law of another (caste) is instantly excluded from his own."[137] Special temporary rules are applicable, however, to obtain subsistence in times of distress.[138]

The proper persons may expand the rules of dharma through interpretation.

> If it be asked how it should be with respect to (points of) the law which have not been (specially) mentioned, (the answer is), 'that which Brâhmanas (who are) Sishtas propound, shall doubtlessly have legal (force).'
>
> Those Brâhmanas must be considered as Sishtas who, in accordance with the sacred law, have studied the Veda together with its appendages, and are able to adduce [rational] proofs perceptible by the senses from the revealed texts.
>
> Whatever an assembly, consisting either of at least ten, or at least three persons who follow their prescribed occupations, declares to be the law, the legal (force of) that one must not dispute. . . .[139]
>
> Even if thousands of Brâhmanas, who have not fulfilled their sacred duties, are unacquainted with the Veda, and subsist only by the name of their caste, meet, they cannot (form) an assembly (for settling the sacred law).[140]

133. *Id.* at 327.
134. *Id.* at 386.
135. *Id.* at 401.
136. *Id.* at 402.
137. *Id.* at 423.
138. *Id.* at 420-30.
139. *Id.* at 509-10.
140. *Id.* at 510-11.

In conclusion, "[a] twice-born man who recites these Institutes, revealed by Manu, will be always virtuous in conduct, and will reach whatever condition he desires."[141]

8. The Mahābhārata

The Mahābhārata, the great (mahā) epic story of the battle of the Bhāratas tribe,[142] is the largest epic poem extant in any language.[143] It is a frame story, i.e., a set of narratives in which several successive stories are nested within more inclusive narratives.[144] It is attributed to Vyāsa, also called Krsna Dvaipāyana, who was a mythical saint, of doubtful historicity, who was supposed to have arranged the Vedas.[145] The didactic passages which deal most directly with Hindu jurisprudence most often are attributed to Bhishma, one of the key figures in the story, who symbolizes wisdom, righteousness and selflessness.[146] Occasionally, however, these passages are attributed to other characters in the story.

The core story must date from before 500 B.C.,[147] though the present text contains many later additions, so that it is almost impossible to date the various portions exactly.[148] A date somewhere between 200 B.C. and 200 A.D., roughly contemporaneous with Manu,[149] sometimes is used.[150]

The Mahābhārata is divided into eighteen smaller parts (parvans).[151] Jurisprudential passages are scattered throughout the entire work,[152] but most are found in the twelfth part,

---

141. *Id.* at 513.

142. B. Van Nooten, The Mahābhārata attributed to Krsna Dvaipāyana Vyāsa 4 (1971).

143. *Id.* at 2.

144. *Id.* at 46.

145. *Id.* at 43.

146. *Id.* at 141.

147. I (Pt. I) P. Kane, *supra* note 10 at 366 & 372.

148. *Id.* at 363. "[T]he Mahābhārata assumed its present form certainly before the Christian era, but how much earlier it is difficult to say." *Id.* at 374. *See generally* B. Van Nooten, *supra* note 142 at 43-45.

149. *Supra* note 101.

150. U. Ghoshal, *supra* note 5 at xxi.

151. B. Van Nooten, *supra* note 142 at 3-4 lists them with titles in Sanskrit and English translation.

152. U. Ghoshal, *supra* note 5 at 188-257, paraphrases these passages, based on the critical edition of the Mahābhārata published in 19 volumes by the Bhandarkar Oriental Research Institute at Poona between 1929 and 1966, edited by Vishnu S. Sukthankar, *et al.* *Id.* at 571. *See generally* B. Van.Nooten, *supra* note 142 at 135.

the Santi Parva, the part dealing with "Peace."[153] In the first 129 chapters of this part, Bhishma discourses on the duties of kings (rajadharma); the next 38 chapters deal with special duties applicable in times of distress (ãpaddharma); and the final 186 chapters, of less jurisprudential interest, deal with release from earthly existence (mokshadharma).[154]

Chapter 15 of the Santi Parva discusses legal punishment (danda).[155] "[E]verything is dependent on the rod of chastisement [danda]," for "[i]f the rod of chastisement did not protect people, they would have sunk in the darkness of hell."[156] "For keeping men awake (to their duties) and for the protection of property, ordinances . . . have been established in the world, under the name of chastisement (or punitive legislation)."[157] "The Brahmacharin [student] and the householder, the recluse in the forest and the religious mendicant, all these walk in their respective ways through fear of chastisement alone."[158] "[T]he acts of all creatures become crowned with success only when the policy of chastisement is properly applied. If chastisement were abolished from the world, creatures would soon be destroyed."[159]

The Mahãbhãrata, like most traditional Hindu jurisprudence, is built on a pessimistic view of human nature. It assumes that "[a] person naturally pure and righteous is scarce."[160] "Chastisement was ordained by the Creator himself for protecting religion and profit, for the happiness of all the four orders, and for making them righteous and modest."[161] On the other hand, "[i]f chastisement did not uphold and protect, then ravage and confusion would have set in on every

---

153. The present discussion relies on 8 THE MAHABHARATA OF KRISHNA-DWAIPAYANA VYASA (P. Roy pub. K. Ganguli transl. 1883-96 3d ed. 1975), Santi Parva pt. I. Though this usually is known as the P.C. Roy translation, it was executed in fact by Kesari Mohan Ganguli. 1 THE MAHÃBHÃRATA: THE BOOK OF THE BEGINNING xxxvi (J. van Buitenen ed. & transl. 1973). The 1975 reprint contains 12 volumes.

154. B. VAN NOOTEN, *supra* note 142 at 38. The well known *Bhagavad-gîta*, which is found in chapters 23-40 of the sixth parvan (the Bhishma parvan), also deals with moksha. *Id.* at 73.

155. 8 THE MAHÃBHÃRATA OF KRISHNA-DWAIPAYANA VYASA, *supra* note 153 at 25-28.

156. *Id.* at 25.

157. *Id.*

158. *Id.*

159. *Id.* at 26.

160. *Id.* at 27.

161. *Id.*

side, and all barriers would have been swept away, and the idea of property would have disappeared."[162] Therefore, "[i]f chastisement did not uphold and protect, no one, to whatever mode of life he might belong, would observe the duties of that mode as declared (in the scriptures) . . . ."[163]

Hope for human improvement requires strict application of punishment. Thus, "where foe-destroying chastisement is well applied, no sin, no deception, and no wickedness is to be seen."[164] "All our acts, without doubt, are dependent on wealth [artha]; [but] that wealth again is dependent on chastisement."[165]

The king who applies punishment properly will be rewarded. "Having studied all the Vedas and the other scriptures duly, having protected the kingdom properly, and having caused all the four orders to adhere to their respective duties, a king becomes sanctified and finally sports in heaven."[166]

> . . . Morality [dharma], Profit [artha], and Pleasure [Kāma] are dependent on kingly duties [rajadharma]. It is also clear that the practices that lead to emancipation [moksha] are equally dependent on them.[167]

"Kings should protect the four orders in the discharge of their duties. It is the eternal duty of kings to prevent a confusion of duties in respect of the different orders."[168]

In the original "state of nature," men were good and punishment was not necessary, but this Golden Age did not endure, decline followed, and law became necessary.

> [I]n the Krita age sovereignty first began. At first there was no sovereignty, no king, no chastisement, and no chastiser. All men used to protect one another righteously. . . . [T]hey found the task (after some time) to be painful. Error then began to assail their hearts . . . . [T]heir virtue began to decline. When their perceptions were dimmed and when men became subject to error, all of them became covetous. . . . When they became subject to lust [of acquisitions], another passion,

162. *Id.*
163. *Id.*
164. *Id.*
165. *Id.*
166. *Id.* at 46.
167. *Id.* at 114.
168. *Id.* at 117.

named anger, soon soiled them. Once subject to wrath, they lost all consideration of what should be done and what should not. . . . When this confusion set in amongst men the Vedas disappeared. Upon the disappearance of the Vedas, Righteousness was lost. When both the Vedas and righteousness were lost, the gods were possessed by fear. . . . [They said to Brahmana], "we are about to descend to the level of human beings. Men used to pour libations upwards while we used to pour rain downwards. . . ." [Brahmana] then composed by his own intelligence a treatise consisting of a hundred thousand chapters. In it were treated the subject of Virtue [dharma], profit [artha], and Pleasure [kâma]. . . . He treated of a fourth subject called Emancipation [moksha] . . . . Chastisements [danda] of two kinds, *viz.*, open and secret, were indicated. . . . Having composed that highly beneficial treatise, . . . [Brahmana said], "Assisted by chastisement, this science will protect the world."[169]

If punishment did not maintain proper standards of conduct, they might be lost. Thus, "[i]f the science of chastisement [dandanîti] disappears, the Vedas will disappear. All those scriptures also that inculcate the duties of men [would] become lost."[170]

If the king maintains the social order through punishment, mankind will be happy.

[A]ll creatures live happily in the world, protected by kings exercising Kshatriya duties like children protected by their parents. Kshatriya duties are the foremost of all duties. Those eternal duties, regarded as the first in the world, embrace the protection of every creature. Themselves eternal, they lead to eternal emancipation [moksha].[171]

Those who do not naturally behave in accordance with their proper social role should be forced to do so. "Those men who disregard all wholesome restraints and who are too much attached to the pursuit of worldly objects [artha] are said to be of the nature of brutes. They are compelled to act with justice by the exercise of kingly duties."[172]

The king who sees that dharma is maintained will earn appropriate religious merit.

169. *Id.* at 122-25.
170. *Id.* at 137.
171. *Id.* at 140.
172. *Id.* at 141.

> All the merits . . . that belong to persons practising the duties of the four modes of life, attach . . . to righteous kings. . . . In consequence of the protection of all creatures as also of the proper protection of his own kingdom, a king earns the merit of as many sacrifices as the number of creatures protected . . . .[173]
>
> That king who duly adheres to the duties laid down by the Creator, obtains the blessed merits of all the modes of life. . . . On the other hand, if kings . . . do not protect the righteous people within their dominions, they then take the sins of the latter (of omission and commission).[174]

The king is, to some extent, a god on earth. Proof of this is found *inter alia* in the coronation ceremony. "The *Srutis* declare that in crowning a king, it is Indra that is crowned (in the person of the king). A person who is desirous of prosperity should worship the king as he should worship Indra himself."[175] "No one should disregard the king by taking him for a man, for he is really a high divinity in human form."[176]

The king is entitled to just taxes and fines, but in return must care for his subjects.

> With a sixth part upon fair calculation, of the yield of the soil as his tribute, with fines and forfeitures levied upon offenders [i.e. losing litigants], with the imposts according to the scriptures, upon merchants and traders in return for the protection granted to them, a king should fill his treasury. Realising this just tribute and governing the kingdom properly the king should, with heedfulness, act in such a way that his subjects may not feel the pressure of want.[177]

The king is not to rule alone, or merely with his ministers, but must work with the brâhmins who know the appropriate social standards. Requiring the king to appoint a personal priest represents one way to accomplish this. Thus, "[t]he king, with an eye to both religious merit and profit whose considerations are often very intricate, should, without delay, appoint a priest possessed of learning and intimate acquaintance with the Vedas and the (other) scriptures."[178]

---

173. *Id.* at 143.
174. *Id.* at 144.
175. *Id.* at 145.
176. *Id.* at 149.
177. *Id.* at 157.
178. *Id.* at 160.

More generally, the king must work with the brâhmin class to ascertain dharma and see that it is followed.

> Ruin overtakes the kingdom of the Kshatriya when the Brahmana and Kshatriya contend with each other. . . . The Brahmana and the Kshatriya are connected with each other naturally, and each protects the other. . . . When each helps the other, both attain to great prosperity. If their friendship, existing from days of old, breaks, a confusion sets over everything. . . . The four orders of men become confounded and destruction overtakes all.[179]

"In consequence of a disunion between Brahmanas and Kshatriyas, unbearable griefs afflict the people."[180] "That kingdom enjoys true felicity where the invisible fears of the subjects are dispelled by the Brahmana and all visible fears are dispelled by the king with the might of his arms."[181] "Between them [the Brahmana and Kshatriya] they are the rightful owners of every thing in the universe."[182]

The king serves, to some extent, as a model for his subjects: if he lives according to his dharma, they are more likely to live in accordance with theirs. Thus, "[i]f the king regards it, righteousness becomes regarded everywhere. Whatever acts and things are liked by the king are liked by his subjects."[183]

To some extent the king is an "insurer" of the property of his subjects: if their property is stolen, he is partly at fault. "If a king fails to restore to a subject the wealth that has been stolen away by thieves, he should then compensate the injured from his own treasury, or, in case of inability, with wealth obtained from his dependents."[184]

Special rules apply in special times of distress, and the brâhmins may even assume political power. Thus, "in seasons of distress a Brahmana may support himself by the practice of Kshatriya duties. . . . When a Brahmana loses his means of support and falls into distress, he may certainly betake himself to the practices of a Vaisya and derive his support by agriculture and keeping cattle, if, of course, he is incompetent

---

179. *Id.* at 161.
180. *Id.* at 162.
181. *Id.* at 163.
182. *Id.* at 164.
183. *Id.*
184. *Id.*

for Kshatriya duties."[185]

Standards of proper kingly behavior are loftly and specific, including special duties to provide for the poor and oppressed.

> The enjoyment of good things after sharing them with others, paying proper honours to the [king's] ministers, and subjugation of persons intoxicated with strength, are said to constitute the great duty of a king. Protecting all men by words, body, and deeds, and never forgiving his son himself (if he has offended), constitute the great duty of the king. The maintenance of those that are weak by sharing with them the things he has, and thereby increasing their strength constitute the duty of the king. . . . Never to forgive a person, however dear, if he has committed an offense by act or word, constitutes the duty of the king. Protecting those that solicit shelter, as he would protect his own children, and never depriving one of the honours to which he is entitled constitute the duty of the king. . . . Wiping the tears of the distressed, the helpless, and the old, and inspiring them with joy, constitute the duty of the king. Aggrandising friends, weakening foes, and honouring the good, constitute the duty of the king.[186]

Proper conduct normally is the ultimate standard for kingly performance regarding both ends and means. Thus, "[a]mongst these three objects, *viz.*, Virtue [dharma], Profit [artha], and Pleasure [kâma], Virtue is the foremost."[187]

> The righteous should always act righteously towards those that are righteous. . . . If a Kshatriya, whose duty it is to fight righteously, wins a victory by unrighteous means, he becomes sinful. . . . Even he that is wicked should be subdued by fair means. It is better to lay down life itself in the observance of righteousness than to win victory by sinful means.[188]

"A victory stained by unrighteousness is uncertain and never leads to heaven."[189] "[T]hat Kshatriya who destroys righteousness and transgresses all wholesome barriers does not deserve to be reckoned as a Kshatriya and should be driven from society."[190]

---

185. *Id.* at 169.
186. *Id.* at 200.
187. *Id.* at 201.
188. *Id.* at 207.
189. *Id.* at 208.
190. *Id.*

Special times, however, may require special measures. Thus,

> [t]he person who supports himself at ordinary times by following the practices primarily laid for him, may in seasons of distress support himself by following the practices laid down in the alternative. In a season of distress, . . . a Kshatriya may live by even unjust and improper means.[191]

Finally, some redistribution of wealth to reward the good and punish evil, is appropriate. Thus the king "who makes himself an instrument of acquisition and taking away [of] wealth from the wicked [and] gives them [i.e., it] to those that are good is said to be conversant with the whole science of morality."[192]

9. Yâjñavalkya

The work attributed to Yâjñavalkya was written in the name of that illustrious ancient sage,[193] probably between 100 B.C. and 300 A.D.[194] It could hardly have been written by its namesake.[195] It is in the form of a smrti and largely systemizes and condenses Manu[196] and, to a lesser extent, Kautîlya.[197] The later Mitâksarâ commentary on the Yâjñavalkyasmrti became the preeminent statement of Hindu law during the British colonial period.[198] The basic jurisprudence of Yâjñavalkya, however, is consistent especially with that of Manu.[199]

Yâjñavalkya holds that "[t]he Purânas [semihistorical and religious legends], the Nyâya [logic or reasoning], the Mimansâ [rules for correctly interpreting the Vedas], the

---

191. *Id.* at 281.

192. *Id.* at 290.

193. *See, e.g.*, the well known conversation of Yâjñavalkya concerning the pantheistic Self in the "great forestbook" of the Upanisads, the concluding portion of the Vedas, probably written between 800 and 600 B.C., reprinted in A SOURCE BOOK IN INDIAN PHILOSOPHY, *supra* note 1 at 80-89.

194. 1 (Pt. I) P. KANE, *supra* note 10 at 443 & 447.

195. *Id.* at 423 & 454.

196. *Id.* at 430-31.

197. *Id.* at 438 & 441.

198. *Id.* at 457.

199. *See generally* U. GHOSHAL, *supra* note 5 at 157-87.

The present discussion relies primarily on YAJNAVALKYA SMRITI WITH THE COMMENTARY OF VIJNAEŚVARA CALLED THE MITAKSARA AND NOTES FROM THE GLOSS OF BÂLAMBHATTA, BK. I, THE ÂCHÂRA ADHYÂYA (S. Vidyârnava transl.) in 21 THE SACRED BOOKS OF THE HINDUS (B. Basu ed. 1918 repr. 1974), which translates the first 368 stanzas (ślokas) of the 1,010 stanzas in the Yâjñavalkya Smriti. *Preface* to *id.* at iii.

Dharma Śâstra [science of dharma], together with the [six] Angas [the auxiliary sciences of: correct pronunciation and accentuation; aphorisms concerning Vedic ritual, etc.; grammar; Vedic etymology; Vedic metrics; and astronomy] and the [four] Vedas are the fourteen seats or sources of sciences and of Dharma."[200]

Standards of conduct are relative, to some extent, and subject to various conditions. Thus, "[w]hatever thing is fully given in [the] (proper) country, at [the] (proper) time, with [the] (proper) means, accompanied by faith [in the after-life], to [the] (proper) person, that all is the cause of Dharma."[201] "The Śruti [Vedas], the Smriti [things remembered in books of sacred law], the conduct of good men, what appears pleasant to one's own self [regarding optional matters], and the desire [not contrary to scriptures] which springs from a good resolution, are said to be the roots of Dharma."[202] The highest dharma, however, beyond all works and conduct, is "that one should see the Self [true knowledge] by Yoga."[203]

Legal institutions to interpret and apply the standards of dharma are provided for. Thus, "[f]our persons who know the Vedas, or who know only the three [Vedic] sciences, constitute a 'Parsad' (a legal assembly). What it says is Dharma. Or that which even one person, who is best among the knowers of spiritual sciences, declares."[204]

The traditional basic caste system is explained as follows: "[t]he castes are the Brâhmanas, the Ksatriyas, the Vaiśyas and the Sûdras. Only the first three (of these) are twice-born . . . ."[205] "Because they are first born from the mother and the second time from the binding of [the] sacred girdle [ceremony], therefore, the Brâhmanas, Ksatriyas and the Vaiśyas are called Dvijas or the twice-born."[206] "To the twice-born, the Vedas are the highest agent of benefaction (the means of attaining salvation) because (they all teach) sacrifices, austerities and good works."[207]

---

200. *Id.* at 6.
201. *Id.* at 12.
202. *Id.* at 13.
203. *Id.* at 15.
204. *Id.* at 16. *See* note 92 *supra* on the three Vedic sciences.
205. YAJNAVALKYA SMRITI . . ., *supra* note 199 at 18.
206. *Id.* at 84.
207. *Id.* at 85.

General standards applicable to the king are explained as follows:

> The ruler of men (a king) . . . should be righteous and without bad habits . . . . (He should be) well-versed in the knowledge of Anvîksiki [the self], in Danda-rule (in the theory of punishment), in vârtâ (in [political] Economy) and also in the three-fold [Vedic] sciences called Trayî [the three Vedas]."[208]

Ministers of the king must meet certain standards. "He should appoint his ministers who are intelligent hereditary servants, steady and pure. In consultation with them, he should administer the kingdom, so also with the Brâhmana . . . ."[209] "He should appoint the Purohita (family priest) who is an astrologer, who is highly exalted, who is well-versed in the theory of punishment, as well as in the Atharva-angiras [ritual sciences]."[210]

The king is rewarded for proper behavior, and punished for improper behavior. Thus, the king "takes the sixth part of the virtuous deeds (of his subjects) by protecting them with justice."[211] "When not protected, whatever sin, subjects commit[,] from that verily goes to the king the half because he takes taxes from them."[212] The sovereign who increases his treasury by illegal exaction from his kingdom soon bereft of good luck, goes to destruction along with his kinsmen."[213]

Special rules are applicable to the king who administers conquered territory. Thus, "[a]ll that very merit of the sovereign which he acquires in protecting his own kingdom is gained by him when becoming master of another kingdom, (and [when he] treats the conquered justly)."[214] "Whatever be the custom, laws and family usages in a country, those verily should be observed by him when the country has come under his control."[215]

The king must administer punishment properly, but this requires that he be of good character. "[H]aving obtained that

---

208. *Id.* at 394. *See* note 92 *supra* on the three Vedas.
209. YAJNAVALKYA SMRITI . . ., *supra* note 199 at 396.
210. *Id.* at 397.
211. *Id.* at 412.
212. *Id.* at 413.
213. *Id.* at 414.
214. *Id.* at 415.
215. *Id.*

([any] kingdom) let the king hurl the Rod [of punishment] on evil-doers; because justice (dharma) in the shape of the rod (punishment) was created of yore by Brahmâ himself."[216] "To wield that (rod) equitably is not possible to one who is greedy or of unimproved mind. It is possible only for him who is true to his promise, pure, well-assisted and wise."[217] "That (rod) gladdens the whole world of Devas [gods], Asuras [evil spirits] and men when employed according to scriptures. But otherwise it produces wrath (throughout) the world."[218]

If the king administers punishment properly he will be appropriately rewarded here and hereafter. "The unrighteous punishment destroys the heaven, the glory and the worlds of the king. But the proper punishment procures him victory, glory and heaven."[219] "The king who punishes the punishable properly, who slays those who deserve death, has, as if, performed many sacrifices finished with best gifts."[220]

The king cannot delegate all of his power to punish evildoers. "[T]he king having thus duly thought over the reward of sacrificial merit, should personally investigate judicial proceedings daily in the company of his assessors, separately."[221] "The families, castes, the Śrenis [guilds], the Ganas [trading societies], and the Janapadas [rural communities] who have deviated from their duty, should be disciplined and set in the right path."[222]

Finally, Yâjñavalkya holds the traditional view that "[t]he science of dharma [dharmaśâstra] is of greater authority than the science of material gain [arthaśâstra]."[223]

10. Nârada

Nârada is the name of an ancient sage,[224] but the smrti

216. *Id.* at 424.
217. *Id.* at 425.
218. *Id.*
219. *Id.* at 426.
220. *Id.* at 427.
221. *Id.* at 428.
222. *Id.*
223. Yâjñavalkya Smrti: Ein Beitrag zur Quellenkunde des indischen Rechts 2.2.21 (H. Losch ed. 1927) reprinted in 1 Sources of Indian Tradition 208 (W. de Bary ed. 1958 repr. 1970). *See also* I (Pt. I) P. Kane, *supra* note 10 at 434 that Yâjñavalkya "*lays down the dictum that where dharmaśâstra and arthaśâstra conflict, the former shall prevail* . . . ."
224. *Id.* at 467.

work bearing that name probably was written between 100 and 300 A.D.,[225] shortly after that attributed to Yâjñavalkya.[226] Nârada follows Manu to a considerable extent, though the version of Manu used differs in some respects from that available to us.[227] Works by the same author dealing with politics and the duties of a king (rajadharma) have not yet been discovered.[228] Therefore, we must extract the general jurisprudential ideas of Nârada from his more technical work on legal procedure (vyavahâra).[229]

The preface, in prose, explains the origin of the work, as follows:

> Holy Manu, in order to promote the welfare of all beings, composed a book here, which was to become the foundation of the established rule of conduct. . . .
>
> Holy Manu, after having thus (composed) that (book) in a hundred thousand slokas . . . delivered it to the divine sage Nârada. He having learnt it from him, reflecting that a work of this kind could not be remembered easily by mortals on account of its size, abridged it in twelve thousand (slokas) and delivered it to the great sage Mârkandeya.
>
> He having learnt it from him, and reflecting on the (limited duration and) capacity of human life, reduced it to eight thousand (slokas), and delivered this (abridgment) to Sumati, the son of Bhrigu.
>
> Sumati, the son of Bhrigu, after having learnt (this book) from him and considered what human capacity had been brought down to through the (successive) lessening of life (in the four ages of the world), reduced it to four thousand (slokas).
>
> It is this (abridgement) which Manes [divine ancestral spirits] and mortals read, whilst the gods, Gandharvas [musicians to the gods], and other (exalted beings) read in extenso the (original) code, consisting of one hundred thousand (slokas).[230]

---

225. *Id.* at 477. 1 (Pt. II) P. Kane, *supra* note 9 at xxi.

226. 1 (Pt. I) P. Kane, *supra* note 10 at 474.

227. *Id.* at 472.

228. *Id.* at 477-78.

229. For textual problems, *see, e.g., id.* at 478 & 482.

The present discussion relies on Nárada (J. Jolly transl.) in 33 The Sacred Books of the East: The Minor Law-Books, Pt. I, Nárada [&] Brihaspati 1-267 (F. Max Müller ed. 1889 repr. 1969).

230. *Id.* at 1-3.

The introduction, attributed to the divine sage, Nārada, states that "[w]hen mortals were bent on doing their duty alone and habitually veracious, there existed neither lawsuits, nor hatred, nor selfishness," but "[t]he practice of duty having died out among mankind, lawsuits have been introduced; and the king has been appointed to decide lawsuits, because he has authority to punish."[231]

Nārada rank orders the standards which should be used in deciding private lawsuits, as follows: "[v]irtue, a judicial proceeding, documentary evidence, and an edict of the king are the four feet of a lawsuit" and "[e]ach following one is superior to the one previously named."[232]

The traditional rewards of a just king also apply to the king who decides private lawsuits justly. Thus, "a king who acts justly must neglect error when it is brought forward, and seek truth alone, because prosperity depends on (the practice of) duty."[233] A "self-restrained king who passes just sentences at trials" will obtain "[r]eligious merit, gain, fame, esteem among men, reverence on the part of his subjects, conquests, and an everlasting residence in paradise. Therefore let a king, after having seated himself on the judgment seat, be equitable towards all beings, discarding selfish interests and acting the part of (Yama) Vaivasvata, (the judge of the dead)."[234]

In applying dharma, it may be necessary to resort to custom or reason from general principles.

> Where the rules of sacred law [dharma] and the dictates of prudence [artha] are at variance, he [the king] must discard the dictates of prudence and follow the rules of sacred law.
>
> When it is impossible to act up to the precepts of sacred law, it becomes necessary to adopt a method founded on reasoning, because custom decides everything and overrules the sacred law.
>
> Divine law has a subtile nature, and is occult and difficult to understand. Therefore (the king) must try causes according to the visible path [of reasoning].[235]

Deciding lawsuits properly is not easy, but rewarded well. Thus, "[t]hat king . . . who is intent on doing his duty, must

231. *Id.* at 5.
232. *Id.* at 7.
233. *Id.* at 14.
234. *Id.*
235. *Id.* at 15-16.

be particularly anxious to discover what is right and what is wrong, because there is a variety of dispositions among mankind."[236] "Thus a king constantly trying lawsuits with attention, will acquire widespread and brilliant renown in this life and the abode of Indra after his death."[237] "He passes a divine sentence who acts up to the dictates of law. If he delivers a fair opinion, a member of the court will incur neither hatred nor sin. But if he speaks otherwise he at once incurs both."[238]

> The members of a royal court of justice must be acquainted with the sacred law and with rules of prudence, noble, veracious, and impartial towards friend and foe.
>
> Justice is said to depend on them, and the king is the fountain head of justice. Therefore the king should try causes properly, attended by good assessors.
>
> When lawsuits are decided properly, the members of the court are cleared from guilt. Their purity depends on the justice (of the sentences passed by them). Therefore one must deliver a fair judgment.
>
> Where justice is slain by injustice, and truth by falsehood, the members of the court, who look on with indifference, are doomed to destruction themselves.[239]

Judges of private lawsuits risk religious penalties if they reach the wrong results. Thus, "[t]hat man [on a judicial assembly] who either stands mute or delivers an opinion contrary to justice is a sinner."[240] "One quarter of the iniquity goes to the offender; one quarter goes to the witness; one quarter goes to all the members of the court; [and] one quarter goes to the king."[241]

Proper methods of acquiring private property depend on caste status:

> The pure wealth peculiar to a Brahmin is declared to be threefold: what has been obtained as alms, by sacrificing, and through (instructing) a pupil.
>
> The pure wealth peculiar to a Kshatriya is of three sorts likewise: what has been obtained in the shape of taxes, by fighting, and by means of the fines declared in lawsuits.

236. *Id.* at 23.
237. *Id.* at 24.
238. *Id.* at 36.
239. *Id.* at 37.
240. *Id.* at 38.
241. *Id.*

The pure wealth peculiar to a Vaisya is also declared to be threefold: (what has been acquired) by tillage, by tending cows, and by commerce. For a Sûdra it consists of what is given to him by the members of the three higher castes.

These are the legitimate modes of acquisition of wealth for all the (four) castes severally. If one caste should take to the occupations of another caste, it is a criminal proceeding, except in extreme cases of distress.

In times of distress, a Brahman is allowed to gain his substance in the mode prescribed for the caste next to him in rank; or he may gain his substance like a Vaisya. But he must never resort to the mode of livelihood prescribed for a member of the lowest caste.[242]

Documents are the preferred means of proofs, especially of land grants. Even this legal procedure has a divine origin; "[i]f the Creator had not created writing as an excellent eye (as it were) [for ascertaining truth], the affairs of this whole world would not take their proper course."[243]

The king is to see that the social order is maintained.

When any caste should remain (behind the rest) or exceed the limits (assigned to it, the king), seeing that it has strayed from its path, shall bring it back to the path (of duty).

So also, when other wicked acts, opposed to the dictates of the sacred law, have been committed, the king, after having reflected (upon the matter) himself, shall inflict punishment on those who deserve it.

What is opposed to revealed and traditional law, or injurious to living beings, must not be practiced by the king; and when it is practiced (by others), he must check it.[244]

Maintenance of the natural order depends on performance of these kingly duties.

If the king were remiss in dictating punishments to (members of) any caste, when they have left the path (of duty), the created beings of this world would perish.

Brahmans would leave the sacerdotal caste, and Kshatriyas would forsake the Kshatriya caste. The stronger would eat up the weaker, like fish on a spit.

The Vaisyas would abandon their work, and the Sûdras eclipse all (the rest), if the kings did not visit their subjects

242. *Id.* at 54-56.
243. *Id.* at 58-59.
244. *Id.* at 215.

with punishment (when they have committed an offence).

To show favour to the virtuous at all times and to oppress the wicked, that is declared to be the duty of kings . . . .[245]

The concluding portions of the Nãrada smrti seem to emphasize the divinity and authority of the king. "Whatever a king does is right, that is a settled rule; because the protection of the world is entrusted to him . . . ."[246] "It is for the establishment of order that various laws (karitra) have been proclaimed by kings" but "[a] royal order is declared to overrule such laws even."[247] "A ruler has purchased his subjects through (the practice of) austerities; therefore the king is their lord. For that reason, his bidding must be obeyed; their livelihood even depends on the king."[248] Still, "[h]is duties are, the protection of his subjects, honouring the aged and wise, the trial of lawsuits, and to make (each caste) abide by the duties assigned to it."[249]

A good king apparently achieves the same caste status as a brâhmin. Thus, "between a Brahman and a king, who are both devoted to their duty, there is no difference of any sort, when they protect mankind (acting) in accordance with the sacred law."[250]

Again, Nãrada emphasizes the divine nature of the king. "How should a king be inferior to a deity," he asks, rhetorically, "as it is through his word that an offender may become innocent, and an innocent man an offender in due course?"[251] Finally Nãrada refers to "the divine nature of the king,"[252] and includes the king among eight sacred objects; "[t]hese one must always look up to, worship and honour them personally, and turn the right side towards them, in order that one's existence may be prolonged."[253]

C. *Illustrative Deviations from Composite Statement*

For the most part, the ten classical works of traditional

245. *Id.* at 216.
246. *Id.* at 217.
247. *Id.*
248. *Id.*
249. *Id.* at 218.
250. *Id.* at 220.
251. *Id.* at 221.
252. *Id.*
253. *Id.* at 222.

orthodox Hindu jurisprudence excerpted in Part B above[254] are consistent with the basic composite approach to law set forth in Part A above.[255] Several eminent Indologists have described these and other texts in historical order, and then reclassified their ideas into a relatively unified comprehensive exposition of Hindu legal philosophy, noting individual deviations.[256] Their Herculean efforts far exceed the capabilities of this author, and will not be repeated or summarized here. This essay, in contrast, excerpts in order the key jurisprudential texts found in ten leading Hindu classics, arranged in putative historical order, to allow the reader to gain directly, through the filter of available English translations (of varying quality), some feeling for the style and content of these Hindu works themselves. As one side benefit, this procedure enables isolation of some individual differences among, and historical developments in, the ideas expressed in the ten works excerpted.

Many of the works excerpted in Part B above develope only some of the specific features of the complete composite traditional orthodox Hindu legal philosophy set forth in Part A. All of them, however, are generally consistent with that composite statement and seem to presuppose it in expounding their individual portions of this subject. In general, however, later works build on earlier ones and add additional details, though that is not always the case.

Variations among traditional orthodox Hindu legal philosophers generally concern relatively minor details. The following examples illustrate some respects in which some of the Hindu legal philosophers excerpted in Part B deviate in emphasis from the composite general statement of Hindu legal philosophy set forth in Part A above. Though dharma generally provides the ultimate standards for the regulation of human behavior, some passages in Kautilya[257] and the Mahābhārata[258] seem to treat artha as superior to dharma. Some

254. *See supra* notes 10-253 and accompanying text.

255. *See supra* notes 2-9 and accompanying text.

256. *See, e.g.*, U. Ghoshal, *supra* note 5, and I (Pt. I) P. Kane, *supra* note 10, I (Pt. II) P. Kane, *supra* note 9, II P. Kane, History of Dharmaśāstra (2d ed. 1974), III P. Kane, *supra* note 3, IV P. Kane, History of Dharmaśāstra (2d ed. 1973), V (Pt. I) *id.*, *id.* (1958) & V (Pt. II) *id.*, *id.* (1962).

257. *See, e.g.*, text accompanying note 95 *supra*.

258. *See, e.g.*, text accompanying note 165 *supra*.

passages in Nãrada[259] treat custom as superior to dharma, though generally that is not the case.[260] Similarly some passages in Kautilya[261] and Nãrada[262] treat edicts of the king as superior to dharma. Manu,[263] the Mahãbhãrata,[264] and especially Nãrada[265] even deify the king, and Nãrada also assimilates the good ksatriya raja to the brãhmin caste.[266]

Some passages in Yãjñavalkya place considerable emphasis on faith[267] and attaining direct knowledge through Yoga,[268] rather than traditional rational interpretation of Vedic revelations. Finally, Yãjñavalkya extends his legal theory to the proper conduct of the king in governing conquered peoples,[269] as well as those within his original kingdom.

Perhaps some of these illustrative deviations from the traditional composite Hindu jurisprudential point of view could be explained by differences among various regions,[270] schools of Vedic interpretation[271] and historical time periods.[272] A few, perhaps, may be due to the greater tendency of traditional Sanskrit authors to juxtapose conflicting opinions without choosing between them, than is acceptable in the West.[273]

D. *Concluding Observations*

Legal theory is indeed theory, and need not accurately describe beliefs generally held or those which actually are put into practice. It may be the case that local customs in fact did

259. *See, e.g.*, text accompanying note 235 *supra*.

260. Note 3 *supra* and accompanying text.

261. *See, e.g.*, text accompanying note 97 *supra*.

262. *See, e.g.*, text accompanying notes 232, 246 & 247 *supra*.

263. *See, e.g.*, text accompanying note 119 *supra*.

264. *See, e.g.*, text accompanying notes 175 & 176 *supra*.

265. *See, e.g.*, text accompanying notes 251-53 *supra*.

266. *See, e.g.*, text accompanying note 250 *supra*.

267. *See, e.g.*, text accompanying note 201 *supra*. *See generally* text accompanying note 70 *supra*.

268. *See, e.g.*, text accompanying note 203 *supra*.

269. *See, e.g.*, text accompanying notes 214-15 *supra*. *See generally* the full paragraph text preceding note 5 *supra*.

270. *See, e.g.*, I (Pt. I) P. KANE, *supra* note 10 at 147-48 for basic differences in social conditions between northern and southern India.

271. *See generally* Smart, *Indian Philosophy*, in 4 THE ENCYCLOPEDIA OF PHILOSOPHY 155-69 (P. Edwards ed. 1967).

272. *See, e.g.*, I (Pt. I) P. KANE, *supra* note 10 at 474-75 that Nãrada may have deified the king to prop up the Imperial Gupta authority.

273. *Id.* at 333.

determine most of the behavioral standards in village India, regardless of what the king and the brâhmins thought. Also, specific rules of Hindu law in various places and at various times may or may not have been consistent with the general principles expounded by the Hindu legal philosophers. Though these general principles were to apply throughout Aryan India, during most of its history the Indian sub-continent was divided politically among many independent kingdoms, and there usually was no great king (mahârâja), emperor or king of kings (maharajatiraja) capable of assuring uniform interpretation and application of these jurisprudential principles. Hence these general principles were bound to be applied somewhat differently in different kingdoms, in practice. The extent to which a particular principle of Hindu jurisprudence was put into practice in various places may affect its importance in world intellectual history; but these historic facts do not add to, or detract from, its status as a basic principle of Hindu jurisprudence.

Modern Western legal philosophers are not used to a jurisprudence based on a rigid caste system and fixed life stages, or any other theology than monotheism. We do not believe in rebirth or natural chaos resulting from violation of proper social standards.

Yet the idea of extra-legal standards against which positive laws are measured, is not strange to us, nor is divine institution of royal punishment to control the evil tendencies of mankind or special limitations on divine rights of kings. We also must work out some reconciliation of ideal standards, positive laws and customs, in normal and exceptional times, and justify legal institutions which interpret these principles and apply them to specific disputes, using reason *inter alia* and legal science. We, too, must deal with institutions for changing law, and ultimately with the possibility of tyrannicide, principled revolution, and civil disobedience.

The ideas of the Hindu legal philosophers presented here may give us a different perspective on some of these perennial problems.[274] In any event they show us how men of a different culture, in different times, worked out what seemed to them a

274. For an excellent comprehensive comparison of Hindu and Western political and legal theory, *see* U. GHOSHAL, *supra* note 5 at 529-68.

satisfactory jurisprudential system by which their behavior and that of their rulers could be justified and judged.

[3]

Surya Prakash Sinha, White Plains, N.Y.

Non-Universality of Law

The Indian way of life

The uniquely Indian way of life is the result of its own particular historicity. Its definition occurred in the ancient or pre-Muslim period[33] and its fundamental principles abide to this day.

About 3000 B.C., agriculturists settled in villages in the upland valleys of Baluchistan and the plains of the Makran and the lower Indus. The Harappa Culture extended in a stretch of about 950 miles from north and south of the Indus valley. Outside of it, the Baluchistan's village cultures continued in their own patterns. This civilization was conservative and theocratic. It enjoyed a continuity of government, possessed a script of some 270 characters, and had contact with Mesopotamia. Some animals and certain trees were sacred, as in the Hinduism of today. There was a horned god, the Proto-Shiva, who is quite akin to the Shiva of later Hinduism. Phallic worship was prevalent, as in later Hinduism. Harappa people were the first in the world to use cotton, wild rice, water buffalo, and domestic fowl. About 2000 B.C., Harappa cities were invaded by the Aryans, who were among the invading tribes was a group of related tribes under the chiefhood of the Bharatas, who had perfected a poetic technique of composition of hymns to be sung at sacrifices in praise of their gods. These were handed down orally and collected and arranged in the early part of the 1st millennium B.C., though not reduced to writing. This collection, called Rg Veda, is the most sacred text of the Hindus which, along with the subsequent oral religious literature of the first half of the 1st millennium B.C., constitutes part of the living Hindu tradition.

The Aryans came to India already possessed of a class division in their tribal structure. Faced with settling among the darker aboriginals, they stressed purity of blood. These class divisions hardened and excluded the Dasas, the hated survivors of the Harappa Culture, as well as those Aryans who intermarried with them. By the end of the Rg Vedic period, the society was divided into four hierarchical classes

33 Commenting upon this period, Historian A. L. Basham concludes that "[a]t most periods of her history India, though a cultural unit, has been torn by internecine war. In statecraft her rulers were cunning and unscrupulous. Famine, flood and plague visited her from time to time, and killed millions of her people. Inequality of birth was given religious sanction, and the lot of the humble was generally hard. Yet our overall impression is that in no other part of the ancient world were the relations of man and man, and of man and the state, so fair and humane. In no other civilization were slaves so few in number, and in no other ancient lawbook are their rights so well protected as in the *Arthasastra.* No other lawgiver proclaimed such notable ideals of fair play in battle as did Manu. In all her history of warfare Hindu India has few tales to tell of cities out to the sword or of the massacre of non-combatants. The ghastly sadism of the kings of Assyria, who flayed their captives alive, is completely without parallel in ancient India. There was sporadic cruelty and oppression no doubt, but, in comparison with conditions in other early cultures, it was mild. To us the most striking feature of ancient Indian civilization is its humanity." A. L. Basham, *The Wonder That Was India*, 8–9 (1954).

34 They began emigrating by about 2000 B.C., due to the pressure of their population on the exhausted pastoral land. Some remained in their old home and became the ancestors of the later Baltic and Slavonic peoples. Some invaded Europe and became the ancestors of the Greeks, Latins, Celts, and Tentons. Some went to Anatolia and, mixing with the original inhabitants there, became the ancestors of the Hittities. Some moved south to Caucasus and the Iranian tableland, from where they attacked the Middle Eastern civilizations. Those who invaded India called themselves Arya, a word anglicized into Aryan. The ancient Persians called themselves that name, too, which survived in the word Iran. Eire represents the most westerly reach of the Indo-European peoples in the ancient times.

which, in the descending order, were the priest (*brahman*), warrior (*kshatriya*), peasant (*vaishya*), and serf (*shudra*). This division exists to this day.

The fundamentals of caste had been well established during this period, to which is linked the modern caste organization. The foremost identification of a person was his caste, rather than a state or its king. The caste did not have territorial boundaries or internal administration. As a result, political and territorial administration was only of secondary importance. The basis of kingship lay in human need and military necessity, the king's first duty being to lead his people in war.

The idea of a divine cosmic order already existed in the Rg Vedic period. The later concept of *dharma* became the most important basis for ordering social relations. *Dharma* is an untranslatable word with many meanings, ranging from the general meaning of righteousness to the legal meaning of divinely ordained norm of good conduct or the sacred law. It prevailed over other bases of obligation, namely, contract, custom, and royal ordinance. The king was the protector of *dharma*, rewarding the righteous and punishing the evildoer. It was the king's duty to maintain *dharma* by *danda* (stick), which meant force, coercion, or punishment.

The *brahmans* had written the texts (such as the *Dharma Shastras*) which laid down the rules of conduct for the four classes, mentioned above, retaining for themselves the highest honor, precedence, and privileges. The *kshatriyas*, also known as *rajarya* in the Vedic period, were the ruling class. The two classes provided a check upon each other's pretensions. This ruling class was made up of all classes and ranks, including those of the invaders as well as those on the margins of the Aryan civilization, such as the Greeks (*Yavana*), the Scyths (*Shaka*), and the Parthians (*Pahlava*). The *vaishya* class was made up of merchants who ranked below the first two, although they were entitled to the sacred thread initiation. It originated in the peasant tribesmen but grew to other occupations than farming and cattle raising, such as dealing in jewels, metals, threads, spices, perfumes, and other merchandise. The *shudras* were not twice-born and were denied initiation. They included groups that refused to accept the rigid customs of the *brahmans* and adhered to the objectionable customs of meat eating, widow remarriage, and so on. The excluded *shudras* (*nirvasita shudra*) were considered outside the society and were assimilated with those who later were regarded as untouchables. The pure or not-excluded *shudras* (*anirvasita shudras*) were assigned the duty to wait on the other three classes and lived off the master's left-over food, cast-off clothing, and discarded furniture. While they could not hear the Vedas, they could hear the Epics (Mahabharata and Ramayana) and Puranas.

Outside this social structure were numerous groups, later called the untouchables or outcasts, such as the *chandala*, who lived outside the boundaries of an Aryan village and cremated corpses and executed criminals, and the *mleccha*, the outer barbarians, who were despised as invaders but for whom an improvement was hoped.

The caste (*jati*) system, which did not develop out of the four *varnas*, *mentioned* above, is an association developed over thousands of years on the basis of region, race, profession, or religion. It is characterized by (i) endogamy, wherein legitimate marriage is possible only within the caste, (ii) commensality, wherein one receives food or eats it only in the presence of a member of the same or higher caste, and (iii) craft-exclusiveness, wherein one practices the trade of one's own caste and not another. It is independent of government. Its most severe sanction is social ostracism. This has enabled the Hindu to live under the political order of the day imposed from above throughout his history and yet retain his cultural individuality. Attempts to break this system have failed.

Thus, there exist the dual systems of *varna* and *jati*, and the relationship between the two has never been harmonized.

The family was a joint family, which is still generally the case today. It was a patriarchal family and it included parents, children, grandchildren, uncles and their descendants, collaterals on the man's side, and, sometimes, adopted children. They lived together and held the property in common. The family, not the individual, was the primary unit of society.

The essential principle of individual and communal life of most Indians is *dharma*. The word is untranslatable, but its concept is certainly not that of law in the Western sense. It originated at the very beginning of the Indian civilization. *Rta* denoted the universal cosmic order, which was immanent, pre-existent, and independent of any other force and *dharma* upheld that which existed in that order (*rta*). *Rta* offered an order to apprehend man's phenomenal surrounding and to structure irregular phenomena into a form of regularity. Gods gave examples of *dharma* to uphold that which existed in order (*rta*), thereby making man conscious of his own active, though ordered, way of life.

The Vedas expressed *dharma* as a complex of action, conduct, ordinance, and principle of regularity in various situations. As such, it had three aspects, namely, an expression of nature's most active parts, an expression of natural and human phenomena, and an expression of abstract as well as concrete relations of pure knowledge and human affairs. The Upanishads shifted the emphasis to the life of man in all its aspects. While they recognized *dharma* as the supreme force of the world, they transformed it into an all-embracing support of life in this world. The Vedic *dharma* was, thus, related to practical necessities of everyday life. The principle of *karma* operated within the all-embracing function of *dharma*, thereby elaborating *dharma* into the many precepts and rules for human affairs. *Karma* sustained by *dharma* led to *moksha*, *i.e.*, the release from the cycle of life, death, and rebirth. The basis for a life of good actions lay in the man's efforts to conform to his duty.

The Vedas, Brahmanas, Aranyakas, and Upanishads constituted the *shruti* (heard) literature. The subsequent *smriti* (remembered) literature elaborated *dharma* further, adapting it to the changing conditions of life. The earliest *smriti* literature on *dharma* consisted of the *dharma sutras*, which were in the nature of manuals of the precepts of *dharma* stated in the form of aphorisms. The subsequent *dharma shastras* presented more detailed compositions in verse form, the most important of which was named after the ascetic Manu as the Manu-Smriti, usually translated in a misleading fashion as The Laws of Manu or the Code of Manu. These *dharma shastras* also included the secularly conceived *Arthashastra* of Kautilya, mentioned above.

All the various teachings of *dharma* addressed themselves to the issue of how to follow a way of life that would be in accordance with *dharma*. The sources of *dharma* were *shruti*, *smriti*, *achara* (good custom), and *atma-tushti* (self-satisfaction). We have mentioned *shruti* and *smriti* above. *Achara* consisted of widespread and unambiguous practice followed by the virtuous upon a firm belief in *shruti* and *smirti*. *Atma-tushti*, or self-satisfaction, was considered unimportant by the authoritative mode of interpretation (*mimansa*). There were three kinds of *dharma*: *svadharma*, which consisted of one's individual duty as determined by his *varna* (discussed above) and *ashram* (stages of life, which were four, namely, *brahmcharin* (early life of celibacy and austerity), *grahastha* (householder), *vanaprastha* (living as a hermit in the forest), and *sanyasin* (wandering homelessly in a total separation from the material world); *sadharma dharma*, which guided man's conduct for the benefit of the community as a whole and benefitted his own being as part of that whole, and whose most cardinal virtues were *ahimsa* (non-violence or abstention from injury) and *satyam* (truth); *purushartha*, which related to attaining the ends of man, namely *dharma*, *artha* (material possessions), *kama* (pleasure), and *moksha* (salvation).

Thus, in the ancient or pre-Muslim period of India we find the definition and development of the Indian way of life and its fundamental principles which abide to this day.[35]

In the Muslim period (8th century to 18th century), the Hindu social system, characteristically, accommodated the Muslim conquerors by putting them into just another caste. However, the Muslim rule affected Hinduism in a variety of significant ways. First, it became more public and popular, since Muslim rulers drove it out of the temples by pillaging them. The religious ceremonies took to public squares and town/village streets, thereby strengthening the popular emotional excitement which Islam failed to snatch. Second, some thinkers, such as Kabir (d. 1518) or Nanak (the founder of Sikhism), attempted to synthesize Hinduism with Islam by grasping what was the truth in the two systems and repudiating what was false. Finally, the popularization of Hinduism was further strengthened by a shift from the classical Sanskrit language for religious purposes to the vernacular languages, such as Hindi and others. However, while Hinduism thus continued to survive, it no longer enjoyed the patronage of the ruling courts and official culture. Consequently, it declined in its literature and architecture, while its Islamic counterparts flourished.

Hinduism received a new and vigorous adoration through the works of holy men and poets, especially the poets. For example, the saint Chaitanya (d. 1527) repudiated caste distinctions and other objectionable manifestations of the traditional religi-

35 Basham, *Wonder*; B. and F. R. Allchin, *The Birth of Indian Civilization: India and Pakistan Before 500 B.C.* (1968); R. E. M. Wheeler, *Early India and Pakistan, to Ashok* (1959); R. E. M. Wheeler, *The Indus Civilization*, The Cambridge History of India, Supplementary Volume (3d ed., 1968); R. C. Majumdar and A. D. Pusalker, eds., *History and Culture of the Indian People, I: The Vedic Age* (1951); J. H. Hutton, *Caste in India: Its Nature, Functions, and Origins* (1946); K. A. Nilakanta Sastri, *A History of South India from Prehistoric Times to the Fall of Vijaynagar* (3d ed., 1966); S. Dasgupta, *A History of Indian Philosophy*, 5 vols., (1932–1955); V. A. Smith, *Early History of India* (4th ed., 1924); V. G. Childe, *The Aryans: A Study of Indo-European Origins* (1926); V. G. Childe, *New Light on the Most Ancient East* (4th ed., 1952); L. Renou, *Religions of Ancient India* (1965); B. B. Lal, "The Indus Civilization, in A. L. Basham, ed., *A Cultural History of India*, 11 (1975); T. Burrow, "The Early Aryans,", *id.*, 20; J. P. Marr, "The Early Dravidians," *id.*, 30; A. L. Basham, "Medieval Hindu India," *id.*, 51; S. Radhakrishnan, "Hinduism," *id.*, 60; B. Sangharakshita, "Buddhism," *id.*, 83; A. N. Upadhyaye, "Jainism," *id.*, 100; S. N. Dasgupta, "Philosophy," *id.*, 111; J. D. M. Derrett, "Social and Political Thought and Institutions," *id.*, 124; R. May, *Law and Society East and West, Dharma, Li, and Nomos* (1985); P. V. Kane, *History of Dharmashastra*, vols. 1–5 (1930–1962, 2d ed., 1968); J. D. M. Derrett, *Essays in Classical and Modern Hindu Law* (1977); J. D. M. Derrett, "The Concept of Duty in Ancient Indian Jurisprudence," in W. D. O'Flaherty and J. D. M. Derrett, eds., *The Concept of Duty in South Asia*, 3 (1978); F. Edgerton, *The Beginnings of Indian Philosophy* (1965); P. T. Raju, "The Concept of Man in Indian Thought," in S. Radhakrishnan and P. T. Raju, eds., *The Concept of Man: A Study in Comparative Philosophy*, 220 (2d ed., 1966); R. Lingat, *The Classical Law of India*, trans. J. D. M. Derrett (1973); K. V. R. Aiyangar, *Some Aspects of the Hindu View of Life According to Dharmashastra* (1952); G. Tha, *Hindu Law and Its Sources*, Vol. I (1930); N. C. Sengupta, *Evolution of Ancient Indian Law* (1953); J. D. M. Derrett, *Dharmashastra and Juridical Literature* (1973); W. T. deBary, ed., *Sources of Indian Tradition* (1958); D. N. Majumdar, *Races and Cultures of India* (4th ed., 1961); T. M. P. Mahadevan, *Outlines of Hinduism* (2d ed., 1960); S. Radhakrishnan, *The Hindu View of Life* (10th impression, 1957); E. Conze, *Buddhist Thought in India* (1962); J. L. Jaini, *Outlines of Jainism* (1916, rev. ed., 1940); A. L. Basham, *The Origins and Development of Classical Hinduism* (1989); G. M. Bongard-Levin, *Ancient Indian Civilization* (1985); K. Jettmar, *The Religions of the Hindukush*, tr. by A. Nayyar (1986)

on. Through a substantial following, he promoted intensely emotional public ceremonies. This, in Bengal, succeeded in stopping conversion to Islam. Therefore, as the Indian society expanded eastward beyond the Ganges delta, it was Hinduism, not Islam, that embraced the new people. While Chaitanya's influence was limited to one sect, the revivifying influence of poets Sur Das (d. 1563) and Tulsi Das (d. 1623) was more widespread. They took themes of the Hindu tradition and developed them in Hindi verse. These verses were quite understandable to the Hindi-speaking population of the north and provided a rich treasure of chants and hymns for use in religious celebrations. These poets did not repudiate the ancient Sanskrit piety and Brahmanical ritual; they simply left them to the professional priests. Sur Das wrote about Lord Krishna and Tulsi Das wrote about Lord Rama. Since both were incarnations of Lord Vishnu, there was no doctrinal conflict.

In the end, the overwhelming majority of Indians remained Hindu, following the traditions of their ancestors and organizing their social life along their indigenous structures.[36]

When the British came to rule India, the Hindus did not find this change of their masters particularly important. Characteristically, they put the Europeans, too, in yet another caste. The official British policy, on its part, left the social institutions and relationships alone. *Dharma* was applied to such matters of the Hindus as marriage, inheritance, the caste system, and religious usages and institutions. Correspondingly, Muslim law was applied to the Muslims. In other matters, a newly created territorial law applied to all subjects, regardless of their religious status. The idea of a territorial law, wherein law existed as an autonomous body independently of religion, was an alien concept to Indian traditions.

English law courts operated in the Presidency towns of Bombay, Calcutta, and Madras and applied English law as it existed in 1726, modified by regulations of local authorities and subject to its applicability to Indian conditions. In the rest of India, the *Mofussil* courts, under the Governor-General's Regulation of 1772 for the Administration of Civil Justice, applied Hindu law and Muslim law in matters of inheritance, marriage, caste, and religious usages and institutions, and general principles of justice, equity, and good conscience in other matters. The Indian High Courts Act of 1861 reorganized the court system throughout the colony. An intensive legislative activity for India occurred after the revolt of 1857. Various Codes were adopted, such as the Indian Code of Civil Procedure (1859), which was replaced by the Civil Code of 1908, the Criminal Code (1860), the Code of Criminal Procedure (1861), the Limitations Act (1859), the Succession Act (1865), the Contract Act (1872), the Evidence Act (1872), the Specific Relief Act (1872), the Negotiable Instruments Act (1881), the Transfer of Property Act (1882), the Trusts Act (1882), and so on.

All this made for an efficient colonial administration by an imperial power. Some urban Indians became fashionably English in their attitudes and mannerism. However, the social contact between the ruling English and the subject Indians was extre-

36 V. A. Smith, *The Oxford History of India* (3d ed., 1958); P. Spear, *India: A Modern History* (1961); W. M. Moreland, *From Akbar to Aurangzeb* (1923); W. H. McNeill, *A World History* (2d ed., 1971); S. A. A. Rizvi, "The Muslim Ruling Dynasties," in A. L. Basham, ed., *A Cultural History of India*, 245 (1975); S. A. A. Rizvi, "Islam in Medieval World," *id.*, 281; J. T. F. Jordons, "Medieval Hindu Devotionalism," *id.*, 266; H. McLeod, "Sikhism," *id.*, 294; R. C. Gupta, *Hindu Society and Influence of the Great Epics* (1991)

mely limited. Most Indians continued to live their lives in accordance with their own traditions.[37]

The independence from the British, though cataclysmic due to partition of the country into India and Pakistan, was not abrupt. Limited self-government had already been established. A secular Constitution was adopted in 1950 and it provides for the maintenance of the former law (Section 372). New legal activity has followed. The tendency has been to replace the religious laws with a secular law. There has been a vigorous activity of industrialization, commercialization, and modernization, with its concomitant structures of Western-style law. There have also been efforts to abolish the undesirable features of such institutions as the caste system. Increased contact with the West has had its influence on life-styles, especially in urban centers. However, about eighty percent of the Indians live in villages and continue to conduct their lives through traditional institutions, traditions, and beliefs. Even in urban centers, where the changes are most evident, there has been a peculiarly Indian blend of Western ways with the Indian traditions in which the fundamental principle of *dharma*, the institution of joint family, the social organization of castes, and other traditions and customs are very much alive and practiced.

Part II
Aspects of Hindu Law and Legal Theory

[4]

HARROP A. FREEMAN

An Introduction to Hindu Jurisprudence

This article intends to be introductory to other more specific studies and, to that end, briefly surveys Hindu jurisprudential theory. It seeks an orientation, recalls the development of Hindu legal institutions, and examines "schools" of jurisprudence in ancient India. It turns to an analysis of ancient Hindu thought on common jurisprudential issues (the state, law and the rule of law, punishment and procedure) and finally attempts to reveal something of modern Hindu jurisprudence's growth, richness, and diversity and its similarity to our own.

(1) *An Orientation.* The practice has become prevalent in American academic writing to set off East and West as opposites. It is said that the West places its reliance on reason and the scientific method; the East, on supersensory experience and intuition.[1] This tends to emphasize, to borrow F. S. C. Northrop's phrase, "ideological differences."[2] Even if a writer concludes that natural law is at the foundation of both Eastern and Western legal orders he still treats them as different—one "known by immediate apprehension," and the other "known postulationally."[3] This leads to the conclusion that attempts to combine Oriental and Occidental economic, political, aesthetic, and religious values end in failure.[4]

HARROP A. FREEMAN is Professor of Law, Cornell Law School.

[1] C. Watts Cunningham, "How Far to the Land of Yoga? An Experiment in Understanding," 57 The Philosophical Review (1948) 513; P. T. Raju contrasts the "inwardness" of Indian philosophy with the "outwardness" of "Western" philosophy, "The Western and Indian Philosophical Traditions," 56 The Philosophical Review (1947) 127; John C. Archer, Faiths Men Live By (New York, 1943).

[2] F. S. C. Northrop, The Meeting of the East and West (1946) and Ideological Differences and World Order (New Haven, 1949). Thus, Professor Northrop once attempted to explain the attitudes of America and India on Korea on the basis that American law, derived from the Christian concept of an all good God against an all evil devil or right opposed to wrong, required a determination of "wrong" or "aggression" and "punishment." On the other hand, India, which recognized no God vs. Devil theology, emphasized compromise and settlement without determination of right and wrong. ("Asian Mentality and United States Foreign Policy," 276 Annals 118, 1951). In my work in India with lawyers, law schools, and courts, I found law as litigious as in America. The ratio of litigation to settlement was greater than in my own practice; the proportionate cost of litigation was higher; the minuteness of legal detail at issue was greater; the insistence on vindication of legal "rights" was comparable. In fact, I felt completely at home with the bench and bar of India and South Asia generally.

[3] Gray L. Dorsey, "Two Objective Bases for a World-Wide Legal Order" in Ideological Differences and World Order (New Haven, 1949); Jean Escarra, "Law, Chinese," in Encyclopedia of the Social Sciences and Le Droit Chinois (Paris, 1936).

[4] See, for example, Commencement Address of F. S. C. Northrop, "Understanding the Contemporary World," Univ. of Hawaii, July 1949; *id.*, "Obstacles to a World Legal Order and Their Removal," 19 Brooklyn L. Rev. (1952) 1; *id.*, The Taming of the Nations (1952). Of course, this posits the issue whether Socialist and Marxist legal

The more I study, the more I find no sharp dichotomy between Eastern and Western basic legal theory. Eastern thought is no more supersensory or less reasoning than Western thought. In law, as in religion and matters philosophical, the reply of Dr. Nitobe to Kipling's famous "The East is the East and the West is the West," is more accurate:

> "The East is in the West and the West is in the East;
> There are no points of compass in the human soul."[5]

Elsewhere it has been suggested that world jurisprudence might properly ground itself on basic elements common to all great religions and cultures.[6] This still allows for differences in specific laws just as there are differences within the Anglo-American system, for example, as to the rule against perpetuities.[7]

(2) *Early Development of Legal Institutions.* In this paper, Indian legal thought is briefly considered to show that much the same jurisprudential development, schools of jurisprudence, and theories of law occur as in our traditional Western pattern.

Sir Henry Maine in *Ancient Law* made comparison after comparison between the development of Hindu legal institutions and the development of legal systems of Europe. In fact, he was able to point out from his study certain characteristics of primitive legal systems and certain fundamental stages in their early growth: the prevalence of co-ownership and the intermixture of personal and proprietary rights; the confusion of public and private duties; the importance of the family; the

theory is a part of the "East" or "West", and where China and India fit into the classification. These writers have tended to rule the communist world out of their systems and to seek a world law for half-a-world. Northrop, "Naturalistic and Cultural Foundations for a More Effective International Law," Yale L. J. 1430.

[5] T. M. P. Mahadevan, "Indian Philosophy and the West," 22 The Philosophical Quarterly, No. 3, 137; E. A. Burtt, "Intuition in Eastern and Western Philosophy," 2 Philosophy East and West, No. 4, January, 1953; George P. Conger, Toward the Unification of the Faiths (Calcutta, 1957) 116; Max Muller, Vedas, p. 4; Vincent Sheean, Lead Kindly Light (New York, 1949) 287; Report, East-West Philosophers' Conference (1948), 115; U. S. Ghoshal, Hindu Political Theories (1927) 7; Manu 2.224 (William Jones translation).

[6] "The United Nations Organization and International Law," 31 Corn. L. Q. 259.

[7] I would be the first to admit the value of the taking of differences. The whole technique of the lawyer is based on recognizing differences—millions of them. What I hope we avoid in comparative law is the mistake comparative religion made, and has not yet rectified, of emphasizing differences to prove that one's own system was *summa cum*. Thus Western religion emphasized its belief in a Supreme Being compared to a pervading presence revealed in many avataras, a man centered compared to a cosmic universe, condemnation of idolatry compared to image worship, original sin and salvation compared to Karma, immortality compared to reincarnation, a religion of material well being compared to asceticism. I venture to suggest that actually all religions have had (and have) in them each of the elements mentioned and that comparative religion is only now discovering its oneness. See note 5 *supra* and E. A. Burtt, Man Seeks the Divine (New York, 1957).

continuous tutelage of women; the growth of the law through fiction.[8] His historical jurisprudence is grounded in Hinduism.

In the early development stages of all legal systems there is no clear distinction between legal rules and religious commands. The story of the Hindu Code of Manu and Moses' Ten Commandments is strikingly similar.[9] Manu's life is a combination of Noah, Jonah, and Moses. The avowed assumption of the old textbooks of Hindu law is that the law is eternal. The primary source of the law is the scriptures—the Vedas.[10] In keeping with the religious view of law, the second source of law is the teaching of the religious leaders and, after that, conscience.[11] There was no clear distinction between legal duties and moral duties. Law embraced all of life and was synonymous with virtue. The Hindu word for law—"dharma"—shows this derivation.[12]

The same relationship can be illustrated by the development of legal literature. The oldest sources of Hindu law are the Vedic hymns based on social custom and divine inspiration. The Aranyakas and Upanishads contain some law, but mainly philosophy and ritual. The Sravta and Grihya Sutras come next and do spell out Aryan custom and rules relating to the social organization. The final stage in the evolution toward ancient Hindu law is the Dharmasūtras, which come near to being lawyer's law. They prescribe detailed rules governing all four stages of life, though chiefly that of Garhasthya or householder. The Dharma Sastras, or Legal Institutes of the Hindus, actually cover civil and criminal law (in Vyavahára), but also social and religious observances (in Achára) and expiation for sin (in Práyaschitta). Smritis, of which eighteen are known, provided numerous commentaries on the Sastras—widely varied by geography, tradition, and culture (somewhat comparable to the glossators on the Roman Code). A practice (e.g., marriage with a maternal uncle's daughter) might be common practice in South India and condemned in the North, and both glossators would find support in the Sastras. In fact, writers from the earliest times up to and including the present debate on the Hindu Code Bill have always sought support of the Sastric norms to justify and approve, or to oppose and challenge practices or proposals of the society in which

[8] Sir Henry Maine, Ancient Law (Everyman ed.) 156; "The ancient German law, like Hindu jurisprudence, makes the male children co-proprietors with their father, and the endowment of the family cannot be parted with except by the consent of all its members," p. 116; widow frequently becomes ward of sons, p. 90; adoption used to expand family into community, p. 16 and ch. 5.

[9] Manu 10.63.

[10] Manu 2.1.

[11] Manu 12.108; Manova-dharma-sastra, VII, v. 6; N. S. Sen-Gupta, Sources of Law and Society in Ancient India (Calcutta, 1914); Morley's Digest of Indian Cases, vol. I, cxcvii.

[12] A. S. Nataraja Ayyer, "Dharma Protects Him Who Maintains It," 4 Vyavahara Nirnaya (1955) 65; "What holds together," "the basis of all order," "the right way," are translations of Dharma.

they live. One of the real strengths of Hindu law has been its reliance on ancient law (religion) while changing it to meet social demands.[13] I shall leave further illustrations of ancient Hindu law and its transition to sections (4) and (5) of this article.

(3) *"Schools of Jurisprudence" in Ancient India.* If you recall that in Anglo-American jurisprudence the earliest legal writings did not differentiate schools and that our scholastic jurisprudence took shape only in the nineteenth century and became recognizable as "schools" in the prolific writing of Dean Pound in the twentieth, and that the chief exponents of some of our schools appeared only within the last forty years (realist, pure theory), you will understand my conclusion that there were no "schools" of jurisprudence in ancient India. Many writers on Indian legal theory have pointed out that the ancient writers would have been surprised to be told that they belonged to a particular "school,"[14]—just as, I suppose, Cicero did not know he was a "natural law" man. Yet these same writers have illustrated the degree to which one can find, in the earliest Hindu writings, matter which presents the natural law, historical, philosophic, analytical (and every other) school of legal thought.[15] But, we ought not to labor a point which should be fairly obvious. Perhaps a quotation from one of India's great modern legal scholars will suffice.[16]

---

[13] This note can do little more than refer to a few of the source materials for the above paragraph: Sen-Gupta, Evolution of Ancient Indian Law (London and Calcutta, 1953); McNaughton, Hindu and Mohammedan Law (9th ed., 1885); Seymour Vesey-Fitzgerald, "Law, Hindu" in 9 Encyc. of Soc. Sci.; V. P. Kané, The Dharma Sastras, (Bombay, 1935).

[14] Dr. Burnell (a Sanskrit scholar and lawyer) in his translation of the Varadraja observed, "Another principle deduced by English lawyers is the doctrine of the Schools of Law. This is unnecessary and foreign to the original texts and digests." J. C. Ghose, The Principles of Hindu Law (Calcutta, 1917) 15 agrees. This is also clear from N. C. Sen-Gupta's first Tagore Lecture, 1950, Evolution of Ancient Hindu Law, Introductory (Calcutta, 1953).

[15] N. C. Sen-Gupta in "Sources of Law and Society in Ancient India" (Calcutta, 1914) and Evolution of Ancient Indian Law (Calcutta, 1953) points out much the same factors. Taking random sentences from the introductory chapter of the latter book we find him referring to "the social background of the law" (p. 2 ff.); "positive law grows and ultimately develops into an elaborate code" (p. 3); "Law existed then not as rules administered by kings but as rules developed in fact by custom and usage . . ." (p. 3); "Transgression of these rules (anrita) is not a mere violation of human laws . . ." (p. 3); "the development of law . . . was conditioned by historical events and by the pressure of environments and circumstances, amongst which were the changing needs of society" (p. 18), etc. See notes 8–11 *supra* on historical jurisprudence.

[16] Sri C. P. Ramaswami Aiyar recognizes all these jurisprudential concepts in ancient Hindu law:

> "The importance of 'natural law' and of conscience is recognized by way of guidance in matters of doubt where the Vedas, usage and custom and divine commands do not furnish any help. . . . Dharma is obeyed as such because of the coercive might of the State and the Dharma Sastras of India (the legal text books) like those of Manu, Vaynavalkya, Narada, Brihaspathi and others acquire the validity of statutes on the recognition of their authenticity and authority by the State.

(4) *Ancient Hindu Thought on Typical Jurisprudential Issues.* This section takes several issues with which jurisprudence has always concerned itself to show the degree to which, in approaching these, Hindu thought has evidenced the same theories as has the West, namely (a) the nature of the State and the ruler, (b) punishment and procedure, and (c) the nature of law and the "rule of law."

(a) *Hindu Theories of King and State.* One of the earliest issues to which Hindu jurisprudence addressed itself was the position of the King and State. Originally the king had no divine attributes. From Manu onward he was supposed to rule by divine right.[17] The king was first considered as a judge, taking over the administration of justice from the Kulas and gilds.[18] Vedic theory did not view the king as either the source or repository of the law. He was under and subject to the law and, failing to maintain it, was destroyed by the law.[19] Frequently referred to as checks on the king were religion, custom, pragmatism, natural justice.[20] The right to overthrow a bad king came to be recognized.[21] This view broadened into a true Hobbesian "contract" theory. One of the earliest statements of the political theory that the state of nature was one of might and war and that the state and

---

> "In Europe, law has been regarded sometimes as the embodiment of eternal justice and as part of the natural heritage of man and embodying natural reason. Another school of thought is that law is that which is brought into existence by the fiat of a law-maker. In other words, that law is obeyed not merely because it is just or good but because it has been laid down by the State. In this way arises the distinction between positive law and ethics. The ethical conception of law was the first to be expounded by Indian law-givers and philosophers. .. . Later on, theories were supplemented by the concept of positive law and there is a long catena of Indian law-givers, including Narada, Sukra and Jaimini who hold that the performance of duty for its own sake having fallen into disuse in the course of human history positive law (vyavahara) was introduced and the King became the superintendent of the law, the wielder of the power to punish (dendadhara). Kautilya lays down that dharma or law is Regnam Agnya—the command of the Ruler."

"The Philosophical Basis of Indian Legal and Social Systems," East-West Philosopher's Conference, 1949, p. 9.

[17] Rigveda IV, 42; Puranic Story of King Vena; Manu 7. 3–13; Majumdar, Chandhuri and Datta, Advanced History of India (London, 1950) 120 ff. Brihatparasara and Ramayana ii, 67 quoted in Ghoshal, note 5, *supra,* at 121, 185.

[18] N. C. Sen-Gupta, Evolution of Ancient Indian Law, 39 and authorities cited.

[19] Manu 8. 15; Sukra, i. 121, quoted in Ghoshal, p. 217; Sen-Gupta, pp. 39–41; Rangaswami Aiyanger, Rajdharma, p. 43.

[20] The most quoted religious aphorism is "Dharma is the king of kings" (Brihadaranyaka Upanishad). Beni Prasad, The State in Ancient India (Allahabad, 1928) 506 demonstrates how both religion and custom controlled the king from the time of the Vedic Hymns. Many of the early apologists for kingship, e.g., Kautalya, emphasized the right of subjects to revolt, their disaffection to the enemy and like pragmatic considerations why the king should act properly, Prasad, 507; Manu 12.108; A. S. Nataraja Ayyar, Dharma Protects Him Who Maintains It, 4 Vyavahara Nirnaya (1955) 65, 83; Sen-Gupta, Sources of Law and Society in Ancient India (Calcutta, 1914) 64–78.

[21] Prachetasa Manu, Ghoshal, p. 138; Mahabharata and Santiparvan, Anusasana 61.32–3, Ghoshal, p. 142; Ghoshal, ch. 4 generally.

ruler were created to destroy anarchy is known as the doctrine of the fishes (Matsya Nyaya) or the two destructive demons (Sundopa) that in nature the larger devour the smaller. The people "assembled together and made compacts (samayal) mutually undertaking to expel from their midst persons guilty of abuse, assault, and connection with other men's wives, as well as those who should break the compact. Afterward they collectively (sahitah) approached the God Brahma . . . (and) the God appointed Manu to rule over them."[22] An examination of the early theorists will show further reliance on contract and utilitarian theory. Thus, the taxes which the king is permitted to collect are said to be his wages for a return agreement to protect the subject.[23]

Although the Mahabarata considers absolute monarchy as the sole Vedic theory of government, writers have demonstrated that the monarchy was limited and that every other form of government existed in ancient India. The king did not rule alone but with a highly organized Sabha, as Sen-Gupta thoroughly documents.[24] Beni Prasad concludes that Indian polity "was saturated through and through with the principles of what for convenience may be called federalism and feudalism."[25] K. P. Jayaswal in his classic *Hindu Polity* discusses the republican forms of government in ancient India. The dedication of the book is interesting: "To the memory of the republican Vrishnis, Kathas, Vaisalas, and Sakyas, who announced philosophies of freedom from devas, death, cruelty, and caste." [26] Some of the forms of government which he finds discussed in ancient Hindu literature are: the *Bhaujya* or cabinet form, membership in which was elected not hereditary;[27] *Pettanika,* similar to the *Bhaujya* form but with hereditary leadership;[28] presidential form (Svarajya) in Northern and Western India, the *Taittiriya Brahmana* describing the president as "the leader of equals";[29] the *Viruddha-rajjani* in which the state is ruled by parties;[30] the *Arajaka*

[22] Sataptha Brahmana, xii.6.24; Ghoshal, p. 127; Santi Parva, chs. 67–68; Ramayana ii.67; K. M. Panikar, Indian Doctrines of Politics (Calcutta, 1940) 4 ff. This is prominent in the Mahabharata.

[23] Bandhayara, i.10.18.1, Govindaswamin comment (Ghoshal, p. 40); Manu 8.144 (Ghoshal, p. 40); Santi., 71.10 (Ghoshal, p. 137); Aparka commenting on Yaj. i.366 (Ghoshal, p. 194).

[24] Sen-Gupta, *supra,* 41–47.

[25] Beni Prasad, The State in Ancient India (Allahabad, 1928) ix, 504, 580ff. See also K. P. Jayaswal, Hindu Polity (2d ed., Pangalore, 1943) 36–39; Edward A. Freeman, History of Federal Government (London, 1863) xl, 721; D. G. Karve, Federations (London, 1932) 24–26; Ramesh'Chandra Majumdar, Corporate Life in Ancient India (Poona, 1922) xi, 414; Radhakumud Mookerji, Local Government in Ancient India (London 1920) xxv, 338; Sir Henry Sumner Maine, Village Communities in the East and West (New York, 1889) xii, 413.

[26] Jayaswal, Hindu Polity, note 62.

[27] *Id.*, 79.

[28] *Id.*, 85.

[29] *Id.*, 80.

[30] *Id.*, 88.

or extreme democracy, where the law was ruler and there should be no man-ruler;[81] the Buddhist assemblies, practicing a form of parliamentary government.[82] A government in which the whole population took the consecration of rulership apparently did exist in Nepal—the *Vairajya* or "kingless constitution."[83] Perhaps there is no better way to point up the continuity of this past with the present than to mention the Village Panchayats, often referred to as "village republics." These were the most ancient indigenous village organizations in India. They placed on chosen wise men of each village extensive civil, criminal, and administrative jurisdiction in small matters. They functioned largely in an arbitral manner and seemed to have handled 75–80% of all disputes and government. They combined executive, legislative, judicial, and "administrative" functions, operated without fixed rules of law, and applied a form of local equity or custom. They have continued even under the British, are reconstituted by Article 40 of the Constitution, and are presently efficient in most villages as shown by recent studies.[84] This diversity and yet continuity of past and present seems similar to that in our own tradition, and leads me to deny that the jurisprudence of any country or region has grown so unitary that it is essentially at variance with theories employed in other regions. Our own Graeco-Judeo-Christian jurisprudence contained enough variety to produce Stoic-Republicanism, Hegelian-Nazism, Marxian-Communism, Hobbesian-Monarchism, and at one time even Jeffersonian-Democracy.

(b) *Punishment and Procedure.* There are those who distinguish primitive from civilized law by the degree to which the system embodies well-organized patterns of punishment and procedure. Without accepting this test of civilization, it is to be pointed out that on both scores the earliest Hindu society had a highly organized system. As early as Manu, there is extensive jurisprudential discussion of the king's relation to punishment, judgment on him who uses punishment unjustly, an organized police force, a detailed catalogue of punishments under four titles (admonition, reproof, fine, corporeal) and rules for the use of each.[85]

In our own jurisprudence, we have done much to demonstrate that

[81] *Id.*, 86.

[82] Marquis of Zetland quoted by Professor Rawlinson in The Legacy of India (London, 1937) xi.

[83] Jayaswal, *supra*, 81.

[84] India (Government Reference Annual) (Delhi, 1955) 84 ff; D. Thorner, Panchayats, Indian Yearbook, 1953;

Statistics for Uttar Pradesh up to March 1954 show 13,000 cases handled by Panchayat adalats (courts), revision asked for in 3% of the cases and granted in 1%.

[85] Manu, 8.129, 8.130, 7.14–15, 7.20–22. E.g., "If the king were not without indolence to punish the guilty, the stronger would roast the weaker like fish on a spit."

"The whole race of men is kept in order by punishment; for a guiltless man is hard to find; through fear of punishment this universe is able to enjoy its blessings."

a "right" is a protected interest, that procedure is at the very heart of substance, and that the more highly developed the procedure the more complete is the jurisprudential system. In India, so complete are the records, we can almost place the exact time at which a thorough procedural system comes into being. Apasthamba, Gautama, Vasistha, and Visnu contain few procedural rules (though they develop some rules of evidence); they are still speaking of ordeals and compurgation, (there is slight reference to witnesses).[36] Manu developed an extensive code of evidence but otherwise little procedure.[37] With Jajnavalkya and Narada, the law of procedure becomes complete. Thus in Yajnavalkya we find procedure classified under Plaint, Answer, Proof and Decision.[38] The detail of rules can be seen from the following:

(1) No recrimination or counterclaim is allowed until the complaint is discharged;

(2) No departure from pleading is permissible.

(3) Counterclaim or recrimination is permitted in certain criminal charges.

(4) Each party is required to find a surety for satisfaction of judgment.

(5) Where a contesting defendant loses, he pays an amount equal to the claim to the king; while, where the complaint is found to be false the complainant pays double the amount to the king.

(6) Distinction between cases which have to be tried immediately and those where decision is to be adjourned.

(7) Order of examination of witnesses, plaintiff's witnesses first examined.[39]

Fraud nullifies litigation; the parties are held to their pleadings; sureties may be required; lack of capacity of children and others is known; subpoena, injunction, dismissal on motion, fatally splitting or joining causes of action are all provided for; rules fix parties, classes of complaints, available defenses.[40] The list could be greatly expanded. Perhaps we can make the modern Anglo-American lawyer feel completely at home by the four classes of answers: (a) Admit (Satya), (b) Deny (Mithya), (c) Confession and avoidance (Pratyavasakandana) and (d) *Res judicata* or previous decision (Pranguyaya).[41]

---

[36] Gautama, Dh. S. XI, 23–25; XIII, 1–6; Apastamba, Dh. S. II 5–7, 11, 29; Manu 8. 1–10; Rigveda VII, 14–15, 105; Vasistha (May. ed. Mandlik, 9). Note the 5 classes of ordeal (Divya): fire (agui), emersion (Apah), balance (Tula), poison (Visa), and drinking (Kosa).

See Gautama Dh. S. XIII, 43 (2 Sacred Books of East, p. 246).

[37] Manu 8.24–26, 46–47, 50–57.

[38] Sen-Gupta, Evolution of Ancient Indian Law, 50.

[39] Vajnavalkya, II, 6–11; Sen-Gupta, 50.

[40] Narada (Jolly Intro., II, 24); Yajnavalkya II, 9–10, 19, 31–32, Mitaksara, Yaju II, 5–6; Kané, Katyayanasmriti, 15–16, 142.

Sen-Gupta, 50–58 and authorities cited.

[41] Narada II, 5–6, I, 62.

Evidence is particularly well and early developed. As early as Gautama, the rules are detailed.[42] From Visnu on, we find classification into real evidence, witnesses, and presumptions. The rules refer to best and secondary evidence, qualification of witnesses, order of proof, cross-examination, burden of proof, *res ipsa loquitur,* hearsay, perjury, demeanor.[43] The point need not be labored further.

(c) *Meaning of "Law"; the "Rule of Law."* In Indian literature, one can find all the conflicting meanings of law which the West has formulated: *lex* and *jus;* justice, legislation, right, duty; natural, divine, enacted.[44] Although we shall turn our attention in a later section to the continuity of modern Hindu jurisprudence with the past, perhaps we can here illustrate these views of law by the opinions of the five India Supreme Court Justices in the famous case of *Gopalan v. Madras,* 1950 S.C.R. 88. Three judges, speaking through Justice C. J. Kania, expressed their view that "law" as used in the phrase "procedure established by law" in Art. 21 of the Constitution meant *"lex"*—laws passed by the legislatures, not *"jus"*—law in the general sense of the principles of natural justice or natural law:

> "To read the word 'law' as meaning rules of natural justice will lead one into difficulties because the rules of natural justice as regards procedure are nowhere defined."

Justice Sastri said that while the word "law" did not mean *jus naturale* it was not limited to law as passed by the legislature but included "settled usages" and "normal modes of proceeding." Justice Fazal Ali held that "law" did mean principles of natural justice.

What has already been said illustrates the extent to which the rule of law obtained in ancient India.[45] This point on "rule of law" may be

---

[42] Gautama XIII (Sacred Books of East, II p. 246).

[43] See authorities collected in Sen-Gupta, pp. 66–77. Also Manu 8. 24–26, 46–47, 50–57; Vajnavalkya 6–7, 13–15, 17, 23 (Gharpure's ed. Mitakshara); Narada I 63–64.

[44] Manu 8. 15; Rangaswami Aiyanger, Rajdharma, 43; P. V. Kané, Hindu Customs and Modern Law (Bombay, 1950); N. C. Sen-Gupta, Evolution of Ancient Indian Law, 39 ff; A. S. Nataraja Ayyer, Dharma Protects Him Who Maintains It, 4 Vyavahara Nirnaya (1955) 65; "The Hindu Conception of Law," 17 Bombay L. J. (1939) 41.

[45] I may summarize this ancient and continuing Hindu experience and why some see in India the future hope for the rule of law by reference to the paper of my former student, Professor Chandra P. Gupta, University of New Delhi, *"The History and Present Status of the Rule of Law in India"* presented at the Fourth International Conference of Comparative Law, Chicago, 1957:

> "Through the centuries, the one supreme guiding principle of the Hindu system was that the conduct of the authority, as of the subject, must conform to law or 'Dharma.' 'Dharma,' a word difficult to translate into English, includes the concepts of justice, law, right and duty, and acting according to Dharma means the duty of acting in a way, in the sphere of one's activity, that would best lead the individual to his self-realization—Moksha or Nirwana." . . .
>
> "In shaping the development of the rule of law in our system, the traditions of the English system, acquired during the British rule, the influence of the American Constitutional system, with its 'due process,' our own ancient traditions and the

concluded by reference to two positions of the Indian courts and parliament in the critical years, 1950–53. First, although the Supreme Court refused to accept natural justice as a definition of "law,"[46] it has set aside a decision of a labor tribunal, which failed to allow the parties to produce evidence, as contrary to the rule of law;[47] it issued certiorari to determine whether a tribunal acted contrary to[48] and in other cases followed the established principles of natural justice.[49] Second, the courts in 1950–51 held certain provisions of the land reform acts, adopted under constitutional authority, invalid as not providing proper compensation.[50] Although there was wide criticism in India of the decisions, which held up the much needed land reform program, and many lawyers and political figures believed the decisions thwarted the purposes of the constitution, the country showed its respect for the rule of law and the independence of the judiciary by amending the constitution to remove any ambiguity which the Court had found in the original constitution.[51]

(5) *Modern Hindu Jurisprudence; The Great Synthesis.* We have already objected to the tendency to refer to Asian jurisprudence as though we were discussing the year 500 B.C., which assumes that if Confucius says "X" or the Dharma Sastras contain "Y" or Buddhism teaches "Z," then these must characterize the legal philosophies of modern countries. We have even attempted to show that, properly understood, ancient Hindu jurisprudence is not "ideologically different" from our own. But, it is insisted that, important as antecedents may be, nothing could be wider of the truth than that we should ground

economic and social conditions in the country, have all played an important role. . . .

"In an ideal sense, rule of law implies a social order in which the individual can best attain his self-realization. . . . So long as there is poverty and ignorance, hunger and disease, and so long as there is crime and coercion, force and violence and the denial of basic freedoms, the rule of law is not fully established. Rule of Law is an ideal to be constantly struggled for. In its pure form, it can only exist in a society based on truth and non-violence." See also Judge Ram Keshar Ranade, Pres. Address, Judicial Conference, Godhra, 45 A.I.R. Jour. 37:

"It may sound platitudinous but it is absolutely true that the success of democracy in our country pivots substantially, if not wholly, on the success of the rule of law.' " Nehru, "The Tragic Paradox of Our Age," N.Y. Times Mag., Sept. 7, 1958, p. 13.

[46] Gopalan v. Madras, 1950 S.C.R. 88.

[47] Bharat Bank v. Employees of Bharat Bank, 1950 S.C.R. 459,500.

[48] Veerappa Pillai v. Raman & Co. Ltd. (1952) S.C.A. 287.

[49] Parry & Co. v. Commercial Employees (1952) S.C.A. 299; J. L. Kapur, "Concept of Natural Justice," 6 Indian L. Rev. (1952) 27; Justice William O. Douglas, We the Judges (1957) 28.

[50] State of Bihar v. Kameshwar, A.I.R. 1952 (S.C.) 252.

[51] Constitution (First Amendment) Act, 1951; Constitution (Fourth Amendment) Act, 1955; State of West Bengal v. Subodh Gopal, 1954 S.C.R. 587; Dwarkadas v. Sholapu Spinning and Weaving Company, 1954 S.C.R. 674; State of West Bengal v. Bela Banerjee, 1954 S.C.R. 41; Saghir Ahmad v. State, 1954, S.C.R. 1218. The Indian Law Reviews during the period 1950–1955 contain over one hundred articles on this.

our discussion solely in ancient history. We are concerned with modern law, and modern law is the product of growth and synthesis. Nowhere is this more true than in India.

So much has been written of the English influence on Indian law that it is necessary to do little more than recall its major outline. In the footnotes there is somewhat more extensive consideration of certain fields of law on which American articles are not likely to appear for some time. With British rule in India, English public law, criminal law, law of torts, and procedure were imported wholesale.[82] English influence extended even into Hindu law of family, property, and inheritance, though the Acts declared that Hindu or Mohammedan law was to be applied in these areas.[83] The law of wills is chiefly a British

[82] See generally, S. V. Gupta, Hindu Law in British India (Bombay, 1947).

Law of Torts: Any collection of Indian cases or statutes will show that English cases and concepts are being applied, e.g. defense of act of State (Secretary of State for India v. Kamachee Boyce Sohiba, 7 M.I.A. 476 (1859)) or of judicial act (Judicial officer's Protection Act, 1850) or of quasi-parental authority of teacher (Sankunni v. Swaminatha Paltar, 45 Mad. 548 (1922)) or necessity (Greyvensteyn v. Hattingh, [1911] A.C. 355). Also whether a tort survives death (Legal Representatives Suit Act, XII of 1855; Indian Succession Act, XXXIX of 1925). Or liability for acts of an independent contractor (Dhondita v. Municipal Comm. of Bombay (1892) 17 Bomb. 307); but if the English doctrine, e.g. common employment, is not clear Indian courts may not be bound to follow it (Sect of State v. Rukhamini Bai (1938) Nag. 54). We could go through the law of torts and see that down to the smallest detail the law is essentially English law—nuisance, Rylands v. Fletcher, negligence, lateral support, libel and slander, forms of action, vicarious liability.

Law of Crimes: The basic acts are the Indian Penal Code of 1860 and Code of Criminal Procedure of 1861. The law as it has been carried over today is well and briefly surveyed in A. Gledhill, The British Commonwealth, vol. 6, India, ch. 12, pp. 173–187. Again, an examination of cases shows the complete similarity:

Moti Lal Mallik v. Emperor, 39 C.W.N. 199—where no murder intent but intent to commit felony.

Emperor v. Kastya Rama, 8 Bom. H. C. 63—territorial limits of criminal jurisdiction.

Emperor v. Gopalia, 26 Bom. L. R. 138—mistake as defense.

Emperor v. Kursin-Bux, 3 W.R. 12 and Gokool Bowree, 5 W.R. 33—amount of force useable as defense.

Emperor v. Sathe, 1 Bom. L. R. 351, and Mokit Pandey, 3 N.W.P. 316—abetment.

Emperor v. Bal Gangadhar Tilak (1908) 10 Bom. L. R. 848—sedition.

Emperor v. Chaube Diukar Rao (1933) 55 All. 654—bribery.

Emperor v. Venkatrao (1922) 24 Bom. L. R. 386—contempt of court.

Emperor v. Govinda (1876) 1. Bom. 344—distinction between culpable homicide and murder.

Emperor v. Nemai Chattraj, 27 Cal. 1041—kidnapping.

Emperor v. KaleeModock, 18 W.R. (Cr) 61—deceit.

Public Law: This will be dealt with in a later article, Gledhill *supra*, starts his discussion of the public law: "it may be a matter of surprise that India, now mistress of her own destinies, should be willing to retain the law, the legal system, and the institutions which Britain imposed on her." p. 147.

[83] Compare N. C. Sen-Gupta, Evolution of Ancient Indian Law, chs. VIII–IX, "Law of Inheritance," with A. Gledhill, *supra*, chs. 15–16. The degree of modification can be seen from the following list of statutes: The Caste Disabilities Removal Act, 1850;

development. The concepts of common law and equity became the common property of Indian law.[54] The association of Colebrooke and Jayannath Tarkapanchanan in translating the last of the great Sanskrit digests in 1797 marked the beginning of a new period. The courts treated Sanskrit legal texts as statutes, whereas previously they were considered merely evidence of unwritten eternal law. The doctrine of *stare decisis* took on all its English rigor.

The Hindu Widows Remarriage Act, 1856; The Native Convert's Marriage Dissolution Act, 1866; The Special Marriage Act, 1872; The Indian Majority Act, 1875; The Transfer of Property Act, 1882; The Guardians and Wards Act, 1890; The Hindu Disposition of Property Act, 1916; The Indian Succession Act, 1925; Inheritance (Removal of Disabilities) Act, 1928; The Hindu Law of Inheritance (Amendment) Act, 1919; The Child Marriage Restraint Act, 1928 (Sarda Act); The Hindu Gains of Learning Act, 1930; The Hindu Women's Right to Property Act, 1937; The Arya Marriage Validation Act, 1937; The Hindu Marriages Disabilities Removal Act, 1946; Hindu Married Women's Right to Separate Residence and Maintenance Act, 1946; Hindu Marriages Validity Act, of 1949.

As India gained her independence the movement was under way to enact a Hindu code relating to personal and family law. The interest it aroused and the degree to which it was debated can be seen from a partial list of Law Reviews and books: Hamid Ali, The Law of Marriage, A Short Study in Comparisons and Contrasts (Hyderabad (Decan), 1944); Vesey-Fitzgerald, S. G., "Projected Codification of Hindu Law," 29 J. Comp. Leg. & Int'l L. (3d ser., 1947) 19–32, 2 India L. R. (1948) 109; Durai, J. C., "Hindu Law: Should It Be Reformed?," 16 J. Comp. Leg. & Int'l L. (3d ser., 1934) 140–4; Rankin, S., "Hindu Law Today, 27 J. Comp. Leg. & Int'l L." (3d ser., 1945) 1–13; Chiu, H. P., "The Roman, Hindu, and Chinese Law of Adoption," 10 Nat. Univ. L. R. (1930) 3–35, 11 Nat. Univ. L. R. (1931) 3–22; Derrett, J. D. M., "Legal Status of Women in India from Most Ancient Times to the Present Day," 43 A.I.R. Journal (1956) 73; Attekar, A. S., The Position of Women in Hindu Civilization (Benares, 1938); Gharpune, J. R., Rights of Women Under Hindu Law (Bombay, 1943); Burway, R. G., "The Present Position of Hindu Women and the Means of Ameliorating Their Lot," 19 Bombay L. J. (1941) 56–67, 98–114.

Specifically on Hindu Code Bill: Tope, F. K. and Ursekar, H. S., Why Hindu Code? (Bombay, Sharma Mandal, 1950); Haksan, Sir Kailash, "Our Law and the Need for Reform," 1 Indian L. R. (1947) 40; Pusalkar, R. N., "Hindu Code: Is The Reform Imminent?," 37 A.I.R. Jour. (1950) 42; Mehta, Lehar Singh, "Some Implications of the Hindu Code Bill, 1948," 37 A.I.R. Jour. (1950) 26; Parekh, Vallabhadas P., "Desertion is No Ground for Dissolution of Marriage Under the Hindu Code Bill—Its Effect," 38 A.I.R. Jour. (1951) 48; Divan, Paras, "Divorce Law of Hindus, Contemplated Reforms and a Few Suggestions," 40 A.I.R. Jour. (1953) 7; Harhare, Gunde Rao, "Hindu Law and Its Codification," 41 A.I.R. Jour. (1954) 2; Gajendragadkar, K. B., "Observations on the Draft Hindu Code," 23 Bombay L. J. (1945) 307; Gajendragadkar, K. B., "Discrepancies and Anomalies in Hindu Law: Need for Codification," 20 Bombay L. J. (1942) 191; Dubey, Thakur Prasad, "Some Criticism on the Two Bills Proposed to be Introduced in the Assembly," 29 A.I.R. Jour. (1942) 53; Gajendragadkar, K. B., "The Two Bills of Hindu Law," 29 A.I.R. Jour. (1942) 61; Hajela, Rai Bahadur K. S., "The Draft Hindu Code, Its Exposition, Comment, and Criticism," 36 A.I.R. Jour. (1949) 64; Kathalay, B. D., "Hindu Law and Codification," 31 A.I.R. Jour. (1944) 13; Balbir Sahar Sinka, "Codification of the Personal Laws," 16 Sup. Ct. Jour. (1953) 9; Paras Diva, "Hindu Law of Marriage, Divorce and Alimony," 18 Sup. Ct. Jour. (1955) 261; S. V. Fitzgerald, "The Projected Codification of Hindu Law," 2 Indian L. R. (1948) 109.

Some of the provisions were enacted; see Hindu Marriage Act of 1955, Hindu Succession Act of 1956; See Divan, Paras, "The Hindu Marriage Act, 1955," 6 Int. & Comp. L. Q. R. (1957) 263; Derrett, Legal Status of Women, *supra*.

[54] A. Gledhill, "The Influence of Common Law and Equity on Hindu Law Since 1800," 3 Int. & Comp. L. Q. (1954) 576.

Anyone who has taught or studied in an Indian law school knows that the modern jurisprudence is distinctly English oriented. The texts are Salmond and Austin. Even the 26-page *Manual of Jurisprudence* by P. S. Atchuther Pillai, which nearly every Indian student uses to cram for examinations, discusses not only analytical, historical, ethical or critical, or teleological, comparative, sociological, functional realist, and natural jurisprudence but also "economic," "psychological," "ethnological" jurisprudence, and pure science of law. It reviews the positions of Austin, Holland, Salmond, Hohfeld, Kocourek, Kant, Kelsen, Allen, Savigny, Maine, Bentham, Bryce, Comte, Spencer, von Jhering, Ehrlich, Weber, Pound, Stone, Hobbes, Goodhart, and others.

It may be objected that the discussion, while showing a familiarity and acquaintance with English and American jurisprudence, lacks depth of insight. However, if one reads the Indian law journals, he will find depth as well as breadth in Indian jurisprudential thinking. The law reviews are replete with articles on such specific concepts as *"Juristic Personality of the Hindu 'Idol.'"*[55]

The broad juristic philosophy of an emergent socialist state could be seen in many current law reviews.[56] This progressive outlook is shown by numerous excellent articles on criminology, psychology and social ideals. *"Crime and Punishment"* by B. K. Bhattacarjee is one example.[57] He is able to discuss the Soviet penal experience with a detachment not often found in American writings. In *"Social Ideals*

[55] Bijan Kumar Mukherjea, "Juristic Personality of the Hindu 'Idol,'" Indian L. Rev. (1947) 277; A. S. Nataraja Ayyar, "The Juristic Personality of Deities in Hindu Law," 3 Vyavahara Nirnaya (1954) 106.

[56] 4 Indian L. Rev. (1950) 300. Consider the review by Justice P. B. Mukharji of Simpson and Stone's, *Law and Society:*

> "Materials in the pronouncements of the new school of American thought so ably expressed in the superb judgments of such great Judges of America like Holmes, Brandeis, Cardozo, Murphy and Frankfurter do not appear to have provoked the authors to a clearer idea of the shape of things to come in juristic thought.
>
> "The law is the calling of thinkers and jurisprudence, not a mere survey either of cases or of individual decisions determining particular rights. One learns from law an amiable latitude with regard to psychology, beliefs and tastes and acquires that catholic outlook whereby men may be pardoned for the defects of their quality if they have quality in their defects. To be able to see so far as one may and to discern the great forces that are behind every detail makes all the difference between philosophy and disputation and between legal compilation and jurisprudence. . . .
>
> "Excessive preoccupation with the purpose of law (Bentham's 'utilitarianism,' Pound's 'social engineering,' and Jhering's 'means to an end' are referred to), unrelated to the source from where it originates has caused much unnecessary mystification about 'executive legislation,' 'New despotism' and 'Administrative Law.' . . .
>
> "It appears that the future jurisprudence will have for its major concern the functional view of the law which alone can reconcile the demands for change with the demands for security."

[57] 5 Indian L. Rev. (1951) 149.

and the Law," Radhaknal Mukerjee gives a penetrating analysis of law and modern psychology[58] and in other articles[59] it is advocated that the bar receive training in psychology. A glance at any current Hindu law journal will reveal that the articles tend to be more jurisprudential than our own.

Elsewhere, it has been pointed out how India has borrowed from the world in framing its constitution.[60] It has drawn on the common law of England and the civil liberties cases of the United States. Some say that it has taken the concept of preventive detention from Russia. I might digress a moment to show how complete has been the synthesis on preventive detention. The oldest existing statute of which I know is the Bengal Regulation of 1818, though some date its Indian antecedents to 1795. Numerous Provincial Maintenance of Public Order Acts existed in the 19th and 20th centuries, and the British Defence of the Realm and Defence of India Acts (under which Ghandi was imprisoned) were continued and finally embodied in the 1950 Preventive Detention Act (to meet partition's problems). Local, Russian, British law have all contributed.[61]

Though India is evolving many original rules of her own, it need not be assumed that her appetite for imported legal principles is exhausted. She will doubtless pick and choose among the systems with which her citizens become acquainted. India has always shown a tolerance and hospitality for other cultures, even those forced upon her. Hardly a writer facing Indian jurisprudence but remarks on this.[62]

[58] 2 Indian L. Rev. (1948) 229.

[59] Bimul Kumar Bhattacharya, "Insanity and the Criminal Law," 6 Indian L. Rev. (1952) 41.

[60] H. A. Freeman, New Constitutions of Europe, Asia and South America, 34 Corn. L. Q. (1948) 1; H. A. Freeman, Review, Basu, Cases on the Constitution of India, 53 Col. L. Rev. (1953) 292.

[61] V. G. Ramchandran, The Law of Preventive Detention, Supreme Court Jour., p. 181; A. Gledhill, The British Commonwealth, vol. 6, India, p. 173; A. K. Gopalan v. The State of Madras, A.I.R. 37 (1950) S.C. 27.

[62] Seymour Vesey-Fitzgerald, "Law, Hindu," 9 Encycl. of the Soc. Sciences, p. 262.

> "The greatest contribution to posterity made by the Hindu tradition was the broad-mindedness, sympathy, and the toleration of different viewpoints exhibited almost alone in India amongst the civilized communities of the earlier days.
>
> "The modern Hindu lawyer, regarding his ancient law with patriotic pride, looks upon English law also with possessory affection. He would not separate even if he could the two systems of which he is the living synthesis, and in adapting his inherited conceptions to the needs of today he is merely doing openly and with modern tools what in another age and another fashion was done by the sages and commentator before him, above all by Vijnanesvara."

In the concluding chapter of *Hindu Polity,* Jayaswal writes:

> "The constitutional progress made by the Hindus has probably not been equalled much less surpassed by any polity of antiquity. The great privilege of the Hindu at the same time is that he is not yet a fossil; he is still living with a determination which a great historian has characterized as a tenacity which bends but does not break. The Golden Age of his polity lies not in the Past but in the Future." K. P. Jayaswal, *Hindu Polity,* 2d ed., Bangalore, 1943, pp. 366–7.

A Suggested Approach. Perhaps the essence of my approach can now be stated. It is to recognize that we are concerned with modern law, even when we review ancient law for comparison; that modern law in all countries is a synthesis of old and new, Western and Eastern; that for adequate study we divide law into subjects, some of which are deeply rooted in old traditions and culture and some of which are related to, but largely replace, those traditions; that we should clearly distinguish the area studied and the approach needed; that we recognize that in areas like "family law" which are closest to custom, the variations between two states in America or two sections in India may be as great as the dissimilarities between East and West; that in many areas no one can tell from what law a given quotation comes. I venture to say that there is no Eastern or Western philosophy and no Eastern or Western law.

[5]

THE PLACE OF HINDU LAW IN COMPARATIVE JURISPRUDENCE.

THE distinguished jurist who surveys the Law of Rome in the Cambridge Mediaeval History (vol. ii. ch. 3) speaks almost plaintively of the lack of any independent standard of comparison by which to gauge the overwhelming greatness of his subject. Modern European systems of law have improved on classical models in various directions; but they have usually been indebted to the Romans not least when they have surpassed them. It has even been suggested—though this is open to question—that the Islamic law of wills is directly borrowed from the Roman doctrines of *donationes mortis causa* and *inofficiositas* as those doctrines were in force in what had once been outlying provinces of the Empire. Hindu law, however, is entirely free from the suggestion of Roman influence, except in so far as non-Hindu rulers in recent times may have looked at it through spectacles tinted by Rome; and in Hindu law surely Dr. Roby might have found what he was seeking. Granted that it would be absurd to suggest comparison on a footing of equality; we postulate only a standard by which 'the Roman greatness forth to measure,' not a rival to set up in opposition. But such a standard may perhaps be found in a system which shows in its principal features its descent from the same prehistoric stock as that of Rome; which has been inspired by ideals in marked contrast to those of Rome; which has held for centuries the contented allegiance of more numerous and as varied peoples in territories wider spread than the Empire of Trajan; and has been expounded by commentators whose work, in spite of all shortcomings, is illuminated by flashes of juristic insight not unworthy of the great Antonine jurisprudents. For an instance of such insight, out of hundreds which could be given, we may refer to the unhesitating way in which the commentators quoted in *Girjabai* v. *Sadashiv* (L. R. XLIII. I. A. 151) make a juristic act—the acquisition of property by partition of the joint family—depend not on any formality but on a state of mind and its unequivocal declaration. For another instance compare Manu

VIII. 151 with Codex IV. xxxii. 10 (Caracalla), Pandects XII. vi. 26 (Ulpian), etc. And though the codification of Hindu law remains a dream—Utopia or nightmare, whichever you please—a comparison of Hindu and Roman law may suggest a kindlier feeling than is sometimes expressed for that genius of the paste-pot and scissors called Tribonian.

Public Law.

At the earliest period at which we have any certain knowledge of Rome we may fairly speak of her in terms borrowed from the Hindus. The stage is occupied by the revolt of an inferior against a superior caste. The patricians were bound together by ties of clanship and sacraments (especially *confarreatio*) which they denied to their inferiors; they claimed, as by hereditary right, to monopolize all the offices and privileges of government, political, religious and social alike; and between them and the *plebs*, until the *Lex Canuleia*, stood the barrier most distinctive of caste, namely, that intermarriage was impossible. Patrician and plebeian faced one another in much the same manner as 'twice-born' and sudra; and even as at the present day there are sudra tribes bearing the same names as the proudest Rajput clans, so also there were plebeian families with patrician surnames—but not recognized as any sort of kindred on that account. By speaking thus for a moment of Rome in terms borrowed from India we place in a clearer light the foundation on which the greatness of the former stands. The *dharmashastras* are full of the highest ideals of duty. No sterner course of self-discipline has ever been put before the world than that which they prescribe for the Brahman student. But the duties which they enjoin are something which priest and king owe to themselves and their caste rather than to their people at large. The secessions and victories of the *plebs* established once and for all the great principle (utterly foreign to India) that power and duty are conferred from below; the proudest and most autocratic of the Cæsars claimed no more than to wield the sovereignty of the people because the people had placed it in his hands.

The idea of caste half raised its head again in the Middle Ages. It was a common conceit of mediaeval writers which divided mankind into *oratores*, *bellatores*, *mercatores* and *aratores* (= Brahman, Kshatriya, Vaisya and Sudra). That the danger never became acute is due in the main to the splendid fight of Pope Gregory VII against the tendency to a hereditary priesthood. But something also may be attributed to the contractual theory of government which, as Maine teaches us, Feudalism derived in part at least from Roman law. It is significant that while Langland in 'Piers Plowman' speaks in one place of the caste-duties of 'lorde, lerede and lewede' in almost Hindu terms, elsewhere he represents those duties under the legal phraseology of offer and acceptance of a covenant (*cf*. C. Passus X. 219-230 with IX. 25-37).

None the less, it must be admitted that the tendency of Roman law in the later Empire and subsequent times was to remember the maxim *Quod principi placuit legis habet vigorem* and to forget the justification on which that maxim had originally been based. The 'Reception' commonly brought with it an increase in irresponsible despotism and a decline in the popular side of government; thereby repeating among the nations which received her law the process by which the free institutions of Rome herself had degenerated.

Rome was a city, *Bharat Varsha* a continent; and it is perhaps unfair to censure the Hindus because they failed to work out a principle which Rome learnt on a small scale before she attempted to apply (and then forgot it) on a big one. Let us beware also of speaking contemptuously about the 'stationary' civilizations. Even admitting that any civilization is ever really stationary, it is from a purely legal point of view a queer criticism which objects to a system of law because the people subject to it are so contented that they desire no change. Progress may be either uphill or down; and stability is not necessarily a defect; nor can we accuse India of being stationary in any sense in which that epithet could not equally be applied to Byzantium. The great demerits of the caste system have always been obvious; but its merits are perhaps better understood to-day than they were when Maine in 'Ancient Law' spoke of it with such scorn. It is indeed the only logical foundation for pride of blood; it is a gigantic experiment in eugenics, or at least in one aspect of eugenics, which has met with a considerable measure of success. In the past it has filled, and to some extent it still fills, the place of a poor law; and also the place in the system of police which was filled in Saxon and Norman England by the view of frankpledge. And our own restless civilization can hardly fail to admire its matchless power of teaching contentment, and therefore happiness, even to those who by our standards have less than nothing with which to be content.

The Indian village community, too, like the caste system and almost everything else in Hindu polity, is based on the unflinching application of the hereditary principle. Every office in the village, from those of headman and priest down to those of scavenger and drummer-boy, descends from father to son; every *watan*,[1] or hereditary right, however humble, is a source of pride. Hence the stubborn vitality of Indian village life, against which despotism and anarchy beat alike in vain. Even the great catalytic of British rule has done little as yet to break down that vitality; though one of the gravest injustices which we have done India is to import the English law of Terms into a country which regarded agricultural tenancies as a matter of status rather than contract. The Tenancy Acts of our various provinces have all been attempts, more or less thorough, to rectify this blunder.

Rome, or rather Byzantium, forgot her popular principles in a despotism bridled only by the cumbrous character of the bureaucracy through which it worked; Hindu polity seems never to have had any popular principles to forget. If the *Arthashastra* (chs. 8-9)[2] can be accepted as giving a fair picture, the Maurya Empire rested on a system of *delatio* or espionage as paralysing as that of Tiberius or Domitian. For all that we mean by self-government the world is indebted to the barbarians of the North; to the Frank, the Anglo-Saxon and the Dane. To many of the best Hindu minds, even to-day, the idea of popular election to public office is an indecency. In one feature and one only of Indian life is there any approximation to what we regard as healthy ideas of local government. Sir Frederick Pollock, in his notes to Maine's 'Ancient Law,' compares the Indian *panchayat*, or council of five men, to the 'reeve and four men' of our English villages. The justice of the comparison lies in the fact that the *panch*, alone among Hindu institutions, are not hereditary, but are chosen *ad hoc* on account of their personal eminence by a rudimentary public opinion. But the number five is only ideal; and they have no necessary connexion with the village organization. They may be chosen from a village, or a caste, or the worshippers of a temple, or the two families concerned in a question of marriage or divorce; or, indeed, from any circle, however vague, which has an internal dispute and wishes to refer it to arbitration. Their business is internal, to arbitrate; not, like the reeve and his companions, to represent their people in some higher assembly. The varying esteem in which Hindus hold this ancient customary institution

[1] I use the word in its Marathi sense.
[2] For references to the Arthashastra I am indebted to Dr. F. W. Thomas.

may be gauged by comparing the Hindi proverb '*Panch mukh bhagwan*' (In the mouth of five is God) with the Gujarathi slang *panchayati*, the proceedings of a *panchayat*; that is to say, a riotous and disorderly assembly. Such as it is, however, the *panchayat* has been rightly taken up by many Anglo-educated Indian reformers as affording some promise for the education of the people in managing their own affairs. In a similar manner Sir Stamford Raffles[2] endeavoured to create a jury on the English model out of the *panch* which he found still flourishing among the debris of Hindu civilization in Java.

Family Law.

Sir Henry Maine in 'Ancient Law' speaks as if the original Aryan family was governed by a despotic patriarch such as the early Roman *paterfamilias*. The resemblance between the positions of a son and a slave was due, he thinks, not to the slave being treated with consideration as a member of the family but to the son being subject to as grinding a tyranny as the slave. Warde Fowler, on the other hand, gives an idyllic picture of a Roman agricultural family in days before capitalism had brutalized the relations of a slave-owner to his slaves. The *Lar Familiaris* himself became the family god because he was introduced to the hearth by the slaves. Maine was the pioneer of historical jurisprudence; and it is no detraction from his greatness to say that he seems to have been misled into this extreme view partly by excessive reliance on Roman law to the depreciation of other sources of information, partly by his desire to expose the falsity of certain wild theories of human origins then in vogue but now discredited. Moreover the evidence from other sources is often ambiguous; in reading the *dharmashastras* it is sometimes difficult to distinguish between the moral duty of honouring a father and legal subordination to his authority. In Berar at the present date a father is in law little more than *primus inter pares* among his own sons; yet he is hedged about with great respect and in legal documents is usually spoken of under the high-flown Sanskrit title *tirthrup* (the abode of reverence).

But the controversy has rolled away from the fields on which it was fought in Maine's day; and we are no longer content to ask what was the earliest form of human society. The patriarchal theory has won a conclusive victory over its rivals. The question before us is, rather, How did early Aryan society

[2] See his Java, vol. 1, p. 293 (edition 1817).

differ from that of other prehistoric peoples? The Book of Genesis and the still existing customs of Arab tribes, described by Doughty, show that the Semitic races had a *patria potestas* as severe as that of Rome; and the same is true of other races also. The distinctively Aryan note is not, as Maine seems to imply, the power of the father, but the corporate unity of the whole family and the absolute rights of its other members even against their head; that is to say, the love of family is no longer quite the same thing as the love of domestic domination. Roman law itself preserves this idea in the phrase *suus heres*; and the Salic law (chapter lix, *De Alodis*) makes it clear that the succession of sons is on quite a different footing from any other, father and son having a sort of joint property. The house communities of the southern Slavs—family republics after the Mitakshara model, in which the patriarch is merely a president—are well known and have been recently described afresh by Sir Paul Vinogradoff (Hist. Jur. I. 269). We may fairly claim that here at least Hindu law is truer to its origins than that of Rome. Nay, more, India successfully avoided a definite juristic fallacy into which Rome fell when she succumbed to the temptation to identify the early corporation aggregate, the family, with a single human personality.[3] That she did so, we need not regret, since it placed her law on an individualist basis and therefore contributed in the end a powerful factor to the cause of human freedom. But the history of Roman law is a series of attempts to remedy this initial mistake, as from one point of view we may fairly call it. Our English practice, whenever we can, is to tie up family property from generation to generation in settlements: and this has had its latest influence on legislation in the intestacy provisions of Lord Birkenhead's Act. In modern France the law insists on the children's right to the greater part of their parents' inheritance, and we are told that as a matter of convenience it is not unusual for them to enjoy that inheritance in common in a manner which bears a strong resemblance to that of a family under Dayabhaga law, though not to the more thorough-going communism of the Mitakshara. Here, then, we have not merely a clear-cut contrast between two widely opposed ideals of law; the usefulness of our contrast is enhanced

[3] The thorough nature of the corporate conception of the Mitakshara family may be illustrated. ABCD is a joint family of four brothers. A, who has no separate property, separately borrows money for his private purposes and dies, leaving no sons. The creditor can recover nothing from BCD, for they are not successors to A; his interest in the family property has simply terminated; and their interests are in theory no larger than they were before his death. Even A's son would only be bound by the law of "the pious duty."

by the partial attempts, which the one system has made, to recover the advantages of the other.

The Indian joint-family system presents instructive parallels and contrasts with Roman family law at other points. Adoption, for instance, is of importance not merely as a primitive substitute for the will-making power, but as a necessary part of joint-family law. Over a great part of India the need for a will-making power is very rarely felt even at the present day—so well does Mitakshara law cater for the natural instincts and affections of those subject to its sway. But where the family is more important than the individual, fictional means of perpetuating the family must be found when natural means have failed. In India, therefore, as in Rome, *adoptio naturam imitatur*; and the attempt to make the fiction look as like the reality as possible has led to some curiously artificial rules. For instance, generally speaking, I may not adopt a son whose mother at the time of her virginity I could not have married. In primitive Rome the pith of the whole ceremony was expressed in the *detestatio* and *adoptio sacrorum*; to-day over the greater part of India the ostensible reason for adoption is to acquire a son, *putra*, who by due performance of the *shraddh* may save his father's soul from hell, *put*. To the Hindus the religious side of their law remains a reality; to the Romans it soon became merely a nuisance. Thus it is that among Hindus an only son should not, and an orphan cannot be adopted; in Rome the vigilance of the pontiffs for the *sacra* of the natural family soon became a mere form.[4]

Again, where the family is the usual subject for the inherence of rights a branch of law must deal with those rights which inhere in a smaller subject, the 'family-member'; and we can profitably compare the Roman law of *peculium* with its counterpart, the Hindu law of 'obstructed inheritance' and self-acquired property. As the Hindu father never degenerated into an autocrat like the Roman *paterfamilias*, he stands in the same class as his sons in this respect; and the general rule is that any member of a Mitakshara joint family may deal as he pleases with property acquired through his own exertions without detriment to the family estate. In each case the question arose, what property is so acquired? The characteristic Roman answer was, first, *peculium castrense*, the spoils of war; and, secondly, *quasi-castrense*, the emoluments and perquisites of high public

[4] Perhaps we should add a further parallel. According to the Arthashastra adoption was *imperio magistratus*.

office. The equally characteristic Brahman answer, while it admitted more or less as an afterthought that loot might justifiably be the *peculium* of a Kshatriya, concentrated its attention on the 'gains of learning'—the offerings which a Brahman may acquire by his skill in the vedas. Such learning was acquired in the days of the Rishis by little expenditure and great self-denial. But it is one of the still unsolved legal problems of British India how this law is to be applied when Western learning has been acquired by one member of a joint family often at the cost of a heavy drain on family funds.

Hindu law, like Roman law, has also its *peculium adventitium* —which does not seem to call for comment. *Peculium profectitium* is of course impossible under the Mitakshara.

Yet another topic, on which Roman and Hindu family law can be better understood by the light which they throw on each other, is the position of women. It was one of the exaggerations of the last generation of anthropologists to maintain that the family was founded entirely on the proprietary jealousy of the dominant male; and just as they treated as typical the Roman ownership of the whole family property by the father, so also they laid stress on those barbarous customs, such as the *niyoga*, which revealed a wife in the light of a chattel rather than a partner with feelings and a dignity of her own. O. Schrader, in his 'Prehistoric Antiquities of the Aryan Peoples,' by a process which can only be described as selection of evidence, arrives at the conclusion that the early Aryan idea of marriage was 'a harsh and cruel slavery from which modern sentiment recoils in horror.' Much of Schrader's argument is undeniably sound; a marked degradation of women must have existed. But the passages in ancient Hindu law which prove this are purely permissive; they give the husband a power but they do not force him to use that power; and they do not exclude the possibility of exalted and depraved ideas of matrimony existing side by side from early times, just as (for that matter) they do to-day. This is the position taken up by the author of Manu IX 64, 65, in regard to the *niyoga*, when, after discussing the law of appointing a stranger to raise up seed, he goes on to say that that custom has been reprobated among the best people from the time of the Vedas. This position is, one may venture to suggest, historically correct; even if those verses are, as Max Müller and Jolly thought, an interpolation. For the rest it is merely begging the question to suggest, as Schrader does, that woman was despised because the early Aryan root means 'bearer of children'—as if there were necessarily anything degrading in bearing children; or that the honorific '*patni*' is only 'a meaningless' feminine of *pati* (one might as well say that 'lady' is only a meaningless feminine of 'lord'). And he is demonstrably in error when he maintains that out of the eight forms of marriage given by Manu *arsha* (or rather *asura*)[5] and *rakshasa* are in any way older or more typically Aryan than *brahma* or *prajapati*.

It is not too much to say that Manu's list of the eight forms of marriage is one of the must unreal things in the frequently unreal atmosphere of the *dharmashastras*. It omits at least one form of marriage which we know to have been common in the heroic age, the *swayamvar*: it includes a devilish exhibition of lust, the *paisacha*, which it is perfectly incredible can ever have been regarded as matrimony[6] among human beings; and it is not a classification at all, for it confuses ceremonies with previous considerations. The so-called *Brahma* marriage of the present day, for instance, appears to combine the characteristics which Manu calls *brahma* and *prajapati*; and if a price has been paid for the bride (as it often is, either secretly or openly), not all the sacramental ceremonies in the world will prevent the marriage being *asura*. The types of marriage in vogue among Hindus at the present day are three, *brahma*, *asura*, and *pāt*[7]; and they bear a striking resemblance to the three modes of acquiring *manus* in early Rome, if we accept Warde Fowler's statement that even in *coemptio* and *usus* marriage religious ceremonies were not entirely dispensed with in early times. *Asura* and *pāt* are only available for sudras, just as *coemptio* and *usus* were originally confined to plebeians. *Asura* is identical with *coemptio*. It is tempting, but perhaps unsafe, to identify *pāt* marriage with *usus*. There is at least this much resemblance, that in some of the castes which practice it the marriage may, if childless, be dissolved by consent within a fixed period, *e.g.* a year; after which time the intervention of a *panchayat* is required.

But infinitely the most important parallel (which Schrader calmly ignores) is between the sacramental marriage of the Roman patrician, *confarreatio*, and the sacramental marriage of

[5] In *arsha* the bride-price of *asura* has been reduced to a customary present.

[6] I do not overlook, of course, Sir E. Trevelyan's suggestion that this and *rakshasa* find their place in the list for the sake of the children.

[7] *Pat* is not found in the law-books, but is recognised (after some hesitation) as valid by custom in Bombay, Berar, the Central Provinces and Punjab. It is also known under the names of *chaddar* and *churipahinao*, and is specially appropriate to the remarriage of widows. In addition to these, permanent concubinage has among sudras certain rights just as it had in Rome. There is a danger in identifying sudra and plebeian customs in that the sudra is mainly non-Aryan.

the twice-born Hindu, *brahma vivah*. Sir Paul Vinogradoff has rightly pointed out that the identity in ceremonial detail between these two forms is so great as to leave no doubt that they descend from a common stock. But the identity is even deeper; since it is an identity not only in outward and visible form but in the inward and spiritual significance of the sacrament, and proves that an exalted idea of the union of husband and wife is one of the most ancient possessions of the Aryan race. The *far* of the Romans is the *pinda* of the Hindus, no mere meal but the bread of sacrament and sacrifice which husband and wife can now offer together; and the Hindu husband makes the perfect offering to the souls of his ancestors (or the Roman to his family gods) only when he fulfils his first duty to them by marrying a wife who now joins for the first time in his *sacra privata*. *Flamen* implies *flaminica* in the public religious worship of Rome and these two must be joint in their private worship also, *non nisi ex farreatis leguntur*; just as in India to-day *pati* implies *patni*, the latter word being defined by Panini as meaning a wife who takes part in the sacrifices of her husband. In Rome the religious marriage gradually disappeared; and Tacitus in a famous passage classes *matrimonia* and *stupra* together as *lascivia principis*. In India sacramental marriage has banished all other forms from the high castes, so that a wife of a different caste, possible according to the law-books, is now forbidden since she could not assist in her husband's religious duties. And the tendency is to regard even the marriage of a sudra as sacramental; it is a common saying that marriage is the only sacrament open to him and incumbent on him.

Family sentiment goes far beyond the bounds of the immediate joint family. Vinogradoff quotes the case of Mr. Justice Chaudhri supporting a family of some seventy or eighty poor relations (though his salary as a Judge is legally his own to do as he likes with); and the claim of even the most distant kindred on a successful Hindu is usually acknowledged in the most ungrudging manner.[8] It is not surprising, therefore, that family sentiment colours the law, even after the immediate joint family is extinct. This is the explanation of the limited estate which the sonless widow of a separated Hindu takes in her husband's inheritance, an estate which exceeds a life estate only for pur-

[8] It is characteristic of the sardonic nature of Indian humour that the word *bhaobandi* (brotherly love) is used in common speech with two opposite connotations (i) nepotism, (ii) envy hatred malice and all uncharitableness.

poses which would be binding on the joint family if it still existed and are therefore binding on the larger family circle. The limitations on her power are not due to *levitas animi*, but to exactly the same causes as produced the Roman *tutela mulierum*, namely, a desire to protect the interests of the family. Indeed, Manu V. 148[9] seems to show that the Hindu law at one time approximated even closer to the Roman model: 'In childhood must a female be dependent on her father; in youth on her husband; her lord being dead, on her sons; *if she have no sons, on the near kinsmen of her husband; if he left no kinsmen, on those of her father; if she have no paternal kinsmen, on the sovereign;* a woman must never seek independence.' The words in italics are Kulluka's gloss. Maine, 'Ancient Law,' seems to have thought that this law was still in force.

Nor is it only in the case of women that guardianship is based on a consideration for the interests of the reversioners. The maxim *ubi emolumentum successionis, ibi onus tutelae,* has its application in Hindu as well as in Roman law; and places the motherless orphan in the hands most likely to protect the integrity of his property, but not always those most likely to protect his person. Fortunately, our own Guardians and Wards Act allows the District Court to separate the guardianship of the person from that of the estate[1]; and Judges who administer that Act meet with frequent illustrations of the essential truth of our old English folk-tale of the Wicked Uncle and the Babes in the Wood.

To sum up; the Roman and the Hindu family spring from the same source, and were both clothed with a religious sanction outwardly identical; though, if Warde Fowler's[2] estimate be correct, different in this that the veneration of ancestors had no place, or only a very minor place, in primitive Rome. They diverged because India remained religious and agricultural, while in Rome a distinctly irreligious and commercial element gained the upper hand. Fictions, it is said, have their origin in the religious law; but Hindu energy is devoted to strengthening that law; while an important chapter in the history of Rome might be filled with the legal devices by which her citizens escaped from a bondage in which they had ceased to believe.

[9] Sir Wm. Jones's translation.

[1] Where the minor is a member of a joint family the Court cannot interfere; but as he has no separate property of his own, no interference is needed.

[2] Religious Experience of the Roman People.

Origins other than Family Law.

Enough has been said to indicate the contributions which the Hindu system is capable of making to our knowledge of Aryan family law. Can we expect from it the same assistance in other branches of the study of origins? Can it shed any light, for instance, on the vexed problems of the origin of contract and its relation to conveyance; or suretyship and deposit; or on the growth of compulsory out of optional jurisdiction? These questions have, we believe, never been thoroughly investigated; but the answer to them is likely to be disappointing; nor is that disappointment wholly or even principally due to the fact that we continue to administer Hindu family law while almost completely ignoring other branches of the same system. The true difficulty is that the *dharmashastras* are not really primitive law-books at all. They are neither primitive, nor are they strictly law-books.

A long and honourable civilization had preceded them, at least in the form in which they have reached us. Great Empires had risen and passed away; Hindu civilization had spread not only over the whole Indian Continent: it was embarking about this time on a great overseas expansion—to Burma, Siam, Cambodia, Java and Sumatra.[3] It is hardly wonderful, therefore, that the *Dharmashastras* do not exhibit any of the characteristics of truly primitive law. There is none of the exaggerated formalism which appears *e.g.* in the Salic law (cap. lviii *De Chrene Cruda*), or in the Roman search for stolen property *lance et licea*. The King has a coercive jurisdiction, and an organized police; and he inflicts genuine punishments (Manu VIII, 310). Manu and, still more, Yajnavalkya and Narada, are startlingly modern in their perception of such matters as procedure, the burden of proof, and the weight of evidence; see *e.g.* Manu VIII, 24-26, 46-47, 50-57; Yajnavalkya 6-7, 13-15, 17, 23 (i and ii); Narada I, 63-64;—the last-named refers to forgery, not exactly a savage crime. Even the art of cross-examination was not unknown, Yajnavalkya 13-15.[4] All this is really conclusive of the existence of a developed jurisprudence.

The ground on which the *dharmashastras* have often been

[3] Prof. Washburn Hopkins (Camb. Hist. Ind. I. xii.) dates Manu about our era, Yajnavalkya 300 A.D., Narada 400 A.D. The Brahman kingdom of Cambodia was founded not later than the second century A.D. the Hindu kingdoms in Burma and Siam earlier. The oldest Burmese laws quote as their authority 'Manu Lord of the Rishis'; and appear (according to Jardine and Forchkammer) to be quoting from an earlier version of our Manu.

[4] References to Yajnavalkya are to the heavy type in Gharpure's edition of the Mitakshara.

treated as primitive is well stated by Dr. Jolly (Narada pref. pp. ix-x): 'The separation of moral precepts from laws is everywhere, and especially among such a religious nation as the Hindus, the work of a comparatively late period.' With the utmost respect one may venture to question this statement. There is not a word of morality in the oldest of our Leges Barbarorum, the Lex Salica; and it is not until the outstanding characteristic of primitive law, formalism, has been blunted that there is any room for confusing morality with law. It was not till the fourteenth century that the ecclesiastics of our own Court of Chancery began to meddle with strict legality in the name of conscience; nor was it till long after the XII Tables that Stoic philosophy embarked the Roman praetor on a similar course of action. The priests of barbarians, like their law, are usually taken up with ceremonial and outward considerations. Morality, like jurisprudence, is a late development; and both are well advanced even in Manu.

The authors of the Shastras were not lawyers but holy ascetics.[4] It is true that even Narada, the most legal-minded of them, constantly mingles law and ethics; but it is hardly fair to say that even Manu confuses them. The fact is that the rishis are not directly interested in either law or ethics in our sense of the words, but in something which transcends and includes both; namely, *dharma*, caste-duty, the central concept of Hindu life. This explains the apparently haphazard classification of Manu and Narada, decried by James Mill. It is not a classification of the whole of law, but merely a list admittedly incomplete (Manu VIII, 8) of 'heads of dispute,' of cases as they present themselves in court before the king or judge whose caste-duty makes it necessary for him to decide them. It regards a dispute, not as a Roman jurisprudent would from the moment of the first acts-in-law out of which it arose, but as something already existing, and deals with the duty of the man who has to decide it. Similarly, Narada speaks of the eternal residence in heaven of a just king (I, 28); and (II, 10 and foll. esp. 18) of the litigant's iniquity falling in part upon his judges and the king when they decide amiss. Thus it is, too, that Manu sanctions perjury to save a life (VIII, 104) in spite of his impressive statement (*ibid.* 81-86) of the duty of truth; the permitted perjury being explained in Kulluka's gloss as a defence against 'the known rigour of the king even though the fault arose from inadvertence or errour.' It is not only in ancient India that

[4] Nor is it only for mnemonic reasons that they composed in verse. They sometimes rise to poetry.

perjury has been the shield of the oppressed against injustice; and manifestly the *dharma* and the law of such a case might differ. The supremacy of *dharma* rather than law also accounts for the importance of family matters and the comparatively minor place of commercial law. Neither the Rishis nor their pupils were usually drawn from the caste whose *dharma* included commerce. To the latter it was enough to know that they must respect and uphold settled usage (see *e.g.* Manu VIII, 164) without requiring their preceptor to tell them what that usage was. Finally the fact that these books were composed by holy men, not by lawyers, makes it difficult always to be certain whether the author is expounding the law or preaching a sermon, or merely spinning cobwebs out of his own inner consciousness. We have already referred to the unreal atmosphere of some of the classifications; and when Vijnaneswar in the Mitakshara explains Yajnavalkya as meaning something quite different from what Yajnavalkya says, it is not easy to guess whether he is really recording a reform of the law, or merely the survival of an alternative which had always existed side by side with that which the Lord of the Yogis preferred to describe; see *e.g.* the Mitakshara (in Gharpure's edition, pp. 182 and following) on the subject of a father's right to make an unequal division among his sons.

A detailed examination of earlier Sanskrit literature would undoubtedly yield larger results, especially if it were made by a scholar skilled both in philology and jurisprudence. But a few chance illustrations only, of what we already know from other sources, are the most that can be expected in this direction from the Shastras, or even from the Sutras which preceded them. Thus Manu VIII, 68, though as it stands it refers to witnesses, is clearly inspired by the same sentiment which made compurgation reasonable: 'Women should regularly be witnesses for women; twice-born men for men alike twice-born; good servants and mechanicks, for servants and mechanicks; and those of the lowest race for those of the lowest.' Similarly the ordeals by water and by fire of Manu are substantially the same as those of Anglo-Saxon England. Manu VIII, 158, is aware of sureties for the appearance of a debtor before his creditor, who are not sureties for payment. Slavery for the payment of debt was familiar, and men sold themselves for bread in the evil times;—just as they would to-day in famine if left to their own devices; see *e.g.* Narada's list of the fifteen kinds of slaves, II v, 24-26, including 'one maintained in a famine . . . one relieved from a great debt . . . one who has offered himself saying "I am thine" . . . a slave for a fixed period . . . one self-sold.' Again the Roman *manus injectio* and the wagering of the *actio sacramenti* are clearly brought to mind by the following of Narada:—

I. (i) 43: 'A claimant may arrest his adversary until the arrival of the summons, if the latter tries to evade the claim he is about to prefer or does not refute his charge.'

I. (i) 6: 'In a lawsuit made by wager, the loser has to pay the wager made by himself and a fine to the king.'

Finally, though jurisdiction is compulsory, not optional, and though the caste-duty is such that the conjuring of the judges by the litigants is unthinkable, we may find something of the feeling which produced the *tancono* of the Salic[5] and other primitive Teutonic law in Narada's description (I. ii. 17) of 'judges who after having repaired to court sit there in silent meditation and do not deliver a candid opinion as they ought.'

Unwritten custom may give us a few more hints, though chiefly from non-Aryan sources. In Java and Sumatra Raffles and Marsden found a regular scale of wergilds; and compurgation with oath-helpers was a common mode of trial; but it would be rash to ascribe either of these customs to Hindu sources in the absence of positive proof of their having ever existed in India. Each is a custom which would almost inevitably spring up under certain conditions. As a Judge, the present writer has frequently been struck with the attitude of witnesses who were produced not because they really knew anything about the issue but merely to support their principal's oath; not wilful perjurers, of whom of course there are always plenty, but men acting in all good faith. He has also frequently been moved to sanction 'cross-cousin' marriage of his wards on the ground that it was auspicious. The levirate, marriage by simulated capture, service for a wife, the tabu of an elder brother, all these and a thousand other anthropological details are part of the daily pabulum of mufassil courts. But from the point of view of jurisprudence they are rather illustrations of what we know already than light on dark places.

S. G. VESEY-FITZGERALD.

[5] L. S. LVII. i.

[6]

MANU'S OMNISCIENCE: ON THE INTERPRETATION OF *MANUSMRTI* II, 7

ALBRECHT WEZLER

1. "The smṛti of Manu is", as J.D.M.Derrett has aptly stated ,[1] "the most famous of the lawbooks. Its unique quality is its combination of all the features beloved by Hindu society in a treatise on Duty.... It is plain to the western eye that Manu ingested productions of centuries and his present text was not composed in one piece...." "The name of Manu has nothing to do with his fame. The compiler's achievement has brought lustre to the name."

Scholars in the West, though for convenience still using expressions like "the smṛti of Manu" or "Manu says", etc., have learnt to look at this 'lawbook' rather as at another text of the vast "anonymous literature"[2] India has produced. This dismissal of the conceptions the Indians have traditionally formed of the author of this Smṛti is, no doubt, demonstrably justified, but it may at the same time also lead to a total neglect of the Indian tradition itself. Ideas, however, do not at all lose their historical significance when later scholars of a quite different civilisation come to the conclusion that they are phantastic, fanciful, mytho-

[1] *Dharmaśāstra and Juridical Literature* (*A History of Indian Literature*, ed. by J.Gonda, part of Vol. IV), Wiesbaden, 1973, p. 31 and 33.

[2] This term was coined by P.Hacker; cf. his article "Zur Methode der geschichtlichen Erforschung der anonymen Sanskritliteratur des Hinduismus", in: *ZDMG* 111 (1961), p. 483 ff. (= Kleine Schriften, ed. by L. Schmithausen, Wiesbaden, 1978, p. 8 ff.).

logical, etc., i.e. altogether untenable. On the contrary, insights of such kind may and, to be sure, should pave the way for an unbiassed study of these ideas, their development and reception, i.e. the effects they historically had within the civilisation they arose in. I do not, of course, want to denigrate in the least the achievements of Western research as regards the problem of the authorship of the Manusmṛti; but I think the time has come to stress that a study of the indigenous Indian ideas about its alleged author is likely to yield results that are most instructive, i.e. from which one may learn much about Indian culture in general and the tradition of Dharmaśāstra in particular; information we would irresponsibly neglect by merely stating that historically it is nonsense.

There is no dearth of material on Manu, or Manus, material mostly found in religious or mythological texts; on the contrary, as only too often in Indian philology, one is confronted with an embarrassingly abundant variety of heterogenous information (much of which has already been collected by Kane).[3] In order to find one's path through this jungle, it is advisable to concentrate first on the data the Manusmṛti itself contains. Of particular interest in this connection is the frame story ("Rahmenerzählung") of the first Adhyāya; but as it has already been given due attention,[4] another statement of Kane's may be taken up for

[3] *History of Dharmaśāstra*, Vol. I (revised and enlarged), Pt. 1, Poona, 1968, p. 306 ff.

[4] Viz. by P. Hacker; cf. his articles "The Sāṅkhyization of the Emanation Doctrine. Shown in a Critical Analysis of Texts", in: WZKSO 5 (1961), p.75 ff. (= Kleine Schriften, p. 167 ff.) and "Two Accounts of Cosmogony", in: *Jñānamuktāvalī. Commemoration Volume in Honour of Joh. Nobel*, ed. by C.Vogel, New Delhi, 1963, p. 77 ff. (= Kleine Schriften, p. 389 ff.). - Hacker's important contributions have unfortunately been overlooked by J.W. Laine; cf. his article "The Creation Account in Manusmṛti" in *ABORJ*, Vol. LXII (1981), p. 157-168.

consideration here, viz. that "Manu is said to be omniscient".[5]

2. The reference is to M. II,7, a verse which is indeed usually taken to explicitly state the omniscience of Manu. It runs as follows:

yaḥ kaścit kasyacid dharmo manunā parikīrtitaḥ /
sa sarvo 'bhihito vede sarvajñānamayo hi saḥ //

No variants seem to exist.[6] Bühler translates:[7]

"Whatever law has been ordained for any (person) by Manu, that has been fully declared in the Veda: for that (sage was) omniscient."

It is apparently this interpretation that has found the widest acceptance in the West, and it is the one that is

[5] Op. cit., p. 309. Cf., however, Vol. III, p. 827, where Kane takes M. II,7 to state "that whatever dharma has been ordained for any person by Manu, all that has been entirely declared in the Veda, for the Veda is full of all knowledge."

[6] At least, according to J. Jolly, *Mānava Dharma-Śāstra. The Code of Manu,* London, 1887. - However, in Hemādri's *Caturvargacintāmaṇi* (Vol. III, Pt. 1, ed. by Pt. Yogeśvara Tarkaratna and Pt. Kāmākhyānanātha Tarkavāgīśa, Calcutta, 198o, p. 2o7) M. II, 7 is quoted with *vihito* in the place of *'bhihito*; yet, this variant is obviously of later origin. -
The fact that Kullūka in commenting on *pāda* c says *sa sarvo vede (pratipāditaḥ)* does not, of course, point to his having read it differently; similarly, Govindarāja's *yaḥ....[kaścid].....dharmaḥ kasyacid.... manunā kathitaḥ sa sarvair vedair uktaḥ....* has to be taken as a paraphrase of the *mūla*, and not as attesting to a variant reading; this applies also to Sarvajñanārāyaṇa's *sarvajñānaprāyo*.

[7] *The Laws of Manu, translated with Extracts from Seven Commentaries* (Vol. XXV, SBE, ed. by F. Max Müller), Oxford, 1886, repr. Delhi, 1964 and 1967, p. 3o; cf. also "Introduction", p. XIII.

usually taken to correspond to the intention of the author.[8] There is hardly any need to remark that Bühler in this case, as often in others, too, has relied on the explanation of Kullūka though he does not fail to point out[9] that "the last clause is taken differently by Gov., who explains it, 'for that (Veda) is made up, as it were, of all knowledge'" and that "Medh. gives substantially the same explanation". Indeed, the other commentators seem all to follow Kullūka with the exception of Rāghavānanda, Govindarāja[10] and Rāmacandra, the last one adding a second explanation.[11]

A problem is actually posed only by the final clause, viz. by the very last word *saḥ* which is taken by the commentators to refer either to *vede* or to *manunā*. In fact, no other alternative is really conceivable, for *dharmaḥ* can be safely ruled out in view of the causal particle *hi* and the general content of the verse. Thus it is between two alternatives only that one has to make a reasonable choice. The relative chronology of the different commentators cannot, of course, yield any proof in the matter;[11a]

[8] Cf. e.g. J. C. Heesterman's "Die Autorität des Veda", in: *Offenbarung, geistige Realität des Menschen. Arbeitsdokumente eines Symposiums zum Offenbarungsbegriff in Indien*, hrsg. von G. Oberhammer, Wien, 1974, p. 3o f.; cf. also p. 89 of the same book (G. Oberhammer).

[9] Op. cit.,l.c. footnote.

[1o] His explanation is quoted below in part 3, see fn. 28a.

[11] Viz: ... *sa vedaḥ sarvajñānamayaḥ sarvaṃ jānātīty arthaḥ / yad vā sa manuḥ sa sarvajñānamayaḥ* /. - Actually Kullūka himself seems to accept both interpretations; see below, p. 94 f.

[11a] The relative date of some of the commentators is not yet known; but even if the relative chronology of all were known and if, in addition, the earlier commentators would unanimously give one interpretation only and the later ones, in the same manner, the other one, this could not be taken to furnish more than a working hypothesis in favour of the earlier interpretation.

instead one has to pose the following question: is it more probable that the assumed author of the Manusmṛti in the course of time "has become omniscient" or that he, albeit originally conceived of as "omniscient", has later been denied this extraordinary quality? One is admittedly tempted to opt unhesitatingly for the first alternative. Such a decision might, however, be precipitous, at least as long as the specific motive for this change in the conception of Manu has not been discovered.

But before studying the commentators' explanations more closely with the aim of eventually unveiling this motive, one should first examine M. II,7 by itself. One cannot then fail to realize that the predicate *sarvajñānamayo* goes more naturally, as I have already stated elsewhere,[12] with a nonpersonal subject, i.e. with *vedaḥ*. Had the author thought of Manu, one would expect him to have used the expression *sarvajña* instead of *sarvajñānamaya*; and it is worth noting that Kullūka on his part does in effect meet this expectation in that he substitutes the former expression for the latter, only that he gives no explanation for the semantic equivalence thus assumed (see below p. 95).

2.1. The Petersburg Dictionary lists only one more occurrence of the expression *sarvajñānamaya*, viz. "R. 7,23, 1,82", i.e. verse 82 of the first Adhyāya of those inserted after 7.23 (= Vol.7, Appendix I, No.1, line 114 of the critical edition) of the Rāmāyaṇa. It is obvious that here the expression, like *sarvadevamaya*, *sarvabhūtamaya* and *sarvalokamaya* of the same verse, is used with reference to a divine person, namely god Viṣṇu, and therefore it seems to have the meaning given in the PW, viz. "alles Wissen in sich enthaltend". Hence it is not possible in interpreting M.II,7 to have recourse to the assertion, appealing though it is at first sight, that the form *sarvajñānamaya* can never be predicated of a person. In the given context of an eulogistic description of god Viṣṇu's cosmic, all-embracing great-

12 In my review of the book mentioned in fn. 8, published in *IIJ* Vol. 24 (1982), p. 142 ff.

ness,[12a] however, this expression is not equivalent to "omniscient". "To know everything" is evidently not the same thing as "to contain all knowledge within oneself", and what apparently is meant by this attribute of Viṣṇu's is that he is the source of each and every type of (human) knowledge, perhaps including liberating insight.

On the other hand, the assumption suggests itself that this usage might be due to a fusion of two different concepts, the theistic idea of a personal god and the mechanistic of a *materia prima*. Yet in the Rāmāyaṇa passage under discussion there is no element that clearly attests to even a partial deviation from the conception of Viṣṇu as divine person.

2.2. That *sarvajñānamaya* should, nevertheless, in 'correct' Sanskrit be predicated of a non-personal subject only is, however, fully corroborated by the manner in which the expression *jñānamaya* is used. For according to the PW it qualifies *tapas* in Muṇḍ.Up.1.1.9 (where *sarvajña* and *sarvavid* stand in the same verse, but, significantly they are predicated of a personal subject); *nidhi* in Mbh. 12.298.7, viz. in the phrase *ajñānāt paripṛcchāmi* (= Janaka), *tvaṃ* (= Yājñavalkya) *hi jñānamayo nidhiḥ*; *vahni*, the "sacrificial fire", in Raghuvaṃśa 8.2o; and finally Viṣṇu's *mukhāmburuhāsava*, the "juice of his face-lotus", of which the worshippers (*saumya*) have drunk, in Bhāg.P. 2.4.24.

2.3. Inspite of this most welcome confirmation, additional arguments should as far as possible be adduced in order to fully warrant the point at issue, i.e. that *saḥ* in M. II,7 does really refer to *vede*. Now, what this verse obviously aims at is a statement as to the relation in which the Manusmṛti as a whole[13] stands to the Veda. The expression

[12a] These descriptions seem to be influenced by *Bhagavadgītā XI*.

[13] In its present context, at least, this verse cannot but be taken to refer to the *Manusmṛti* as such and not to some particular teaching ascribed to Manu.

sarvaḥ, used here either attributively or, rather, predicatively, is clearly meant to emphasize what in a circumlocutory manner is already stated by the initial *yaḥ kaścit kasyacid dharmo*, viz. that without exception each and every 'norm' prescribed by Manu is contained in the Veda. The verb used in this connection, viz. *abhi-dhā*, however, can hardly have the meaning "to say or state e x p l i c i t l y", since such an assertion could easily be shown to be wrong; besides, the Manusmṛti would then amount to no more than a jejune repetition of explicit statements contained in the Veda, its value consisting in nothing but simply collecting in one work, for the sake of convenience, *dicta* already found in the Vedic texts themselves, only that there they are scattered far and wide.[14] Rather what the author must have had in mind was the well-known idea that the different elements of *dharma* are either explicitly taught in the Veda or are to be deduced from certain *liṅgas* contained in it or must go back to corresponding passages in Vedic texts no longer extant. Consequently, what the author wants to intimate is that the whole of *dharma* as taught in the Manusmṛti is solely based, directly or indirectly, on the Veda, i.e. that it has no other source one might conceive of. Hence it follows that M. II,7 is opposed to M. II,6 where in a descending scale after the "whole of the Veda" (*vedo 'khilaḥ*)[15] "the recollection, i.e. the tradition based on recollection, and the virtuous character[16] of those who know [the Veda]" (*smṛtiśīle ca tadvidām*), "the conduct of (morally) good people" (*ācāraś caiva sādhūnām*) and finally

[14] Cf., however, Medhātithi on M. II,6: ... *ity evaṃ viprakīrṇānāṃ manvādayo 'ṅgopasaṃhāraṃ sukhabodhārthaṃ cakruḥ* /.

[15] Explained by Medhātithi on M. II,6 to mean: *kṛtsnaḥ / na kiṃcit padaṃ varṇo mātrā vā yan na dharmāya* /!

[16] Medhātithi on M. II,6 first quotes an explanation according to which *śīlam* means *rāgadveṣaprahāṇam*, but gives later his own (*vayaṃ tu brūmaḥ*) - problematic - interpretation, viz.: *samādhiḥ śīlam ucyate / tathāhi 'śīla samādhāv' iti dhātuṣu* [viz. Dhātupātha I 556] *paṭhyate* /.

ātmanas tuṣṭir (eva ca)[17] are enumerated as each forming "the root of *dharma*" (*dharmamūlam*).

Now, if at all a reason is to be adduced for the quite different assertion of M. II,7 a-c, [17a] what could it be like? Certainly not Manu's omniscience; for, if one would have to be omniscient in order to be able to correctly interpret the *dharma* as indicated or hinted at in Vedic texts, this would hold good for anyone consulting these texts for information on the *itikartavyatā*. Nobody in his right mind could have thought of substantiating this assertion, viz. that the whole of *dharma* taught in the Manusmṛti is based on Vedic *diṣṭa*, by pointing out that Manu was omniscient! And if one takes into account the context, i.e. the extant sequence of M. II,6 preceding II,7, and the palpable contrast in which the latter verse stands to the former, there cannot be the least doubt that what actually calls for a convincing justification is the rather bold contention that the Veda is not merely the foremost of sources of *dharma* as expounded by Manu, but rather the only one. Precisely this, however, is ultimately accomplished by the final clause of M. II,7, provided that *saḥ* is correctly taken to refer to *vede* and not to *manunā*!

As to the relation between M. II,6 and 7, it should, of course, be added that the latter verse does not contradict M. II,6 in every regard; rather M. II,7 is meant to point out a peculiar feature of *dharma* as taught by Manu, viz. that it is exclusively based on the Veda whereas that exposed by other *smṛtikāras* flows from other springs be-

[17] On this term cf. P. Hacker in his article "Dharma im Hinduismus", in: *ZMR* 49 (1965), p. loo ff. (= Kleine Schriften, p. 5o3 ff.).- On *ātmārāma* cf. B. Schreiner in: *ZDMG* 2 XIX, Supplement III, Deutscher Orientalistentag. ..., Vorträge, hrsg. von W. Voigt, Wiesbaden, 1977, p. 941 ff.

[17a] Surely if *saḥ* were in fact to refer to Manu, the argument would have to run thus: "What has been taught by the Veda has been expounded by Manu, for Manu is omniscient"!

sides. The Manusmṛti is thus said to have a peculiar excellence, a clear superiority over all the other Smṛti texts;[18] and this claim has in fact been recognized not only by *dharmaśāstrins*, as can easily be ascertained when considering the predominant rôle this text has played in the history of Dharmaśāstra or when looking into the Tantravārttika of Kumārilabhaṭṭa who states:[19] "Man beobachtet, daß ausser den Purāṇen, dem Mānavadharmaśāstra und dem

18 Cf. also the verses:
vedārthopanibaddhatvāt prādhānyaṃ hi manoḥ smṛtam /
manvarthaviparītā tu yā smṛtiḥ sā na śasyate //
tāvac chāstrāṇi śobhante tarkavyākāraṇāni ca /
dharmārthamokṣopadeṣṭā manur yāvan na dṛśyate // ,
ascribed to Bṛhaspati and quoted among others by Medhātithi and Kullūka on M. I,1. - This view is, however, not shared by all the later Dharmaśāstrins; e.g. Hemādri (op. cit., l.c., see fn. 6) refutes it by stating:
yat tāvat uktaṃ manusmṛteḥ śrutitulyatvena vidheḥ smṛtyantarebhyo balīyastvam iti tat kalpamātram / bṛhaspativacana[ṃ]
[Hemādri refers to the first of the verses quoted above]
manvarthaviparītānāṃ budhādismṛtīnām aprāmāṇyam āha /
nanu śiṣṭatraivarṇikasvīkṛtānāṃ kātyāyanādismṛtīnāṃ vedārthapratibaddhatvād ity aprāmāṇyahetvavidyamānatvād ato manuśabdenātra sarve vedārthasmartāraḥ kātyāyanādayo 'bhyupalakṣyante /
athavā 'māna jñāne' iti dhātupāṭhād [viz. IV 67] *vedārthajñānavān munir manur ucyate /*.
One has, of course, to read *buddhādi*° and not *budhādi*° as the reference is not to the spurious Smṛti of Budha (on which cf. P.V.Kane, op. cit., p. 286 f.), but to the Buddhist '*dharma*'; cf. also *Tantravārttika*, ed. by G.Y. Nātū, *ĀSS* 97, Poona 197o, p. 113 f. [on MS 1.3.4.].

19 I quote the translation given by G. Oberhammer, op. cit. (see above, fn. 8), p. 42. The original runs as follows (*Tantravārttika*... ed. by Mm. Pt. Gaṅgādhara Śāstrī, *BSS*, Nos. 5 ff; Benares, 19o3, p. 179. 17 - 22 = *TV* (Pt. 2), ed. by Gaṇapatarāv Yādavarāv Nātū, *ĀSS* 97, Poona, 197o p. 172. 7 - 11 [on MS 1.3.15]):

Itihāsa, die von Gautama, Vasiṣṭha usw. verfassten Dharmaśāstras und Gṛhya-Werke jeweils nur in bestimmten vedischen Schulen studiert werden, so, wie dies für die Prātiśākhyas typisch ist. So wird das Dharmaśāstra des Gautama und Gobhila nur von den Chandogas angenommen, das des Vasiṣṭha von vielen Ṛgvedins, das von Śaṅkha und Likhita von den Vājasaneyins und das von Āpastamba und Baudhāyana von den Taittirīyas."

3. Turning now to the explanation of M. II,7 as offered by the commentators, it is primarily two aspects on which interest should be focused, viz. on the motive for attributing omniscience to Manu and on the opinions as regards the main purport of this verse in its given context. Since there would be little sense in quoting all of them (so far as their works have been preserved or edited), I shall discuss only two of them, viz. Medhātithi and Kullūka, for they represent the two divergent interpretations noted by me at the outset.

3.1. Medhātithi says:[20] *yad uktaṃ vedavitsambandhena smṛteḥ prāmāṇyaṃ tad anena prakaṭayati*/ yaḥ kaścid dharmo[21] *varṇa-*

19 (cont.) *purāṇamānavetihāsavyatiriktagautamavasiṣṭhaśaṅkhalikhitahārītāpastambabaudhāyanādipraṇītadharmaśāstrāṇāṃ gṛhyagranthānāṃ ca prātiśākhyalakṣaṇavat praticaraṇaṃ pāṭhavyavasthopalabhyate / tadyathā gautamīyagobhilīye chandogair eva <ca> parigṛhīte / vāsiṣṭhaṃ bahvṛcair eva śaṅkhalikhitoktaṃ ca vājasaneyibhiḥ / āpastambīyabaudhayanīye taittirīyair eva pratipanne....*

[cf. also P.V. Kane, op. cit. (fn. 3), p. 2o and in: *JBBRAS* (N.S.), (1925), p. 96]. - Oberhammer's rendering of *bahvṛcaiḥ* has to be emended to just "Ṛgvedins".

20 I quote from: *Manu-Smriti* with Nine Commentaries...; Vol. 1, *Bhāratīya Vidyā S.*, No. 29, ed. by J.H. Dave, Bombay, 1972, p. 177.

21 As to the different aspects of the concept of *dharma* in Hinduism, analyzed by P.Hacker (in his article mentioned in fn. 17), it should be noted that already Medhātithi has clearly distinguished

dharma *āśramadharmaḥ saṃskāradharmaḥ sāmānyarūpo viśeṣarūpaś ca* kasyacid *brāhmaṇāder varṇasya* / manunā parikīrtitaḥ / sa sarvo 'pi vede 'bhihitaḥ *pratipāditaḥ / yathā caitat tathā pūrvaśloka uktam* / sarvajñānamayo hi saḥ / *sarveṣāṃ jñānānām adṛṣṭaviṣayāṇāṃ hetur nimittaṃ vedaḥ / sarvair jñānair nirmita iveti jñāne tadvikāratvam adhyāropya mayaṭ kṛtaḥ / yo hi yadvikāraḥ sa tanmayas tatsvabhāva ity ucyate / vedaś ca jñānahetutvāt tanmaya iti / satkāryadarśane kāraṇaṃ kāryasvabhāvam iti / athavā sarvajñānād dhetor āgataḥ 'hetumanuṣyebhyaḥ'* (Pāṇ. 4.3.81) *iti mayaṭ kriyate* //.

"By this [verse the author, i.e. Manu] makes clear what has been said [in the preceding verse, viz.] that tradition based on recollection is authoritative [as regards *dharma*] due to [its] relation to [persons] who know the Veda. 'Whatever *dharma*', [i.e.] *dharma* relating to the *varṇas*, *dharma* relating to the stages of life, *dharma* relating to the *saṃskāras*, general (i.e. valid for all) and special, 'has been fully described by Manu', 'whichever [the person], i.e. whichever the *varṇa* [involved], beginning with [that of] the Brahmins; 'all this' without exception (*api*) 'is stated, [i.e.]

21 (cont.)

between "*dharma* im Vollzug" and "*dharma* nach dem Vollzug"; for in his commentary on M. II,6 he remarks (p. 172):

uktam asmābhir dharmaśabdo 'yaṃ smṛtikāraiḥ kadācid vidhiniṣedhaviṣayabhūtāyāṃ kriyāyāṃ prayujyate, kadācid tadanuṣṭhānajanye āphalapradānāvasthāyini kasmiṃścid arthe /;

the reference is to his explanation of M. I,2, where he had stated (p. 9):

dharmaśabdaḥ kartavyākartavyayor vidhipratiṣedhayor adṛṣṭārthayos tadviṣayāyāṃ ca kriyāyāṃ dṛṣṭaprayogaḥ /:

obviously, he also has seen the difference between "*dharma* vor dem Vollzug" and "*dharma* im Vollzug". Therefore, Hacker's statement "diese Unstimmigkeit besteht nur für unsere Denkgewohnheiten" (l.c., p. 1o2/2o5) has to be slightly revised: the Indians themselves were fully aware of important distinctions of the term *dharma*, although they would not, of course, have subscribed to the opinion that these differences amount to an "Unstimmigkeit".

is expounded, 'in the Veda'. As to how this [is done], that has been taught in the preceding verse."

Medhātithi's explanation of the final *pāda* of M. II,7 is rather difficult. Obviously G.Jhā [22] was not able to clear the hurdle. One has to realize that Medhātithi, as regards the first of the two interpretations he gives, tacitly refers to Pāṇ. 4.3.143 and 4.2.134.[23] Because of his introductory remark (*sarveṣāṃ jñānānām adṛṣṭaviṣayāṇāṃ hetur nimittaṃ vedaḥ*), resumed later by *jñānahetutvāt*, and in view of the fact that in referring to the *satkāryavāda* it is the cause (*kāraṇa*) he makes the subject of the phrase, one arrives at the conclusion that what he wants to say is this: "'For he is *sarvajñānamaya*': the Veda is the cause (*hetu*), the source (*nimitta*) of all knowledge the object of which is not seen / not visible. [The affix] *maya(ṭ)* has been added [to *sarvajñāna-* in accordance with Pāṇ. 4.3. 143 and 4.3.134] by superimposing on knowledge the character of having it (i.e. the Veda) as [its] product-of-change; [that is to say, the affix is added] in the sense of '[the Veda] is, only as it were, produced by all knowledge'; for what is the product-of-change of something is said to be 'that-*maya*', [i.e.] to have its nature (i.e. the same nature as that). And the Veda because of being the cause of knowledge has the nature of it (i.e. knowledge). This [is what is meant by the expression *sarvajñānamaya*] (*iti*). For (*iti*), according to the [Sāṃkhya] view that the product exists [already] in its cause [and only becomes manifest], the cause has the nature of [its] product."

22 Manu = Smṛti. *The Laws of Manu with the Bhāṣya of Medhātithi*, Vol. 1, Pt. 1, Calcutta, 192o, p. 2o8.

23 On this meaning of the secondary affix *maya(ṭ)* cf. also my article "Paralipomena zum *sarvasarvātmakatvavāda*.I. Mahābhāṣya zu Pāṇ. 4.3.155 und seine einheimischen Erklärer", to be published in: *WZKS*, XXVI (1982).

That is to say, the gist of Medhātithi's interpretation is: the Veda is the cause of all knowledge; according to the Sāṃkhya theory of causation every cause contains in itself its product(s) and can, hence, be said to have its/their nature. Applied to 'Veda' and 'all knowledge' this means that the Veda, though in fact being the cause of all knowledge, nevertheless has the *svabhāva* of its product, i.e. all knowledge; therefore the Veda can be said to be made up of knowledge, but it cannot be said to be produced by all knowledge, but to be produced by it o n l y a s i t w e r e . Accordingly, it has to be assumed that the addition of the affix *maya(ṭ)* is caused by an *adhyāropa*, i.e. by superimposing on (all) knowledge the character of being the *prakṛti* of the Veda that in its turn is looked at as though it were its product-of-change. That is to say, according to Medhātithi the affix *maya(ṭ)* as equivalent to *tasya vikāraḥ* is used here but figuratively. Yet he might have felt that this interpretation is not completely satisfactory so that he offers another one, viz.:

"Or [alternatively / rather (?) the affix] *maya(ṭ)* is added in accordance with Pāṇ. 4.3.81 [and 82 in connection with 4.3.74], [i.e. what is meant by *sarvajñānamaya* is that the Veda] has proceeded from all knowledge as its cause".

Of particular importance are the following elements in Medhātithi's explanation: *1.* He specifies *jñāna* as *adṛṣṭa-viṣaya*, thus making clear that the context is that of *dharma* and not of knowledge in general. *2. abhihitaḥ* is paraphrased by *pratipāditaḥ*, an expression that seems to have been consciously chosen as it does not imply any limitation as regards the means by which the *dharma* is "made understood" in the Veda. *3.* The verse is taken to elucidate one of the constituent parts of M. II,6, viz. the authoritativeness of *smṛti* as one of the sources of *dharma* (due to its relation to *vedavids*). It is plain to the Western philologist that by this interpretation, i.e. by obliterating the contrast be-

tween both these verses, Medhātithi is but pursuing the aim, characteristic of commentators, of bringing out in relief the assumed internal consistency of the *mūla* text.
4. Medhātithi is the only commentator who gives a detailed explanation of the expression *sarvajñānamaya*,i.e. who by implicitly or explicitly referring to the relevant *sūtras* of Pāṇini's accounts for the functions of the secondary affix *maya(ṭ)*. He offers two alternative explanations, that is, he takes into consideration only two functions of this affix out of the four distinguished by Pāṇini. Indeed, Pāṇ. 5.2.47 cannot be applied here as its scope is limited to numerals only. But what about Pāṇ. 5.4.21 (together with 22)? By the indigenous Indian grammarians, this *sūtra* is not taken to assign to *maya(ṭ)* the meaning "made up of" or "consisting in" (as some Western interpreters would have it);[24] instead they assign to it the meaning "prepared in plentiful supply" or "at which there is plentiful supply of something".[25]

[24] E.g. O. Böhtlingk, *Pāṇini's Grammatik*,Leipzig, 1887, and L. Renou *La Grammaire de Pāṇini*, Paris, 1966, the last one, however, pointing out that this sūtra is interpreted differently by "les commentaires".

[25] Cf. e.g. the *Kāśikā* and *Siddhāntakaumudī* on Pāṇ. 5.4.21, as well as the *Bṛhacchabdenduśekhara* on the latter (ed. by Dr. Śrīsītārāma Śāstrī, *Sarasvatībhavanagranthamālā* 87), Varanasi, 1960, p. 1537. where Nāgojībhaṭṭa remarks:
yady api prakṛtam eva prastutam, tathāpi 'yādṛśasya prakṛtasya loke mayaṭā vacanaṃ [=] pratyāyanaṃ tatra' ityarthakavacanagrahaṇasāmarthyalabhyaṃ vyākhyānalabhyaṃ ca vivakṣitam artham āha prācuryeṇ - *eti ... :*
I think the indigenous interpretation has to be preferred, not only because of the Pāṇinīyas' better feeling for words, but also because Pāṇ. 5.4.21 as understood by Böthlingk and Renou would be a mere repetition of Pāṇ. 4.3.143 (together with 4.3.134).

Since Medhātithi seems to have considerable knowledge of the Aṣṭādhyāyī and probably also of some of its commentaries as also of later grammatical works, it is hardly possible to assume that he simply overlooked this latter *sūtra* of Pāṇini's; he must have consciously ruled out this possibility, and the reason, or at least an important reason,[26] cannot but be the prior member of the compound, i.e. *sarva-*, by which, at least in the given context, total completeness is expressed in such a way that the additional idea of plenitude would simply be nonsensical. Therefore, when one keeps to the obviously more precise and accurate description Pāṇini has given of the function of *maya(ṭ)*, or when one follows Medhātithi's interpretation in this respect (and I do think one should follow it), *sarvajñānamaya*[27] can only mean "product-of-change of all knowledge" or "proceeded from all knowledge as its cause". It is to be admitted that both these meanings ultimately amount to "containing all knowledge [within itself and hence being the source of all knowledge]"; none of them, however, is compatible with a personal subject (at least a personal subject other than God). Thus we gain a further argument in favour of the interpretation of M. II,7 as stating that it is the Veda that is *sarvajñānamaya*.

3.2. Kullūka, on the other hand, gives the following explanation:[28] *vedād anyeṣāṃ vedamūlatvena prāmāṇye 'bhihite 'pi manusmṛteḥ sarvotkarṣajñāpanāya viśeṣeṇa vedamūlatām*

[26] Another reason might be that in the given context it is already *a priori* more probable that by the word ending in *-maya* a specific, viz. 'causal' relation is expressed as obtaining between *sarvajñāna* and the subject predicated by it.

[27] Its use in the Rāmāyaṇa (see above, p.83) may be either due to an unconscious fusion of the two concepts, or may be taken as another piece of evidence for what we often find elsewhere also in later Sanskrit, viz. 'semantic expansion'.

[28] I quote from the edition mentioned in fn.2o.

āha yaḥ kaścid *iti* / yaḥ kaścit kasyacid *brāhmaṇāder* manunā dharma *uktaḥ* sa sarvo vede *pratipāditaḥ* / *yasmāt sarvajño 'sau manuḥ* / *sarvajñatayā cotsannaviprakīrṇapaṭhyamānavedārthaṃ samyag jñātvā lokahitāyopanibaddhavān* / *govindarājas tu* sarvajñānamaya *ity asya sarvajñānārabdha iva veda iti vedaviśeṣaṇatām āha* //

"Although [in/on the preceding verse] it has been said that [the sources of *dharma*] other than the Veda are authoritatively valid because of having the Veda as [their] root, he (i.e. Manu) states in this verse that [his] Manusmṛti is based to a higher degree on the Veda in order to impart [what otherwise couldn't easily be realized, viz. that his Manusmṛti] surpasses all [the other Smṛti works]. 'Whatever *dharma* [as valid] for certain' [people, i.e.] the Brahmins, etc., has been taught 'by Manu, all that' has been expounded 'in the Veda', for he [i.e.] Manu, is omniscient; and by being omniscient he has come to know correctly the content [not only] of the Veda which is [still] recited [nowadays, but also] of that [Veda] of which [the oral tradition] has ceased or which is scattered far and wide, and then he has expounded it [in his work] for the benefit of men. Govindarāja, however, has taken *sarvajñānamaya* to qualify *veda*, [that is to say, he has taken the final clause] to mean '[for]the Veda is, as it were, produced from all knowledge'."

In contradistinction to Medhātithi, Kullūka works out the peculiar relation in which this verse stands to the preceding one: for he observes, most acutely, that M. II,7 is meant to point out that Manu's work is superior to all other Smṛtis and this is something we cannot but accept. Yet at the same time it has to be noted that this his opinion is not connected with the interpretation he himself offers for the predicate *sarvajñānamaya*. This is indicated by the fact that he does not hesitate to quote Govindarāja's divergent view which he seems to regard as at least likewise possible; obviously, Kullūka did not fear that the view of the older commentator could ultimately affect what he himself had said about the central purport of M. II,7, although Govindarāja's interpretation of this verse differs considerably from his own.[28a]

Further, Kullūka in his paraphrase simply replaces the crucial expression *sarvajñānamaya* by *sarvajña* without the least attempt at accounting for this semantic equation. Yet, it has to be admitted that he obviously has reflected to some extent on the reason underlying the view that Manu is omniscient. The explanation he gives is, however, not at all convincing: even if a particular element of *dharma* taught by Manu could be said to be based on an (injunctive) passage in a Vedic text no longer extant (*utsanna*), the question would still arise why one should not assume that this text was still recited when Manu composed this his Smṛti. If, however, by *utsanna*° are meant Vedic texts that were no longer handed down even in the times of Manu himself, one would have to draw attention to the fact that commentators of other Smṛti texts do not scruple to infer the former existence of relevant Vedic texts without assigning omniscience to the assumed authors of these Smṛti texts. And why should it be only Manu who has to be omniscient in order to be able to understand the *artha* of the Veda, still recited in his times (*paṭhyamāna*)?[29]

Therefore, one cannot help arriving at the conclusion that what Kullūka suggests is not the true motive for Manu's omniscience, i.e. that the origin of this idea must

28a After having stated that M. II,7 is meant to show that the other sources of *dharma*, enumerated in the preceding verse, are in their turn based on the Veda, Govindarāja explains the *pādas* a - c accordingly and finally says :
yasmāt sarva-[read sarvā-] *dṛṣṭārthajñānahetutvāt* sarvajñānamayaḥ *sarvajñānārabhha iva vedaḥ* / ...

29 In this respect Hemādri's argument (see above, fn.18) that in that case all the *smṛtikāras* would have to be taken to be omniscient sounds plausible.

lie elsewhere. It is even possible to venture the opinion that the real motive must either be of such a kind that it could not be utilized in interpreting M. II,7 or was simply no longer known to Kullūka.

4. While studying some of the numerous textcritical and exegetical problems the Vaiśeṣikasūtra poses, I recently chanced upon a passage in one of the commentaries that might render substantial assistance in discovering the true motive. What I am referring to is the explanation found in the anonymous Vyākhyā [30] on VS 2.1.19 *pratyakṣapūrvakatvāt saṃjñākarmaṇaḥ*. This *sūtra* forms one sentence together with the preceding one (2.1.18: *saṃjñākarma tv asmadviśiṣṭānāṃ liṅgam*), i.e. a single argument, meant to refute the objection of a (fictitious) opponent who calls in question the possibility of proving, by means of inference, the existence of the 'substance' wind. That the interpretation offered by the author of the Vyākhyā can ultimately be shown to be historically wrong [31] does not matter in the present context. What he says is:[32] *asyeyaṃ saṃjñeśvarasyābhipreteti jñānaṃ saṃjnākarma / tac ca nāsmadādīnāṃ yogajadharmanirapekṣendriyavedyatvāsambhavāt / nāpi liṅgajanyam / sṛṣṭyādau manvādibhiḥ parameśvarābhiprāyavyāptaliṅgānavagamāt / tasmān mahādevaprasādāsāditayogajadharmasadhrīcīnamanasā vāyvādayo vāyvādipadair boddhavyā itīśvarābhimatam iti manvādibhir niścīyata iti manvādīnāṃ sarvajñatvasiddhiḥ / ata evāsmadviśiṣṭānām iti bahuvacanam //*

[30] Ed. by Anantalal Thakur, *Mithilāvidyāpīṭhagranthamālā, Prācīnācāryagranthāvalī*, No. 5, Darbhanga, 1957.

[31] I hope to show this in a monograph entitled "Textkritische und exegetische Untersuchungen zum Vaiśeṣikasūtra I. Der sechste Adhyāya" which I am presently working on.

[32] P. 22. 1-5 of the edition referred to in fn. 30.

"*saṃjñākarma* [is a *bahuvrīhi* compound, i.e. is equivalent to *saṃjñā karma* [=] *viṣayo 'sya*,[33] that is to say, what is meant by it is] the knowledge that it is the intention of God that this (i.e. x) be the conventional designation of that (i.e. the object y); and it is not people like us (i.e. common human beings) who [can] have this [knowledge], since it cannot be obtained by the senses without the help of a [particular] *dharma* born of Yoga. Nor can it [have] be[en] obtained with the help of a characteristic mark (i.e. by inference); for, at the beginning of creation Manu and the others could not perceive [any] characteristic mark pervaded by the intention of Parameśvara (i.e. a logical reason from which God's intention could have been inferred by them). Therefore, [the fact] that it is the wish of God that [really existing objects] like wind, etc., are to be understood by the words 'wind', etc., [has been] truly cognized by Manu and the others, [namely] by [their] internal organ favoured by a [particular] *dharma* born of a Yoga that had been achieved by the grace of Mahādeva. Hence it is correctly established that Manu and the others [were] omniscient. [And] for this very reason the plural 'of people superior to us' [is used in sūtra 2.1.18]." [33a]

The objection raised by the opponent is thus refuted by resorting to a peculiar theory of the origination of language. The argument adduced here is tantamount to the statement that the 'substance' wind, although itself not perceivable, does exist because the name 'wind' has been created by God. This language-creating activity of God, however, is confined to the realm of volition. That is to

[33] According to the author's explanation of this term given on VS 2.1.18 (p. 21.6).

[33a] This specific justification of the plural of *asmadviśiṣṭānām* in *VS* 2.1.18 is directed against an interpretation according to which it is an honorific plural referring to Īśvara. Cf. the monograph mentioned in fn. 31.

say, according to this theory, God does not himself teach language to the first men (i.e. by indicating the objects and uttering their designations); rather, his intention has to be cognized, and this cannot be accomplished by 'mere mortals', for God's intention can neither be perceived nor inferred; only persons who are endowed with a peculiar, higher faculty of cognition can have insight into it, and it is they who, in their turn, teach all others how to speak.

These persons - the primeval *vṛddhas* whose *vyavahāra* others observe in order to learn how to speak - are identified as "Manu and the others". It is hardly conceivable that it is Manu, the *smṛtikāra*, who is primarily, if at all, referred to here. In the given context, in connection with the idea of a series of creations, dissolutions (and recreations) of the universe, it should rather be the 'mythological' Manu, or Manus, whom the author has in mind. Indeed, it is more than likely that the author of the Vyākhyā depends here on Vaiśeṣika ideas about creation belonging to an earlier period [34] and traceable back to Praśastapāda, who, for all that is known, seems to have been the first representative of this system to introduce not only the Īśvara doctrine, but also to conceive of the latter's rôle as first of all connected with the creation and dissolution of the universe.[35]

In the process of creation, Maheśvara, according to Praśastapāda,[36] creates "by a mere act of will (*abhidhyānamātrāt*), out of the atoms of fire and earth, a big egg in which he creates...god Brahmā. It is this Brahmā who is

[34] According to A.Thakur, the author of the Vyākhyā himself "seems to belong to about the twelfth or thirteenth century".

[35] Cf. G.Chemparathy's article "The Īśvara Doctrine of Praśastapāda", in: *VIJ* VI (1968), pp. 65-87.

[36] Cf. *Praśastapādabhāṣya* (*Padārthadharmasaṃgraha*) with Commentary of Śrīdharabhaṭṭa, Varanasī, 1963, p. 129 ff.

then entrusted with the creation of the living beings",[37] i.e. who, in his turn, creates "the Prajāpatis, the *mānasān manudevarṣipitṛgaṇān* and finally the four *varṇas* and all the other living beings".[38] The compound *manudevarṣipitṛgaṇān* is explained by Śrīdhara as follows:[39] *manūn, devān, ṛṣīn, pitṛgaṇān*, and the attribute *mānasān* is taken by him to mean *manaḥsaṃkalpaprabhavān*, "whose origin lies in an act of will [of god Brahmā]." Of immediate relevance to the present argument, however, is what Śrīdhara says in a passage following immediately upon his explanation of the wording of the *mūla*. This passage runs as follows:[40]

> *kalpādāv utpannānāṃ prāṇināṃ sarvaśabdārtheṣv avyutpannānāṃ saṃketasyāśakyakaraṇatvāc chābdavyavahārānupapattir iti codanāyāṃ pratyavasthānabījam idam* mānasān *iti / yonijaśarīro hi mahatā garbhāvāsādiduḥkhaprabandhena viluptasaṃskāro janmāntarānubhūtasya sarvasya na smarati / ṛṣayaḥ prajāpatayo manavas tu* mānasā *ayonijaśarīra-viśiṣṭādṛṣṭasambandhino dṛṣṭasaṃskārāḥ kalpāntarānubhūtaṃ sarvam eva śabdārthavyavahāraṃ suptapratibuddhavat pratisandadhate pratisandadhānāś ca parasparaṃ bahavo vyavaharanti / teṣāṃ vyavahārāt tatkālavartināṃ prāṇināṃ vyutpattiḥ, tadvyavahārāc cānyeṣām ity upapadyate vyavahāraparamparayā śabdārtha-vyutpattir ity arthaḥ /*

"Since the living beings that have come into existence at the beginning of a *kalpa* are completely ignorant of

[37] Quoted from Chemparathy's article (see fn.35), p. 8.

[38] The original runs as follows (p. 13o.2-131.3):
sa ca maheśvareṇa viniyukto brahmātiśayajñānavairāgyaiśvaryasampannaḥ prāṇināṃ karmavipākaṃ viditvā karmānurūpajñānabhogāyuṣaḥ sutān prajāpatīn mānasān manudevarṣipitṛgaṇān mukhabāhūrupādataś caturo varṇān anyāni coccāvacāni bhūtāni ca sṛṣṭvāśayānurūpair dharmajñāna-vairāgyaiśvaryaiḥ saṃyojayati... /.

[39] P. 131.13 f. of the edition used (cf. fn. 36).

[40] P. 133.3-1o.

all that pertains to word and meaning [and, hence, of all words themselves] they are not able to create linguistic convention. Therefore, [under such conditions] communication-by-language cannot be adequately accounted for. The [expression] *mānasān* [in the passage of the Padārthadharmasaṃgraha under discussion] forms the germ of the counter-argument directed against this objection (i.e. contains this counterargument in its essence). For,[41] the man, who possesses a body from the womb, does not remember anything of former births, for the impressions (*saṃskāras*) have disappeared owing to the miseries undergone during the stay in the womb, etc.; Ṛṣis, Prajāpatis and Manus, however, possessing unseen (qualities of the soul) which are distinguished by bodies, not born from the womb, clearly perceive the *saṃskāras*, and remember the complete use of word and meaning, just like a man who awakens from sleep; then they, many as they are, having this remembrance, make use [of the words and meanings] when among each other; through their use [of language] the creatures who are contemporaneous with them, get proficient in it; and from their use [of language] others again; thus the proficience in word and meaning originates by tradition of use...".

It is true that this theory is partially different from that referred to by the author of the Vyākhyā in that the intention of God and its cognition by "Manu and the others"

41 In the following, I quote the translation given by B.Faddegon, *The Vaiśeṣika System*, repr. Wiesbaden, 1969 , p. 376, although it is not faithful to the original in every regard; e.g. *mahatā* is left out; *suptapratibuddhavat* should rather be rendered by "like [a man] who has [first] fallen asleep and [later] awakened [from sleep]"; and *pratisandadhānāś ca parasparaṃ bahavo vyavaharanti* means rather "then they, having this remembrance, converse much with each other" (that there are many sages need not be stated anymore; instead, what has to be stressed is that in conversing they cover the whole range of language; that is to say, *bahavo* corresponds to an adverb in English; cf. J.S.Speijer, *Sanskrit Syntax*, repr. Kyoto, 1968, p. 186 (§ 243)).

is not mentioned here. However, one cannot fail to realize that the theory expounded by Śrīdhara is incomplete insofar as it does not account for the very first creation of language.

Now, a fragment preserved in the Tattvasaṃgrahapañjikā of Kamalaśīla,[42] ascribed to Praśastamati (=Praśastapāda)[43] and analyzed by G.Chemparathy [44] clearly shows that Praśastapāda not only attributed the very first creation of language to God, but used this also as one of the proofs for God's existence. Unfortunately, this fragment does not contain any explicit statement on the exact relations between God's creation of language and the "usage of words fixed for each object (such as) for cow, etc.". All that can be deduced with certainty is that according to Praśastapāda communication-by-language as initiated at the beginning of creation presupposes instruction by God; in which way this instruction is accomplished, i.e. whether directly or indirectly, is not stated. In view of Praśastapāda's ideas about the creation (and dissolution) of the universe the assumption seems to be warranted that it was already he who brought in Manu, or the Manus, and other sages as a sort of "go-betweens".

In any case, there cannot be the least doubt that in Vaiśeṣika circles a doctrine existed according to which Manu, or the Manus, and other sages were the first persons who by virtue of an extraordinary cognitive faculty,

[42] Quoted by Chemparathy in his article (see fn. 35), p. 4.- On the general trustworthiness of Kamalaśīla cf. E.Steinkellner, "Zur Zitierweise Kamalaśīlas", in: *WZKSO* VII (1963), p. 116-5o.

[43] That Praśastamati is identical with Praśastapāda is not, as B.K. Matilal (*Nyāya-Vaiśeṣika* [*A History of Indian Literature* ... VI,2], Wiesbaden, 1977, p. 62) says, "a highly debatable point", but well established by A. Thakur, G. Chemparathy and Muni Jambūvijaya.

[44] Cf. his article (fn. 35), p. 4 ff.

i.e. a kind of *yogipratyakṣa*, peculiar to them learnt language which prior to them existed only in the form of God's intention, and thus started the *paramparā* of communication-by-language. And it is this doctrine that adequately explains the origin of the conception of Manu's and the other sages' omniscience and renders it fully intelligible. For, to know God's intention as regards words implies the knowledge of all the *designata*, too, i.e. of everything that has the character of being (*bhāvarūpa*).

Accordingly, what is meant by attributing omniscience to "Manu and the other [sages]" is that they know "the totality of reality *secundum extensionem*". This, however, is precisely the meaning intended by the word *sarvajña(tva)* as applied to God by some early Vaiśeṣikas;[45] and in this regard, Manu and the other sages, on the one hand, and God, on the other are remarkably similar.[46] What has been rightly observed by Chemparathy [47] in analyzing Praśastapāda's ideas about creation, viz. that "all those qualities" (*dharma, jñāna, vairāgya* and *aiśvarya*) "which are ascribed to the Supreme God... by Pakṣilasvāmin" are ascribed by Praśastapāda to Brahmā, who is charged by Īśvara with the creation of the beings, i.e. that Īśvara and Brahmā have qualities in common, holds good for "Manu, etc.", and Īśvara also. Yet, the similarity obtaining between God and "Manu, etc.", seems not to be confined to their omniscience only; for, when Kullūka states that Manu, the *smṛtikāra*, "has expounded it (i.e. the °*vedārtha*) [in his work] f o r

[45] Cf. G. Chemparathy, "Two little-known Fragments from early Vaiśeṣika Literature on the Omniscience of Īśvara", in: *ALB* 33 1969, p. 117-134. - On the likewise narrower sense of the Buddhist concept of omniscience cf. now G. Bühnemann, *Der allwissende Buddha. Ein Beweis und seine Probleme. Ratnakīrti's Sarvajñasiddhi*, (*Wiener Studien zur Tibetologie und Buddhismuskunde*, Hft. 4), Wien, 198o.

[46] An important difference, however, is that eternity is attributed to God and denied of "Manu, etc."

[47] Cf. his article (fn. 35), p. 8 ff.

the benefit of men (*lokahitāya*)", this cannot but imply that Manu has a peculiar regard for all (human) beings; one is, therefore, reminded of Pakṣilasvāmin's conception of God as *āptakalpa*, i.e. as "one who has gained all his wishes" and who, accordingly, does not act for his own sake, but for that of others only, i.e. "who has regard for all beings like a father for his offspring" (*yathā pitāpatyānāṃ tathā pitṛbhūta īśvaro bhūtānām*);[48] there is every appearance that the conception of Manu corresponds in this respect also to that of Īśvara. According to the author of the Vyākhyā it is by the 'grace' (*prasāda*) of God that "Manu and the others" obtain *yoga*, and this word might well be used here in the sense of *samādhi*. Now, this latter is again one of the qualities attributed to Īśvara by Pakṣilasvāmin[49] so that his similarity to Manu and the other sages becomes still more striking.

Chemparathy[50] has likewise already drawn attention to the fact that Praśastapāda apparently "took up the already existing mythological conceptions of the dissolution and creation of the universe in order to give them a philosophical basis and to systematise them". Yet, "his attempt to reconcile the existing mythological conceptions with philosophical thought" is not only indicated by his making not Īśvara, but Brahmā the direct creator of all beings,[51] but also by his keeping to the mytheme of Prajāpatis, Manus, etc.; for, obviously, in this case also he has in a peculiar

48 Quoted from the *Nyāyabhāṣya* on NS 4.1.21, *Nyāyasūtra of Gautama. A System of Indian Logic*, ed. by G.Jha(No. 58, *POS*), p. 253.1.

49 Cf. *Nyāyabhāṣya* l.c., p. 252.2.

50 Quoted from his article (fn. 35), p. 9.

51 According to *Mbh*. III 185.49 f., however, it is Manu who is entrusted by Prajāpati-Brahmā with the creation of all "offspring" (*prajā*), including Gods, demons and men. The problems connected with these divergent mythological conceptions cannot be discussed here.

manner made use of conceptions attested to in mythological texts, in that he assigns to these beings a special function which seemed important to him for philosophical reasons, viz. that of truly cognizing God's intention as regards language and thus establishing the *paramparā* of human speech. Therefore, it is legitimate to assume that by the expression *manvādi* the author of the Vyākhyā, too, refers, at least among others, to the Purāṇic "fourteen Manus", likewise known to Kumārilabhaṭṭa.[52]

Now, one of these, viz. Manu Svāyambhuva, is traditionally, e.g. according to the first Adhyāya of the Manusmṛti itself, taken to be the author of the famous 'lawbook'. Hence, it is not surprising at all that the quality of being omniscient, originally ascribed to the 'mythological' demiurge Manu, has in the course of time been transferred to the assumed author of the Manusmṛti. And, to be sure, it is this latter development that lead to the introduction of Manu's omniscience into M. II,7.

As was pointed out at the outset, this does indeed distort the original intention of the verse.[53] Yet the foregoing remarks, sketchy though they are, do reveal how ideas which historically are essentially distinct and of

[52] Cf. *Tantravārttika* on MS 1.3.7, p. 2o2 and 122 of the two editions (referred to in fn. 18), respectively.

[53] In this connection it should be added that the historically correct interpretation of M. II,7 is met with also outside the range of Dharmaśāstra literature. E.g.,Prabhācandrācārya (98o-1o65) in his *Nyāyakumudacandra*, a commentary on Akalaṅkadeva's I. *Laghīyastraya* (ed. by Pt. Mahendra Kumar Nyaya Shastri (*MDJG* 38/39), Bombay , 1938/41, p. 88), while summarizing - in a *pūrvapakṣa* section - the Mīmāṃsā view that there are no omniscient beings, distinguishes between two kinds of *upadeśa*, viz. a *vyāmohapūrvako yathā svapnopalabdhārthopadeśaḥ*, and a *samyagjñānapūrvakaḥ*, exemplified by him in the following manner:

yathā manvādīnāṃ sakalārthajñānodayavedamūlo dharmādyaśeṣārthopadeśaḥ / te hi nikhilapadārthajñānotpattihetor vedād āvirbhūta viśuddhabodhā dharmādyaśeṣapadārthasārtham upadiśanti .... /.

distinct origin have influenced each other; and how Indian interpreters have attempted to overcome the contradictions by bringing them to a common denominator, in spite of the fact that they clearly realized certain exegetical difficulties.

53 (cont.)

This passage, which almost looks like a commentary on M. II,7, clearly shows that in the 11th century (and perhaps significantly enough among Jains) Manu (and the other *smṛtikāras*) - inspite of the fact that they are said to deal comprehensively with all the topics of *dharma* - were not (yet) regarded as omniscient, and that in accordance with the original intention of M. II,7 it was the Veda that was considered as "the source of knowledge of all things".

[7]

"LAWYERS" IN CLASSICAL HINDU LAW

LUDO ROCHER
University of Pennsylvania

THE CONTROVERSY

THERE CAN BE NO DOUBT that parties to a lawsuit in ancient Hindu law had a right to be represented by other persons. The question arises whether or not the representatives referred to in the ancient texts correspond to the pleaders, advocates, vakils or attorneys of modern India. In other words, did ancient Hindu law have the kind of legal procedure in which the rights of the parties were safeguarded through the services of a class of experts, as is the case in present day India and in most other modern legal systems?

Looking at Hindu law as it became known to the West in the latter half of the 18th century, it did indeed seem as if the question was to be answered in the affirmative. Halhed's *Code of Gentoo Laws* (1777), translating the *Vivadarnavasetu,* did have a section (ch. III, § II) explicitly called "Of appointing a vakeel (or attorney)." Its contents are as follows:

> If the plaintiff or defendant have any excuse for not attending the court, or for not pleading their own cause, or, on any other account, excuse themselves, they shall, at their own option, appoint a person as their *vakeel;* if the *vakeel* gains the suit, his principal also gains; if the *vakeel* is cast, his principal is cast also.
>
> In a cause where the accusation is for murder, for a robbery, for adultery, for eating prohibited food, for false abuse, for thrusting a finger into the *pudendum* of an unmarried virgin, for false witness, or for destroying any thing, the property of a magistrate, a *vakeel* must not be appointed to plead and answer in such cases; the principals shall plead and answer in person; but a woman, a minor, an ideot [*sic*], and he who cannot distinguish between good and evil for himself, may, even in such causes as these, constitute a *vakeel.*

LAW AND SOCIETY REVIEW

> Except the brother, father and son of the plaintiff and defendant, if any other person, at the time of trial, should abet, and speak for either party, the magistrate shall exact a fine from him: if a brother, a father, a son, or a *vakeel*, should assist, and speak for either party, it is allowed.[1]

As we shall see below, this passage comprises most of the ancient rules connected with representation in court. If the English version gave a faithful rendering of the original Sanskrit, little doubt would remain that the present day vakil had his counterpart in ancient India. The answer to this question must, however, be left open at the moment. The only point we want to stress here is this: from the first translated Sanskrit text onward, scholars were confronted with a picture according to which ancient Hindu law had a system of pleaders similar to the one they were so familiar with in contemporary India.

Such an eminent authority as Julius Jolly went one step further, and drew a conclusion which under the circumstances was perfectly logical: "Instead of appearing in person, each party has a right to be represented at the trial; thus, even today the vakils, i. e., advocates, constitute an unusually numerous professional group in India."[2] In other words, Jolly interpreted the particular attraction on the part of contemporary Indians to the legal profession as the natural outcome of a factor that had its root deep in ancient Indian tradition. In his opinion the legal profession in ancient India was an important one, and one that attracted many recruits. In his classical treatise on *Hindu Law and Custom* Jolly does not refer to lawyers explicitly. But at least one passage of the book,[3] and several statements elsewhere (especially in his translations quoted below) clearly suggest that Jolly firmly believed in the existence of a legal profession in ancient India.

Nothing was more natural than that the ideas of the greatest European specialist on Hindu law were drawn upon by other legal historians who had no direct access to the Sanskrit sources and who used Jolly as their main authority. As a result, Jolly's opinion found its way into other Western publications dealing with Hindu law.[4]

The existence of legal practitioners in ancient India has also been maintained, quite independently of Jolly, by Indian scholars. According

1. N. B. HALHED, A CODE OF GENTOO LAWS 93 (1777).
2. J. JOLLY, BEITRAGE ZUR INDISCHEN RECHTSGESCHICHTE. ZEITSCHRIFT DER DEUTSCHEN MORGENLANDISCHEN GESELLSCHAFT 44, at 346 (1890).
3. J. JOLLY, HINDU LAW AND CUSTOM 299 (B. K. Ghosh transl. 1928).
4. J. KOHLER, ALTINDISCHES PROZESSRECHT 20 (1891).

to K. P. Jayaswal, for instance, professional lawyers existed at least from the time of the *Manusmrti* and perhaps even earlier:

> Manu, VIII. 169, shows that professional lawyers were already in existence in the time of the Manava Code. The verse says that the people who suffer for the sake of others are witnesses, sureties and the judges, but that those who are benefited by legislation, are the king ("who gets court-fees"), the creditor ("who gets his decree"), the merchant ("the speculator who supplies money for defence to the defendant and acquires his property in return"), and the Brahmin. This Brahmin is the Brahmin who advised each party on law . . . The definition of *vidya-dhana*, with its history going back to the Dharmasutras, presupposes the existence of the profession much earlier.[5]

The viewpoint of the Indian dean of *dharmasastra* is completely different. Concerning the legal profession in ancient times, P. V. Kane says:

> An interesting question arises whether lawyers as an institution existed in ancient India. The answer must be that so far as the smrtis are concerned, there is nothing to show that any class of persons whose profession was the same as that of modern counsel, solicitors or legal practitioners and who were regulated by the State existed.[6]

However, Kane too admits that, "This does not preclude the idea that persons well-versed in the law of the smrtis and the procedure of the courts were appointed (*niyukta*) to represent a party and place his case before the court." His reasons for this restriction are mainly three. First, from a story narrated in Asahaya's commentary on the *Naradasmrti* (1, 4) "it appears that persons who had studied the smrtis helped parties in return for a monetary consideration to raise contentions before the court." Next, there are "some important rules" in the *Sukranitisara*. And, to these two arguments directly derived from the texts, is then added a general consideration: "The procedure prescribed by Narada, Brhaspati and Katyayana reaches a very high level of technicalities and skilled help must often have been required in litigation."

An equally cautious opinion has been voiced by U. C. Sarkar:

> There is no sufficient indication that at the time of the Smritis there was any legal profession in the modern sense of the term. Persons versed in the science of law could give their opinion for the consideration of the king and his councillors. The system was perhaps most analogous to the Responsa Prudentium of the early Romans. The opinions of the legal

5. K. P. JAYASWAL, MANU AND YAJNAVALKYA. A COMPARISON AND A CONTRAST. A TREATISE ON THE BASIC HINDU LAW 288-89 (1931).

6. 3 P. V. KANE, HISTORY OF DHARMASASTRA 288 (1946).

experts also were not binding on the king. They had no other part to play except giving their opinion.[7]

Others were even much more outspoken. Thus, in P. Varadachariar's opinion: "It is not possible to say anything as to the existence of a legal profession in Ancient India."[8] The same author makes it a point to reject Jayaswal's above mentioned statement according to which the Brahman referred to in *Manusmrti* 8. 169 is "the Brahmin who advised each party on law":

> Mr. Jayaswal thinks that professional lawyers ought to have existed from the days of Manu or at least from the first century A. D. I find it difficult to interpret the reference to *Vipra* in Manu VIII, 169, as a reference to a "Lawyer Brahmin." The commentaries on this verse lend no support to such a reading.

We have quoted opinion about the legal profession in ancient India at some length, mainly to show the degree of confusion to which the problem has led. Various authors working on an identical set of data have been able to draw from them a number of apparently contradictory conclusions. Nothing could be more characteristic in this respect than two passages from an issue of the *Madras Law Journal*. At the yearly "Vakils' Gathering," held in Madras on April 17, 1909, the Advocate-General had this to say:

> The origin of the English Bar is shrouded in the remotest antiquity. It has been traced as far back as Edward I. Turning to the History of India, whether ancient or medieval, you find no glimpses of the existence of the legal profession. For the sake of curiosity, I looked into some of our sacred books. While you find an abundance of rules about causes of action, pleadings, plaints, written statements, burden of proof, rules of trial and judgment, you find no mention whatever of arguments of Counsel.[9]

However, in a discussion of the Advocate-General's address an anonymous author makes the following statement:

> In this the learned Advocate-General would seem to have fallen into an error, and notwithstanding his statement that he had looked into the Sanskrit-books and arrived at that conclusion, we should think there is express authority in the Sanskrit-books the other way. The following passages from the Sukranitisara would clearly show that the Vakils were

7. U. C. SARKAR, EPOCHS IN HINDU LEGAL HISTORY 37 (1958).
8. S. VARADACHARIAR, THE HINDU JUDICIAL SYSTEM 156 (1946).
9. MADRAS L. J. 201 (1909).

> not unknown in ancient or medieval India as the Advocate-General would seem to think.[10]

And he adds an English translation of a number of verses from the *Sukranitisara,* to which we shall return below.

We shall now examine the original data. It is hoped that the mere presentation of these data will demonstrate how the opinions cited above could come to be held. We apologize to those readers who are not familiar with Sanskrit. In each case we shall have to start from the original Sanskrit text, to show how these texts lend themselves to different interpretations according to the general context in which one is willing to place them. Finally we shall add a few general remarks and draw conclusions which, it is hoped, will help to place the problem in its correct perspective.

THE TEXTUAL DATA

Narada

A first point to be noted is that representation in a law court is not referred to before the *Naradasmrti.* Truly enough, the earlier texts on *dharmasastra* are not very explicit with regard to law in general and legal procedure in particular. This absence of explicit data allows of a twofold interpretation. Either representation did exist from an earlier time, but Narada was the first one to mention the institution explicitly, or representation did not exist before Narada. We prefer not to go beyond presenting the alternatives. Tentatively, in view of the silence of Manu (like Varadachariar, we cannot follow Jayaswal's interpretation of Manu 8. 169) and of Yajnavalkya we lean slightly toward the latter alternative.

In the *Naradasmrti* we are faced with two *slokas* which definitely refer to representation in the court. The first verse (Introduction 2. 22) is as follows:

arthina samniyukto va pratyarthiprahito 'pi va
yo na bhrata na ca pita na putro na niyogakrt

In Jolly's translation this means:

> If one deputed by the claimant, or chosen as his representative by the defendant, speaks for his client in court, the victory or defeat concerns the party [himself and not the representative].[11]

10. *Id.* at 153.

11. J. JOLLY, THE MINOR LAWBOOKS 29 (Sacred Books of the East 33, 1889).

LAW AND SOCIETY REVIEW

This is another piece of evidence of Jolly's belief in the existence of a class of lawyers. The words "for his client" are nowhere present in the Sanskrit text; literally the latter says: "for somebody" or "for him," referring thereby to the claimant and the defendant. On the other hand, it is clear that reference is made in the text to two persons who carry on litigation for two other persons, the decision binding the latter and not the former: (1) one who is *samniyukta* by the plaintiff, and (2) one who is *prahita* by the defendant. Both terms are clear without being precise; they refer to persons "appointed," "proposed" by either party.

The second stanza of Narada (Introduction 2. 23) is this:

yo na bhrata na ca pita naputro na niyogakrt
pararthavadi dandyah syad vyavaharesu vibruvan.

Jolly translates:

> He deserves punishment who speaks in behalf of another, without being either the brother, the father, the son, or the appointed agent; and so does he who contradicts himself at the trial.[12]

As in the preceding verse—*yo yasyarthe vivadate*—here too, reference is made to "somebody stating the affair of another" or "somebody speaking for another" (*pararthavadin*). Moreover, among the eventual *pararthavadins* figure: the father, the son, the brother, and the *niyogakrt*. The latter especially is important for our purpose. Jolly, in the light of his idea referred to above, translates: "the appointed agent." We do not dare to go so far, but we do notice that *niyogakrt* ("he who performs *niyoga*") derives from the same verbal root preceded by the same preverb which we already met with in the preceding *sloka:* there it was *samniyukta,* here it is *niyogakrt.* The only, but important, conclusion to be drawn from this is that, according to Narada, a party could give to another person a *niyoga* ("appointment") to speak for him in the court.

Unfortunately, nothing allows us to draw any more specific conclusions. Both verses apparently go together and deal with the same topic, but they have no contextual relation either with the preceding or with the following *slokas.* We would venture to say, with S. Varadachariar, about the first verse: "Such a declaration would be uncalled for if the passages were to refer to a professional class whose profession itself was to represent others."[13]

---

12. *Id.*

13. VARADACHARIAR, *supra* note 8, at 157.

"LAWYERS" IN CLASSICAL HINDU LAW

Before proceeding we must raise an objection to Jolly's translation of the second *sloka*, especially to his final words: "and so does he who contradicts himself at the trial." There is nothing in the Sanskrit text to warrant the inclusion of the conjunction "and"; on the contrary, the grammatical subject of *vyavaharesu vibruvan* is the same as that of *pararthavadi*. However, it is not easy to propose a more correct translation than Jolly's; the point is that *vibruvan* can have two different meanings which give equally different meanings to the verse as a whole. And since no argument can be drawn from the context, the only valid treatment of the passage is to mention both interpretations. Both have found their adherents among the later commentators, but it is not, and never will be, possible to know with certainty, which interpretation was the original one. In the first place, it is possible that the preverb *vi* radically changes the meaning of *bruvan* ("speaking"), so that *vibruvan* means: "speaking wrongly, speaking untruthfully, lying." We ourselves have been tempted by this interpretation, and, when the verse occurred in the *Vyavaharacintamani* (78), we translated: "He who makes false statements in legal procedures while pleading the cause of another person, should be punished, except when he is [the party's] brother, father, son, or express deputy." [14]

We still hold that this is a valid interpretation. However, after having examined the materials which serve as a basis for the present paper, we would prefer terms that are less precise than "pleading the cause" and "express deputy." In any case the verse then indicates that there are two classes of "persons speaking for somebody else," those explicitly enumerated and all others; the former may make false statements in the court without being punished, the others may not. In the second place, it is also possible that the preverb *vi* does not change the meaning of *bruvan; vibruvan* then simply means "speaking." In that case the verse prescribes punishment for anybody who speaks in lieu of a party to a lawsuit, except for the brother, father, son, and *niyogakrt*.

Brhaspati

The *Brhaspatismrti* (1. 142) in its turn contains at least one *sloka* connected with representation:

apragalbhajadonmattavrddhastribalaroginam
purvottaram vaded bandhur niyukto 'nyo 'nyatha narah.[15]

---

14. L. ROCHER, VACASPATIMISRA'S VYAVAHARACINTAMANI 168 (1956).

15. K. V. RANGASWAMI AIYANGAR, BRHASPATISMRTI (Reconstructed) 23 (Gaekwad's Oriental Series 85, 1941).

Jolly translates:

> For one timorous, or idiotic, or mad, or overaged, and for women, boys, and sick persons, a kinsman or appointed agent should proffer the plaint or answer [as his representative].[16]

Again Jolly uses the term "appointed agent," this time to render the Sanskrit term *niyukta.* We on our side merely notice the use of *niyukta,* a variant form for Narada's *samniyukta* and *niyogakrt.*

Brhaspati's stanza raises, however, a number of questions which are important if one wants to understand what he meant by *niyukta.* First, Jolly's translation omits one word from the Sanskrit text: *'nyo* ("other"). Since we no longer have access to the original context, we cannot a priori reject either of the following interpretations: (1) a kinsman, or another man who is *niyukta, i. e.,* either a kinsman or somebody who is not a kinsman but a *niyukta;* (2) a kinsman or another *niyukta, i.e.,* anybody who had been *niyukta* by the party. In the former alternative *niyukta* might eventually refer to a specific class of representatives; in the latter alternative it could mean no more than "designated" generally.

A second problem raised by Brhaspati's text is connected with a variant reading found in the *Vyavaharacintamani* (no. 74 of our edition) and in the *Viramitrodaya* on *Yajnavalkyasmrti* 2. 6. Here the second line reads: *purvottaram vadet tadvad aniyukto 'thava narah.* That means: "In the same way even a person who has not been deputed may speak first or last for . . ." In this case too, *aniyukta*—and, for that matter, *niyukta*—comes closer to the general "designated" than to the technical meaning of an "appointed agent."

Katyayana

Of all *dharmasastras,* the *Katyayanasmrti* seems to have been most prolific in connection with representation. P. V. Kane[17] collected no less than seven *slokas* on the subject; in his translation[18] he arranged them under the title "Substitutes or recognised agents of parties."

The first two distichs (Katyayana 89-90) are as follows:

samarpito 'rthina yo 'nyah paro dharmadhikarini
prativadi sa vijneyah pratipannas ca yah svayam.
adhikaro 'bhiyuktasya netarasyasty asamgateh
itaro 'py abhiyuktena pratirodhikrto matah.

16. JOLLY, *supra* note 11, at 288.
17. P. V. KANE, KATYAYANASMRTI ON VYAVAHARA (law and procedure) 14-15 (1933).
18. *Id.* at 133-34.

Kane translates:

> A person though other [than the defendant,] if put forward by the defendant before the judge [as defendant] should be regarded as the defendant and he also who is accepted [by the plaintiff] himself [as the defendant]. It is the right of the person charged [to give a reply] and not of another person, since the latter is unconnected [with the dispute]; [but] even a stranger may be allowed [to have the right to defend] if he is put forward [as the defendant] by the person charged [by the plaintiff].

These verses, the original of which is lost, present a number of variant readings in the later commentaries in which they have been quoted. Several Sanskrit words are problematic and might be given different translations from those proposed by Kane. A detailed discussion of all these problems is not relevant here. We must, however, remark that the words "a stranger" used by Kane are definitely too precise and too strong; the Sanskrit words *itaro 'pi* say nothing more than "even another person" without any further specification.

Katyayana 91 does not present any new problem: it corresponds word for word with Narada (Introduction 2. 22). In view of Varadachariar's remarks quoted above, we can hardly agree with Kane's statement that "this verse contains the germs of the modern profession of pleaders." [19]

Katyayana 92 reads as follows:

dasah karmakarah sisya niyukta bandhavas tatha
vadino na ca dandyah syuh yas tv ato 'nyah sa dandabhak,

i.e., in Kane's translation:

> Slaves, menials, pupils, persons deputed, and relatives, these should not be punished when they speak [on behalf of another, their master, etc.]; any one other than these [if meddling in litigation] deserves punishment.

Here we have a clear enumeration of those who may represent a party: (1) *dasah,* (2) *karmakarah,* (3) *sisyah,* (4) *niyuktah,* and (5) *bandhavah.* Thus, a *niyukta* is a specific kind of representative (*vadin* or *prativadin*), along with slaves, menials, pupils, and relatives; all others are excluded.

Katyayana 93-95 deal with the same subject:

19. *Id.* at 133.

brahmahatyasurapanasteyagurvanganagame
anyesu catipapesu prativadi na diyate;
manusyamarane steye paradarabhimarsane
abhaksyabhaksane caiva kanyaharanadusane
parusye kutakarane nrpadrohe tathaiva ca
prativadi na datavyah karta tu vivadet svayam.

Kane's translation is as follows:

> A representative [of plaintiff or defendant] is not allowed in [charges of] brahmana murder, drinking wine, theft, sexual intercourse with the wife of an elder [incest] and in other grave sins. A representative should not be given in man slaughter, theft, indecent assault on another's wife, eating forbidden food, kidnapping of a maiden and intercourse with her, harshness . . . , counterfeiting coins and measures, and also in sedition; but the man himself [the plaintiff or defendant] should engage in the dispute.

The interesting point here is that all representatives (*prativadin*), *i.e.*, including the *niyukta*, are excluded in a number of specific lawsuits. The nature of these lawsuits may have its importance for our conclusions; we shall return to it below.

Vyasa

One of Vyasa's *slokas* comes very close to the one by Brhaspati quoted above:

kulastribalakonmattajadartanam ca bandhavah
purvapaksottare bruyur niyukto bhrtakas tatha.

Although this stanza does not seem to have been particularly popular with the commentators (it occurs only in few medieval compilations), it provides us with a new element: the payment of the representative. Unfortunately, again two interpretations are possible. The representatives "who may speak up for women of good family, children, madmen, idiots, and disturbed persons, concerning the plaint and the defense," are either *bandhava* ("a relative"), *niyukta* whom we have met with above, and *bhrtaka* ("a person receiving a remuneration"), or *bandhava* ("a relative"), and *niyukto bhrtaka* ("an appointed person who receives a remuneration"). In the latter case the relative, who is unpaid, is opposed to the *niyukta* who earns a salary. In our view the more faithful interpretation is: a relative, a *niyukta*, and a *bhrtaka*. In that case we do not learn anything new about the *niyukta*, and about the term *bhrtaka* we can merely say that it is connected with *bhrti* ("salary").

Pitamaha

Finally, we must mention two verses by Pitamaha:

pita mata suhrd vapi bandhuh sambandhino 'pi va
yadi kuryur upasthanam vadam tatra pravartayet;
yah kascit karayet kimcid niyogad yena kenacit
tat tenaiva krtam jneyam anivartyam hi tat smrtam,

which were thus interpreted by Scriba:

> The king should conduct a lawsuit when the father, the mother, a friend, a relative, or a servant appear [as representatives].
>
> Whenever somebody appoints another person to act in his behalf, it is as if the act was done by himself, and it cannot be annulled.[20]

The first *sloka* is unambiguous: the king should allow a party to be represented by his father, mother, friend, or relative. But the second stanza, following after the first, again allows various interpretations. Either it means that any one *of those referred to before,* when acting through *niyoga,* acts in the other person's name. Or it indicates that anybody speaking for anybody else through *niyoga* is his real representative. In that case, *niyoga* does not refer to an "appointment" given to a specific class of representatives, but it suggests that anybody can be anybody's *niyukta.*

Commentaries and Nibandhas

Pitamaha's verses conclude our survey of the available materials on representation as far as the ancient *dharmasastras* are concerned. To these we might now add the medieval materials drawn from the commentaries and *nibandhas.* However, after a careful examination of the Sanskrit texts, we decided not to include these materials, since they do not add any really new data to those already discussed. None of the commentaries or *nibandhas* quotes *all* relevant passages from the older treatises. Even those that cite most of them try to adapt them into a coherent system, a task that was not easy and that led to highly varied results. Inasmuch as we have tried to provide all possible interpretations for the *dharmasastra* passages we are confident that we have included all interpretations proposed by the commentators. The latter would be important for our purpose only if they showed a definite development

20. K. SCRIBA, DIE FRAGMENTE DES PITAMAHA. TEXT UND UEBERSETZUNG (1902).

in one direction or another, *e.g.*, in the direction of gradual recognition of real lawyers. This is not the case; here as elsewhere the commentators did not aim at introducing any novelties. Their sole purpose was a correct interpretation of the ancient texts as such.

Arthasastra

Instead of quoting from the commentaries and *nibandhas*, we shall briefly refer to two *arthasastra* passages. Kautilya has no reference at all to representation in the court. The only text which is partly relevant is this (3. 20. 22):

> *devabrahmanatapasvistribalavrddhavyadhitanam anathanam anabhisaratam dharmasthah karyani kuryuh,*

i.e., in R. P. Kangle's translation:

> The judges themselves shall look into the affairs of gods, Brahmins, ascetics, women, minors, old persons, sick persons, who are helpless, when these do not approach [the court].[21]

This faithful rendering makes it clear that Sternbach went too far when, in connection with this text, he spoke of the judges as "official legal advisors."[22]

The situation is completely different in the *Sukranitisara*. Here we are provided with a long passage dealing with representation in the court. In G. Oppert's edition (Madras 1882) the text runs as follows:

> *vyavaharanabhijnena hy anyakaryakulena ca*
> *pratyarthinarthina tajjnah karyah pratinidhis tada.* (4. 5. 108)
> *apragalbhajadonmattavrddhastribalaroginam*
> *purvottaram vaded bandhur niyukto vathava narah.* (109)
> *pita mata suhrd bandhur bhrata sambandhino 'pi va*
> *yadi kuryur upasthanam vadam tatra pravartayet;* (110)
> *yah kascit karayet kimcin niyogad yena kenacit*
> *tat tenaiva krtam jneyam anivaryam hi tat smrtam.* (111)
> *niyogitasyapi bhrtim vivadat sodasamsikim*
> *vimsatyamsam tadardham va tadardham ca tadardhikam;* (112)
> *yatha dravyadhikam karyam hina hina bhrtis tatha*
> *yadi bahuniyogi syad anyatha tasya posanam;* (113)

21. R. P. KANGLE, THE KAUTILIYA ARTHASASTRA, PART II 293 (1963).
22. L. STERNBACH, JURIDICAL STUDIES IN ANCIENT HINDU LAW, PART I 324-25 (1965).

dharmajno vyavaharajno niyoktavyo 'nyatha na hi
anyatha bhrtigrhnantam dandayec ca niyoginam. (114)
karyo nityo niyogi na nrpena svamanisaya
lobhena tv anyatha kurvan niyogi dandam arhati. (115)
yo na bhrata na ca pita na putro na niyogakrt
pararthavadi dandyas syad vyavaharesu vibruvan. (116)
manusyamarane steye paradarabhimarsane
abhaksyabhaksane caiva kanyaharanadusane; (119)
parusye kutakarane nrpadrohe ca sahase
pratinidhir na datavyah karta tu vivadet svayam. (120)

B. K. Sarkar's translation of verse 108 reads:

> Representatives have to be appointed by the plaintiff and defendant who do not know the legal procedure or who are busy with other affairs.[23]

One important word in the text remains untranslated: the representative should be *tajjna* ("knowing it"). It is tempting to have *taj°* ("it") refer to *vyavahara* ("legal procedure") in the first line, and to say that whenever a party is not an expert on legal procedure he should be represented by a person who is an expert on such matters. If this is the case, the verse comes very close to describing a class of professional lawyers. Sarkar himself must have had this in mind when he added the following note to his translation: "Pleaders and lawyers are to represent such persons and state their cases as their own." However, we cannot accept that *taj°* refers to *vyavahara*. From verse 118, in which a son is to be accepted as a representative of his father on the condition that he is *tajjna* ("knowing it"), it is clear that *tajjna* means "knowing the circumstances of the case." In other words, the representative, to be acceptable, must have known the party whom he represents intimately enough to be fully aware of the circumstances in which the contested activities took place. This element will be an important one in our conclusions below.

Verses 109, 110 and 111 bring nothing new; apart from a few insignificant variant readings they are identical with the passages from Brhaspati and Pitamaha quoted above.

Much more important are the following four verses (112-115). This is Sarkar's translation:

23. B. K. SARKAR, THE SUKRANITI (Sacred Books of the Hindus 13, 1914).

> The lawyer's fee is one-sixteenth of the interests involved (*i.e.*, the value defended or realised).
>
> Or the fee is one-twentieth or one-fortieth, or one-eightieth or one hundred and sixtieth portion, etc.
>
> Fees ought to be small in proportion as the amount of value or interest under trial increases.
>
> If there be many men who are appointed as pleaders in combination they are to be paid according to some other way.
>
> Only the man who knows the law and knows the Dharma should be appointed [as pleader].
>
> The king should punish the pleader who receives fees otherwise.
>
> The pleader is to be appointed not at the will of the king.
>
> If the pleader acts otherwise through greed he deserves punishment.

The only problem in these verses is the expression "who receives fees otherwise" in 114. Sarkar duly states the two possibilities in a note to this translation: "He may be punished if he takes exorbitantly or if he practices without knowing the law, etc." After what has been said in the former half of the stanza, we would be inclined toward the second alternative, with Kane: "if the representative takes wages without knowing these."[24] However, the first alternative should not be excluded either: if 112cd-114ab are a more recent insertion into the text (we shall return to this in our conclusions), the latter part of 114 originally belonged together with the former part of 112. In that case "otherwise" means: "otherwise than one sixtieth part."

Verse 116 is identical with Narada's Introduction 2. 23, and verses 119 and 120 correspond to Katyayana 94-95.

Besides the points which we had become familiar with from the *dharmasastras*, we do find in the *Sukranitisara* a number of new and interesting elements: (1) representatives are appointed by parties who are *vyavaharanabhijna* ("who do not know the rules of legal procedure"); (2) the payment of the *niyojita* or *niyogin* is dealt with in great detail; (3) the *niyogin* is to be appointed by the party, not by the king. It hardly needs to be recalled that these elements played an important part in some of the opinions of modern scholars, quoted in our introductory remarks.

---

24. KANE, *supra* note 6, at 158-59.

Interpretation

As indicated at the outset, the principal reason for raising the question of the existence of lawyers in ancient India was the awareness of the existence of such a professional class in modern Indian law, and in Western law as well. Consciously or unconsciously, the general background of the investigations on ancient Hindu lawyers—as of many other aspects of research on Hindu law—has been one of defensiveness. Was it possible that such a wonderful legal system as the one depicted by *dharmasastra* did not include the institution of legal practitioners?

An excellent example of this tendency to look for "the germs of the modern profession of pleaders" is P. V. Kane who, notwithstanding his admirably sound approach, when translating Katyayana 91, could not withhold from adding the note cited above. Even Judge S. Varadachariar, who completely denies the existence of a legal profession in ancient India, unwittingly takes up the defense of Hindu law. He cites examples of various other ancient legal systems that did not know a legal profession either. The underlying idea is that we should not really be surprised if ancient Hindu law had no lawyers, since contemporary systems were not more advanced. Characteristically, the enumeration of the other legal systems ends with the following statement: "In England there was no definite legal profession till more than a century after the Norman conquest." [25]

Our approach to the problem is completely different. We maintain that such an apologetic attitude is not at all necessary. In our opinion, the ancient Hindu legal system was such that a legal profession not only did not exist, but that it was not called for and hardly could have existed. The reasons that led us to assume that a legal profession did not exist in ancient India are at least three in number.

First, the only term which might eventually have referred to professional lawyers was *niyogin*, *niyukta*, or *niyogakrt*. We are not much concerned about the fact that there is no uniformity of nomenclature. There are other examples of well established institutions in ancient Hindu law which did not enjoy a uniform terminology. But we are concerned about the fact that not a single text on *dharma* pays any special attention to the *niyukta* as such. If he had been an important and constant element of the law court, we may be assured that some *dharmasastra* would have elaborated on the qualifications to become a *niyukta*—*e.g.*, under the heading *niyuktaguna*—and on the disquali-

25. VARADACHARIAR, *supra* note 8, at 158-59.

fications which would have prevented a person from entering the profession. All participants in a lawsuit have been duly enumerated and described in the texts; the authors of the *dharmasastras* would have fallen short of their duty if they had not paid attention to one of these participants, the "lawyer."

Secondly, if the main purpose of *niyoga* had been a more effective presentation of the party's interests than he could normally provide himself, we do not see why *niyoga* was so fiercely opposed in what we may call major criminal cases.[26] Katyayana's three *slokas* (93-95) which deal with this aspect of the problem seem to indicate that, when it came to really serious cases, *niyoga* was prohibited. From this we must infer that *niyoga* was allowed only as long as the case was a less serious one. Whenever a party was unable or unwilling to appear in person, he was allowed to be represented by another person in minor cases; but he had to appear personally in major issues. Such a criterion is hardly compatible with the role of a professional legal adviser as we conceive it today.

This second argument leads us to a third, namely, the existence of a class of professional representatives was not called for in Hindu law. This argument is undoubtedly the most important and most basic one. Administration of justice in ancient India was the concern of the king; it was part of *rajadharma*. Several rules in the *dharmasastras* lay down that the king is responsible for punishing those who deserve to be punished. But it is added that the king is also responsible for the innocent not to be punished. Thus, *e.g.*, Manu 8. 126-128, in G. Buhler's translation:

> Let the [king], having fully ascertained the motive, the time and place [of the offence], and having considered the ability [of the criminal to suffer] and the [nature of the] crime, cause punishment to fall on those who deserve it.
>
> Unjust punishment destroys reputation among men, and fame [after death], and causes even in the next world the loss of heaven; let him, therefore, beware of [inflicting] it.
>
> A king who punishes those who do not deserve it, brings great infamy on himself and [after death] sinks into hell.[27]

---

26. L. Rocher, *Ancient Hindu Criminal Law*, 24 J. ORIENTAL RESEARCH MADRAS 15-34 (1955).

27. G. BUEHLER, THE LAWS OF MANU 276 (Sacred Books of the East 25, 1886).

That means that the only person in the court who is responsible for the party's interests being safeguarded is the king, or, in practice, the king's representative: the chief judge. The fact that the parties might not be *vyavaharajna* ("acquainted with legal procedure") and hence unable to defend themselves properly, was no reason why they should be assisted by professional lawyers. The person responsible for the correct course of the case and for safeguarding the parties' interests was the king himself or whoever presided over the court in his name. It is in the light of these considerations that we must also understand the passage from Kautilya quoted above: parties who are unable to appear in person need not, therefore, be represented; the king himself is responsible for their interests.

So, as we see it, professional lawyers did not exist and could hardly have existed. To this we now want to add a restriction. As it so often happens in ancient Hindu law and in Hindu civilization generally, in the case of legal representation too, a certain degree of development must have taken place in the course of the centuries. We are not among those who believe that the more recent *dharmasastras* were composed with the intention to innovate and depart from what had been said by the older ones. On the contrary, we are convinced that the more recent authors tried their very best to maintain the general scheme laid out by their predecessors. But in the meanwhile the actual situation did change, and every now and then authors of more recent *dharmasastras* could not prevent themselves from reflecting some of these changes.

Thus, we believe that at an early date—let us roughly say at the time of the *dharmasutras*—professional lawyers or, to be more precise, specialized *dharmasastrins* could not exist. The Indian sage in those days was a specialist in all of the texts related to a particular Vedic school. His specialized knowledge concentrated on a specific version of the Vedic *samhita* and all its related texts: *brahmana, aranyaka, upanisad, srautasutra, grhyasutra, dharmasutra,* etc. There were no specialists on *dharmasastra*, and, a fortiori, no specialists on law that were part of it.

But the situation changed. The texts on *dharma* grew away from the Vedic schools. Gradually there may have come into being a specialized group of learned men whose main interest was *dharma*, and the various *dharmasastras* as such.

Finally, as the amount of textual material increased, we may assume that certain experts, without detaching themselves completely from other aspects of *dharmasastra* and from Hindu learning generally, accumulated a very specialized knowledge of one aspect of *dharma: vivada* and *vyavahara*, or, in modern terminology, law. It is very possible that at this stage the nature of legal representation (*niyoga*) also underwent a certain change. We do not want to exclude the possibility that, at that moment, in a number of cases legal competence played a role in the choice of a representative. We are even willing to accept that Vyasa refers to the very special circumstance in which the representative was paid for his services. However, no written source allows us to draw the conclusion that the experts on legal matters ever developed into a professional group whose regular activities consisted in representing parties in the court. The impression which we gather from the texts is that, even in cases where the representative was chosen because of his special competence on legal matters, and, a fortiori, in all other cases, the necessary condition for a person to represent a party was the existence, between the former and the latter, of a certain form of close personal relationship.

In this connection we want again to refer to the categories of *niyukta* enumerated by Narada (Introduction 2. 23): brother, father, son, and by Katyayana (92): slaves, menials, pupils, etc. Some of these terms were vague enough to be interpreted very broadly, and we can very well see how a party who wanted to be represented in the court may have tried to fit into these categories a person who knew the *dharma* rather than one who did not. But the main requisite was the personal relationship stressed by the *dharmasastras*, not the representative's legal competence.

Moreover, our point of view offers an adequate explanation for the passage from Asahaya quoted by Kane and referred to above.[28] Here again, it is true that the representative, Smartadurdhara, is said to be an expert on *dharma*, but nothing points to him as a professional lawyer. On the contrary, he is a friend of the family, and, as such, serves as their adviser. He does represent the party in court, but only after having assured the judge that he is entitled to do so because "he and his ancestors were friends of the family." In other words, he does not act as a professional expert (*vyavaharajna*) but as a personal friend (*suhrd*); the fact that the *suhrd* is *vyavaharajna* is purely coincidental.

Finally, our interpretation is also confirmed by the above quoted passage from the *Sukranitisara*, about which we want to add a few words

28. P. N. K. SAHAY, A SHORT HISTORY OF THE INDIAN BAR 4-6 (1931).

here. There is no doubt that, of all sources examined in this paper, the *Sukranitisara* is the one which most strongly reminds us of the modern legal profession. While commenting on it, Kane went as far as to say:

> The rules of Sukra made a near approach to the modern institution of the Bar and the fees prescribed by Sukra are similar to those allowed by the Bombay Regulation II of 1827 and by Schedule III to the Bombay Pleaders' Act (Bombay Act XVII of 1920).[29]

The main support for this statement is the detailed description of the representative's remuneration (verses 112-114). However, it has been so far overlooked that at least part of these verses (112cd-114ab), although reproduced in Oppert's edition, actually occurred in one manuscript only; they were missing in all four other manuscripts and in the printed version used by Oppert. We would not hesitate to consider them as a very recent addition to the original text. As a matter of fact, the entire *Sukranitisara*, as we have it today, is of recent origin.[30] It seems to us that it is a recent compilation, based upon a number of ancient rules—some of the verses are simply identical with those quoted from the *dharmasastras*—but into which were inserted certain very modern ideas, even ideas belonging to the colonial period. We would not be surprised if the rules about the representative's remuneration belonged to this latter category.

Under the circumstances it is all the more noteworthy, as Varadachariar puts it, "that it provides for the appointment of a 'representative' not only on the ground of the party's ignorance of Vyavahara but also on the ground of his being otherwise busy."[31] Thus, even such a very recent text as the *Sukranitisara*, which seems to have known a real professional class of lawyers and does not hesitate to incorporate it into the classical system of *dharmasastra*, does not exclude the idea that the legal representative and the person represented by him should be linked by a personal tie of blood relationship, friendship, etc. This, more than anything else, shows that this traditional element was a very important one, probably the most important of all in legal representation according to classical Hindu law.

---

29. KANE, *supra* note 6, at 290.

30. M. WINTERNITZ, GESCHICHTE DER INDISCHEN LITTERATUR. BAND III 531 (1920).

31. VARADACHARIAR, *supra* note 8, at 157.

CHRONOLOGICAL SURVEY OF SANSKRIT TEXTS[32]

Dharmasutras 600-300 B. C.

Dharmasastras
- Manu 200 B. C.-100 A. D.
- Yajnavalkya 100-300 A. D.
- Narada 100-400 A. D.
- Brhaspati 300-500 A. D.
- Katyayana 400-600 A. D.
- Vyasa 600-900 A. D.
- Pitamaha 600-900 A. D.

Commentaries and *nibandhas*
- Asahaya on Narada 700-750 A. D.
- *Vyavaharacintamani* 1500-1550 A. D.
- *Viramitrodaya* on Yajnavalkya 1615-1645 A. D.
- *Vivadarnavasetu* 1773 A. D.

Arthasastra
- Kautilya 300 B. C.-100 A. D.
- *Sukranitisara* ? [1800 A. D. ?]

32. KANE, *supra* note 6, at XVII-XX.

[8]

STUDIES IN THE VERSES RELATING TO *NIRṆAYA* IN THE *VYĀSASMṚTI*

Heramba Chatterjee Sastri

Of the several *Dharmaśāstras* that have not yet seen the light of the day in their complete form the *Vyāsa-dharmaśāstra* is one. Vyāsa's name is mentioned in the list of writers on *Dharmaśāstra* as presented in the *Yājñavalkya-saṃhitā*.[1] The name of Vyāsa is also included in the list of the writers of *Upasmṛti*.[2] In the absence of the text of Vyāsa in its complete form it is not possible to verify the authenticity of the claim of Vyāsa both as writer of *Smṛti* and *Upasmṛti*. There are other problems associated with Vyāsa. Vyāsa is the celebrated author of the *Mahābhārata*, which also contains in several places directives which partake of the same characteristics as those of the *Dharmaśāstras*. Mm.P.V. Kane has pointed out some such cases where Viśvarūpa, commentator of the *Yājñavalkya-saṃhitā* mentions some verses as of Vyāsa which actually are taken from the *Mahābhārata*. Same is the case with Medhātithi on the *Manu-saṃhitā* and Maskarin on the *Gautamadharmasūtra*. Both of them ascribe verses to Vyāsa which are traced in the *Mahābhārata*.[3] Vyāsa

[1] *Y.S.* 1.4-5. For a discussion on the number of *Dharmaśāstras* *(Smṛtis)* see introduction of my *Dāyabhāga*, Howrah, 1978 , at p. VII, f.n. 1o and 11.

[2] See *Smṛticandrikā*, p. 2; *Sarasvatīvilāsa*, p. 13 for mention of the *Upasmṛtis*. It may be added here that there is hardly any basis for making distinction between the *Smṛtis* and the *Upasmṛtis*. Some of the names are interchangeable.

[3] See *History of Dharmaśāstra*, I,1 (revised ed., 1968), p. 53o.

shares with Bṛhaspati an interesting directive recommending even condemned means of livelihood for the sake of maintenance of old parents, a wife dedicated to pious disposition and a minor son.[4] We have a *Vedavyāsasmṛti* with four chapters (on *Brahmacarya, Stryadhikāra, Gṛhasthāhnika, Gṛhasthāśramapraśaṃsā*) included in the *Smṛtīnām samuccayaḥ* in the A.S.S. (No. 48) published from Punyapattana in 1905 edited out of five manuscripts (pp. 357-371). Pañcānana Tarkaratna published from Calcutta a compilation text under the title *Ūnaviṃśasaṃhitā* (Vaṅgābdha, 1310). The *Vyāsasaṃhitā* is included there in pp. 377-392. In the compilation text edited by Pt. Jīvānanda Vidyāsāgara,[5] the text of Vyāsa is recorded in Part II, pp. 321-342. The texts are more or less the same with variations of minor nature. Unfortunately the portions of the text of Vyāsa containing discussions on *Vyavahāra* have not yet been unearthed and that makes a strong case for a reconstruction of the text of the *Vyavahāra* portion of the *Vyāsasmṛti*.[6]

[4] *vṛddhau ca mātāpitarau sādhvī bhāryā sutaḥ śiśuḥ /*
apy akāryaśataṃ kṛtvā bhartavyā manur abravīt // *Bṛ.S.apaddharma-I;* Vyāsa, quoted in *Kṛtyakalpataru, Gṛhasthakāṇḍa*, p. 229.

[5] *Dharmaśāstrasaṃgraha*. Ed. Jivananda Vidyasagara, Calcutta, 1876.
The Dharmaśāstra, text. vol. I. Ed. Manmatha Nātha Dutta, Calcutta. 1918; *Vyāsasaṃhitā*, pp. 467-488. Text: *Vyāsasaṃhitā*, with English translation, by M. Dutta, Calcutta, 1917.

[6] For earlier attempts on reconstruction of different *Smṛti* texts, the following may be noted:
J. Jolly, collection of Hārīta's *Vyavahāra* materials in the *Bayerische Akademie der Wissenschaften*, p. 18;
Manzini translated the fragments of Pitāmaha in the *Atti del Reale Istituto Venete di Scienze, Lettere ed Arti* 63, pt. 2.
A.A. Führer collected 84 verses of Bṛhaspati with German translation and notes (Leipzig, 1879).
P.V. Kane collected the views ascribed to Śaṃkhalikhita in the *Annals of the Bhandarkar Oriental Research Institute*, Poona, VII-VIII (1926-27); he also collected the text of Kātyāyana as *Kātyāyanasmṛtisāroddhara*, Bombay, 1933.

Dr. B.K. Ghosh published 116 verses of Vyāsa on *Vyavahāra* in *Studia Indo-Iranica, Ehrengabe für Wilhelm Geiger*, München 1931. Another lot of verses on *Vyavahāra* was published by him in the *Zeitschrift für Indologie und Iranistik*, Band 9, Heft 1, Leipzig, 1932. The two taken together were published under the title *Vyāsasmṛti* (*Vyavahāra* chapter) under the editorship of the same editor in the Law Series 1 of Bhāratī Mahāvidyālaya Publications, Calcutta, 1944.[7]

K.P. Jayaswal rightly points out that the verses of Vyāsa on *Vyavahāra* have their importance.[8] Kalpataru quotes about 8o verses of Vyāsa on *Vyavahāra* and significantly a good number of *Vyavahāra* verses of Vyāsa appear in the *Aparārka* commentary on the *Yājñavalkyasmṛti* and in the *Smṛticandrikā*.[9]

6 (cont.)
N.C. Bandopadhyaya also collected verses of Kātyāyana under the title: *Kātyāyanamatasaṃgraha*, Calcutta, 1927.
K.V.R. Aiyangar collected 121 additional verses of Kātyāyana in his paper to the *Kane Festschrift*, pp. 7-17 (Poona Oriental Series, No.75, Poona, 1941); he also collected the verses of Bṛhaspati under the title *Bṛhaspatismṛti*, Baroda, 1941.
See also S.C. Banerjee, 'Reconstruction of the Dharmasūtras', in: *Dharmasūtras, a study in their origin and development*, Calcutta, 1962, pp.237-344.

7 Regarding Vyāsa's verses on *ācāra* and *prāyaścitta* the observations of Dr. Ghosh deserve mention: 'I also collected Vyāsa's verses on *ācāra* and *prāyaścitta*, but now no more than twelve years ago I find any reason justifying the publication of those insipid sayings of a person who probably had nothing but his name in common with the author of the work on *vyavahāra* of which the available fragments preserved in quotations are being presented here.' Introductory note of the editor of the *Vyāsasmṛti*.

8 *Manu and Yājñavalkya*, Tagore Law Lecture, 1917, published in 193o, Calcutta, p.3oo.

9 P.V. Kane while commenting on the quotations of Vyāsa in the Aparārka commentary has the following observations: "But as Aparārka makes no distinction between Vyāsa, the jurist, Vyāsa, the reputed compiler of the Mahābhārata and Vyāsa who wrote on the Saṃskāras, Śrāddha and other topics, it appears that the jurist and the writer on other topics of dharma were separated from him by several centuries." *History of Dharmaśāstra*, I,1, 1968, p. 533.

Without going into the question further it is deemed worthwhile to make reference to certain views ascribed to Vyāsa which may be marked as his own view. Thus with reference to *bhukti* (possession) it has been laid down by Vyāsa that if the owner stays with his capacity to resist, he will lose his ownership if a person other than the owner enjoys the owner's land (let us say, in his presence) for a period of twenty years, when the territory is governed by a king (i.e. when there is no lawlessness).[10] Vyāsa speaks of *bhoga* as having five constituents or characteristics.[11] Again against four types of sureties men-

10 *varṣāṇi viṃśatir yasya bhūr bhuktātha parair iha /*
sati rājñi samarthasya tasya seha na siddhyati // (verse 75 in Ghosh's *Vyāsasmṛti*). Quoted in the Aparārka com., p. 632; *Sm.C.*, p.155 (*Vy.Kā*; Bibliotheca Sanskrita No. 45); *Sarasvatīvilāsa*, p.129. Univ. of Mysore edition; *Vīr. Vy.Pr.*, p. 157, Chowkhamba Sanskrit Series). The portion underlined speaks of a new feature not mentioned by other writers. For detailed discussion on possession see Kane, *H.Dh.*, III, p. 317-329; A. Thakur, *Hindu Law of Evidence*, Calcutta, 1933, pp.220-240.

11 *sāgamo dīrghakālaś cā-vicchedo paravojjhitaḥ /*
pratyarthisannidhānaś ca pañcāṅgo bhoga iṣyate // (verse 84)
Quoted in the *Sm.C.*, p.161, where the significance of the expression *pañcāṅga* has been pointed out in the following form: '*pañcāṅga iti vadan ekāṅga-vaikalye'prāmāṇyam eva bhogasya iti darśayati.*' p.162. The verse has been explained by Mitramiśra in his *Vyavahāraprakāśa*, p.154. Here for the portion underlined the reading is: '... *paribhogo'pi pañcadhā*.' This has also been quoted in the *S.V.*, p.130. This is almost the same as a verse ascribed to Pitāmaha:

sāgamā dīrghakālā ca vicchedoparavojjhitā /
pratyarthisannidhānā ca bhuktiḥ pañcavidhā smṛtā //

Quoted in the *S.V.*, p.130; *Sm.C.*, p.160. See also *Aparārka*, p.630. *Vyavahāra nirṇaya*, p.129, refers to a text of Bṛhaspati of identical nature:

sāgamo dīrghakālaś ca nicchidroparavo dhanam /
pratyarthisannidhānaṃ ca paribhogo'pi pañcadhā // Bṛ.S. VII. 64.
See also *Bṛhaspatismṛti*, VII.23-24.

tioned by Bṛhaspati[12] and five types recognised by Kātyāyana,[13] Vyāsa makes mention of seven varieties.[14] In tune with the provisions made by Kātyāyana that there is equal ownership in respect of the property of the grandfather between the father and the son,[15] and in conformity with what has been stated in categorial terms by Yājñavalkya,[16] as also by Bṛhaspati,[17] Vyāsa expresses his view that in respect of the houses and the landed properties inherited from the ancestor, the father and the sons have equal shares, but the sons cannot claim a share in the property acquired by the father himself in case father does not consent to such a partition.[18]

These are some of the cases to point out that the text of Vyāsa offers enough scope for further verification and

12 *darśane pratyaye dāne ṛṇidravyārpaṇe tathā /*
catusprakāraḥ pratibhūḥ śāstre dṛṣṭo manīṣibhiḥ // Bṛ.S. X. 73.

13 *dānopasthānavādeṣu viśvāsaśapathāya ca /*
lagnakaṃ kārayed evaṃ yathāyogaṃ viparyaye // Kāt., 53o. For a discussion on the number of sureties see Chatterjee, *The Law of Debt in Ancient India*, Calcutta, 1971, pp. 144-151.

14 *lekhye'kṛte ca divye vā dānapratyayadarśane /*
gṛhītabandhopasthāne ṛṇidravyārpaṇe tathā // Quoted in *Vy.Pr.*, 248.
The verse has been explained in the *Smṛticandrikā*, p.347.

15 *paitāmahaṃ samānaṃ syāt pituḥ putrasya cobhayoḥ / Kāt.* 839

16 *bhūr yā pitāmahopāttā nibandho dravyam eva vā /*
tatra syāt sadṛśaṃ svāmyaṃ pituḥ putrasya cobhayoḥ // II. 121

17 *dravye pitāmahopātte sthāvare jaṅgame'pi vā /*
samam aṃśitvam ākhyātaṃ pituḥ putrasya caiva hi // XXVI. 14

18 *kramāgate gṛhakṣetre pitā putrāḥ samāṃśinaḥ /*
paitṛke na vibhāgārhāḥ sutāḥ pitur anicchayā (anicchataḥ) // 248
Nīlakaṇṭha ascribes this verse to Bṛhaspati. (See *Vyavahāramayūkha*, p.59).
First line of Vyāsa's verse quoted in the *Sm.C.*, p.649; in the *Sarasvatīvilāsa*, p.375.
See *Vyavahāracintāmaṇi*, p. 148, for an attempt to explain the eight types.

There are other problems relating to the text of Vyāsa arising out of the mention of *Gadyavyāsa* in the *Smṛticandrikā* (*Āhnika*, p. 224), *Laghu-Vyāsa*, *Bṛhad-Vyāsa*, *Mahā-Vyāsa*, *Dāna-Vyāsa*, *Vṛddha-Vyāsa* and the like (for which reference may be made to Kane, *History of Dharmaśāstra*, I,1, 534). In this short paper it is not possible to discuss those problems and it is proposed to discuss the verses of Vyāsa in respect of *nirṇaya*, which in the *Vyāsasmṛti* edited by Dr. B. K. Ghosh have been introduced as: *vyavahāranirṇaya*.

pramāṇahetucaritaiḥ śapathena nṛpājñayā /
vādisampratipattyā vā nirṇayo'ṣṭavidhaḥ smṛtaḥ // 1

English translation: Decision is regarded as of eight types (i.e. may be arrived at through any of the eight means), such as - three recognized modes of proof (document - *likhita*; possession - *bhukti* and witness - *sākṣi*); circumstantial evidence (*hetu*); established usage or convention (*carita*); oath or ordeal; royal order and declaration of the truth of the claim.[18a]

Notes: Nārada by way of enumeration of the judicial proceedings speaks of *nirṇaya* as the fourth stage, the first being *āgama* (connection or the hearing of the complain - *āgamo'rthivacanaśravaṇam* as explained in the *Sarasvatīvilāsa*, p.75), *vyavahārapada* (ascertainment as to the title of law in which it is to be included) coming next in order, followed by cure and redress of the grievances (*cikitsā* - explained as *pratijñottarapramāṇānāṃ vicāraḥ* in *S.V.*, p. 75) and finally resting with *nirṇaya* (decision - *pramāṇato jayāvadhāraṇam*).[19]

Yājñavalkya speaks of *vyavahāra* as having four feet or constituents (*catuṣpād vyavahāro'yaṃ vivādeṣūpadarśitaḥ*. II.8), the fourth of which has been pointed out by Vijñāneśvara by making reference to a *Smṛti* text, as·*sādhyasiddhi*:

[19] *āgamaḥ prathamaṃ kāryo vyavahārapadaṃ tataḥ /*
cikitsā nirṇayaś caiva darśanaṃ syāc caturvidham // N.S. 1.36.
N.M.S. reads *vivitsā* (1.3o) and Bhavasvāmī explains:
vivitsā niveśitākṣarapративacanavicāraṇā.

bhāṣottarakriyāsādhyasiddhibhiḥ kramavṛttibhiḥ /
ākṣiptacaturaṃśas tu catuṣpād abhidhīyate //

Mitramiśra categorically states that the last constituent, namely, *sādhyasiddhi*, is synonymous with what is otherwise called *nirṇaya*.[20] The *Sarasvatīvilāsa* in clear terms speaks of the fourth *pāda* as *nirṇaya*.[21]

The verse of Vyāsa mentions eight types of *nirṇaya* and in this context it is relevant to state that Bṛhaspati while speaking about *nirṇaya* as of four types refers to the view that according to some it is of eight varieties.[22]

There is nothing wrong if by *kaiś cit* the view of Vyāsa has been referred to. In the *Śukranītisāra*, IV.5.271 *nirṇaya* has been stated to be of six types and by way of justification it may be suggested that Śukra regarded *pramāṇa* in general as one.[23]

It is Bṛhaspati who in clear terms states that decision in doubtful cases is to be arrived at by any one of the four means, namely, *dharma* (moral law), *vyavahāra* (technical judi-

20 *atha nirṇayāparaparyāyaḥ siddhipadaḥ*. *Vyavahāraprakāśa*, p.86.

21 *bhāṣāpādas tu tatrādyo dvitīyo marśanaṃ tathā /*
kriyāpādas tathā cānyaḥ caturtho nirṇayas smṛtaḥ //
Text without authority quoted in the *Sarasvatīvilāsa*, p.62. A verse of identical nature has been ascribed to Bṛhaspati:
pūrvapakṣaḥ smṛtaḥ pādo dvitīyas tūttaras tathā /
kriyāpādas tathā vācyaś caturtho nirṇayas tathā // Bṛ.S. 1.17.

22 The verse of Bṛhaspati has been mentioned by *Aparārka*, p. 611; *Kṛtyakalpataru*, *Vyavahārakāṇḍa*, p. 16 and others:
caturvidhaḥ pūrvapakṣaḥ pratipakṣas tathaiva ca /
caturdhā nirṇayaḥ proktaḥ kaiś cid aṣṭavidhaḥ smṛtaḥ // Bṛ.S. II.36.

23 The importance of *Śukranīti* has of course of late been belittled for which reference may be made to L. Gopal, 'The Śukranīti, A nineteenth-century text', in: *Bulletin of the School of Oriental and African Studies*, XXV, pt.3, 1962, pp. 524-56.

cial formalities), *caritra* (local custom or convention), *nṛpājñā* (a royal edict).[24] Reference has already been made to the description of *vyavahāra* as having four feet or constituents by Yājñavalkya (II.8). Nārada declares that *vyavahāra* is *catuṣpāda*.[25] Kātyāyana also indicates the four feet of *vyavahāra* by making reference to the four stages of processes in a law-suit. They are in the form of the plaint (*pūrvapakṣa*), the reply (*uttara*), the deliberation as to the burden of proof (*pratyākalita*) and the adducing of proof (*kriyāpāda*).[26] Bṛhaspati himself has a verse of identical nature.[27] *pratyākalita* refers to 'the deliberation of the judge and the assessors as to where the *onus probandi* lies and as to the method of proof.' (*pratyākalitam uttarāṅgīkārānantaram api vivadamānayoḥ kasya atra kriyopanyasanam nyāyyam iti prāḍvivākādīnāṃ vimarśanam. Smṛticandrikā, Vy. Kā.* p.27).[28] Nārada has also the four feet

[24] *dharmeṇa vyavahāreṇa cāritreṇa nṛpājñayā /*
catusprakāro'bhihitaḥ sandigdhe'rthe vinirṇayaḥ // *Bṛ.S.* IX.1.

[25] *sa catuṣpāc catuḥsthānaś catuḥsādhana eva ca /*
caturhitaś caturvyāpī catuskārī ca kīrtyate // 1.8.

[26] *pūrvapakṣaś cottaraṃ ca pratyākalitam eva ca /*
kriyāpādaś ca tenāyaṃ catuṣpāt samudāhṛtaḥ // *Kāt.* 31.

[27] *bhāṣāpādottarapādau kriyāpādas tathaiva ca /*
*pratyākalitapādaś** *ca vyavahāraś catuṣpadaḥ* // *Bṛ.S.* II.1.
* This however should not be confused with *pratyākalita* mentioned by Nārada as a supplementary statement:
vādibhyāṃ likhitāc cheṣaṃ yat punar vādinā smṛtam /
tat pratyākalitaṃ nāma svapāde tasya likhyate // *N.S.* II.21

[28] Devaṇabhaṭṭa in his *Smṛticandrikā* refers to another interpretation of the word *pratyākalita*: '*kecid upanyaste pramāṇe pramāṇābhāvaśaṅkāpanodakaṃ jayaparājayanirṇayaphalakaṃ vimarśanaṃ pratyākalitam āhuḥ. tanmate pādasaṃkhyaiva hi vivakṣitā na tu kramaḥ... yat tu Yājñavalkyenoktaṃ - tatsiddhau... anyathā iti tatrāpi siddhiśabdena siddhiphalakaṃ pratyākalitam ucyate.* P. 28
See here the observations of Vijñāneśvara on *Yāj.* II.8:

of *vyavahāra* as *dharma, vyavahāra, caritra* and *rājaśāsana*.[29]

The question that may pertinently be raised is: what is the actual position of four types of *pāda* - *dharma, vyavahāra, caritra* and *rājaśāsana* as stated by Nārada; and the four (*vi*)-*nirṇayas* of the same name as mentioned by Bṛhaspati? Is there any sort of relationship between the four feet and the four *nirṇayas*? The reply to the question is to be sought in the fact that from the explanation offered by Vijñāneśvara on the verse of Yājñavalkya (II.8) already referred to, it is clear that the *pādas* (*bhāṣā; uttara; kriyā* and *sādhyasiddhi*) refer to the gradual procedural steps for arriving at a decision.

nirṇayas are decisions and the eight types of *nirṇayas* are nothing but the eight varieties of methods or proof that are taken to for arriving at the right decision. It would therefore be wise to interpret the verse of Nārada (1.1o) as making reference to the four feet of *vyavahāra* in a secondary sense (*gauṇa*).[3o] Bṛhaspati therefore is more methodical in making out a

28 (cont.)

uttarābhidhānānantaraṃ sabhyānām arthipratyarthinoḥ kasya kriyā syād iti parāmarśalakṣanasya pratyākalitasya yogīsvareṇa vyavahārapādatvenānabhidhānāt vyavahartṛsambandhābhāvac ca na vyavahārapadatvam iti sthitam.

29 *dharmaś ca vyavahāraś ca caritraṃ rājasāśanam /*
catuṣpād vyavahāro'yam uttaraḥ pūrvabādhakaḥ // *N.S.* 1.1o

3o A suggestion to this effect has been made by Kane in his *History of Dharmaśāstra*, III, p.26o.
In this context the following text of Devaṇabhaṭṭa's *Smṛticandrikā* deserves special mention:
nanu pratijñottarapramāṇanirṇayānāṃ vyavahārapadatvaṃ na dharmādīnām iti kim idam uktam ? ucyate, nirṇayapādo dharmādyanusāreṇa caturvidhaḥ. tatra yadanusāreṇa yo nirṇayaḥ saḥ tacchabdena nirdiśyate. tena dharmādibhir eva catuṣpāttvavarṇanaṃ yuktam eva. Vyavahārakāṇḍa, pt.1, p.21.
In his *Vīramitrodaya-vyavahāraprakāśa* (p. 6) Mitramiśra has interesting observations which are relevant in the present context:

clear distinction between the two - the four feet (as recorded in II.1) and the four *nirnayas* (as specifically stated in IX.1).

The four varieties of *nirṇaya* as specifically mentioned by Bṛhaspati have been defined by Nārada (in the form of four feet) and Kātyāyana (as *nirṇaya*) though the latter does not mention the number of *nirṇaya* as four. Bṛhaspati, quite interestingly describes each of these four again in two ways.[31] The eight types of *nirṇaya* as mentioned by Vyāsa in the verse mentioned above include *carita*, and *nṛpājñā* (*rājaśāsana*), which are mentioned and defined by Nārada, Kātyāyana and Bṛhaspati. It is rather surprising that Vyāsa eliminates two very important constituents of *nirnaya*, namely, *dharma*[32] and *vyavahāra*.

30 (cont.)

yadyapi pratijñādīnāṃ vakṣyamāṇānāṃ sākṣād vyavahārasvarūpaghaṭakatvād vyavahārapādatvaṃ yuktaṃ, dharmādīnāṃ tu tatra satye sthito dharma iti nāradoktaprakāreṇaiva nirṇayamātrahetutvān na sākṣād vyavahārapadatvam arham. yājñavalkyādibhir ata eva teṣām eva vyavahārapādatvam uktam... tathāpi nirṇayākhyacaturthavyavahārapādahetutvena gauṇam eva vyavahārapādatvam eṣām atroktam. vyavahārapadena nirṇaya eva vā lakṣyate. taddhetutvaṃ tatpādatvam iti draṣṭavyam.

31 *ekaiko dvividhaḥ proktaḥ kriyābhedān manīṣibhiḥ /*
aparādhānurūpaṃ tu daṇḍaṃ ca parikalpayet // *Bṛ.S.* IX. 2.

32 Nārada speaks of *dharma* as based on truth (*tatra satye sthitho dharmaḥ*, *N.S.* 1.11) Asahāya in his *bhāṣya* by way of elaboration points out that where both the parties adhere to truth in their statements there is no further necessity of judicial procedure, written proof or royal edict. This point has further been explained in clear terms by Bhavasvāmī in his commentary: ..*tathābhūtākhyāne ubhayor api pratipattau sākṣyādibhiḥ prayojanābhāvāt dharmavyavahāraḥ. yathā kaś cit brūyāt mamāsau dhārayati dāpyatām iti; svāmināhūya pṛṣṭaḥ sa cāha: satyaṃ dhārayāmi dadāni ceti samāpto dharmavyavahāraḥ.*

Kātyāyana by keeping in his mind the *vyavahārapada* called *ṛṇādāna* defines the *dharma* variety of *nirṇaya* wherein in a dispute, say, relating to debt, the offender (here the creditor) admits his own fault (in the form of lending of the sum from the party concerned) and the person lending out the money (accordingly) gets back his money:

We may feel tempted to offer the suggestion that the *nirṇaya* of the type of *vādisampratipatti* as we shall have occasion to show, partakes of the nature of the *dharma* variety of *nirṇaya* as defined by Kātyāyana. This gets strenghthened by the interpretation of the verse of Kātyāyana (no. 35),[33] by Mitramiśra where actually the expression *'sampratipatti'* has been used.

Bṛhaspati, as already stated, describes each of these four types of *nirṇaya* as having two characteristics. So far as *dharma* is concerned, Bṛhaspati describes the first variety of *dharma* (*nirṇaya*) as one when the matter in dispute is decided correctly after due deliberation (*yuktyā*) and when it is examined thoroughly through oath or ordeal.[34]

32 (cont.)

doṣakārī tu kartṛtvaṃ dhanasvāmī svakaṃ dhanam /
vivāde prāpnuyād yatra dharmeṇaiva sa nirṇayaḥ // Kāt. 35.
The appositeness of the appellation may be observed here in as much as the offender impelled by moral sense deems it to be his duty to admit his offence and as such the adjudicators have not to trouble themselves much for determining the truth. It may be stated here that this definition by Kātyāyana is in conformity with the definition of *dharma* variety of *nirṇaya* of the second type:
prativādī prapadyeta yatra dharmaḥ sa nirṇayaḥ. Bṛ.S. IX. 4.

33 *vākpāruṣyasteyādidoṣakārī vyavahārapravartanam antareṇaivānutāpādinā dharmābhimukho'dharmād bhītaś ca svasya doṣakartṛtvaṃ svayam abhyupaiti. yatra dhanasvāmī dharmābhimukhād adharmabhīroś cādharmaṇāder vyavahāraṃ vinaiva svakīyaṃ dhanam āpnoti, tarobhayatra sampratitapattyuttara iti yāvat. dharmeṇaiva nirṇaya ity arthaḥ. at evoktaṃ tatra satye sthito dharmaḥ.* Vyavahāraprakāśa, p. 7.

34 *samyag vicārya kāryaṃ tu yuktyā samparikalpitam /*
parīkṣitaṃ tu śapathaiḥ sa jñeyo dharmanirṇayaḥ // Bṛ.S. IX. 3.
The interpretation offered by Devaṇabhaṭṭa is simply a synopsis of the verse of Bṛhaspati without going into the details. Thus far it is clear that in this type of decision it is truth which is ascertained through the examination of facts:

The second definition of *dharma* by Bṛhaspati deserves our special attention. According to the second definition of *dharma-nirṇaya* the defendant admits the accusations levelled against him or furnishes clear evidence of his innocence by passing through an ordeal or oath.[35] The difference between the two definitions of *dharma* presented by Bṛhaspati lies in the fact

34 (cont.)

saha tattvānusaraṇena kṛtaḥ prathamo dharmākhyaḥ nirṇayaḥ.
Smṛticandrikā, *Vy.Kā.* p.22.

It is interesting that Bṛhaspati here insists on the ascertainment of facts and it may be stated that this is strictly of general nature common to all types of *nirṇaya*. More interesting is the fact that Bṛhaspati in his delineation of this variety of decision has introduced two more elements, namely, *yukti* and *śapatha* (oath or ordeal). As we shall have occasion to see, *hetu* may be equated with *yukti*. *śapatha* rightly may be included under the *pramāṇa* on the basis of the statement of Yājñavalkya:

pramāṇaṃ likhitaṃ bhuktiḥ sākṣiṇaś ceti kīrtitam /
eṣām anyatamābhāve divyānyatamam ucyate // II. 22.

Bṛhaspati more clearly differentiates between them, the first three falling under *mānuṣa pramāṇa* and the last under *daiva:*

sākṣiṇo likhitaṃ bhuktir mānuṣaṃ trividhaṃ smṛtam /
ghaṭādyā dharmajāntā tu daivī navavidhā kriyā // Bṛ.S. IV. 7.

35 *prativādī prapadyeta yatra dharmaḥ sa nirṇayaḥ /*
divyair vā śodhitaḥ samyag dvitīyaḥ sa udāhṛtaḥ // Bṛ.S. IX. 4.

The reading of the verse in Aiyangar's edition has not been accepted here and the text quoted in the *Smṛticandrikā* (p. 22) is adopted.

In both the definitions there is provision for the administering of oath or ordeal, which however does not suit well the context. Even if somehow its appropriateness in the first variety may be justified, it does not at all fit in well with the first line of the second definition of *dharma*, which by any means may be taken as self-sufficient to represent the true characteristics of *dharma-nirṇaya*. *'divyair vā śodhitaḥ'* may pertinently be taken out to stand independently conveying the meaning that correct decision consists in the case where the facts (even admitted) are strengthened by oath or ordeal. (This may be gathered from the reading accepted in Aiyangar's ediiton of the text in the second line: *'divyair viśodhitaḥ samyaṅnirṇayaḥ samudāhṛtaḥ'*.)

that whereas in the first definition stress has been laid on the proper ascertainment of fact by the adjudicators, who are to be led by logic, ratiocination and if necessary by accepting an oath or ordeal in addition; in the second variety the major part is played by the defendant himself by way of admitting the charge, reminding us of the supposed golden age[36] in this land where people were dedicated to dharmic ideals. This is the most desirable *nirṇaya* and therefore is mentioned first in the list by Nārada, Kātyāyana and Bṛhaspati.

Non-mention of *vyavahāra* variety of *nirṇaya* by Vyāsa may be accounted for. Nārada is brief in his short exposition '*vyavahāras tu sākṣiṣu*' (1.11), which means that a judicial proceeding rests on the statements of the witnesses. Bhavasvāmī in his commentary does not enlighten us more on the point when it is stated: *visaṃvāde sākṣibhir nirṇīyate, sa sākṣivyavahāraḥ*. It is Mitramiśra who rightly points out in this context that the word *sākṣiṣu* in the text of Nārada should stand for the *pramāṇas* in general: *sākṣigrahaṇaṃ pramāṇopalakṣaṇam*. (*Vy.Pr.*, p.7)

Decision of the *vyavahāra* variety, according to Kātyāyana, arises in the case where the persons in charge of executing the

35 (cont.)

The interpretation offered by Devaṇa is just a summarisation of the verse of Bṛhaspati: *vinā tattvānusaraṇaṃ satyottareṇa vā divyapramāṇena vā kṛto dvitīyaḥ*. *Smṛticandrikā*, p. 22.

By taking into consideration the definition of *dharma-nirṇaya* by Nārada as also by Kātyāyana (already mentioned) it is wise to accept the common element in the three by accepting 'admission by the defendant' as the principal character of *dharmanirṇaya*. As already indicated, this then stands in adjustment with the statement of Vyāsa in '*vādisampratipattyā*.'

36 See in this context the text of Nārada:
dharmaikatānāḥ puruṣā yadāsan satyavādinaḥ /
tadā na vyavahāro' bhūn na dveṣo nāpi matsaraḥ // 1.1.
See also here the statement of identical design by Bṛhaspati:
dharmapradhānāḥ puruṣāḥ pūrvam āsann ahiṃsakāḥ /
lobhadveṣābhibhūtānāṃ vyavahāraḥ pravartitaḥ // *Bṛ.S.* 1.1.

sacred law (the judges) take use of the modes or methods mentioned in the *Smṛti* texts for arriving at a correct decision.[37]

Bṛhaspati, as already stated, speaks of each variety of *nirṇaya* as having two characteristics. So far as *vyavahāra* is concerned, the first variety of the same (*vyavahāra*) consists in the case where a sentence is founded on an examination of the evidence. The second variety of *vyavahāra* arises when the defendant tells a lie or makes no answer.[38]

[37] *smṛtiśāstraṃ tu yat kiñcit prathitaṃ dharmasādhakaiḥ /*
kāryāṇāṃ nirṇayārthe tu vyavahāraḥ smṛto hi saḥ // Kāt. 36.
Devaṇabhaṭṭa in his *Smṛticandrikā*, p. 22, explains the implication of the verse of Kātyāyana thus: *dharmaśāstranirūpitapratijñottarādyanusāreṇa nir yo vyavahārākhya ity arthaḥ.*
Mitramiśra is much more lucid in his expostion when it is stated: *dharmasādhakaiḥ sabhyaiḥ smṛtiśāstraṃ sākṣyādikriyāpratyāyakam arthipraty rthinoḥ kāryanirṇayārthaṃ prathitaṃ prakhyāpitaṃ yatra catuṣpādvyavahārapravartanena nirṇayakaraṇam iti yāvat.* *Vyavahāraprakāśa*, p. 7.

[38] *pramāṇaniścito yas tu vyavahāraḥ sa ucyate /*
vākcchalānuttaratvena dvitīyaḥ parikīrtitaḥ // Bṛ.S. X. 5.
Devaṇa speaks of *pramāṇa* as having reference to secular modes of proof: *pramāṇam atra mānuṣaṃ vivakṣitam, divyaniścitasya dharmanirṇayakoṭitvāt.* *Smṛticandrika*, p. 23.
There is however no significant difference between the two varieties of *vyavahāra* mentioned by Bṛhaspati. The main point in both the definitions is that here the decision is arrived at through the examination of different modes of proof as recognised in the *Śāstras*. Whereas in the firs case the modes of proof are mentioned in general, in the second definiti there is mention of possible circumstances under which such *pramāṇas* are to be applied. What is intended is that in *vyavahārapramāṇas*, whatever that may be, are to be resorted to by the adjudicators when the defenda instead of a positive reply in the form of admission as in *dharma* adopt a tactics of remaining silent (*anuttara*) or of telling a lie. Practical speaking, these are the possible cases where the utility of *pramāṇa* is be understood.

Vyāsa therefore did not perhaps think is necessary to make separate mention of *vyavahāra* by taking into consideration the fact that it is already included in the category of *pramāṇa* mentioned by him.

The next question that deserves our attention relates to the mention of *hetu* as a separate variety of *nirṇaya*, not mentioned by Nārada, Kātyāyana and Bṛhaspati in the same form. Vyāsa himself explains the meaning of *hetu* by supplying the synonyms in the form of *anumāna* and *tarka*.[39] It is of interest to note that amongst the writers on *Dharmasūtra* it is Gautama who has used the term *tarka*.[40] Kātyāyana almost in tune with the view of Vyāsa applies the word *hetu* and observes that the king should arrive at a decision in all cases of dispute

[39] *anumānaṃ vidur hetuṃ tarkāñ ceti manīṣiṇaḥ*. *V.S.* verse 2. The reading 'tarkaś ceti' as recorded in the *V.S.* (ed. Ghosh) is wrong. His comments in the foot-note are equally insubstantial inasmuch as he has missed the page 117 of the *Sarasvatīvilāsa* (ed. R. Shama Sastry) where the line has been attributed to Kātyāyana. (See verse 242 of the *Kātyāyanasmṛtisāroddhāra*, ed. Kane). Ghosh mentions that in the *Smṛticandrikā (Vyavahārakāṇḍa*, pt. 1, p. 23; ed. L. Srinivasacharya) this verse has been attributed to Vyāsa. Here also the editor wrongly places '*tarka*' in the nominative form. Same is the case with the *Vīramitrodaya-vyavahāraprakāśa* (p.87) where the editor injudiciously uses both *hetu* and *tarka* in the nominative in place of the accusative case.

[40] *nyāyādhigame tarko'bhyupāyaḥ. tenābhyūhya yathāsthānaṃ gamayet.* *Gautamadharmasūtra* XI. 23-24
In this context the text of Bṛhaspati deserves attention in as much as it is stated that the adjudication devoid of rationication from the dharmic point of view is unjustifiable:
kevalaṃ śāstram āśritya na kartavyo vinirṇayaḥ /
yuktihīne vicāre tu dharmahāniḥ prajāyate // *Bṛ.S.* 1.114.
The comments of Devaṇabhaṭṭa are: *atas tarkānugṛhītam eva śāstrārtham āśritya nirṇetavyam iti arthād uktaṃ bhavati*. *Sm.C.*, *Vy.Kā*. p. 55.
A text of an anonymous author has been quoted in the *Smṛticandrikā*:
Yas tarkeṇānusandhatte sa dharmaṃ veda netaraḥ. p.55.

through the application of the *pramāṇas* or through *hetu* (inference) or even through ordeals.[41] In his definition of *hetu* Kātyāyana shares with Vyāsa the same text that *hetu*, *anumāna* and *tarka* are synonymous.[42] Bṛhaspati, while making mention of *anumāna* by name, observes that by arriving at a decision through the application of witnesses, documents and *anumāna* a king earns fame. It is interesting that while mentioning the modes of *nirṇaya* Bṛhaspati observes silence in respect of *hetu* or *anumāna* probably for the reason that *caritra* mentioned as one of the four constituents of *nirṇaya* according to him (IX.1), as we shall have occasion to see, refers to a decision arrived at through *anumāna*. (IX.6).[43]

[41] *pramāṇair hetunā vāpi divyenaiva tu niścayam /*
sarveṣv eva vivādeṣu sadā kuryān narādhipaḥ // Kāt. 241.
It may be observed here that the word *niścaya* in the verse of Kātyāyana can be taken as equivalent to *nirṇaya* in his verse.

[42] Verse 2 of the *Vyāsasmṛti* is exactly the same as the verse 242 of Kātyāyana:
likhitaṃ sākṣiṇo bhuktiḥ pramāṇaṃ trividhaṃ smṛtam /
anumānaṃ vidur hetuṃ tarkaṃ caiva manīṣiṇaḥ //
In another place Kātyāyana refers to *anumāna* in connection with the respective strength of the *pramāṇas:*
anumānād guruḥ sākṣī sākṣibhyo likhitaṃ guru /
avyāhatā tripuruṣī bhuktir ebhyo garīyaṣī // Kāt. 315.

[43] *sākṣilekhyānumānena prakurvan kāryanirṇayam /*
Vitatyeha yaśo rājā bradhnasyāpnoti viṣṭapam // Bṛ. S. IX. 33.

Bṛhaspati in continuation of his discussion on *nirṇaya* speaks of it as a sacred task on the part of the king:
yatraivaṃ vetti nṛpatiḥ nirṇayaṃ tu vratādhvaram /
so'smin loke yaśaḥ prāpya yāti śakrasalokatām // Ibid. IX. 34.
In another verse Bṛhaspati refers to *anumāna* along with witness and document:
aparādhānurūpaś ca daṇḍo'tra parikalpitaḥ /
sākṣilekhyānumānena samyag divyena vājitaḥ // Bṛ.S. IX. 25.

Before discussing in detail the position of *anumāna* at the hands of Bṛhaspati, it is desirable to cast one's glance at Manu on the point. While instructing that the king in his act of adjudication should pay full attention to truth, to the object of dispute itself, to himself, to the witnesses, to the place, time and to the aspect,[44] Manu stresses the importance of inference (*anumāna*) by way of instituting the position of the hunter. What he states is this: 'As a hunter traces the lair of a (wounded) deer by the drops of blood, even so the king shall discover on which side the right lies by inferences (from facts),[45] Manu states in particular that[46] the internal

[44] *satyam artham ca saṃpaśyed ātmānam atha sākṣiṇam /*
deśam rūpaṃ ca kālañ ca vyavahāravidhau sthitaḥ // Manu VIII. 45.

[45] *yathā nayaty asṛkpātair mṛgasya mṛgayuḥ padam /*
nayet tathānumānena dharmasya nṛpatiḥ padam // Manu VIII. 44.

[46] *bāhyair vibhāvayel liṅgair bhāvam antargataṃ nṛṇām /*
svaravarṇeṅgitākārais cakṣuṣā ceṣṭitena ca // Manu VIII. 25.

ākārair iṅgitair gatyā ceṣṭayā bhāṣitena ca /
netravaktravikārais ca gṛhyate'ntargataṃ manaḥ // Manu VIII. 26.
Medhātithi in his interpretation of the first verse (VIII. 25) observes: *anumānenāpi satyānṛtavāditā vyavahārataḥ sākṣiṇāṃ ca niścetavyā iti ślokārthaḥ. ataś ca svarādigrahaṇaṃ pradarśanārtham. tena yan niścitaliṅgaṃ tenaiva paricchindyād ity uktaṃ bhavati, na punaḥ svarādibhir eva, savyabhicāritvāt teṣām.*
Bhārucī, supposed to be the oldest of the commentators of the *Manusmṛti*, has a discussion on the importance of *anumāna* which deserves our attention here. What he says is this:
kecit tv āhuḥ, savyabhicāritvād anumānasya vyavahārasthitiḥ sākṣibhiḥ syāt, avidyamāneṣu tu sākṣiṣu anumānam apy āśrayaṇīyam. tad etad anyāyyam; yady anumānaṃ vyabhicāri dṛṣṭam nanu sākṣivacanāgamo'pi tathā dṛṣṭaḥ. athātra vivekayatnān nirṇayaḥ, evam anumānādiṣu api bhaviṣyati. yadi cānaumnaṃ vyabhicāri katham avidyamāneṣu sākṣiṣu tannirṇayārtham upādeyam ity ācakṣītā. tasmād yuktopadeśam anumānam. tathā ca kṛtvā vyavahārād anyatrāpi laukikaiḥ.
See *Bhāruci's Commentary on the Manusmṛti*, Vol. I: *The text;* Vol. II: *The translation and notes* (Franz Steiner Verlag GmbH, Wiesbaden, 1975) edited creditably by J. Duncan M. Derrett.

disposition of men should be ascertained by means of external signs, by their voices, their colour of countenance, their motions, their aspects, their eyes and their gestures. Yājña-valkya too while speaking about the nature of false witnesses mentions the signs that are to be the ascertaining factor for a false witness. All these cases clearly speak in favour of the utility and importance of *anumāna*.[47] In the section *strī-saṃgrahaṇa* the utility of *liṅga* has been categorically emphasised by Yājñavalkya.[48] Reference in this context should be

[47] *deśād deśāntaraṃ yāti sṛkkiṇī parileḍhi ca /*
lalāṭaṃ svidyate cāsya mukhaṃ vaivarṇyam eti ca // Yāj. II. 13

pariśuṣyatskhaladvākyo viruddhaṃ bahu bhāṣate /
vākcakṣuḥ pūjayati no tathoṣṭhau nirbhujatyapi // Ibid. II. 14

svabhāvād vikṛtiṃ gacchen manovākkāyakarmabhiḥ /
abhiyoge'tha sākṣye ca duṣṭaḥ sa parikīrtitaḥ // Ibid. II. 15
See here the comments of Vijñāneśvara:
etac ca doṣa sambhāvanāmātram ucyate, na doṣaniścayāya svābhāvikanaimittikavikārayor vivekasya durjñeyatvāt.

[48] *pumān saṃgrahaṇe grāhyaḥ keśākeśi parastriyā /*
sadyo vā kāmajaiś cihnaiḥ pratipattau dvayos tathā // Yāj. II. 283.
Vijñāneśvara comments: *keśākeśikrīḍanabhāvenābhinavaiḥ kararūhadaśanādikṛtavraṇaiḥ rāgakṛtaliṅgaiḥ dvayoḥ saṃpratipattyā vā jñātvā saṃgrahaṇe pravṛtto grahītavyaḥ.*
In this context the statement of Vijñāneśvara regarding inclusion of *bhukti* under **anumāna** deserves to be refuted. What he says is this: *Nanu likhitasya sākṣiṇāṃ ca śabdābhivyaktidvāreṇa śabde'ntarbhāvāt yuktam prāmāṇyam, bhuktes tu kathaṃ prāmāṇyaṃ - ucyate, bhuktir api kaiś cid viśeṣaṇair yuktā svatvahetubhūtakrayādikam avyabhicārād anumānayanty anupapadyamānā vā kalpayantīty anumāne'rthāpattau vāntarbhavatīti pramāṇam eva.* (on Yāj. II. 22). Aparārka has the same line of approach (p. 628). This view does not appear quite justifiable on the ground that Bṛhaspati in course of his discussion on the respective strength of the *pramāṇas* makes independent mention of both *anumāna* and *bhukti* in:
anumānād varaḥ sākṣī sākṣibhyo likhitaṃ guru /
avyāhatā tripuruṣī bhuktir ebhyo garīyasī // Bṛ.S. VII. 34.

made to the statement of Āpastamba wherein it has been averred that in case of doubt decision in disputes may be arrived at through *liṅga* or ordeal.[49] Āpastamba does not offer any direct clue as to what he likes to mean by *liṅga*, but Haradatta in his *Ujjvalā* commentary explains it as *anumāna*. It is therefore quite evident that as early as Āpastamba the value of *liṅga* or *anumāna* as independent means of proof has been recognised. This shows further that direct evidence and circumstantial evidence went side by side and were regarded as of equal force.

While we pass on to Kauṭilya's *Arthaśāstra* we come across several references to circumstantial evidence. Thus in the section dealing with *daṇḍapāruṣya* it has been held by Kauṭilya that witnesses are to be regarded as authoritative, but if the witnesses are not available the decisive factors would be injury or the indications of the scuffle. Thus Kauṭilya recognises the importance of witnesses and at the same time lends due consideration to circumstantial evidence.[50] Kauṭilya insists on examin-

48 (cont.)
Reference may also be made of another verse of Bṛhaspati:
anumānaṃ vasaty atra sākṣī cāmaraṇād bhavet /
avyāhataṃ lekhabhogaṃ pramāṇaṃ tu tripauruṣam // Ibid. VII. 35.

49 *sandehe liṅgato daiveneti vicitya.* *Āpastambadharmasūtra,* II. 11.29.6. (ed. J. Bühler, 3rd edition, Bombay Sanskrit Series, Vol. XLIV, 1932)
Ujjvalā commentary:
te ca nirṇayantaḥ sandehasthaleṣu liṅgato'numānena daivena taptamāṣādinā...

50 *pūrvaṃ paścād vābhigatasya sākṣiṇaḥ pramāṇam, asākṣike ghātaḥ kalahopaliṅganaṃ vā.* Arthaśāstra III. 19.21.
Again in the context of deposit (*aupanidhikam*) Kauṭilya has used the term *upaliṅgana* in the following rule: *dravyabhogānām āgamaṃ cāsyānuyuñjīta, tasya cārthasya vyavahāropaliṅganam abhiyoktuś cārthasāmarthyam. Ibid.* III. 12.51. Translation: 'And the judge should question the source of the objects used (by the defendant), and inquire into indications of that object being involved in the transaction, as well as the capacity of the complainant to (own) the object.' We have in the *Arthaśāstra* again reference to *upaliṅgana* in the context of the fee for a harlot: *labheta puṃścalī bhogaṃ saṅgamasyopaliṅganāt.* III. 13.37. Translation: A harlot should get a fee in accordance with the indications of union.

ation of the cases through indications (*hetu*).[51] Thus in the section on *Śaṅkārūpakarmābhigraha* (arrest on suspicion, with the stolen article and by indications of the act) Kauṭilya concludes the topic by stating that the magistrate along with the village and divisional officers, should make a search of thieves outside, and the city-super-intendent (should do it) inside the fort, according to the indications mentioned in the section. Again in the section entitled *kanyāprakarma* (violations of maidens) Kauṭilya while speaking on adultery observes that adultery should be understood as committed when there is mutual caressing of the hair or from indications of bodily enjoyment.[52] The idea almost in the same form appears in the text of Nārada, where amongst others reference to *keśākeśi* has been made.[53] Devaṇabhaṭṭa in his *Smṛticandrikā* (p. 221) and Mitramiśra in his *Vīramitrodaya-vyavahāraprakāśa* refer to the statement of Śaṅkhalikhita having almost same idea and expression.[54] Nārada does not categorically recognise *anumāna* or *hetu* as *pramāṇa* but in his directives there are several cases which testify to his acceptance of circumstantial evidence. Thus

51 *sagopasthāniko bāhyaṃ pradeṣṭā coramārgaṇam / kuryān nāgarikaś cāntadurge nirdiṣṭahetubhiḥ* // *Arthaśāstra* IV. 6.2o.
It is of interest to note that in the section - *āśumṛtakaparīkṣā* (inquest on sudden deaths) the directives of Kauṭilya regarding examination of the cases are more or less on the line of circumstantial evidence. See the section in *A.Ś.* IV. 7.

52 *keśākeśikaṃ saṃgrahaṇam, upaliṅganād vā śarīrabhogānāṃ tajjātebhyaḥ strīvacanād vā. Arthaśāstra*, IV. 12.35.
See in this context the similarity of approach by Kauṭilya and Yājñavalkya II. 283 for a discussion on which see f.n. 48.

53 *keśākeśgṛhītaś·ca yugapat pāradārikaḥ. Nāradasmṛti* IV. 173.
For other detail in this respect see the discussion that follows in the context of Nārada.

54 *keśākeśigrahaṇāt pāradārikaḥ, ulkāhasto'gnidaḥ, śāstrapāṇir ghātakaḥ loptrahastaś caura iti.* P. 168.

while speaking about the six different kinds of proceedings where witnesses are not required, it has been held that the wise accept indications of the crime committed as the evidence of witnesses. By way of illustration it has been held that a person carrying a firebrand in his hand is to be regarded as incindiary; one with a weapon in hand a murderer, and where a man and another woman are observed to be in playful mood through grasping of hair mutually, the person is to be taken as adulterer. Several such cases have been mentioned by Nārada in this context.[55] Reference should also be made to other directives of Nārada in connection with the laws of debt in the form of *yuktileśa*. Thus it has been held that in the case where because of negligence of the creditor there is neither any document (executed) nor any witnesses and the opponent denies his being a party to such transaction, three methods are to be adopted.[56] The three methods are: a timely reminder, argument and an oath.[57]

[55] *asākṣipratyayās tv anye ṣaḍvivādā prakīrtitāḥ /*
lakṣaṇāny eva sākṣitve yeṣām āhur manīṣiṇaḥ //

ulkāhasto'gnido jñeyaḥ śastrapāṇis tu ghātakaḥ /
keśākeśigṛhītaś ca yugapat pāradārikaḥ //

kuddālapāṇir vijñeyaḥ setubhettā samīpagaḥ /
tathā kuṭhārapāṇiś ca vanacchetta samīpagaḥ //

pratyakṣicihno vijñeyo daṇḍapāruṣyakṛn naraḥ /
asākṣipratyayāḥ hy ete ....// IV. 172-175; *N.M.S.* IV. 151-154.

Bhavasvāmī in his commentary explains the true import of the word underlined in the following way:
tatra sākṣiṇaḥ santi, katham tarhi te'sākṣiṇaḥ; lakṣaṇaiḥ cihnaiś te paricchidyante, na darśanaśravaṇānubhavaiḥ. Ato lakṣaṇāny eva sākṣitvaṃ sākṣikāryaṃ kurvantīty arthaḥ. On *N.M.S.* IV. 151.

[56] *pramād dhanino yatra na syāl lekhyaṃ na sākṣiṇaḥ /*
arthaṃ cāpahnute vādī tatroktas trividho vidhiḥ // IV. 235.

[57] *codanāsā-pratikālañ ca yuktileśas tathaiva ca /*
tṛtīyaḥ śapathaḥ proktas tair enaṃ addhayet kramāt // IV. 236.

We have other texts of Nārada which deserve mention in this context.[58] Kātyāyana first speaks of three *pramāṇas* and in that reference refers to ordeal and *yukti*, the last of which has been described by him as 'the consideration of certain characteristics which cannot be explained otherwise (than on the hypothesis propounded)'.[59] Mitramiśra in his *Vyavahāra-*

57 (cont.)

In the *Smṛticandrikā* as also in the commentary of Bhavasvāmī on the *N.M.S.*, the reading is: *codanāḥ pratikālam* where the two words have been pronounced as separate and this appears relevant while the compounded form explained by Mitramiśra is more or less inappropriate.

According to him: *codanāpratikālasvarūpaṃ tu codanāyā dhanadānādiviṣayaka-preraṇayā apratikālo'pratiṣedhaḥ. So'pi yady ayam asya ṛṇādisambandhī na syād yācyamānas enaṃ na nirākuryāt anirākaraṇād asty asyānena sambandha ity arthāpattividhayā'numānavidhayā vā ṛṇādisambandhaṃ sādhayan bhavati pramāṇam iti.* *Vyavahāraprakāśa*, p. 168.

See here the comments of Bhavasvāmī on *N.M.S.* IV. 212:

kāle kāle (here the reading is *pratikalam* as separate) *mahājanasamakṣaṃ codanā dehīti hetus tattvāvagame. bhūyo bhūyo'muṣyāmuṣya sakāśe codito'yam iti vibhāvite sa paricchidyate dhārayatīti. yuktileśaḥ kasyacid ekadeśasya kadācid ādānam amunā preṣitena matsakāśāt gṛhītvāmutrāmutra ca vyayitam iti.*

See also Devaṇabhaṭṭa's interpretation on the same line in his *Smṛticandrikā*, *Vyavahārakāṇḍa*, p.118.

58 *abhīkṣaṇaṃ codyamāno yaḥ pratihanyān na tadvacaḥ /*
triś catuḥ pañcakṛtvo vā parato'rthaṃ sa dāpayet // IV. 237

An identical text of Kātyāyana should be remembered here:

arthinābhyarthito yas tu vighātaṃ na prayojayet /
tricatuḥpañcakṛtvo vā paratas tad ṛṇī bhavet // Kāt. 336

Nārada has another text:

codanāpratighāte tu yuktileśais tam anviyāt /
deśakālārthasambandhaparimāṇakriyādibhiḥ // IV. 238

Cf. the text of Kātyāyana:

ṛṇe lekhyaṃ sākṣiṇo vā yuktileśādayo'pi vā /
daivikī vā kriyā proktā prajānāṃ hitakāmyayā // Kāt. 233

59 *likhitaṃ sākṣiṇo bhiktiḥ pramāṇaṃ trividhaṃ viduḥ /*
leśoddeśas tu yuktiḥ syād divyānīha viṣādayaḥ // Kāt. 214

Par.Mā., 111, p. 91 reads: *liṅgoddeśas tu ...*

prakāśa makes the meaning of *yukti* clear.[6o] Kātyāyana refers to the cases where such *yukti* is to be applied.[61] According to him persons committing crimes in secret and of heinous type should be examined through the means of ordeal or reasoning or gestures or outward manifestations or voice or eye or by movements. Kātyāyana interestingly uses the term *hetu* and read in the light of his verse (no. 214) already referred to, it may be treated as synonymous.[62]

So far as Bṛhaspati is concerned, he is more categorical in his recognition of *anumāna* as a *pramāṇa* by name. Thus in the context of *mānuṣa-pramāṇa* he states that they are three

6o *leśo'nyathā'nupapanno dharmas tasyoddeśo vimarśo yuktir ity arthaḥ*. *Vy.Pr.*, p. 82.

61 *guḍhasāhasikādīnāṃ tu prāptaṃ divyaiḥ parīkṣaṇam* / *yukticihneṅgitākāravākcakṣuśceṣṭitair nṛṇām* // *Kāt*. 23o. Mitramiśra reads the word underlined as *yuktileśeṅgitākāra*. *Vy. Pr.*, p. 84.

62 Kātyāyana states that in all sorts of dispute the king should ascertain the facts through the employment of *pramāṇas*, the ordeals or by *hetu* (inference):
pramāṇair hetunā vāpi divyenaiva tu niścayam /
sarveṣv eva vivādeṣu sadā kuryān narādhipaḥ // *Kāt*. 241.
For the words underlined the *Sarasvatīvilāsa* (p. 1o7) has the reading *sarveṣv arthavivādeṣu*, which appears inappropriate in view of the fact that in such a case the scope of such *pramāṇas* becomes restricted. Reference here should made to the means mentioned by Kātyāyana regarding the establishment of claim through indirect proof:
dānaṃ prajñāpanābhedaḥ sampralobhakriyā ca yā /
cittāpanayanam caiva hetavo hi vibhāvakāḥ // *Kāt*. 337.
Mitramiśra reads *vittāpanayanam* (see *Vy.Pr.* 169).
eṣām anyatamo yatra vādinā bhavito bhavet /
mūlakriyā tu tatra syāt bhāvite vādinihnave // *Kāt*. 338.
Mitramiśra has explained the significance of each item for which see p. 169 of *Vyavahāraprakāśa*.

namely, witness, document and *anumāna*.[63] Of them witnesses are stated to be of twelve varieties, documents of eight and *anumāna* of three.[64] We do not however come across the names and classifications of the varieties of *anumāna* in the available text of Bṛhaspati. It is intersting that Bṛhaspati in another verse makes mention of *yuktileśa* and the like in ascertainment of the litigation relating to debt.[65] Other verses where references to *anumāna* are made, are noted below.[66]

63 *dviprakārā kriyā proktā mānuṣī daivikī tathā /*
ekaikā'nekadhā bhinnā ṛṣibhis tattvavedibhiḥ // Bṛ.S. IV. 6.
sākṣilekhyānumānaṃ ca mānuṣī trividhā kriyā. Ibid. IV. 8.

64 *sākṣī dvādaśa bhedas tu likhitaṃ tv aṣṭadhā smṛtam /*
anumānaṃ tridhā proktaṃ navadhā daivikī kriyā // Ibid. IV. 8-9.
For the underlined word there is as a variant reading *dvividhah* for which see f.n. 3, p. 46 of the *Bṛhaspatismṛti*, ed. K.V.R. Aiyangar.
See *Vyavahāranirṇaya* of Varadarāja wherein it has been stated: *bhuktiḥ kaiś cid viśeṣaṇair viśiṣṭā svatvahetuḥ, sā tu krayasākṣilekhyādikam avyabhicārād anumāpayati anupapadyamānā vā kalpayatīty anumānaṃ dvividham iti bhuktir evoktā.* P. 73.

65 *ṛṇe lekhyaṃ sākṣiṇo vā yuktileśādayo'pi vā /*
daivikī vā kriyā proktā prajānāṃ hitakāmyayā // Ibid. IV. 2o.
It is to be noted here that only in the *Vyavahāramayūkha* this has been attributed to Bṛhaspati, while the digest-writers like Devaṇabhaṭṭa, Mādhava and Pratāparudra speak of it as of Kātyāyana. See Kātyāyana 233 and the notes by Kane in his *Kātyāyanasmṛtisāroddhāra*, p. 32.

66 *likhite sākṣivāde ca sandigdhir jāyate yadi /*
anumāne ca sambhrānte tatra divyaṃ viśodhanam // Bṛ.S. IV. 17.

cirantanopāṃśukṛte ciranaṣṭeṣu sākṣiṣu /
praduṣṭeṣv anumāneṣu divyaiḥ kāryaṃ viśodhayet // Ibid. IV. 21.

aparādhānurūpaś ca daṇḍo'tra parikalpitaḥ /
sākṣilekhyānumānena samyag divyena vā jitaḥ // Ibid. IX. 25.

sākṣilekhyānumānena prakurvan kāryanirṇayam /
vitatyeha yaśo rājā bradhnasyāpnoti viṣṭapam // Ibid. IX. 33.

Reference in this respect is to be made to the texts of Nārada[67] and Kātyāyana.[68]

From the discussion made above in the light of the texts of the writers on *Dharmaśāstra* beginning with Gautama right up to Bṛhaspati, it is clear that willingly or otherwise the ancient legislators directly or indirectly had to lend recognition to circumstantial evidence for which the terms employed by different writers were *anumāna*, *hetu*, *tarka* and *yukti*.

The point that should receive our attention at this stage is the appropriateness or otherwise of the application of circumstantial evidence. Nārada rightly points out that some people sometimes come to the level of inflicting wounds and injuries on their own persons by way of accusing others and therefore in such cases special examinations have been prescribed.[69] Kauṭilya points out that there may be cases where, persons having association with persons indulging in illegal and immoral activities are likely to fall victim to the wrong application of inferential mode of proof. The case of Māṇḍavya has been referred to in this context.[7o]

67 *Nāradasmṛti* IV. 193-196; again in *Cauraprati̇ṣedhaprakaraṇa*, 1o-11 (*N.M.S.*, *Prakīrṇaka*, 7o-71).

68 Kātyāyana 385-386.

69 *kaś cit kṛtvātmacihnaṃ dveṣāt param upadravet / <u>hetvarthagatisāmarthyais</u> tatra yuktaṃ parīkṣanaṃ //* IV. 176 (*N.M.S.* 1.155). For the word underlined we have in the *Smṛticandrikā* the reading: *'yuktihetvarthasambandhaiḥ'*. *Vy.Kā.*, p. 56. Explanation offered is: *yuktir arthāpattiḥ; hetur anumānam ...*

7o *dṛśyate hy acauro'pi coramārge yadṛcchayā saṃnipāte coraveṣaśastrabhāṇḍasāmānyena gṛhyamāṇo dṛṣṭaḥ corabhāṇḍasya upavāsena vā, yathā hi māṇḍavyaḥ karmakleśabhayād acoras corosmīti bruvāṇaḥ.* *Arthaśāstra* IV. 8.12
His direction in this respect is:
tasmāt samāptakaraṇaṃ niyamayet. Ibid. IV. 8.13
In other words, punishment should be inflicted only in the cases where proof is fully obtained. The case of Māṇḍavya has been recorded in the *Mahābhārata*, *Ādi*, 63, 92-93, Cr. ed. 57; 1o1; *Anuśāsana*, 18. 46-5o; *Mārkaṇḍeyapurāṇa*, chap. 16 (where the name referred to is Aṇimāṇḍavya).

Nārada here directs that often truth has the tendency of being veiled under untruth and it is therefore desirable that proper examination of the facts should be made without relying merely on inference.[71] He has in this connection attempted to explain the position with reference to an illustration.[72] It has been contended that even perception turns out to be misleading, which shows that examination of facts is essential.[73] Nārada in this reference states that the nature of *dharma* is very subtle,[74] and the case of Māṇḍavya has been referred to by Nārada.[75] Māṇḍavya's story also finds its place in the text of Bṛhaspati.[76]

71 *asatyāḥ satyasaṃkāśāḥ satyāś cāsatyasannibhāḥ* (*darśanāḥ*) /
dṛśyante vividhāḥ bhāvāḥ tasmāt yuktaṃ parīkṣaṇam // 1. 71 (*N.M.S.* 1.62).
For an identical statement of Pitāmaha:
asatyās satyasaṃkāśāḥ satyāś cāsatyasannibhāḥ /
dṛśyante bhrāntijanakās tasmād yuktaṃ parīkṣaṇam //
See *Smṛticandrikā*, *Vy.Kā.* p.55
See also the text of Bṛhaspati:
asatyāḥ satyasadṛśāḥ satyāś cāsatyasaṃnibhāḥ /
dṛśyante bhrāntijanakās tasmād yuktyā vicārayet // 1. 117.

72 *talavad dṛśyate vyoma khadyoto havyavāḍ iva* /
na talam vidyate vyomi na khadyote hutāśanaḥ // 1. 72 (*N.M.S.* 1. 62)

73 *tasmāt pratyakṣadṛṣṭo'pi yuktam arthaḥ parīkṣitum* /
parīkṣya jñāpayann arthān na dharmāt parihīyate // 1. 73 (*N.M.S.* 1. 64)

74 *sūkṣo'pi bhagavān dharmaḥ parokṣo durvicāraṇaḥ* /
ataḥ pratyakṣamārgeṇa vyavahāragatiṃ nayet // 1. 41 (*N.M.S.* 1. 35 where the reading is a bit different: *sūkṣo'pi balavān dharmo durvicāras tv atīndriyaḥ*)

75 *yāty acauro'pi cauratvaṃ cauraś cāyāty acauratām* /
acauraś cauratāṃ prāpto māṇḍavyo vyavahārataḥ // 1. 42 (*N.M.S.* 1. 36)

76 *cauro'cauraḥ sādhv asādhur jāyate vyavahārataḥ* /
yuktiṃ vinā vicāreṇa māṇḍavyaś coratāṃ gataḥ // *Bṛ.S.* 1. 116.
For systematic treatment of circumstantial evidence see,

Caritra variety of *nirṇaya* deserves our attention at this stage. From Kātyāyana we have clear definition of *caritra* to the effect that herein practices are followed either according to the letters of the sacred law or in consonance with the established convention of the country.[77] We have almost an identical definition of *caritra* from Pitāmaha as recorded in the *Smṛticandrikā*.[78] In this context it is quite befitting to refer to the directives of the Śāstrakāras regarding the recognition accorded to the customs and conventions of the country. Manu, while speaking about the sources of *dharma* recognises *sadācāra* along with the *Veda*s and the *Smṛtis*.[79] In another verse Manu speaks of *ācāra* as most authoritative and Yājñavalkya directs the king to recognise and retain the local usages of the country.[80] Gautama[81] however adds a condi-

76 (cont.)

A. Thakur, *Hindu Law of Evidence*, Calcutta, 1933, pp. 25-32.

P.V. Kane, *History of Dharmaśāstra*, III, pp.354-357.

Wills, *Principles of Circumstantial Evidence* (English and Indian edition combined), seventh edition, pp. 39-48.

77 *yad yad ācaryate yena dharmyam vādharmyam eva vā /*
deśasyācaraṇān nityaṃ caritraṃ tat prakīrtitam // Kāt. 37.

78 *yad yad ācarati śreṣṭho dharmyaṃ vādharmyam eva vā /*
kulādideśācaraṇāc caritraṃ tat prakīrtitam //

grāmagoṣṭhapuraśreṇīsārthasenānivāsinām /
vyavahāraś caritreṇa nirṇetavyo bṛhaspatiḥ // Sm.C., p. 58 quotes the text of Pitāmaha.

79 *vedaḥ smṛtiḥ sadācāraḥ svasya ca priyam ātmanaḥ /*
etac caturvidham āhuḥ sākṣād dharmasya lakṣaṇam // II. 6
See also: *ācāraḥ paramo dharmaḥ śrutyuktaḥ smārta eva ca /*
tasmād asmin sadā yukto nityaṃ syād ātmavān dvijaḥ // *M.S.* 1. 1o8

8o *yasmin deśe ya ācāro vyavahāraḥ kulasthitiḥ /*
tathaiva paripālyo'sav yadā vaśam upāgataḥ // *Y.S.* 1. 343.

81 *deśajātikuladharmāś cāmnāyair aviruddhāḥ pramāṇam;*
karṣakavaṇikpaśupālakusīdikāravaḥ sve sve varge;
tebhyaś ca yathādhikāram arthān pratyāhṛtya dharmavyavasthā. *G.D.S.* 11. 2o-22. We have from Vasiṣṭha also the rule:
deśajātikuladharmān śrutyabhāvād abravīn manuḥ. *V.D.S.* 1. 17.

tion to the effect that usages of the country may be regarded as authoritative only when they do not go against the directives of the *Śrutis*. There are other texts of Manu emphasizing the importance of local customs and usages.[82] Bṛhaspati pertinently presents the reason that disregard to these customs by the head of the state is likely to incur displeasure of the subjects.[83] We have the directives of Kauṭilya that due recognition should be given in the formulation of the laws of inheritance to the customs.[84]

Kātyāyana distinctly directs the king to administer the state first in accordance with the principles of *Śāstra* and in the absence of any positive direction of the scriptures, to

[82] *pratyahaṃ deśadṛṣṭaiś ca śāstradṛṣṭaiś ca hetubhiḥ /*
aṣṭādaśasu mārgeṣu nibaddhāni pṛthak pṛthak // M.S. VIII. 3.

jātijanapadān dharmān śreṇīdharmāṃś ca dharmavit /
samīkṣya kuladharmāṃś ca svadharmaṃ pratipādayet // Ibid. VIII. 41..
cf: *yasmin deśe pure grāme traividye nagare'pi vā /*
yo yatra vihito dharmas taṃ dharmaṃ na vicārayet // Devala, quoted in the *Smṛticandrikā*, 1, p. 10.

[83] *pratilomaprasūtānāṃ tathā durganivāsinām /*
deśajātikulādīnāṃ ye dharmās tatpravartitāḥ // Bṛ.S. I. 126.

tathaiva te pālanīyāḥ prajā prakṣubhyate'nyathā /
janāparaktir bhavati balaṃ kośaś naśyati // Ibid. I. 127.
In this reference Bṛhaspati mentions several such customs which are interesting:
uduhyate dākṣiṇātyair mātulasya sutā dvijaiḥ /
madhyadeśe karmakarāḥ śilpinaś ca gavāśanāḥ // Ibid. I. 128.

matsyādāś ca narāḥ pūrve vyabhicārāratāḥ striyaḥ /
uttare madyapa naryaḥ spṛśyā nṛṇāṃ rajasvalāḥ // Ibid. I. 129.

sahajātāḥ pragṛhṇanti bhrātṛbhāryām abhartṛkām /
anena karmaṇā naite prāyaś-cittadamārhakāḥ // Ibid. I. 130.

[84] Kauṭilya's directive has special reference to the laws of inheritance:
deśasya jātyāḥ sanghasya dharmo grāmasya vāpi yaḥ /
ucitas tasya tenaiva dāyadharmaṃ prakalpayet // Arthaśāstra III. 7. 40.

take to the customs and usages of the country.[85] In this context Kātyāyana himself explains the significance of the word *deśadṛṣṭa* and according to him it stands for custom of the country which has a background of being introduced since long time and which is not in opposition to the directives of the *Śāstra* in the line suggested by Gautama as already referred to.[86] Kātyāyana is more methodical and prudent in realising the difficulties that may crop up every now and then if customs are given recognition in deciding tha cases. What he suggests is that people in general should sit together to decide which of the customs are to be accepted as authoritative. The best course then is to put them in writing for record with the royal seal embossed on the same.[87] Once recognition is accorded to the customs it should be the sacred duty of the king to preserve them and to be guided by them in cases of doubts. The king should not reverse them.

85 *tasmāc chātrāṇusāreṇa rājā kāryāṇi sādhayet /*
vākyābhāve tu sarveśāṃ deśadṛṣṭena sannayet // Kāt. 45.
For different readings see *Kātyāyanasmṛtisāroddhāra*, p. 9, f.n. 45.

86 *yasya deśasya yo dharmaḥ pravṛttaḥ sārvakālikaḥ /*
śrutismṛtyavirodhena deśadṛṣṭaḥ sa ucyate // Kāt. 46.
Other verses of Kātyāyana deserve reference in this context. While accepting the importance of the customs Kātyāyana quite appropriately states that even by deciding cases in accordance with the customs, the king should make it a point to adopt Śāstric laws in case of dispute or difference:
deśapattanagoṣṭheṣu puragrāmeṣu vāsinām /
teṣāṃ svasamayair dharmaśāstrato'nyeṣu taiḥ saha // Kāt. 47.

87 *deśasyānumatenaiva vyavasthā yā nirūpitā /*
likhitā tu sadā dhāryā mudritā rājamudrayā // Kāt. 48

śāstravad yatnato rakṣyā tāṃ nirīkṣya vinirṇayet /
naigamasthais tu yat kāryaṃ likhitaṃ yad vyavasthitam // Kāt. 49.

tasmāt tat saṃpravarteta nānyathaiva pravartayet // Kāt. 5o.

pramāṇadeśadṛṣṭaṃ tu yad evam iti niścitam /
apravṛttaṃ kṛtaṃ yatra śrutismṛtyanumoditam /
nānyathā tat punaḥ kāryaṃ nyāyāpetaṃ vivarjayet // Kāt. 51.

In his gloss on the *Manusaṃhitā* Medhātithi refers to several usages of the country which deserve our attention here.[88]

In the light of this discussion and background, the description of *caritra* by Vyāsa is to be understood. According to him *caritra* stands for an established usage of the country.[89]

Bṛhaspati, as already stated, has assigned two characteristics to each of the four *nirṇayas* (IX.2). In respect of *caritra* one characteristic is in full agreement with what has been defined by Kātyāyana as discussed above. The other mentioned by Bṛhaspati is not very clear.[90] According to him a decision arrived at through the application of inference is

88 *sā ca vyavasthā dvividhā, sādhāraṇy asādhāraṇī ca. deśabhedāśrayabhedā sāpi dvividhā, aviruddhā viruddhā ca. aviruddhā yathā keṣāñ cid dākṣiṇātyānām aputrā strī bhartary uparate sabhāsthānum upārohati, tam upārūḍhādhikṛtaiḥ parīkṣitā kṛtalakṣaṇā tatkṣaṇāntaraṃ sapiṇḍeṣu ṛkthaṃ labhate. tathodīcāṃ labhyamānāṃ kanyāṃ yācamānāya bhojanaṃ yadi dīyate tata iyāṃ tubhyaṃ dattety anukte'pi pratiśrutā bhavati. viruddhā ca. kvacid deśe vasante dhānyaṃ prayujyate śaradi dviguṇaṃ pratyādīyate. tathānujñātabhoga ādhir dviguṇe'pi tadutthadhane praviṣṭa āmūlahiraṇyadānāt bhujyata eva. eṣā hi 'aśītibhāgaṃ gṛhṇīyāt', kusīdavṛddhir dvaiguṇayaṃ nātyeti viruddhā.* Medhātithi on Manu VIII. 3.

89 *deśasthitiḥ pūrvakṛtā caritraṃ samudāhṛtam.* Vyāsa, verse 3.

For an illuminating discussion on the point, see the section: 'Custom and Law in Ancient India', included in *Religion, Law and the State in India* by Prof. J.D.M. Derrett, pp. 148-17o.

9o *anumānena nirṇītaṃ cāritram iti kathyate /*
deśasthityā dvitīyas tu śāstravidbhir udāhṛtaḥ // Br.S. IX. 6.
The second definition is what is recognised by all other writers on law in respect of *carita*, but it cannot be accounted for exactly how a decision passed on the basis of inference (circumstantial evidence) has been termed by Bṛhaspati as *carita*. Bṛhaspati, as already pointed out, recognises the *anumāna* as one the three *mānuṣa-pramāṇas*. It may humbly be suggested that when an established usage is made use of in the desision of a case, the judicators are expected to be guided by circumstantial evidence so to say

called *caritra*, and the wise conversant with the śāstric precepts regard the usages of the country as the second variety *caritra*. One may note with interest that the digest-writers hardly attempt to be clear in their expositions in cases like this and the only explanation that may be offered is that they were so much outdistanced from the ancient legislators that when they entered into the field the original meaning of the terms might have been passed into oblivion.

While referring to the accepted view of the *Smṛtikāras* regarding the meaning of the *caritra* variety of decision, Kane refers to the Nasik Inscription in the following way. He says: 'This seems to be the sense of *caritra* in *'phalakevāre charitroti'* occurring in the Nasik Inscription No. 12 in *Ep. Ind.*, Vol. VIII., p. 82. In *prakīrṇaka*, 24 Nār. seems to give the same sense: *'sthityartham pṛthivīpālaiś caritraviṣayāḥ kṛtāḥ.'* (*History of Dharmaśāstra*, III, 260).

Nārada's definition of *caritra* may at this stage invite our attention here. According to him, the usages attain validity when after proper discernment they are written down for record for future guidance. (*Caritraṃ pustakaraṇe*. *N.S.*, 1. 11).[91] This is in full agreement with what has been directed by Kātyāyana as already stated.

The fifth variety of *nirṇaya* according to Vyāsa is *śapatha* (oath or ordeal), which has been spoken of by Raghunandana in

90 (cont.)
at least in respect of inferring in any form a *śruti* directive at any stage. It is known that the Mīmāṃsakas recognise the authoritativeness of the *ācāra* by relying on *anumiti* (i.e. presumption of a *śruti* background but for which a custom cannot stand the test of time for long). For a highly scholastic discussion regarding the authoritativeness of the *ācāras* on the basis mainly of the *Śabarabhāṣya* and the *Tantravārtika* see Kane, *History of Dharmaśāstra*, vol. III, p. 841 ff.

91 Bhavasvāmī offers the following explanation of the statement of Nārada: *lekhyena nirṇīyate tac caritram. caritraṃ saṃgrahaḥ puṃsām iti pāṭhāntaram.* On *N.M.S.* 1.11.
Mitramiśra refers and criticises the reading accepted by Caṇḍeśvara thus:

his *Divyatattva* as a decision which may be resorted to even when there is scope for human modes of proof.[92] It should be noted that the first great safeguard which law provides for the ascertainment of truth in ordinary cases consists in requiring all evidences to be given under the sanction of an oath. This imposes strongest obligation upon the conscience of the witness to declare the whole truth that human wisdom can devise; a wilful violation of truth exposes him at once to temporal and to eternal punishment.

Legislators of ancient India recognised the importance of this divine mode of proof and we may trace the utilisation of this variety of decision in the Vedic period.[93] Before mentioning other references to *divya* by the writers on *Dharmaśāstra* it is worthwhile to pursue the interesting line of dis-

91 (cont.)

atra mādhavīye 'caritraṃ tu svīkaraṇe' iti pāṭhaṃ likhitvā deśācāraś caritraṃ tatsvīkāre tad eva nirṇayahetur iti vyākhyātam... caṇḍeśvareṇa tu 'caritraṃ pustakaraṇam' iti paṭhitvā pustaṃ pañjikety arthaḥ. tatkaraṇam adhikaraṇaṃ yasyeti vyākṛtam. tad rūḍhihīnatvād vacanāntarāsambādāc ca heyam. *Vyavahāraprakāśa*, p. 7.

It is not very easy however to accept the reading recorded in the *Arthaśāstra* of Kauṭilya in the following way:

tatra satye sthito dharmo vyavahāras tu sākṣiṣu /
caritraṃ saṃgrahe puṃsāṃ rājñām ajñā tu śāsanam // III. 1. 140.

Read in the light of the verse of Nārada (1. 11) this may mean 'the view commonly accepted by men'. The reading however may be taken as doubtful.

92 *mānuṣapramāṇanirṇayasyāpi nirṇāyakaṃ yat tad divyam iti lokaprasiddham. apinā mānuṣapramāṇasattve'pi yatra caiva ghaṭādyaṅgīkāras tatrāpy etad bhavatīti sūcitam.* *Divyatattva*, p. 574.

93 See *Atharvaveda* II. 12. 8:

ā dadhāmi te padaṃ samiddhe jātavadesi /
agniḥ śarīraṃ veveṣṭavasuṃ vāg api gacchatu //

For a discussion on this *mantra* see *Proceedings of the American Oriental Society*, vol. III, pp. CCXXI-XXVI, where the views of Ludwig, Weber and Zimmer have been referred to and criticised.

The story of Vatsa as recorded in the *Tāṇḍyamahābrāhmaṇa* (14. 6. 6) and cussion by Medhātithi on the appropriateness of a trial by ordeal.[94] The *prima facie* position has been stated to be that even by appeal to the inanimate objects like fire, water etc. no positive effect can be expected and as such they are supposed to be utilised to frighten the parties. His conclusion is that ordeals may be relied on as one relies on witnesses and other *pramāṇas*.

93 (cont.)

also referred to in the *Manusaṃhitā* (VIII. 116):

vatsasya hy abhiśaptasya purā bhrātrā yavīyasā /
nāgnir dadāha romāpi satyena jagataḥ spaśaḥ //

may be regarded as the earliest positive reference to decision by ordeal: *vatsaś ca vai medhātithiś ca kāṇvāv āstāṃ, taṃ vatsaṃ medhātithir ākrośad abrāhmaṇo'si śūdrāputra iti. so'bravīt ṛtenāgniṃ vyayāca yataro nau brahmīyāniti. vātsena vatse vyain medhātithena medhātithis tasya na loma ca nauṣat.*

Reference in this context should be made of the *Chāndogya Upaniṣad* wherein we come across the incident of proving the innocence in respect of theft through holding by hand of a heated axe. *Chāndogya*, VI. 16. 1.

94 *manu caurā api na dahyante, sādhavo'pi dahyamānā dṛśyante; tat kathaṃ śapathe āsvāsaḥ? ucyate, na dṛśyena vyabhicāreṇa vyavastheyam apanetuṃ śakyate, kadācitkatvād vyabhicārasya. pratyakṣādiṣv api pramāṇeṣu dṛśyata eva tādṛśo vyabhicāraḥ. na ca tāni na pramāṇam; atha vyabhicāravanti naiva pratyakṣādiśabdavācyāni yad vyabhicarati na tat pratyakṣam, yat pratyakṣam na tad vyabhicaratīti vacanāt. ihāpi śakyate tad vaktum, yad vyabhicarati nāsau śapatho, yaḥ śapathaḥ sa na vyabhicaratīti. kaḥ punaḥ śapathaḥ, yaḥ samastetikartavyatāmātrādyapagraheṇa nirūpitakuhakaḥ stambhanābhāvaḥ. viparīto'śapathaḥ. na tādṛśasya vyabhicāro'sti. athāpi syāt tatrāpi prākkṛtasya karmaṇaḥ phalavipāko bhavati, nimittatvāt. kṛtāparādhe'pi pūrvakṛtena garīyasā śubhena mucyate, akṛtāparādho janmāntaradoṣeṇa nigṛhyate. vicitrā hi karmaṇāṃ phalapākābhivyaktihetavaḥ, sahasrād eko mithyā gṛhyate, utsargatas tv amithyātvam. putreṣṭikārīryādiṣv apy etatsamānam. tasmāt sākṣivat śapathe'pi pratyetavyam te'pi kadācin mithyā vadanti. na bhayadarśanamātram etat. ruḍhyā śapathā uktāḥ satyaṃ pratiṣṭhita iti.*

Medhātithi on Manu VIII. 116. Medhātithi is supposed to have before him the commentary of Bhārucī where there is discussion of the same type.

Ordeal as a *pramāṇa* has been recognised in the texts on *Dharmaśāstra* and *Arthaśāstra*. Kauṭilya states that the following are helpful in arriving at decisions in a case. They are: an offence distinctly noticed; voluntary admission (similar to *vādisampratipatti* as mentioned by Vyāsa in verse no.1); straightforwardedness in questions and answers to one's own and the opposite party; reasoning (*hetu* - similar to that mentioned by Vyāsa) and oath.[95]

Other references to oath and ordeal from the *Dharmaśāstras* are being mentioned here in bare outline.[96]

[95] *dṛṣṭadoṣaḥ svayaṃvādaḥ svapakṣaparapakṣayoḥ /*
anuyogārjavaṃ hetuḥ śapathaścārthasādhakaḥ // A.Ś. III. 1. 46.
See in this context Kauṭilya's provision of penalty for a person putting questions to suspects on oath without authorisation:
śapathavākyānuyogam aniṣṛṭaṃ kurvataḥ... pūrvaḥ sāhasadaṇḍaḥ. A.Ś. III. 2o. 17.

[96] *Āp.Dh.Sū.* II. 11. 29. 6, where *daiva* has been used by name.
Manu VIII. 113-116, where the expression *śapatha* has been used and there is reference to ordeal by fire and water. Nārada however ascribes to Manu five types of *divya:*
Sandigdhe'the'bhiyuktānāṃ pracchanneṣu viśeṣataḥ /
daivaṃ pañcavidhaṃ jñeyam ity āha bhagavān manuḥ // IV. 251.
He himself in the next verse (IV. 252) speaks of five varieties of *divya*, and two more are referred to again in IV. 337 and 343. Yājñavalkya II. 95 also is in favour of five *divyas: tulāgny āpo viṣaṃ kośo divyānīha viśuddhaye*. See also Viṣṇu IX-XIV. Kātyāyana uses both the terms *śapatha* (verse 463) and *divya* and for the latter has elaborate discussion covering verses 411-461. In the context of the *pramāṇas* Kātyāyana refers to *divya* in verses 214, 216-22o; 223-225 etc. Bṛhaspati speaks of nine varieties of *divya: ghaṭādyā dharmajāntā ca daivī navavidhā kriyā*. VIII. 2, verses VIII For other elaborate discussion on the nature and technicalities of *divya* see VIII. 5-32. Bṛhaspati speaks of *śapatha* and is of opinion that *śapatha* as distinct from *divya* is to be resorted to in disputes of trifling matte while in serious ones like debt etc. *divya* is the *pramāṇa* to be adopted:
satāṃ vāhanaśastrāṇi gobījakanakāni ca /
devabrāhmaṇapādāś ca putradāraśirāṃsi ca // VIII. 33. Cf. Nārada IV. 248.

Nārada makes mention of both *divya* and *śapatha* thereby emphasising that there is difference between the two[97] Nārada interestingly refers to cases of *śapatha* adopted by the divine and semidivine beings. Thus, Vasiṣṭha took an oath when he was accused of having assumed the shape of an evil spirit. The seven Ṛṣis resolutely took an oath together with Indra in order to clear themselves mutually of suspicion when each was suspected by the rest of having taken lotus fibres:

> *śapathā hy api devānām ṛṣīṇām api ca smṛtāḥ /*
> *Vasiṣṭhaḥ śapathaṃ śepe yātudhānena śaṅkitaḥ* // IV. 243
>
> *Saptarṣayas tathendreṇa puṣkarārthena śaṅkitāḥ /*
> *Śepuḥ śapatham avyagrāḥ parasparaviśuddhaye* // IV. 244

Treatment of trial by ordeal is exhaustive in the texts of Nārada (see verses IV. 247 ff.); Yājñavalkya (II. 96-113; Kātyāyana (verses 411-463); Bṛhaspati (VIII. 1-92) as also in the *nibandha* texts ot which the *Divyatattva* of Raghunandana, the *Vyavahāraprakāśa* of Mitramiśra and the *Vyavahāramayūkha* of Nīlakaṇṭha may be of special interest (pp. 169-221).

The text of Vyāsa with reterence to *śapatha* should be referred to here. It is stated there oaths and ordeals of different types are to be applied proportionate to the amount of money involved about which dispute has taken place.[98] For cla-

96 (cont.)

ete ca śapathāḥ proktāḥ alpārthe sukarāḥ sadā /
sāhaseṣv abhiśāpeṣu divyāny āhur viśodhanam // VIII. 34.

For other informations on *śapatha* see Bṛhaspati VIII. 35 ff. The idea of Bṛhaspati has been derived from Nārada, who in turn refers to Manu:

ity ete śapathāḥ proktā manunā svalpakāraṇe /
pātakeṣṭābhiyoge ca vidhir divyaḥ prakīrtitaḥ // IV. 25o, also see:
mahāparādhe divyāni dāpayet tu mahīpatiḥ /
alpeṣu tu nṛpaśreṣṭhaḥ śapathaiḥ śrāvayen naram // IV. 249.

97 *yadā sākṣī na vidyeta vivāde vadatāṃ nṛṇām /*
tadā divyaiḥ parīkṣeta śapathaiś ca pṛthagvidhaiḥ // IV. 247

98 *arthānurūpāḥ śapathāḥ smṛtāḥ satyadhaṭādayaḥ*. Vyāsa, verse 3. Quoted in the *Smṛticandrikā*, *Vy.kā.*, p. 222. (Mysore edition)

rification we may here refer to the text of Yājñavalkya which states about the application of ordeal in terms of dispute relating to money.[99]

Kātyāyana is clear in his statement in this respect. Thus he holds, after ascertaining the price of things (the subjects of dispute) he (the judge) should trace their equivalent in gold and then the proper ordeal should be prescribed.[100] Bṛhaspati also has the same directive to the effect that ordeals are to administered by taking into consideration the time, the place and the amount of money involved.[101]

The reference to *satya* in the expression *satyadhaṭādayaḥ* in the verse of Vyāsa (no. 3) may be explained in a better way if the verse of Manu regarding the different modes of oath in respect of different castes is considered. According to this verse a Brāhmaṇa is to undertake an oath in the name of truth[102]

98 (cont.)
Devaṇabhaṭṭa in this context refers to the text of Nārada as having the same implication as that of Vyāsa (p. 222):
yuktiṣv asamarthāsu śapathair eva nirṇayet /
arthakālabalāpekṣam agnyambusukṛtādibhiḥ // *N.S.* IV. 239.
The reading in the edition of Jolly as also in the *N.M.S.* (215) is different in the words underlined. For *nirṇayet* the reading is *ardayet*; and for artha° the reading is deśa°. Devaṇa's interpretation of Vyāsa's *arthānurūpam* is as follows:
arthāpekṣaṃ sisādhayiṣitārthālpatvamahattvarūpam ity arthaḥ. (p. 222)

99 *nāsahasrād dharet phālaṃ na viṣaṃ na tulā tathā*. II. 99.

100 *sarvadravyapramāṇaṃ tu jñātvā hema prakalpayet /*
hemapramāṇayuktaṃ tu tadā divyaṃ niyojayet // *Kāt*. 417.
See in this context other verses of Kātyāyana 418-421.

101 *yasmād devaiḥ prayuktāni duṣkarārthe mahātmabhiḥ /*
aham uddeśatāṃ vacmi sandigdhārthaviśuddhaye //
deśakālārthasaṃkhyābhiḥ prayuktāny anupūrvaśaḥ // *Bṛ.S.* VIII. 5.
See in this context other verses of Bṛhaspati VIII. 29-32.

102 *satyena śāpayed vipraṃ kṣatriyaṃ vāhanāyudhaiḥ /*
gobījakāñcanair vaiśyaṃ śūdraṃ sarvais tu pātakaiḥ //Manu VIII. 113.

(Bühler: 'Let the judge cause a Brāhmaṇa to swear by his veracity ...'). Nārada also makes mention of *satya* of course without specific mention of the caste of the person making such oath.[103] In an earlier verse of course Nārada shares with Manu a verse where there is reference to the castes and the different procedures of oath.[104]

While declaring that the different modes of oath are to be administered for different castes, Bṛhaspati almost in the same language prescribes the different formalities.[105]

102 (cont.)

Medhātithi describes here the nature of *śapatha* and *satya* thus:
nanu yady aham evaṃ kuryāṃ tadidam aniṣṭaṃ āpnuyām iti saṃkīrtanakriyā śapathaḥ... 'satyena śape 'satyādinibandhano'yaṃ, 'dharmo vā me niṣphalaḥ syād'iti.

103 *satyaṃ vāhanaśāstrāṇi gobijakaṇakādi ca /*
devatāpitṛpādāś ca dattāni sukṛtāni ca // IV. 248.

mahāparādhe divyāni dāpayet tu mahīpatiḥ /
alpeṣu tu nṛpaśreṣṭhaḥ śapathaiḥ śrāvayen naram // IV. 249.

104 Nārada IV. 199 = Manu VIII. 113. The next verse of Nārada is interesting. According to him, the king should inspire the persons with ancient sacred texts, extolling the excellence of truth, and with the denouncement of the sinfulness of falsehood:
purāṇair dharmavacanaiḥ satyamāhātmyakīrtanaiḥ /
anṛtasyāpavādaiś ca bhṛśam uttrāsayed imān // N.S. IV. 200.

105 *varṇānurūpaiḥ śapathaiḥ śapanīyaṃ pṛthak pṛthak / Bṛ.S.* VIII. 38.
Bṛ.S. VIII. 36 = Manu VIII. 113.
We may here note that all the oaths were principally imprecatory and the imprecation was in a form 'adapted to the peculiarities of the influences by which each individual might be presumed to be most affected.' Best in his *Evidence* questions the utility of imprecation thus: 'Imprecation is however, no part of the essence of an oath, but is a mere adjunct of questionable propriety as calculated to divert attention from the true meaning of the ceremony and fix it on some external observance.' (p. 45). For a discussion on the point see, A Thakur, *Hindu Law of Evidence*, Calcutta, 1933, 136 ff.

satyadhaṭādayaḥ in the verse of Vyāsa has evidently reference to *satya* (the nature of which was just explained) and others beginning with *dhaṭa*. We should therefore in this context make a passing reference to the number of such ordeals, which have already been indicated in *f.n. 96*. The most common are the ordeals by balance (*tulā* or *dhaṭa*) historical reference to which is available from the Silimpur stone slab inscription of the time of Jayapāladeva at about 12oo A.D. (See *Ep. Ind.*, Vol. XIII, p. 283, at pp. 291-292). The others are ordeal by fire;[1o6] by water;[1o7] by poison; by *kośa* (drinking of holy water); by *taṇḍula* (rice grains); by *taptamāṣa* (heated piece of gold); by *phāla* (ploughshare) and by *dharma* (images or pictures of *dharma*).

The next variety of decision as mentioned by Vyāsa is *nṛpājñā* and *rājājñā*, which is similar to *rājaśāsana* of Nārada

1o6 Kane in his *History of Dharmaśāstra*, III, 377-8 refers to a Marathi publication entitled '*Vatanpatreṃ, nivāḍapatreṃ* etc.' (pp. 45-56)., ed. P. V. Mavjee and D.B. Parasnis (19o9) which contains a document describing in great detail the ordeal of fire in Śake, 1666 Pauṣa bright 11th, Thursday in 1745 A.D. and interestingly the opponent was made to pass a document of victory to the *śodhya* called '*yejitapatra*'. There are other references of ordeals in the same text.

1o7 Interestingly Devaṇabhaṭṭa records that by his time (12oo-1225 A.D.) the ordeal by water and poison was already out of use:
atra jalaviṣayor utsannānuṣṭhānatvāt tadvidhim anākhyāya kośavidhir ucyate Introductory portion of *kośavidhi*, in *Sm.C.*, p. 271. See here Stephens, *History of Criminal Law of England*, vol. 1, p. 73. In p. 3oo of the same text it has been stated that the Assize of Northampton presribed ordeal of water for murder, robbery etc. but ordeals were abolished in England since 1215 A.D.
P.V. Kane in the third volume of his *H.Dh.*, pp. 375-378 has collected epigraphic and other records relating to application of different śāstric modes of ordeals. Other references to the treatment of ordeals may be four in: *Divyatattva* of Raghunandana; we should refer here to the critical ed. the *Divyatattva* by Richard W. Lariviere, Delhi, 1981; D.C. Sircar, *The successors of the Sātavāhanas*, Calcutta, 1939, Appendix, pp. 354-376.

(1.1o) and *nṛpājñā* of Bṛhaspati (IX.1) and *rājaśāsana* of Kātyāyana (verse 38).[108]

Nārada speaks of it as an edict which depends on the pleasure of the king.[109] Kātyāyana declares that a righteous royal edict is made by the king which is not in conflict with the rules of justice and with the usages of the country.[110] Here the decision is arrived at by the king by relying on his own intellect.[110a] Such case has been indicated by Kātyāyana when after observing the usage as opposed to the sacred law, the king overrules the same by his command.[111]

Bṛhaspati, as already pointed out, has two definitions of *rājājñā*, as he has two definitions for each of the *nirṇayas*. According to one of the definitions, a decision based on the edict of the king is ordained for those cases in which no evidence is available.[112] The second variety of royal edict is

1o8 In the absence of the aforesaid *pramāṇas* decision is to be made through royal proclamation:
teṣām abhāve rājājñāṃ nirṇayaṃ tu vidur budhāḥ. Vyāsa, verse 3.

1o9 ... *rājājñāyāṃ tu śāsanam*. Nārada, 1. 11. This has been explained in the commentary of Bhavasvāmī as: *rājñām ājñā rājājñā, tatra sthitaṃ śāsanam. rājña icchā yathā tathājñāsiddhiḥ*.
Asahāya comments here that the suit which has been decided by an edict from the king himself, is superior to all the rest, according to the saying- 'what has been decided in a village, goes to the town; what has been decided in the town, goes before the king. What has been decided by the king, though wrongly decided, cannot be tried anew.'

11o *nyāyaśāstrāvirodhena deśadṛṣṭes tathaiva ca /*
yaṃ dharmaṃ sthāpayed rājā nyāyyaṃ tad rājaśāsanam // Kāt. 38.

11oa Devaṇabhaṭṭa brings out the meaning of the verse of Kātyāyana thus: *mānāntarāviruddho rājabuddhimātraparikalpito nirṇayo rājaśāsanam ity ucyate*. *Sm.C., Vy.Kā.*, p. 22.

111 *viruddhaṃ nyāyato yat tu caritraṃ kalpyate nṛpaiḥ /*
evaṃ tatra nirasyeta caritraṃ tu nṛpājñayā // Kāt. 42.

112 *pramāṇarahito yas tu rājājñā nirṇayaḥ smṛtaḥ*. *Bṛ.S.* IX. 7. The reading accepted by Aiyangar (in his ed. of the *Bṛ.S.*) as *pramāṇasamatāyām* appears not to be very happy.

to be applicable when the law-books and the judges are at variance with one another.[113] The contention as contained in both the definitions is that royal intervention in the form of edict can only take place when other *nirṇayas* are not available in any form or when there are differences of opinion on a point. This also at the same time indicates that normally such edicts were not resorted to. Nārada's directive that the *nirṇaya* mentioned later in the list should be treated as superior to one previously named (*uttaraḥ pūrvabādhakaḥ, N.S.*, 1.11) has been discussed by Devaṇabhaṭṭa in his *Smṛticandrikā* (*Vyavahārakāṇḍa*, pp. 23-25).[114]

Kauṭilya in his *Arthaśāstra* has dealt with royal edicts in his section on *Śāsanādhikāra* (II.1o). It is stated that *śāsanas* (edicts) are intended for issuing royal orders (*śāsane śāsanam ity ācakṣate. A.Ś.*, II.1o.1). It has further been stated that the kings principally depend on such edicts in as much as peace and war depend on it (*śāsanapradhānā hi rājānaḥ, tanmūlatvāt sandhivigrahayoḥ.* II.1o.2). Kauṭilya mentions different varieties of *śāsana*.[115]

113 *śāsrasabhyavirodhena tathānyaḥ parikīrtitaḥ. Bṛ.S.* IX. 7. The reading in the Aiyangar's edition of the *Bṛ.S.: 'śāstrasabhyāvirodhena caturtha parikīrtitaḥ'* appears to be unhappy as in the first line of the verse. Translation of the verses by Jolly in *S.B.E.*, vol. XXXIII, Oxford, 1889 p. 286 may be stated in support.

114 See in this context the following verse of Bṛhaspati:
śāstraṃ kevalam āśritya kriyate yatra nirṇayaḥ /
vyavahāraḥ sa vijñeyo dharmas tenāpi bādhyate // 1. 19

deśasthityānumānena naigamenānumatena ca
kriyate nirṇayas tatra vyavahāras tu bādhyate // 1. 2o

vihāya caritācāraṃ yatra kuryāt punar nṛpaḥ /
nirṇayaṃ sā tu rājājñā caritaṃ bādhyate tayā // 1. 21
see also Kātyāyana, verses 39-43.

115 *prajñāpanājñāparidānalekhas tathā parīhāraniṣṭilekhau /*
prāvṛttikaś ca pratilekha eva sarvatragaś ceti hi śāsanāni // II. 1o.

anena vijñāpitam evam āha tad dīyatāṃ ced yadi tattvam asti /
rājñaḥ samīpe varakāram āha prajñāpanaiṣā vividhopadṛṣṭā // II. 1o. 39

159

While speaking about documents Bṛhaspati makes mention of three kinds - those written by the king, those written in a particular place and those written (by a person) in a particular place.[116] Bṛhaspati speaks of three varieties of royal edicts.[117] Vasiṣṭha classifies the documents under two heads, *laukika* and *rājakīya*,[118] of which the latter has been classified into four groups - *śāsana*, *jayapatra*, *ājñāpatra* and *prajñāpanapatra*.[119]

115 (cont.)

bhartur ājñā bhaved yatra nigrahānugrahau prati /
viśeṣeṇa tu bhṛtyeṣu tad ājñālekhalakṣaṇam // II. lo. 4o

yathārhaguṇasaṃyuktā pūjā yatropalakṣyate /
apy ādhau paridāne vā bhavatas tāv upagrahau // II. lo. 41

jāter viśeṣeṣu pureṣu caiva grāmeṣu deśeṣu ca teṣu teṣu /
anugraho yo nṛpater nirdeśāt tajjñaḥ parīhāraḥ iti vyavasyet // II. lo. 42

nisṛṣṭisthāpanā kāryakāraṇe vacane tathā /
eṣa vācikalekhaḥ syāt bhaven naisṛṣṭiko'pi vā // II. lo. 43

vividāṃ daivasaṃyuktāṃ tattvajāṃ caiva mānuṣīm /
dvividhāṃ tāṃ vyavasyanti pravṛttiṃ śāsanaṃ prati // II. lo. 44

dṛṣṭvā lekhaṃ yathātattvaṃ tataḥ pratyanubhāṣya ca /
pratilekho bhavet kāryo yathā rājavacas tathā // II. lo. 45

yatreṣvarāṃś ādhikṛtāṃś ca rājā rakṣopakārau pathikārtham āha /
sarvatrago nāma bhavet sa mārge deśe ca sarvatra ca veditavyaḥ // II. lo. 46

116 *rājalekhyaṃ sthānakṛtaṃ svahastalikhitaṃ tathā /*
lekhyaṃ tat trividhaṃ proktaṃ bhinnaṃ tad bahudhā punaḥ // *Bṛ.S.* VI. 4.

117 *saptadhā laukikaṃ lekhyaṃ trividhaṃ rājaśāsanam.* Ibid. VI. 5
These three are: *śāsana, jayapatra* and *prasādapatra*. For elaboration see *Bṛ.S.* VI. 2o-29.

118 *laukikaṃ rajākīyaṃ ca lekhyaṃ vidyād dvilakṣaṇam.* Q. in *Sm.C.*, p. 125.
See also the same view of Saṃgrahakāra recorded in *Sm.C.*, p. 125.

119 *śāsanaṃ prathamaṃ jñeyaṃ jayapatraṃ tathāparam /*
ājñāprajñāpanapatraṃ rājakīyaṃ caturvidham // Q. in *Sm.C.*, p. 125.
For fivefold classification see *Sarasvatīvilāsa*, pp. 111 ff. For detailed information relating to documents reference may be made to:

Reference has already been made to *sampratipatti* in the context of our discussion on *dharma*. Some more references are being noted here. The last of the *nirṇayas* recognised by Vyāsa is *vādisampratipatti* (Vyāsa, verse 1) i.e. admission by the person accused. Vyāsa himself in the context of delineating different varieties of *uttara* (reply) defines *sampratipatti* as admission by the accused of the charge levelled against him.[12o] In such a case, as is quite evident, the adjudicators are not to be in trouble of demanding other modes of proof and going through the technicalities for the ascertainment of truth, as rightly pointed out by Vijñāneśvara having support from the text of Hārīta.[121] This step helps us to understand Nārada's

119 (cont.)

Yāj. II. 84-94; Nārada IV. 69-75; Kāt. verses 249-312; see also Kane *History of Dharmaśāstra*, III, pp. 3o8-312; specially, A. Thakur, *Hindu Law of Evidence*, pp. 2oo-21o.

12o *sādhyasya satyavacanaṃ pratipattir udāhṛtā*. Vyāsa, verse 24. The same line with identical wordings has been attributed to Kātyāyana by Vijñāneśvara on Yāj., II. 7. See *Kātyāyanasmṛtisāroddhāra*, verse 168. It should be noted in this context that uttara has been classified as of four types: *mithyā, sampratipatti, pratyavaskandana* and *pūrvanyāya*. See Nārada, II. 4; Kāt. verse 165; Bṛhaspati III. 6. Bṛhaspati has the following definition of *sampratipatti* type of reply:

śrutvābhiyogaṃ pratyarthī yadi tat pratipadyate /
sā tu sampratipattis tu (°ḥ syāt) śāstravidbhir udāhṛtā // Bṛ.S. III. 18. S
anuktvā kāraṇaṃ yatra pakṣaṃ vādī prapadyate /
pratipattis tu sā jñeyā kāraṇaṃ tūttaraṃ pṛthak // Ibid. III. 14.

Devaṇabhaṭṭa refers to a text of Prajāpati for the definition of this uttatra: *asyaiva deyam evaitat nāsadbhāṣitam arthinā /*
iti sampratipattyākhyaṃ dvitīyam idam uttaram // Sm.C., Vy.Kā.,

121 *ataś ca sampratipattyuttare sādhyābhāvena bhāṣottaratvādinor dvayor apy arthitvābhāvāt sādhananirdeśa eva nāstīti tāvataiva vyavahāraḥ parisamāpyata iti gamyate*. On Yāj., II. 7. The text of Hārīta has been quoted in support: *prānnyāyakāraṇoktau tu pratyarthī nirdiśet kriyām /*
mithyoktau pūrvavādī tu pratipattau na sā bhavet //

statement relating to the *dharma* variety of *vyavahāra* that *dharma* is based on truth (*satya*) (Nārada 1.11).[122]

From an analysis of the verses of Vyāsa relating to *nirṇaya* it may be stated that in adjustment with the four varieties of *nirṇaya* of Bṛhaspati (1.18), the eight types of *nirṇaya* propounded by Vyāsa (verse 1) may be explained to be practically of four types, of course with the addition of a new one, namely, *hetu*. *Pramāṇa* and *śapatha* of Vyāsa may be stated to be included under *vyavahāra*; and *sampratipatti* under *dharma*. *Caritra* and *nṛpājñā* are directly mentioned both by Bṛhaspati and Vyāsa. *Hetu* or *anumāna* is an additional one, but on this point it may be stated that this has been recognised by all the writers on law in some form or other.

In this context a question connected with *nirṇaya* should be hinted at. Whatever be the decision, it is befitting that it should have a record for future reference. Nārada accordingly states that a *jayapatra* (a document of victory in the suit) should be issued to the victorious party in a particular form.[123] One should note with interest that Varadarāja in his

122 The text of Kauṭilya is helpful in interpretation where the term used is *svayaṃvāda*: *dṛṣṭadoṣaḥ svayaṃvādaḥ svapakṣaparapakṣayoḥ /*
anuyogārjavaṃ hetuḥ śapathaś cārthasādhakaḥ // *A.Ś.* III. 1. 46

123 *sabhyair eva jitaḥ paścād rājñā śāsyaḥ svaśāstrataḥ /*
jayāne vāpi deyaṃ syād yathāvaj jayapatrakam // *N.S.* II. 43.
Bṛhaspati has definition of *jayapatra* as also of the contents of the same in the following lines:
pūrvottarakriyāvādanirṇayānte yadā nṛpaḥ /
pradadyāj jayine lekhyaṃ jayapatram tad ucyate // *Bṛ.S.* VI. 26

yad vṛttaṃ vyavahāre tu pūrvapakṣottarādikam /
kriyāvadhāraṇopetaṃ jayapatre'khilaṃ likhet // Ibid. VI. 27

sādhayet sādhyam arthaṃ tu catuṣpādanvitaṃ jaye /
rājamudrānvitaṃ caiva jayapatrakam iṣyate // Ibid. VI. 28

anyavādyādihīnebhya itareṣāṃ pradīyate /
vṛttānuvādasaṃsiddhaṃ tac ca syād jayapatrakam // Ibid. VI. 29
We have also from Vyāsa some verses relating to *jayapatra* thus:

123 (cont.)

vyavahārān svayaṃ dṛṣṭvā śrutvā vā prāḍvivākataḥ /
jayapatram tato dayāt parijñānāya pārthivaḥ // Verse 5o

pūrvottarakriyāpādaṃ pramāṇaṃ tatparīkṣaṇam /
nigadaṃ smṛtivākyaṃ ca yathāsabhyaṃ viniścitam //
etat sarvam samasena jayapatre vilikhayet // Verse 51

jaṅgamam sthāvaram yena pramāṇenātmasātkṛtam /
bhāgābhiśāpasandigdhe yaḥ samyag vijayī bhavet /
tasmai rājñā pradātavyam jayapatraṃ suniścitam // Verse 52.

Verse 5o of Vyāsa has also been ascribed to Kātyāyana for which see Kātyāyana's *Smṛtisāroddhāra* (verse 476). Kātyāyana refers in this context to a judgement called technically *paścātkāra*, wherein the prescribed modes of proof are resorted to by the litigant:

anena vidhinā lekhyaṃ paścātkāraṃ vidur budhāḥ /
nirastā tu kriyā yatra pramāṇenaiva vādinā /
paścātkāro bhavet tatra na sarvāsu vidhīyate // Kāt. 264.

Jayapatra, according to Kātyāyana, is issued to those who are'cast off (in their cause) because they aver something other (than that was first stated) and other *hīnavādīs* and which contains a recital of what happened':

anyavādyādihīnebhyaḥ itareṣāṃ pradīyate /
vṛttanuvādasaṃsiddhaṃ tac ca syād jayapatrakam // Kāt. 265.

For an informative discussion on *jayapatra* see the commentary of Vijñāneśvara on *Yājñavalkya* II. 91. For interesting facts relating to documentary evidences of *jayapatras* see Kane, *History of Dharmaśāstra*, III, p. 381 ff. where there are references to Jolly's communication regarding a *jayapatra* in ancient Javanese as recorded in 25 *Calcutta Weekly Notes*, pp. CXLII-III; K.P. Jawaswal's paper in the same Journal in No. 24, pp. CXLIX-CLVI relating to a *jayapatra* granted by the Hindu Court in Mithilā in Śake 1716 (1794 A.D.) and in *Journal of the Bihar and Orissa Res. Soc.*, vol. VI, pp. 246-258. These records show that such *jayapatras* conform strictly to the formalities prescribed in the *śāstras*. It is interesting that the judgement was written and signed by the Chief of the Judges, named therein as Sacalamiśra and was addressed to the *dharmādhyakṣas* - the members constituting the assembly, as also to the *paṇḍitas*, seven of whom recorded their *sammati* (concurrence) at the top of the document.

For informations relating to nine such Sanskrit *jayapatras* from the courts

Vyavahāranirṇaya expresses his view that in the case where a dispute is decided by a domestic tribunal a *nirṇaya**-*patra* in place of a *jayapatra* is to be issued.[124]

123 (cont.)

of Mithila in the 18th and 19th centuries, see *Journal of the Bihar and Orissa Research Society*, vol. XXVIII, 1942.

Reference here should be made to *hīnapatra*, perhaps a document of defeat, mentioned by Vijñāneśvara (on *Yāj*. II. 91):

yatra tu hīnatā... tatra na jayapatrakam asti, api tu hīnapatrakam eva. tac ca kalantare daṇḍapraptyartham, jayapatraṃ tu prānnyāyavidhisiddhyartham iti viśeṣaḥ.

For more scholastic discussion on the point see: A. Thakur, *Hindu Law of Evidence*, pp. 21o-219.

124 *kulādibhir nirṇaye* jayapatrābhāvāt nirṇayapatram tatra kāryam, pratta-patram* (dif. reading: *vṛttapatram) iti yāvat*. p. 85.

For the word *kulādi* see Nārada 1. 7:

kulāni śreṇayaś caiva gaṇaś cādhikṛto nṛpaḥ /
pratiṣṭhā vyavahārāṇāṃ gurv ebhyas tūttarottaram //

List of abbreviations

Arthaśāstra = *A.Ś.*

Bṛhaspatismṛti = *Bṛ.S.*

Gautamadharmasūtra = *G.D.S.*

Kātyāyanasmṛtisāroddhāra = *Kāt.*

Manusmṛti = *M.S.*

Nāradasmṛti = *N.S.*

Nāradīyamanusaṃhitā = *N.M.S.*

Sarasvatīvilāsa = *S.V.*

Smṛticandrikā = *Sm.C.*

Vasiṣṭhadharmaśāstra = *V.D.S.*

Vīramitrodaya, vyavahāraprakāśa = *Vīr.Vy.Pr.*

Yājñavalkyasmṛti = *Y.S.; Yāj.*

Bibliography of texts utilised

Original texts - Smṛtis

Manusmṛti, with the commentary of Medhātithi, ed. G.N. Jha (B.I. Series, Calcutta, 1939).

Manusmṛti, with the commentary of Bhāruci, ed. J.D.M. Derrett, Wiesbaden, 1975.

Yājñavalkyasmṛti, with the comm. of Vijñāneśvara, ed. N.R. Acharya, Bombay, 1949.

Nāradasmṛti, with extracts from *Asahāyabhāṣya*, ed. J. Jolly, (B.I. Series, Calcutta, 1885).

Nāradīyamanusaṃhitā, with the comm. of Bhavasvāmī, ed. K. Sambasiva Sastri, (T.S.S., 1929).

Kātyāyanasmṛtisāroddhāra, ed. P.V. Kane (with English translation and notes), Bombay, 1933.

Bṛhaspatismṛti, ed. K.V.R. Aiyangar, (G.O.S., LXXXV, Baroda, 1941).

Vyāsasmṛti, *Vyavahāra* chapter, ed. B.K. Ghosh, Calcutta, 1944.

Digests - Nibandhas

Smṛticandrikā by Devaṇabhaṭṭa, *Vyavahārakāṇḍa*, pt. I, ed. L. Srinivasacharya, Mysore, 1914.

Sarasvatīvilāsa, *Vyavahārakāṇḍa* by Pratāparudra, ed. R. Shama Sastry, Mysore, 1927.

Vīramitrodaya (Vyavahāraprakāśa) by Mitramiśra, ed. V.P. Bhandari, Chowkhamba Sanskrit Series, Benares, 1932, vol. VIII.

Dāyabhāga by Jīmūtavāhana, ed. H. Chatterjee, Calcutta, 1978.

Divyatattva, ed. Richard W. Lariviere, Delhi, 1981.

vyavahāracintamaṇi, ed. Ludo Rocher, Gent, 1956.

vyavahāranirṇaya by Varadarāja, ed. K.V. Rangasvami Aiyangar and A.N. Kr Aiyangar, Adyar, 1942.

Vyavahāramayūkha by Bhaṭṭa Nīlakaṇṭha, ed. P.V. Kane, Poona, 1926.

Texts other than Dharmaśāstra

Arthaśāstra of Kauṭilya, ed. in two vols. R.P. Kangle (University of Bom Series, pt. I, 197o; pt. II, 1972), the second part contains English tra lation and critical notes.

Translation of texts

Translation of the *Nāradasmṛti* and the *Bṛhaspatismṛti* by J. Jolly in the Series of Sacred Books of the East, vol. XXXIII, Oxford, 1889.

J. Duncan M. Derrett, *Bhāruci's Commentary on the Manusmṛti*. Vol. 1: *The Text*; Vol. 2: *The Translation and Notes*, Wiesbaden, 1975.

Secondary sources

J.D.M. Derrett, *Religion, Law and the State in India*, London, 1968. *Essays in Classical and Modern Hindu Law*, Leiden, 1976.

P.V. Kane, *History of Dharmaśāstra*, vol. I, pt. I, (revised and enlarge edition) Poona, 1968.

P.V. Kane, *History of Dharmaśāstra*, vol. III, Poona, 1946.

A. Thakur, *Hindu Law of Evidence*, Calcutta, 1933.

H. Chatterjee, *The Law of Debt in Ancient India*, Calcutta, 1971.

D.C. Sircar, *The successors of the Sātavāhanas*, Calcutta, 1939.

[9]

Matrimonial Property Law Among Hindus

RAM SINGH, LL.M.†

Since the dawn of early civilization women in India have enjoyed an elevated position so far as their proprietary rights are concerned. In certain legal systems, history bears sufficient witness to the perpetual tutelage and constant dependence of married women on men. This dependence is often attributed to their inherent weaknesses,[1] and their physical incapacities.[2] A married male, normally the bread winner in a Hindu family, has a distinct advantage in disposing of his matrimonial property and few cases ever reach the courts for adjudication. But as various complex problems arise in the fast developing industrial world, the normal control exercised by the Hindu husband over the matrimonial property is bound to be weakened by an egalitarian approach of the courts.

Thus, for the coming generations of jurists, the relationship of husband and wife with respect to their matrimonial property shall depend on the social and economic values attained by society. Here one is reminded of the caveat against setting forth too much legislation in the field.[3] Economic independence of married women in certain societies has given them

---

†Member of the Faculty of Law, University of Delhi, India.

EDITOR'S NOTE: *The editors wish to acknowledge the invaluable assistance of Mr. Deba Prasad Patnaik, Lecturer, University of Louisville, in translating the sanskrit portions of the footnotes to this article.*

1. *Laws of Manu*, IX, 311:

   "Women are not capable of living independently. In childhood the parents look after them; when grown-up the husbands take care of them; and when they are old the sons nurse and protect them."

   Yagnavalkyasmrti, I, 8:

   "The father, the husband, and the son are the only ones to support the wife, therefore in want or suffering women can seldom have independence."

2. Bhattacharya, Introduction to Hindu Jurisprudence 368:

   "But the physical incapacity caused by the bearing of children and by the cares of maternity places women at a disadvantage; and they are generally obliged to sacrifice their freedom and individuality to the male members of the community who take the utmost advantage of their position."

3. Freund, "*Matrimonial Property Law in England*," Matrimonial Property Law (Friedmann ed. Stevens and Sons, Ltd. 1955):

   "In a normal family it does not matter very much to the husband or the wife or their children what technique the law uses to regulate their property relations. It may be, however, very important for the husband's or the wife's creditors and for other outside persons. . ."

a legal control over their matrimonial property, and naturally the systems applied to determine the respective rights to property during the subsistence of the marriage or even after its dissolution seem to be leaning towards the wife. The various systems operating in different jurisdictions have been elaborately analyzed by the Royal Commissioners in their report on marriage and divorce.[4] Even this study, though nicely delineating a few jurisdictions,[5] has reached only a few broad generalizations about a few prevailing systems.

Matrimonial property law as it operates in various jurisdictions cannot be engineered into water-tight compartments, and realistic social and economic conditions do not permit such labels as "Community of Property System"[6] or "Separation of Property System."[7] At the utmost what can be indicated is merely the degree of control which either spouse possesses in relation to matrimonial property. Nonetheless, the separation

4. Royal Commission on Marriage and Divorce, Report 1951-1955, App. III, 392:

> "18. The other systems which a husband and wife may choose to regulate their property rights in the marriage contract are:
> (a) the system without community;
> (b) the system of separate property;
> (c) the dotal system;
> (d) the system of community of 'acquets.'
> 19. Under the system without community, there is no common fund but the husband is entitled to administer his own and his wife's separate property.
> 20. Under the system of separate property, husband and wife retain ownership of their separate property and may enjoy, manage, and dispose of it alone.
> 21. Under the dotal system the wife's property is divided into dotal property. The husband is entitled to the management and enjoyment of the dotal property, the ownership of which remains vested in the wife. The dotal property cannot in principle be alienated, but either spouse may apply to the court for authority to do so. The wife has full rights of administration and disposal over her personal property.
> 22. Under the system of community of 'acquets' there is a common fund, as in a full community system, but the fund is restricted to property acquired by onerous title (for instance, by purchase) during the marriage. In other respects the statutory rules of the community system apply."

5. Mentioned in a little detail in the Report are four different kinds of matrimonial property systems based on community of property: 1. Southern Rhodesia; 2. France; 3. Norway; 4. Louisiana (U.S.).

6. Friedman, "*Family Law*," Law in a Changing Society (1959) 239: ". . . Community property means largely that 'husband and wife are one and the husband is the one.' "

7. Freund, *supra*, 268:

> "It is difficult to imagine any system of law which, in its regulation of the impact of marriage on property, could completely ignore these elementary social facts; it is confined to a strict rule of 'Separation of Property' in the sense that marriage has no effect on the property of the spouses at all."

of property system has led to many innovations toward the goal of emancipating women, and has saved them from the treachery of being treated as a mere chattel as under Roman law.[8] In very early times in India women fortunately did not suffer much in the hands of their husbands with respect to their matrimonial property, and even under the system of land law recognition of separate property is found. This factor has given women a great amount of freedom in the field of their property rights and has succeeded in maintaining their independence, which was often a subject of contempt, particularly in the eyes of jurists.[9]

The legal history of India remarkably shows the unique independence of Hindu women with regard to their property rights. The whole range of property of a married woman known as "Stridhan," whose intricacy has lured a large number of jurists to deal with its subtleties, indicates where the systems of "Separate Property" and "Community Property" seem to be intertwined.

After going through the *Commentaries* of Blackstone on the laws of England and other treatises of his time, one is led to the irresistible conclusion that a married woman in England lacked capacity to acquire, hold, or dispose of property, and for all such transactions was dependent on her husband. It was through a gradual development in equity that the common law recognized separate property of a wife and gave her a right to dispose of it at will; in 1882 an English statute gave her authority over all her real and personal property acquired either before or after marriage.[10] This lead by Britain was followed by the United States, Canada, and other parts of the British Empire wherever common law carried the grass-roots concept of separate and equal rights of a married woman over her property.

"Stridhan"—A Landmark of Proprietary Rights of Married Women

An attempt to trace the germs of stridhana[11] has been

8. According to the marriage laws of Manu the wife was treated as the daughter of the husband, and the husband was treated as having control over the wife like *patria potesta*. Of course in Roman marriage, or marriage known as free marriage, the husband was not given any right to administer the property of the wife and he was also free from the obligation to maintain the wife of such marriage. For a detailed discussion see, Lee, Elements of Roman Law (3rd. ed. 1952) 68.

9. See Altekar, The Position of Women in Hindu Civilization (2nd ed.) 391.

10. For historical background see, Johnson, Family Law (1958) 85-91.

11. In an analogy stridhan may be understood as "peculium" in Roman Law or bride's "pin money" in England.

made even in the Vedic literature.[12] I shall presently discuss what constitutes stridhan and how far Hindu law has allowed the married woman to exercise her dominion over it. The term literally means "woman's property," but with the *smrti* and other writers it has almost acquired a technical meaning. An attempt has been made here to include only a definite class of property as the woman's property. To discuss its details would amount to a serious digression from the purposes of this article.[13]

Katyayana is possibly the first writer among the *smrtikaras* who has taken enough pains to devote at least 27 verses to an elaborate treatment of the subject. His classification of stridhan as "saudayika" and "asaudayika"[14] indicates the extent of

12. Kane, History of Dharmashastra, Vol. III, Ch. XXX, p. 770. Professor Jolly, however, traces its origin in presents made to the wife. See Jolly, Hindu Law and Customs (1928) 227.

13. Those who are interested in its niceties and subtleties may find an elaborate and interesting discussion of the subject in Benerjee, Marriage and Stridhan (Tagore Law Lecture); see also Kane, *supra*.

14. "That is known as saudayika which is obtained by a married woman or by a maiden in her husband's or father's house from her brother or from her parents." Katyayana, "Dayabhaga," ch. 4, sec. 1, para. 19. However, gifts made by a stranger during coverture, and property acquired by mechanical arts during coverture, were excluded by Katyayana from the category of stridhan:

> "The wealth which is earned by mechanical arts, or which is received through affection from a stranger, is subject to her husband's dominion. The rest is pronounced to be stridhana."

Vijneswar later took a more liberal view and included in the list of stridhan some five other kinds of property as stridhana:

> "That which was given by the father, by the mother, by the husband or by a brother; and that which was presented by the maternal uncles and the rest at the time of the wedding before the nuptial fire; and a gift on a second marriage or a gratuity on account of supersession; and as indicated by the word 'adya' (and the rest), property obtained by (1) Inheritance; (2) Purchase; (3) Partition; (4) Seizure, e.g. adverse possession; and (5) Finding; all this is stridhan according to Manu and the rest."

However, the interpretation which Vijneswar put on the word "adya," which was found in *Yagnavalkyasmrti* and expanded the scope of stridhan by incorporating five additional classes of property, did not find favor with the Privy Council:

> "The Bengal School of lawyers have always limited the use of the term narrowly, applying it exclusively, or nearly exclusively, to the kinds of woman's property enumerated in the primitive sacred texts. The author of Mitakshara and some other authors (that is of the Virmitrodaya and the Mayukha) seem to apply the term broadly to every kind of property which a woman can possess, from whatever source it may be derived." Sheo Shanker v. Devi Sahai (1903) 25 All. 468; 30 I.A. 202.

And thus the Privy Council refused to treat the following kinds of property as stridhan:

A. (i) Property inherited from a male by a woman. Bhugwandeen v. Myna Baee (1867) 11 M.I.A. 139.

(ii) Property inherited from a female by a woman. Sheo Shanker v. Devi Sahai, *supra*.

dominion which a married woman was capable of exercising over such property. A married woman could exercise an absolute and unrestrained control in the disposal of "saudayika" but could only do so with "asaudayika" after obtaining the consent of her lord. The married Hindu woman, who often has been treated contemptuously by the social philosophers for her laxity in matters of sex and morality, thus enjoyed the elevated position of being a full-fledged owner of a certain class of matrimonial property.[15] Relics of the past are still traceable amidst the Indian statutes.[16]

The whole idea of stridhan looms large for the economic independence of women during hard times; it may be able to spare her from want and be a sizeable shelter when she needs it most.[17] Normally ornaments worn by a woman were considered her stridhan even though they were not available for partition according to some authorities.[18] Neither the husband, father, or brother had power to deal with them in any way.

Undoubtedly this type of married woman's property has successfully protected many women from social insecurity and

---

B. Share obtained by widow on partition. Debi Mangal Prasad v. Mahadeo Prasad (1912) 34 All. 234, 39 I.A. 121.

It seems that the expansion suggested by Vijneswar of the word "adya" has been discarded in the above decisions.

15. So Katyayana declares:

> That which is received by a married woman or a maiden, in the house of her husband or of her father, from her husband or from her parents, is termed the gift of affectionate kindred. The independence of women who have received such gifts, is recognized in regard to that property, for it was given by their kindred to soothe them, and for their maintenance. The power of women over the gifts of their affectionate kindred is ever celebrated, both in respect of donation and of sale according to their pleasure, even in the case of immoveables." Katyayana, "Daya-Bhaga," ch. 4, sec. 1, para. 21, in Mitakshara and Daya-Bhaga, Two Treatises on the Hindu Law of Inheritance (Colebrooke trans.) at p. 66.

16. See Hindu Succession Act, 1956, Sec. 14.

17. Professor Jolly finds the germs of emancipation and independence of married women in their stridhan:

> "A gradual independence of the woman in the field of the partition of property is perceptible in the development of the stridhana." Jolly, Hindu Law and Customs (1928) 171.

18. See Kane, *supra*, where Vaijyant is cited as authority. For a more considerate view see Apastambha, II, 14; ix; Visnu, XVII, 22; Laws of Manu, IX, 200, and Katyayana, "Mitakshara", *supra*, at p. 30.

> "The ornaments which may have been worn by women during their husband's lifetime his heirs shall not divide; those who divide them become outcasts." Maxmuller, Sacred Books of the East (Laws of Manu) 372.

during their worst days they have saved themselves from the clutches of ignominy and humiliation. Stridhan has played a very significant role in the history of women's economic emancipation and has succeeded in securing an honorable position for married women in Hindu society. It should be remembered, however, that stridhan, although it has succeeded in maintaining some degree of economic independence, has not made any headway in permitting women to enjoy the equality of either status or sex. This undesirable phenomena was only noticed around the beginning of the twentieth century in this country during the germination of liberal legislation. In other countries the movement was comparatively advanced due to a developed industrial economy, and the married woman was better able to benefit from equality of status and opportunity in those countries.

In the field of law the year 1956 was a year of great achievements in India, particularly for women.[19] The Hindu married woman was placed on a par in regard to property rights with her counterpart in other emancipated countries of the West. The Act of 1956 did away with inequality of property rights based solely on sex. This achievement, a mile-stone on the march of women's economic emancipation, forcibly liberalized the outlook of men, and gave married women greater control over their property by altering the character of property which a married woman could hold under the Act. Now an emancipated Hindu married woman can face men at par, at least with the belief of gaining equal status in an economic sphere. However, a dilemma still remains to be solved. It seems that even such an egalitarian measure has not percolated the rocks of a social structure based on an agrarian economy, in which a married woman has little to do except share the burden of toil which spouses are called upon to share to achieve the basic necessities. This dilemma will haunt future legislators, sociologists, and economists, especially in view of the politically conscious Indian woman who knows that the underlying trend toward equality may become a reality.

19. See Hindu Succession Act, 1956, Sec. 14. It appears that our legislators in 1956 restored the wider view of stridhan, once taken by Vijneswar in his Mitakshara, and even included all sorts of property as woman's absolute which had never been treated as her stridhana, and which they could not precisely exhaust even though they attempted to do so.

Contracts and Spouses

In ancient times Manu, the law giver, seems to have been quite rigid in refusing to accept any kind of property ownership by a married woman, having said that whatever she acquires, she acquires for her husband.[20] Another authority laid down a general rule that nobody was allowed to lend any thing to a woman because her economic position was such that recovery of the debt was impossible, on the basis that women normally did not own any property, and that a debt made by a woman could not be repaid by her.[21] In spite of these injunctions it appears that women in the Hindu community have frequently borrowed to meet several types of unforeseen contingencies, and that the rule admitted certain exceptions. However, these exceptions were well known,[22] and the claim of a third party who has lent the wife anything under such circumstances will not be defeated by the plea of the husband that the debt was never contracted by him but by his wife.

However, there is nothing in the ancient or more modern law which prevents a third party from seeking relief against the separate property of the wife who has contracted a debt or taken a loan. At no time in history was a woman under Hindu law denied contractual freedom so far as her own personal effects and property were concerned. In repayment of debts the general rule had been that a woman was not bound to pay any

---

20. "Whatever is earned by the three — wife, son and slave — belongs to one, to whom they belong." Manu, Chap. VIII, sloka 417.

21. "Let no man lend anything to women, to slaves, or to children. Whatever thing of value has been lent to them, the lender cannot in general recover, without the assent of their master or guardian." Katyayana, as cited by Colebrooke, Digest of Hindu Law (1797) Vol. 1 at p. 16.

22. "Bhrigu ordained that a man shall pay a debt contracted in his remote absence, even without his assent, by his servant, his wife, his mother, his pupil, or his son, provided it were contracted for the subsistence of the family." Katyayana, as cited by Colebrook, Digest of Hindu Law, *supra*. Colebrook, explaining the nature of the debt binding on the husband but contracted by the wife, lays down:

> "Nor do we see any objection against loans made to women who have separate property, on the mortgage of their immovable property. A debt contracted by a woman, whose husband is absent, for her food and apparel, or for the support of her servants, must be repaid by her lord; and debts contracted by the wives of the herdsmen and the like must also be repaid by their husbands; we hold it a rational opinion, that there is no objection against lending money to those women." Digest of Hindu Law, *supra*.

debt except one to which she agreed, or which was contracted by her either jointly with her husband or by herself alone.[23] *Smrti*-writers have often taken a more realistic attitude in determining such issues and did not lose sight of the socio-economic position of a married woman in determining her contractual capacity. In those professions where the man supports himself only with the help of his wife, i.e., washermen, shepherds, actors, and sailors, the debt contracted by the wife is without exception binding on the husband.[24]

In cases where the husband and wife have joint ownership of property, neither of them is entitled to deal with it or alienate it without the consent of the other. This was the law even in the past.[25] In a case where husband and wife held the property in their joint names, it was decided that the property did not devolve on the husband by survivorship, but instead it devolved on her stridhan heirs.[26]

Loans between spouses under Indian social circumstances are beyond imagination, but the possibility of advancing such loans cannot be entirely overlooked. A wife who gives a loan to her husband is entitled to be repaid provided that the loan was not made for a use in which both of them were equally interested, or for the purposes of running the household. Under normal circumstances there seems to be no reason why equity should not come into play and require the husband to repay what he has received and used for some of his own adventures in which the wife has no interest at all; the law will not allow him to utilize the fortunes of the wife on his unwise ventures without incurring any personal liability.[27]

A wife is bound to pay the debts contracted by her husband before his decease, but this liability of the wife, like that of any other heir, extends only to the property which she has

---

23. Yagnavalkya, Book II, Chap. III, V. 49.

24. Yagnavalkya, *supra*, V, 48; Visnu VI, 37; Narada *I*, 16, *xxii*; also see Yagnavalkya, as cited by Colebrooke, Digest of Hindu Law, *supra*, 270.

25. "It is declared that brethren, husband and wife, father and son, cannot become sureties for each other before partition nor reciprocally lend their joint property nor give evidence for each other in matters relating to the common stock." Yagnavalkya, as cited by Colebrooke, Digest of Hindu Law, *supra*.

26. Muthu Ramkrishna Naiken v. Marimuthu Goundan I.L.R. (1915) Mad. 1036.

27. In England the social circumstances permitting such an evil were a precursor of the Married Women's Property Act of 1870, a measure by which the earnings of the wife were put away from the reach of the husband's obligations for certain purposes.

inherited from him. This well-known rule was recognized by jurists[28] even in ancient India, and is now confirmed by statute.[29]

After the advent of the British in India, a well knitted statute relating to contractual obligations came into being, and under that enactment there is nothing which prevents a married woman from entering into contracts.[30] Under the provisions of this enactment, a married woman is treated the same as a "feme sole" as far as her rights and liabilities arising under a contract are concerned.[31] She has full capacity to contract, and any distinction based on the status of being married has been ignored. In this respect she has been very fortunate and did not suffer the disability of like women in England. Although the feminist movement advanced rapidly there under the influence of persuasive writers,[32] England needed a series of statutes to emancipate women,[33] far more than were required for the Hindus in India. Since Christianity was the faith of a few under a colonial power like Great Britain, this necessitated laws designed to have nothing to do with Hindus or Muslims also.[34] Because of their peculiar circumstances,

28. "The heir who takes the heritage as also he who takes the woman (of the deceased) should be made to pay his debts." Yagnavalkya, *supra*, V., 51. The idea of joint liability in such cases is the result of treating the spouses as a single unit, and thus debts contracted when the spouses lived together are presumed to be for the benefit of either of them. Law relating to debts obligates the surviving spouse to pay the debts contracted by the deceased spouse to the extent of the inheritance from the deceased spouse. See Mulla, Principles of Hindu Law (12th ed. 1960) pp. 426-27.

29. Hindu Succession Act, 1956, Sec. 29.

30. Indian Contract Act, 1872.

31. Her position is often better than a "feme sole" in matters of raising loans, as her husband will be liable under quasi-contract or agency for reimbursement or fulfillment of the obligations. See Indian Contract Act, 1872.

32. See John Stuart Mill, The Subjection of Women (1869). The following year after this monograph was published, Parliament enacted the Married Women's Property Act, which protected the "daughters of the poor" who were not able to bring enough along with them at the time of marriage, and whose earnings, before the enactment, were even subject to attachment for the satisfaction of those debts of the husband incurred for his exclusive use.

33. The Married Women's Property Act, 1882, 45 & 46 Vict., c. 75, held women responsible for their contracts. Prior to 1 January 1883, the contract of a married woman was void, as husband and wife were treated as one person, but subsequent enactments progressively separated her capacity and gave her a status equivalent to that of a "feme sole." See the Married Women's Property Acts of 1870, 33 & 34 Vict., c. 93; 1874, 37 & 38 Vict., c. 50; 1882, *supra*; 1893, 56 & 57 Vict., c. 63; 1907, 7 Edw. 8, c. 180; and The Law Reform (Married Women and Tortfeasors) Act, 1935, 25 & 26 Geog. 5, c. 30; and the Married Women (Restraint upon Anticipation) Act, 1949, 12, 13 & 14 Geog. 6, c. 78.

34. Except when Hindus marry under the Special Marriage Act, 1954.

these religions were incorporated as exceptions to a few pieces of property legislation relating to married women.[35]

Contracts of spouses may conveniently be divided into two classes: those entered into between spouses themselves, and those into which a spouse enters with a third party. Further, there is a subdivision of each class of contracts: those made by spouses during coverture, and those made by the intended husband or wife. The following scheme attempts to survey the contractual obligations of the spouses.

Antenuptial Agreements or Law of Sulka[36]

Property which comes to a married woman as a result of an antenuptial settlement executed by her intended husband has been treated as her absolute estate.[37] However, spouses in India are liable to fulfill the obligations arising out of the contracts which they enter between themselves before their marriage, since Indian law does not recognize the principle of fusion of personality by subsequent marriage.

---

35. The Married Women's Property Act, 1874; the Married Women's Property (Extension) Act, 1959. These enactments do not apply to Hindus (see Sec. 2 of the Act of 1874) except for the enforcement of contractual obligations (see Sec. 7 of the Act of 1874). Similarly, the Indian Succession Act, 1925, which also does not apply to Hindus, maintains separate status of spouses and provides them with full liberty to deal with their property in whatever manner they like:

> "20(1) No person shall, by marriage, acquire any interest in the property of the person whom he or she marries or become incapable of doing any act in respect of his or her own property which he or she has done if unmarried.
>
> (2) This section (a) shall not apply to any marriage contract before the first day of January 1866; (b) shall not apply, and shall be never deemed to have applied, to any marriage to one or both of the parties to which professed at the time of the marriage the Hindu, Muhammadan, Buddhist, Sikh, or Jain religion."

36. Sulka: the fee which is variously described (i) as the gratuity for the receipt of which the girl is given in marriage; (ii) as being a special present to the bride to induce her to go cheerfully to the mansion of her lord; and (iii) as what is received as the price of household furniture, conveyance, milch cattle and ornaments. Mayne, Hindu Law and Usage (1955) 727. Presents to the parents of the bride to persuade them to marry their daughters are not uncommon in other countries. In 1963 the Minister for Justice in Kenya, who himself gave handsome presents to the parents of his bride at the time of his marriage, said that he hopes that brides in Kenya would be cheaper now. National Herald, 1963.

37. "They have no doubt whatever that, whether the deed is to construed according to English law, as Russel, J. thought or by Indian law, Kumari Bachubai took under it an absolute estate of inheritance." Lord Davey in Bai Kesherbai v. Hunsraj Morarji, 33 I.A. 176, 187.

Contracts During Coverture

A married woman in British Indian courts was treated as having joint status with her husband, and therefore the husband was liable for contracts made by her, although the trend of the decisions does not appear to be uniform. Generally, a wife cannot bind the husband without his authority. The binding force of such contracts more or less rests on agency principles. A wife is not absolutely prevented from entering into contracts. A Hindu married woman, of course, is not incapacitated in any way from entering into a contract on account of her marriage. There are occasions when the husband may be bound by contracts entered by his wife without authority, such as those of pressing necessity.[38] Normally the liability incurred by the wife as a result of her contracts is to be satisfied out of her separate property, particularly in cases where she has no authority to make such contracts from her husband.[39] Similarly, a married woman can contract jointly with her husband, and in that case her liability extends only to the extent of her stridhan.[40]

Torts Relating to Property and Spouses

Under Indian social circumstances torts between spouses are ignored and there are very few cases which are submitted to the law courts. However, the rapid change in the socio-economic position of women in India, and their growing consciousness of equality in the political and economic spheres, have permitted the resurgence of a new personality of their own, which will ultimately affect their outlook towards their legal rights. In the future, cases of tortious liability, which are thus far unknown, may form a class of litigation among spouses. One is led to believe that any Western impact would necessarily invite this result. Therefore, it will be appropriate to deal in a summary manner with a few of these principles as administered in the English courts.

Under English law a wife could not sue the husband for torts even after termination of their married status. But under the Married Women Property Act, 1882, every married

38. Pusi v. Mahadeo Prasad I.L.R. (1880) 3 All. 122, 124.
39. Nathu Bahi v. Jabher I.L.R. (1876) 1 Bom. 121.
40. Govind Ji v. Lakmi Das I.L.R. (1879) 4 Bom. 318; Narotam v. Nanka I.L.R. (1882) 6 Bom. 473.

woman "shall have in her own name against all persons whomsoever, including her husband, the same civil remedies. . . for the protection and security of her own property as if such property belonged to her as a feme sole but except as aforesaid no husband or wife shall be entitled to sue the other for the tort."[41] Under these exceptional circumstances alone could the wife sue her husband for the detention or conversion of her chattels,[42] or for negligence or malicious injury to her property,[43] in the same manner as she could sue any stranger. A revolution was brought about by the Law Reforms (Married Women and Tortfeasors) Act, 1935, under which a married women could sue for tort or contract but she still cannot be sued by her husband.[44]

In India suits between spouses to enforce contracts and tort interests are maintainable. Particularly among Hindus where the wife is treated as a part (rather half-part) of the body of the husband, marriage alone will not bar such suits, as the Hindu law has completely ignored the fusion of the personality after marriage of the individuals.

Presumption of Advancement between Spouses

If A supplies the money for the purchase of property and the same is conveyed in the name of B, the English law, in the

41. Married Women's Property Act, 1882, Sec. 12.
42. Larner v. Larner (1905) 2 K.B. 539.
43. Weldon v. De Bathe (1884) 14 Q.B.D. 339.
44. Webster v. Webster L.R. (1916) 1 K.B. 714 held that a husband could not get an injunction against his wife to prevent her from pledging his credit. This position was accepted by the Act of 1935. See Baylis v. Blackwell L.R. (1952) 1 K.B. 154, where McNair, J. observed:

> ". . . the observations of Lord Sumner in *Edwards v. Porter* (1925) A.C. 1, 38, to the effect that 'generally speaking the Act of 1882 was a Married Woman's Property Act, not a Married Man's Relief Act,' is in my judgment equally applicable to Part I of the Act of 1935."

However, sympathizing with the position of the husband, he further remarked:

> "Though it is true, as was pointed out in *Nordenfelt v. Maxim-Nordenfelt Guns and Ammunition Co.* (1894) A.C. 535, 553, that public policy may change and, in so far as the old rule against actions between husband and wife was based on public policy, the rule may be said to be no longer firmly founded (though if civil litigation between spouses was unseemly in 1882, it is difficult to see why it should be considered seemly today), yet, nevertheless, there is in my judgment a counter-vailing principle, namely, that the courts should not by over-refined subtlety of reasoning be persuaded merely for the sake of logic to weaken well-established doctrines of the law which have long been acted on by the public and their advisors."

absence of any other facts, will presume that A intended to pass the whole interest in the property to B, and not merely the beneficial interest. This is known as the doctrine of advancement. Therefore, where a husband provides the money to purchase property, but obtains the conveyance in the name of his wife, under English law the wife is treated as a full owner. The doctrine equally applies to the case where the purchase money was provided solely by the husband, but the conveyance is taken in the joint names of the wife and husband. In India, however, this presumption of advancement does not apply; therefore where property was purchased out of the joint funds of wife and husband, it was treated as belonging exclusively to the husband, and his wife was merely a benami for him.[45] Benami transactions are popular in this country, and though they are looked on with disfavor by the courts are nonetheless quite legal.

The doctrine of advancement could not secure a place due to the existence of this indigenous institution among the Indian people. Moreover, the social circumstances of the Hindus left no room for reception of the doctrine so popular in England. The benami closely resemble the resulting trusts which were an invention and perfection of the Court of Chancery in England. In fact, statutory recognition has been accorded to such a practice in the Indian Trusts Act, 1882.[46] But in case the surrounding circumstances of any case are insufficient to explain that by such conveyance the husband intended to pass merely beneficial interest to the wife, it will be presumed that the wife, instead of taking a beneficial interest, has taken an absolute interest in the property, and is no longer a benami for the husband. However, among Hindus it is not uncommon for the husband, either acting as Karta of the family or otherwise, to manage the property belonging to the wife, on her behalf, and therefore the rule cannot be applied without making sufficient room for the exceptions which may be admitted with the help of circumstantial evidence. The rule of benami is certainly not of universal application, and the fact of management and possession in the husband's hands will not disentitle the wife of her property.

In a recent Supreme Court case the husband had provided the money as a gift to the wife, and out of that money an estate

45. Parvati Ammal v. M. R. Sivarama Iyer A.I.R. (1927) Mad. 90 (D, B.); see also Sura Lakshmiah Chetty v. Kothandaram Pillai A.I.R. (1925) P.C. 181.
46. Indian Trusts Act, 1882, Sec. 81, 82.

was purchased in the wife's name, but which was managed by her husband on her behalf until the end of his life. The husband left the estate to certain individuals in his will, and such disposal by testament was challenged by his daughter claiming as the heir of her mother. Delivering the opinion of the court Gajendragadkar, C.J., observed:

> It is true that the actual management of the property was done by the appellant's father; but that would inevitably be so having regard to the fact that in ordinary Hindu families the property belonging exclusively to a female member would also be normally managed by the Manager of the family; so that the fact that appellant's mother did not take actual part in the management of the property would not materially affect the appellant's case that the property belonged to the mother. The rent was being paid by the tenants and accepted by the appellant's father; but that again would be consistent with what ordinarily happens in such matters in an undivided Hindu family. If the property belongs to the wife and the husband manages the property on her behalf, it would be idle to contend that the management by the husband of the properties is inconsistent with the title of his wife to the said properties. What we have said about the management of the properties would be equally true about the actual possession of the properties, because even if the wife was the owner of the properties, possession may continue with the husband as a matter of convenience. . . Therefore, we hold that the property had been purchased by the appellant's mother in her own name though the consideration which was paid by her for the said transaction had been received by her from her husband.[47]

Indeed the decision points in the direction that as a wife becomes a trustee under these circumstances, similarly a husband may also be treated as a mere trustee for the property of the wife. The application of the doctrine must be examined in every case on the facts, and mere facts of possession and management of the property belonging to the wife by the husband will not give him title to this property. At the same time the decision explains the application of the principle laid down in illustration (d) of Section 81 of the Indian Trusts Act, 1882,[48] and indicates that in every case the doctrine of benami

---

47. *Kanakarathanammal* v. *V. S. Loganatha Mudaliar* A.I.R. (1965) S.C. 271, 274.

48. "Illustration: (d) A makes a gift of certain land to his wife B. She takes the beneficial interest in the land free from any trust in favor of A, for it may be inferred from the circumstances that the gift was for B's benefit."

is not to be presumed without examining all the circumstances in which the wife was dealing with the property.

Disposition of Property by a Married Woman

Alienation of property by a married Hindu woman in India is not governed by her personal law alone. The specific statutes[49] as well as her personal law determine her legal capacity to dispose of the property which she owns either separately or jointly with her husband. There is nothing to prevent her from selling immovable property[50] or even that which is movable.[51] Similarly, she is capable of making a mortgage,[52] gift,[53] or an exchange.[54] Under the general law she is capable of making leases other than for agricultural purposes.[55] For agricultural holdings the law throughout India is not uniform, but even here a woman is capable of transferring her interest in agricultural land under certain statutes.[56] In certain cases she is even permitted to let out her agricultural lands provided her husband is suffering from some disability and is incapable of carrying out farming on her behalf.[57]

Gifts Generally

The law relating to gifts among Hindus is not of recent origin. Gifts to a bride at the occasion of her marriage or

---

49. See Indian Sale of Goods Act, 1930, and Transfer of Property Act, 1882.

50. Transfer of Property Act, 1882, Sec. 7.

51. Indian Sale of Goods Act, 1930, Sec. 4.

52. Transfer of Property Act, 1882, Secs. 7, 58.

53. Transfer of Property Act, 1882, Secs. 7, 122.

54. Transfer of Property Act, 1882, Secs. 7, 118.

55. Transfer of Property Act, 1882, Secs. 7, 105. However, the Act does not exclude the possibility of a married woman executing leases for agricultural purposes. This has been provided exclusively by special legislation in various states in India; the Act of 1882 does not govern such leases.

56. For example in Uttar Pradesh the Uttar Pradesh Zamindari Abolition and Land Reforms Act, 1950, allows the superior tenure holders, the "Bhumidhars," to transfer their tenancy interest. Sec. 152 provides: "The interest of Bhumidhar shall be transferable. . ." However, in case the married woman happens to be a "Sirdar" or an "Asami," other inferior classes of tenure holders, she is not allowed to transfer. U.P.Z.A. and L.R. Act, 1950, Sec. 153.

57. Sec. 157. Lease by a disabled person

> (1) A Bhumidhar or a Sirdar or an Asami holding the land in lieu of maintenance under (Sec. 11) who is:
>
> (a) an unmarried woman, or if married, divorced or separated from her husband or whose husband suffers from any of the disqualifications mentioned in clause (c) or (d), or a widow." U.P.Z.A. and L.R. Act, 1950.

Such incapacities of her husband include his lunacy, idocy, or incapacity to cultivate due to blindness or other physical infirmity.

afterwards by her relations, friends, parents, and even her husband, have been a constant source of new acquisitions over which she has exercised unrestrained powers even during her coverture. However, gifts which are often given jointly to bride and bridegroom at the time of their marriage have become a subject of much litigation between spouses.

Katyayana refers to a cross classification of stridhan properties with reference to the independent power of a woman to dispose of it. He terms such properties "saudayika" stridhana. "That which is obtained by a married woman or a maiden in the house of her husband or of her father, from her brother[58] or from her parents, is termed saudayika."[59]

Another cross division of stridhana is "yautaka" and "ayautaka." According to Virmitrodaya, whatever is given at the time of marriage to the bride and bridegroom sitting upon the same seat is called "yautaka," derived from "what belongs to the yutau (or the two united)." "Ayautaka" is that which is not "yautaka."[60] India shares a common experience with other countries in that cases involving gifts made at or about the time of marriage are not easy to decide as a practical matter.[61]

Gifts Between Spouses

A gift made by the husband to his wife normally has been treated as her stridhana, of which she was absolute owner, and which descended to her heirs and not to the heirs of her husband. This rule prevails even now. Often the question has arisen whether the wife took such gift as absolute owner under

58. The Dayabhaga reads "from her husband" instead of "from her brother."

59. Katyayana as cited in Mitakshara, Smrti-Chandrika, Mayukha and Virmitrodaya. For a similar text ascribed to Vyas see Smrti-Chandrika IX, pp. ii, 6.

60. "Yautaka" includes all gifts made during the marriage ceremony, whereas "Ayautaka" includes all gifts made either before or after the marriage. See Muthukaruppa v. Sellathammal I.L.R. (1916) 39 Mad. 298, 300; also Mayne, Hindu Law and Usage (1953) 728.

61. In England, Goddard, C.J., in Hichens v. Hichens, L.R. (1945) pp. 23, 26, observed:

> As everybody knows, it is often difficult to decide questions of property between husband and wife according to their strict rights. The matter very often comes up with regard to wedding presents, which in one sense are given to both spouses. One often has to solve the problem by saying that if a present was given by a friend or relation of the wife's, the property should be given to the wife and that it should be given to the husband if it was a present from a friend or relation of his.

all the circumstances or whether her interest in the property was merely limited. The true answer probably depends on the nature of the property which has been given to her. If the subject matter of the gift was family property, the wife takes merely as a limited owner; the property reverts to the donors after her decease.[62] However, she takes as absolute owner when the words are sufficient to convey an absolute estate.[63] Of course, presumptions and notions of a limited estate in favor of the wife would not apply at all.[64] Such cases deserve a more liberal interpretation.[65]

Partition and Spouses

On account of the system of coparcenary, women in Hindu law are underrated, as they cannot be admitted to coparcenary. What a Hindu woman may get is merely a share, in case the coparceners ever divide, as the widow of a deceased husband who was a coparcener with others.[66] This right to share along with other coparceners is merely a matter of allotment, and she has no claim to it as a matter of right. In case a partition takes place among sons, the widow-mother is entitled

62. Hitendra Singh v. Maharajdhiraj Sir Rameswar Singh A.I.R. (1925) Pat. 625; for a different view see Manika Mudali v. Muthachi Kavandan A.I.R. (1916) Mad. 690. It may depend on the language of the deed. See Jagmohan Singh v. Sri Nath A.I.R. (1928) Oudh 203 (D.B.).

63. Hitendra Singh v. Rameswar Singh A.I.R. (1928) P.C. 112.

64. Ramchandra Rao v. Ramchandra Rao I.L.R. (1919) 42 Mad. 283. For such a presumption see S. Nataraja Sarma v. Rambhadran Naidu Garu A.I.R. (1916) Mad. 646.

65. Chetty v. Naidu (1919) 51 I.C. 217.

66. In fact it would be a misnomer to call her a coparcener because she can never be one, at least in the theory of Mitakshara. The Act of 1937 treats her like a coparcener for a limited purpose, but it certainly does not treat coparceny. Therefore in a Madras case, when the question arose whether on the death of the sole surviving coparcener, she takes the whole of the property to the exclusion of the heirs of such coparcener, it was answered by their Lordships in the negative. While discussing the scope of Sec. 3 of the Act of 1937, their Lordships observed:

> ". . . that the view of the Division Bench was fundamentally opposed to the concept of a coparcener under the Mitakshara system of jurisprudence, where only male members, born in or adopted into the joint family, could be regarded as coparceners. Prior to the enactment of the Hindu Women's Right to Property Act, a woman who married a member of a coparceny did not have any interest in the family property, and, after the death of her husband, she became entitled only to receive maintenance therefrom and not to a share therein. It was with a view to remedying this defect in the law and to confirm better rights on women that the Hindu Women's Right to Property Act was passed." Times of India, February 2, 1964.

to a share equal to that of a son.[67] Similarly, a wife cannot claim partition between herself and her husband, but in case partition takes place between the husband and her son, she is entitled to a share equal to that of the son.[68]

Under normal circumstances among Hindu spouses, or even when the relations are estranged, partition among them is impossible because they are treated as a composite unit, and they therefore possess, hold, and enjoy the property in absolute jointness.[69] If an occasion for separation without breaking the marriage tie ever arises, the husband takes control of the affairs of the matrimonial property, even that which the spouses hold in joint ownership, and at the utmost, the wife is only entitled to maintenance.[70] Of course the rules which apply to the administration of such property after the dissolution of the marriage are quite different. In that case the court, exercising jurisdiction under the Hindu Marriage Act of 1955, may make such orders as it may think just and proper, but only with respect to such property as was presented to the spouses jointly at or about the time of mariage.[71] The practice of courts in England in this respect is of immense value and great

---

67. Damodur v. Senabutty I.L.R. (1882) 8 Cal. 537; Damodardas v. Uttamram I.L.R. (1893) 17 Bom. 271; Chowdhary Canesh Dutt v. Jewach I.L.R. (1904) 31 Cal. 262, 271; Ishee Pershad v. Nasib Koer I.L.R. (1884) 10 Cal. 1017.

68. Dular Koeri v. Dwarkanath I.L.R. (1905) 32 Cal. 234 (suit for partition by son against father); Jairam v. Nathu I.L.R. (1907) 31 Bom. 54; Sumrun v. Chunder Mun I.L.R. (1882) 8 Cal. 17; Partap Singh v. Dalip Singh I.L.R. (1930) 52 All. 594; Dhanabathi Bibi v. Pratapmull Agarwalla I.L.R. (1934) 61 Cal. 1056.

69. The husband and wife are more like tenants-in-common than joint tenants with respect to their joint property, since after the death of either it does not go to the surviving spouse but devolves on the heirs of the deceased.

70. Hindu Marriage Act, 1955, Sec. 24.

71. "In any proceeding under this Act the Court may make such provisions in the decree as it deems just and proper with respect to any property presented, at or about the time of marriage, which may belong jointly to husband and wife." Hindu Marriage Act, 1955, Sec. 27. However, it is to be noted that this section does not authorize the matrimonial causes court exercising jurisdiction under the Act (the District Court and the High Court), to decide cases arising out of disputes relating to matrimonial property. Its ambit only extends to cases in which the question of property presented at or about the time of marriage is involved. Therefore it is only in these cases that the courts exercising jurisdiction can apply their yardstick to determine what is just and proper. In the interest of objectivity the courts may be guided by the principles enunciated in this behalf by the English matrimonial courts. See Derrett, Introduction to Modern Hindu Law (1936) pp. 183-84.

practical importance since it is based on principles of intention, source, and equity.[72]

Property of Spouses and their Testamentary Power[73]

The general rule before the passing of the Hindu Succession Act of 1956 was that a Hindu could not dispose of any interest by will which he could not transfer *inter vivos*. This rule was done away with after the above enactment which authorized a Hindu to dispose of his interest in "any property"

---

72. In Allen v. Allen (1961) 3 All. E.R. (C.A.) Lord Evershed, M.R., who was required to interpret the respective rights of the wife and husband with respect to a residential house, applied the test of intention. Similarly, in Hine v. Hine (1962) 3 All. E.R. (C.A.) where the wife paid part of the purchase price of the house out of her own savings and the husband subsequently paid off the mortgage, Lord Denning, M.R., directed that the surplus of the sale proceeds, after repaying the respective investment of husband and wife, should be distributed equally between them. However, the case determining the respective rights of the spouses are not free from difficulty. Bucknil, L.J., in Newgrosh v. Newgrosh (1950) 210 L.T.J. 108, remarked:

> ". . . (Sec. 17) gives the judge a wide power to do what he thinks under the circumstances is fair and just. I do not think it entitles him to make an order which is contrary to any well-established principle of law, but, subject to that, I should have though that disputes between husband and wife as to who owns property which at one time, at any rate, they have been using in common are disputes which may very well be dealt with by the principle which has been described here as 'palm tree justice'."

Dealing with the problem of wedding presents, Hodson, L.J., in Samson v. Samson (1960) 1 All. E.R. 653, referring to the opinion of Lord Goddard quoted above (fn. 61), remarks in a disapproving mood:

> "If I may say so, with respect, that seems to be eminently sound sense, but it does not purport to be a declaration of law. . . I entirely agree with the observations which purport to have fallen from His Honour's lips. I do not think that, as a matter of law, any intention is to be attributed to the donor. Where there is evidence of intention on the part of the donor, it may well be that wedding presents may be found to have been given either to one spouse or to the other, or to both; but where no intention is clear the court is fully entitled to draw the inference . . . that money and gifts in kind originating from one side of the family were intended for the husband and those from the other side, from friends of that party, were intended for the wife."

73. For a general history of testamentary disposition see Pal, The History of Hindu Law (Tagore Law Lectures of 1930 published by Calcutta University in 1958). For legislative history refer to Tagore v. Tagore (1872) 9 Beng. L.R. 377; Hindu Transfers and Bequests Act, 1914 (Madras Act No. 1 of 1914); Hindu Disposition of Property Act, 1916; Hindu Transfers and Bequests (City of Madras) Act, 1921; and the uniform act for the whole of India, Hindu Succession Act, 1956.

of which he is capable.[74] Even a coparcener was given the right to dispose of his interest in the coparcenary property, which he could not do under the law before 1956.[75] However, even now a Hindu cannot dispose of property to defeat the legal rights of the wife or any other persons whom he is legally bound to maintain.[76]

At one time the question of a wife's capacity to obtain property under a legacy was treated as a highly controversial matter. But it was subsequently settled that a woman who accepts property under an ambiguous will holds it not as a limited owner for life but as an absolute owner. Even under the old law, if the husband passed to his wife an absolute estate in the movable or immovable property, either by will or gift, the same devolved after her death on her heirs as her stridhana,[77] and during her lifetime the same could be disposed of either *inter vivos* or by will.[78] After the enactment of 1956 a wife may become an absolute owner of a variety of property, and under the provisions of that Act she is empowered to dispose of her separate property by will to her husband or to any other person.[79] There are absolutely no fetters on this valuable right of the married woman. With respect to those properties which she owns jointly with her husband, it appears that she can dispose of them by will only to the extent of her interest. In this respect her position can be compared favorably to that of a co-owner. Today she neither takes a limited interest under a will, nor is she incapacitated to dispose of the property belonging to her by testament. A wife stands on an equal footing with her husband in respect to her testamentary power over property; she can alienate it and it is heritable by her heirs. We are ushering in an era full of opportunities for wives, and their testamentary power of disposition is a means by which

74. As a general rule, disposition by testament was unknown among Hindus; under the old Hindu law one could dispose of only interests in property which were capable of being made the subject of a gift. With statutory authorization this position has now been entirely changed. See Tagore v. Tagore, *supra*, and Hindu Succession Act, 1956, Secs. 14, 30.

75. Explanation of the Hindu Succesison Act, 1956, Sec. 30.

76. Hindu Adoption and Maintenance Act, 1956, Secs. 18, 29.

77. Ramasami v. Papaya I.L.R. (1893) Mad. 466; Basant v. Kamikshya (1906) 33 Cal. 23. These cases indicate the validity of a gift made by a person to his female relations.

78. Surajmani v. Rabinath I.L.R. (1908) 30 All. 84; Fateh Chand v. Rup Chand A.I.R. (1916) P.C. 20; Ram Chandra Rao v. Ram Chandra Rao, *supra;* Janki v. Bhairon I.L.R. (1907) 29 All. 217; Damodar v. Purmananddas I.L.R. (1883) 7 Bom. 155.

79. Hindu Succession Act, 1956, Sec. 14.

they could assert their free will to its maximum advantage. Past inequalities in defining a wife's rights under a will have been curtailed, and she has emerged as a free model of self-assertion.[80]

Divorce and Afterwards

In the past divorce other than customary was unknown among Hindus, and questions involving the respective rights of spouses over matrimonial property never arose except where inheritance was involved. However, in the lower section of society where customary divorce was practiced, the wife who deserted her husband was bound to refund to him whatever she had received during the marriage or afterwards.[81] In general, mutual gifts and presents were exceptions to the above rule in all other sections of society.[82] However, it seems that the rules in this respect were not fixed, and the husband had the lion's share in the matrimonial property.

With the coming of the Hindu Marriage Act of 1955 the law was no longer worried about the disposal of matrimonial property, as that Act incorporated divorce as a remedy to terminate the married status of the spouses. To cope with the impending problem of determining proprietary rights, the Act provided that the property jointly presented to the spouses at or about the time of marriage may be disposed of by the court as it may think just and proper.[83] The expression "jointly" in the Act is of significance; it demarcates the limits of the matri-

80. The innumerable inequities suffered by a married Hindu woman with respect to her proprietary rights may be located in the juristic writings of the ancient law-givers. The customs then prevalent in society are today fast withering as a result of the removal of the barrier of sex and the treatment of women at par with men.

81. This practice of refunding chattels and other property is not uncommon with women belonging to Chamar, Pasi, Kori, Dhanuka and other scheduled castes among whom customary divorce is quite in vogue. Apart from refunding the property received from their husbands, they are also often obliged to hand over custody of the children born out of the union.

82. Vatsyayana, speaking about the virgin widow remarried (Punarbhu) prescribes:

> "As to gifts of affection mutually exchanged between the husband and the wife, there is no fixed rule about them. If she leaves her husband after marriage of her own accord, she should restore to him whatever he may have given her, with the exception of mutual gifts. If, however, she is driven out of the house by the husband she should not return anything to him." Vatsyayana, 4 Adhikarana, Ch. 2, V. 46, 47.

83. Hindu Marriage Act, 1955, Sec. 17.

monial courts as well as their jurisdiction over the disposal of such property. This jurisdiction has been narrowed in two respects: first, by limiting it to property which has been given to the spouses either at or about the time of marriage; second, such property must have been given to them jointly. This construction is too thin, and a majority of the cases are left out of the purview of the Act. There are cases relating to various other kinds of property which become the subject matter of dispute between spouses; for example, the property given to them jointly in the form of gifts and presents from any source either "before" or "after" the marriage,[84] property jointly pooled by the spouses during their coverture for meeting the needs of the family and consisting of either their individual earnings or separate property, furniture, utensils, apparel, and other things of personal use which are clearly outside the purview of the Act. Courts are often called upon to adjudicate with respect to these matters while determining the respective rights of the spouses in the wake of the dissolution of their marriage, and no doubt the courts often meet with difficult situations while so doing. The distribution of chattels and other household articles between spouses after a breakup presents still more difficult questions. The better principle seems to be that the specific articles such as clothes, ornaments, and other personal belongings which by their nature are to be used by a particular spouse, may be given to him or her, but property other than this should be treated as belonging to both as co-owners and may be divided between them at the time of the dissolution of their marriage.[85]

The principles applicable in such matters are those of com-

---

84. These words have been carefully avoided in the section, and it seems that the property acquired either "before" or "after" the marriage has been left within the jurisdiction of ordinary civil courts.

85. Referring to such difficulties and their solution, Denning, L.J., as he then was, remarks in Newgrosh v. Newgrosh, (1950) 100 L.J. 525 (C.A.):

> "In the ordinary running of a home, where the parties agree to buy clothes or furniture, they may also agree to whom it is to belong; but if, as so often happens they have left that unsaid, the title to it depends as a rule on the nature of property bought or the investment made. It does not necessarily depend on who provided the money. If clothes are bought for the wife they are of course hers; if money is invested in the wife's name it is presumably hers. Conversely, where money is invested in the husband's name, it is presumably his. But if they invest money in their joint names, or if they buy furniture with it, which it is obviously intended as a continuing provision for the benefit of them together, it may properly be presumed to belong to them jointly. . . Full effect is, therefore, given to their intention by holding them to be joint owners."

mon sense. Application of formal and rigid rules of law will not be of much advantage, and, on the contrary, may perpetuate the trouble. The main reason for this is that spouses never pool their chattels or other similar articles of daily use with a view toward determining their respective shares in them, and their rights cannot be determined on principles of contract as none exist in this situation. As unsound as it may seem, it is nonetheless a fact that spouses never foresee the eventuality of divorce at the start of a marriage. It is also a matter of common experience that spouses do not intend to create any formal legal relationship when they use goods belonging to each other; it cannot be definitely held when one was acting as agent or bailee for the other. These are some considerations which prevent matrimonial courts from deciding the respective claims of spouses on more equitable grounds than the formal principles of law. The courts are rather handicapped in the absence of any fixed set of rules or a clear judicial practice in this area. Naturally, any tendency toward general principles of law and a resort to justice, equity, and good conscience encourages the play of a subjective element in the judiciary. A civil code, perfect in itself,[86] would avoid such mischief to a major extent, and it seems imperative that laws applicable to Hindus should be thoroughly revised and any lacunas or loopholes plugged through the legislative process. The judiciary, of course, might be helpful in doing this, but it inherently suffers from the same weakness for which the process of judicial lawmaking has often been decried: that it moves too slowly in comparison to the legislative process.

In disposing of property cases the civil courts of India generally make good use of general principles of law, particularly those of partnership, agency, bailment, and pledge.[87] General principles of law relating to joint ownership are frequently resorted to while disposing of such property. It cannot be said that this is a happy state of affairs. For a nation which has developed elaborate statutes for governing property relations with respect to its acquistion, enjoyment, and disposal, it seems to be a matter of mere apathy preventing the legislative machinery from establishing rules for disposal of

86. Of course even a perfect Civil Code admits the scope of gaps, and the caution posited by Cardozo, J., in "The Nature of the Judicial Process" will be taken into consideration by the courts on the basis of the peculiarities of each case.

87. See particularly the Indian Partnership Act, 1932, and the Indian Contract Act, 1872, and the case law developed thereunder.

matrimonial property either during the subsistence or after the dissolution of marriage.

The court under the Act of 1955 is required to act in conformity with what it thinks "just and proper." These words indicate their indefinite ambit, and place on the courts the burden of applying principles which may appear to be equitable and just. While handling the problems, the courts, either consciously or unconsciously, scoop precedents set forth by the English courts in this area. A sample survey, analyzing a few Indian cases, will acknowledge this debt. To illustrate by a single example, an Indian court will deny a guilty spouse any claim with respect to property on almost identical principles as those used by most of the courts in England. In brief, some of the generalized rules for enforcing claims of spouses with respect to their matrimonial property after the dissolution of their marriage are as follows:[88]

(1) Where either of the spouses has his or her separate property, this may be retained solely by him or her.

(2) Where the spouses have pooled their property, it should be divided equally between them irrespective of their respective contribution to it.

(3) Where either of the spouses has been found guilty of one of the matrimonial offenses, such as adultery or desertion, the guilty spouse should be enjoined to claim any share in the property.

(4) Gifts and presents made to the spouses, either jointly or singly, before, at, about, or after the marriage, either by parents, relations, or friends, may be disposed of in accordance with the following rules:

(a) Gifts or presents made jointly to spouses should be divided between them in equal shares irrespective of the source.

(b) Gifts or presents made individually to the spouses should be treated as their respective separate and exclusive property, and should not be divided at the time of the dissolution of the marriage.

---

88. The suggestions here in no way indicate an adoption of any particular legal system, but are based on the practice and law of both systems, separate as well as community property, and even more on equitable principles. Nonetheless, they venture to lay down some principles for legislation with regard to the social circumstances prevailing among the Hindu community.

(c) In the case of mutual gifts or presents made by the spouses, where it appears that the intention of the donor at the time of making the gift was merely to allow the other its beneficial use and not to pass the ownership to the donee spouse, such donee spouse must refund the subject matter of the gift to the donor spouse.[89]

The courts in every country face the difficulty of being umpire between husband and wife with respect to their matrimonial property. The tendency of the common law courts has always been in favor of a separate property system,[90] although the adoption of a community property system has been advocated from time to time.[91] Of course the fifty-fifty rule introduces what is known as community property where both work, and when the Court of Appeals in England allowed a deserted to wife to stay in the matrimonial home, it was interpreted as introducing the concept of "new equity." Similarly in *Bendall v. McWhirter*,[92] it was held that a wife's right to occupy the matrimonial roof survives the consortium.

The basis of these various rules of law seems to be the historical growth of the role of a spouse, particularly the economic role which he or she has played inside the family and the community. A survey of England reveals that the agrarian society of the past did not allow the married woman the same rights over property as her husband, whereas in the present in-

89. In Spellman v. Spellman (1961) 2 All. E.R. 498 (C.A.), where the husband purchased a car under a hire-purchase contract and gave the same to his wife as a gift along with the connected papers relating to title, it was held that the husband was still owner of the car and not his wife in proceedings under Sec. 17 of the Married Women's Property Act, 1882. The principal reasons advanced were: (a) the relationship between the two was informal as that of husband and wife usually is, and it was not to be decided by formal rules; (b) it is difficult to say that the husband under the circumstances can pass a title in favor of his wife by way of gift where under hire-purchase he himself does not own the property until all the installments are paid; (c) as papers relating to title were connected with the hire-purchase transaction of the car, possession of them by the wife did not give her a title to the property. Curiously enough the case deals with the modern problems of hire-purchase transactions which are getting wide currency in India these days.

90. The tendency of the textbooks in the field is to discuss the position under common law and the position gained under emancipating statutes. See Bromley, Family Law (1962) 400-41. For a more historical account see Report: Royal commission on Marriage and Divorce (1951-55) Part IX.

91. Lord Fraser's view is that "communio bonorum," i.e., a communion of all the movable property belonging to husband and wife, was an artificial concept and a mere legal fiction which cannot be reconciled with the husband's jus mariti. Fraser, Husband and Wife (2nd ed. 1876) Vol. 1, Ch. IX, cited in the Report, *ibid.*

92. L.R. (1952) 2 Q.B. 466.

dustrially developed society, although she has enslaved herself under the domination of her husband in the economic field, she is treated at par with most of the "feme soles." Now to a large extent she is capable of exercising absolute rights with respect to her separate property which at early common law were denied to her.[93] In the past a woman in England, as in many other countries, was exclusively concerned with the internal management of the home, taking care of the children and, in certain aristocratic families, controlling the domestic labor.[94] Apart from this her role in the economic sphere was negligible. Outside economic life, where the chances for acquisition were greater, was the sole domain of her husband. It is not surprising that under the socio-economic structure of such a society, where a married woman was denied from claiming proprietary rights, or equal status with her husband, that her personality was totally eclipsed by that of her husband in marriage. But now times have changed, and this will have an effect on the status of the spouses and their property relations.

Today a married woman is more secure economically, and she may legitimately take pride in a better status which allows her to exercise rights over her property. While governing the affairs of the home, the woman of today is also working along with her husband in earning the livelihood.[95] He is no longer the only bread earner, and in these changing and complex circumstances her property rights need to be redefined. Among Hindus the circumstances in which a married woman was placed about two or three decades ago are fast vanishing, and the gradual independence which they are gaining in the economic sphere is making them more vociferous in asserting their proprietary rights. This change is not confined to the "feme sole," but is more visible in the cases of divorce.

93. See the married woman's position with respect to her property rights before the passage of the Married Women's Property Act, 1882. Johnson, Family Law, *supra*.

94. It may be taken as a matter of great relief to the fair sex that their role in modern society has not been treated in any way inferior to that of their husbands. The Royal Commissioners record in the Report (1951-55):

> Sec. 644: In the first place, we fully endorse the view that marriage should be regarded as a partnership in which husband and wife work together as equals, and that the wife's contribution to the joint undertaking, in running the home and looking after the children, is just as valuable as that of the husband in providing the home and supporting the family.

95. See Copeman v. Copeman (1953) 103 L.J. 624, which involved a claim for possession of a flat by a wife against her husband, where Judge Howard applied the theory of "substantial bread-winner" to determine the proprietary rights.

For a legal order the problem brought about by this socio-economic revolution is a challenge to draft suitable rules with a view toward determining the "viniculum juris" between the spouses with regard to their matrimonial property. This disparity thus far between their respective rights deserves serious attention, with a view toward ultimately treating them on a par with men. It will not be out of place to mention here that the law governing the relations of spouses in connection with their property rights is meager and insufficient to meet the needs of a changing society. The misery becomes manifold when one comes across the scattered provisions which govern these cases. The factors responsible for this seem to be legislative apathy coupled with significant changes in the socio-economic life of the Hindu community during recent years, which undoubtedly demand more and better laws. The requirement is not to be met by merely falling back upon the general principles of law, but on the contrary calls for incorporating new legislative pieces in the system.

Till now the complexity of this problem among Hindus did not raise its monstrous head, as the women had a form of social security in their "stridhana," and there was little chance that their marriage would dissolve and place them in the position of a destitute or dependent on their paternal relations. In modern times a Hindu woman with the advantage of a liberal education looks at life from a different angle, and naturally the development toward her economic emancipation in the changing socio-political conditions of the country has compelled her to demand a better deal with respect to her matrimonial property, particularly after the dissolution of her marriage.

The Hindu community today needs a redefined, objective, and egalitarian approach to the problem through the legislative process. The opinion that the problem has neither engaged the attention of the community with all its seriousness nor is of great magnitude does not seem to be a sound one. In case due notice is not taken by the legislature, then there may be serious cases of injustice. To sit on the crater of a volcano without knowing the force of eruption and the possible degree of danger involved would surely not be wise. The advent of well-drafted legislative pieces, fully appreciative of the needs of society and meeting the demands which have been created by the changes of time, will always be welcome.

[10]

Hinduism and Human Rights*

Ved P. Nanda**

I. Introduction

Ever since the adoption by the United Nations General Assembly of the Universal Declaration of Human Rights,[1] the universality of internationally recognized human rights norms has been a subject of concern and debate, especially by those espousing cultural and religious relativism.[2] During the preparatory meetings convened in various regions of the world as precursors to the 1993 World Conference on Human Rights in Vienna,[3] governments advocated the view at the Regional Meeting for Asia that human rights be seen in the context of the religious and cultural setting as well as the national and regional setting.[4] It should, however, be noted that the Vienna Declaration and Programme of Action adopted at the Vienna Conference reiterated the universality and indivisibility of human rights.[5]

Thus, human rights concepts as viewed from the perspective of Hinduism is an important subject. As a preface to my discussion of this topic, however, it seems essential to provide the proper context by briefly describing Hinduism and its pertinent major tenets.

II. Hinduism and its Pertinent Tenets

As the oldest living religion, Hinduism, the religion of the Indo-Aryans, is called '*Sanatana*' *dharma* or eternal religion, based on eternal truths. It is also called *Manva Dharma*, the *dharma* of man, which was meant for all mankind.

Dharma, which is hard to define, has been appropriately described by Professor Kane as 'one of those Sanskrit words that defy all attempts at an exact rendering in English or any other [language]'.[6] He considers the conception of *dharma* 'a far-reaching one [which] embraced the whole life of man',[7] and continues:

> The writers on Dharmasastra meant by *Dharma* not a creed or religion but a mode of life or a code of conduct, which regulated a man's work and activities as a member of society and as an individual

*Adapted from a presentation at the Graduate Institute of International Studies, Geneva, in Spring 1995.

**Evans University Professor, Thomson G. Marsh Professor of Law, and Director of the International Legal Studies Program, University of Denver.

and was intended to bring about the gradual development of man and to enable him to reach what was deemed to be the goal of human existence.[8]

Dharma is that which sustains; it is 'the way in which the cosmos or the balance in the cosmos is maintained'.[9]

A modern jurist, M. Ramajois, has recently referred to one of the commentaries in describing *dharma* as that which 'sustains and ensures progress and welfare of all in this world and eternal bliss in the other world. The *Dharma* is promulgated in the form of commands.'[10] He continues:

> Therefore, *Dharma* embraces every type of righteous conduct covering every aspect of life essential for the sustenance and welfare of the individual and society and includes those rules which guide and enable those who believe in God and heaven to attain *moksha* (eternal bliss).[11]

The *Manusmriti*[12] describes the necessity of scrupulous practice of *dharma* in the following words: '*Dharma* protects those who protect it. Those who destroy *Dharma* get destroyed. Therefore, *Dharma* should not be destroyed so that we may not be destroyed as a consequence thereof.'[13] Ramajois explains:

> The principle laid down in this saying is of utmost importance and significance. In the above shortest saying, the entire concept of Rule of Law is incorporated. The meaning it conveys is that an orderly society would be in existence if everyone acts according to Dharma and thereby protects Dharma, and such an orderly society which would be an incarnation of Dharma, in turn, protects the rights of individuals. Rules of Dharma were meant to regulate the individual conduct, in such a way as to restrict the rights, liberty, interest and desires of an individual as regards all matters to the extent necessary in the interest of other individuals, i.e., the society, and at the same time making it obligatory for the society to safeguard and protect the individual in all respects through its social and political institutions. Shortly put, Dharma regulated the mutual obligations of the individual and the society. Therefore it was stressed that protection of Dharma was in the interest of both the individual and the society. Manu warns, 'Do not destroy Dharma, so that you may not be destroyed.' A 'State of Dharma' was required to be always maintained for peaceful co-existence and prosperity.[14]

Roughly 5000 years old, Hinduism prizes the most ancient book, the *Rigveda* ('Universal Principles'), and claims a following of 700 million people. The religion has endured while the ancient faiths of Babylon, Egypt, Greece and Rome have survived only in history books. Its strength lies in its unique ability to adapt itself to changing circumstances by reinterpreting early scriptural texts, while always retaining its core.

An important axiom of Hinduism is that God is omnipresent and immanent in all that exists in the universe.[15] Thus, according to Hinduism, this universal spirit or soul (*Brahman*) manifests itself in all human beings and indeed pervades all creation, as the very first verse of the *Isa Upanishad* declares: 'God covers all that moves in the Universe.'[16] What follows from this fundamental belief in the omnipotent presence of the Supreme Being is pertinent for our discussion of international human rights.[17] As a first corollary Hinduism firmly believes in universal brotherhood. Since God permeates every being, there is unity and equality in diversity, which *Bhagvadgeeta* describes in the following words:

A Seer is he
Who sees the immutable
In the body of all mortals;
And, realising
That the same Being
Equally exists everywhere,
He attains salvation
As he does not slay others
Bringing death to his own Self.[18]

Similarly, *Isa Upanishad* describes it thus:

He moves and is yet Immobile.
He is at once far off and near.
He is within all and also
On the face of all that exist.
Seeing this Supreme Being
As the beginning and end of
All beings and pervading all,
One can have hatred towards none.[19]

Hindu teachings reiterate the human goal of the realization of the Divine in everything, which means the unity of all faiths – that is, not only freedom from any hatred or malice to other human beings, but also an affirmative duty and obligation to serve God's creation if one is to attain the highest level of spiritual attainment in being identified with the Divinity.[20] The well-known Hindu saying, 'All humanity is one family', aptly captures this sentiment.

The second corollary is in Hinduism's belief in the oneness of all religions and hence its advocacy of universal tolerance – indeed, the total acceptance and rejoicing in differences. *Bhagvadgeeta* states it eloquently:

Whoever approaches me
In whatever manner,
I accept him.
All paths men are struggling through
Lead unto Me.[21]

What better expression of human rights, human dignity and catholicity than the following verse in the *Geeta*?

Impartial and equal am I to all beings.
None do I despise nor love more than any other.[22]

That India put this belief into practice is demonstrated by its willingness and ability to welcome and give solace to people of other faiths and religions from abroad, many of whom were facing persecution, such as Judaism, Zoroastrianism, Christianity, Islam, and others that were indigenous to India, such as Buddhism, Jainism, and Sikhism. More recently, it has given refuge to a large number of Tibetans who fled their native country with the Dalai Lama after the Chinese moved into Tibet.

III. Internationally Protected Human Rights in the Context of Hinduism's Basic Tenets

In the light of the tenets of Hinduism noted above, it would be a fair assessment that Hinduism would not find fault with the international Bill of Human Rights – the Universal Declaration of Human Rights,[23] the International Covenant on Civil and Political Rights[24] and its Optional Protocol,[25] and the International Covenant on Economic, Social and Cultural Rights.[26] However, critics are likely to point to some features of Hinduism which seem to be at odds with the modern concept of human rights. One such feature is the caste system. Professor Barnett R. Rubin has recently criticized 'the tenets of Hinduism as interpreted by the priestly stratum, the Brahmins, [which] sanctify inequality as institutionalized in caste'.[27] The second feature which follows from the caste system is untouchability which, in Professor Rubin's words, is '[p]robably the biggest obstacle to human rights ..., which while outlawed, is still widely practised and relegates a whole section of the community to "unclean" status'.[28] The third such feature relates to the status of women who, according to critics, belong first to their fathers and then to their husbands, as in other pre-modern societies.[29] These issues will be specifically addressed next and will be followed by a discussion of slavery and the place of humanitarian law in ancient India.

A. *The Caste System*

There exists a voluminous literature on the origin and development of the caste (*varna*) system in India.[30] After carefully studying the ancient scriptures, Professor Kane concludes that, in the earliest times about which literary record exists, there were only two *varnas* – the *aryas* and their opponents, the *dasyus* or *dasas*, who were later subjugated and given a position subservient to the *aryas*,[31] but that, later, 'owing to cultural advance, division of labour arose and numerous arts and crafts developed and they were in the process of contributing to the complexity of the system by creating numerous sub-castes based upon occupations'.[32]

It is, however, worth noting that, in earlier times, castes were not hereditary, as is demonstrated by a verse in *Rigveda*, where a poet exclaims, 'I am a reciter of hymns, my father is a physician, and my mother grinds corn with stones.'[33] In another verse in *Rigveda*, a poet asks the god Indra, 'O, indra, fond of soma, would you make me the protector of people, or would you make me a king, would you make me a sage that has drunk of soma, would you impart to me endless wealth?'[34] This shows that the same man could be a sage or a nobleman or a king, depending upon his desire and activities. In another ancient scripture, the Brahmanas, Kshatriyas, Vaisyas and Sudras, the four castes, are said to have sprung from the mouth, arms, thighs and feet of the Supreme Lord.[35] In the very next verse the sun and the moon are said to be born from the eye and the mind of the Lord. This shows that the composer of the hymn regarded the division of society into four classes to be as natural and God-ordained as the sun and the moon.

In later periods – no later than about 1000 BC – several castes and sub-castes developed, based on crafts and professions and subprofessions.[36] According to the Greek envoy to the Mauryan empire (around 400 BC), Megasthenes, Indian society was divided into seven castes: (1) philosophers, (2) husbandmen, (3) shepherds, (4) artisans, (5) military, (6) overseers, and (7) councillors and assessors.[37] Professor Kane offers the possible explanation that this mply reflected division of labour in a complex society where castes and sub-castes developed ı response to society's functional needs.[38]

Thus it appears that, during the Vedic period, equality of all human beings was reiterated 'ith no one being superior or inferior, all being considered as equal 'like the spokes of a 'heel of the chariot connecting its rim and the hub'.[39] Later, society came to be divided ıto four *varnas* on functional bases:

. Brahmanas, the class of persons in teaching and other learned professions;
. Kshatriyas, those who were warriors and the ruling class;
. Vaisyas, the class of persons undertaking trade, commerce and agriculture; and
. Sudras, the class of persons rendering all other essential services to the society, such as artisans.

ustice Ramajois explains:

> Even so the superiority or inferiority of an individual by birth in any one of these classes appears to have not been in existence. For instance, Valmiki and Vyasa, the authors of the two great epics, the Ramayana and the Mahabharata, who are regarded as the greatest poets, writers and philosophers of the country and who are held in the highest esteem down to this day by all sections of the society, belonged to the fourth and the second *varna*, respectively. This is also the case as regards the heroes of these two great epics. Rama, belonging to the Kshatriya class, in view of his superb qualities as a man and as an ideal ruler, has won a place in the hearts of one and all for ever. So too Krishna, the greatest of diplomats and warriors, and a great teacher, being the propounder of the immortal Bhagavadgita. Both these are adored and worshipped by all sections of the society as incarnations of God Himself.[40]

. *Untouchability*

'he impact of foreign invasions on Hindu India and the complications for a society striving ɔ keep its identity intact must be kept in perspective. With the onslaught of invasions starting ı 327 BC, India faced foreign armies, including the Greeks, Huns, Arabs, Turks, Afghans, 'ersians, Mongols, Portuguese, French and British, and came under Muslim rule in the ıirteenth century for nearly 600 years until the British takeover of power at the end of the ighteenth century. The practice of untouchability grew as those belonging to the fourth *varna* 'ere denied many privileges, including Vedic and higher education. Justice Ramajois explains:

> At a still later point of time, in the long meandering course of our history, the society got divided into innumerable castes and sub-castes. The evil of discrimination as high and low among men, on the basis of birth, hereditary avocations and other considerations, raised its head and the pernicious practice of untouchability with all its degrading implications came into existence.[41]

With India's independence in 1947 untouchability was constitutionally abolished.[42] The 'onstitution of India confers the right of equality before law and equal opportunity for all, nd prohibits discrimination on the basis of religion, caste, gender and so on.[43] However, ocial reformers, including Sri Chaitnya and Sri Ramakrishna, had been fighting against this vil for quite some time. Indeed, the most well-known of such reformers, Mahatma Gandhi 1869–1948), had as his life's mission the total abolition of untouchability.

C. *The Status of Women*

In ancient India, Hindu women and men had equal status. Professor Kane refers to specific hymns in *Rigveda* as composed by women[44] and cites *Bhadranayaka Upanishad* to show that women actively participated in philosophical discourses.[45] Women studied alongside male students, and women sages and teachers were not uncommon.[46]

During the *Sutra* period (800–400 BC) women routinely recited Vedic mantras. But, later the position of women became that of dependence on men. Women were not considered fit to study the Vedas, and rituals for girls were performed without the recitation of Vedic mantras.[47] However, family rituals required their equal participation with men.

While criticizing pre-modern Indian society, as other pre-modern societies, as discriminating against women, even Professor Rubin acknowledges that

> … [w]omen have a somewhat higher status in Hinduism than in some cultures, as their participation is required in some rituals (not only 'women's rituals') and some variants place great importance on *shakti*, or female power, as incarnated in goddesses such as Kali and Durga.[48]

Moreover, Professor Kane cites several instances where women ruled in various parts of ancient India.[49]

D. *Slavery*

It is possible that the opponents of *aryas*, the *dasas*, when conquered were treated as slaves, although the *Rigveda* does not refer to them as slaves.[50] However, in a later period, there are several references to the humane treatment of slaves, which indicates that, at some time, this practice developed. The *Manusmriti* places a slave

> … on the same level as one's son in the matter of corporal punishment. Thus 'the wife, the son, the slave, a menial servant – these when guilty of wrong may be beaten with a rope or a thin piece of split bamboo, but only on the back and never on the head, and if a person beat them otherwise he would be punished as a thief'.[51]

Slavery could not have been much in evidence in the fourth century BC when Megasthenes from Greece, who was accustomed to the treatment of slaves in his country, visited India, for he thought that there was no slavery. Justice Ramajois explains:

> On the whole, it can be said that, though providing scope for slavery was unfortunate, the provisions declaring forcible slavery illegal, prohibiting the masters from subjecting the slaves to cruelty and getting dirty jobs done by them and specifically enjoining that they be treated kindly, were some of the humane aspects of this pernicious practice.
>
> As regards right to property and right to enter into contract, the position of a slave under the ancient Hindu law was comparable to dependants in a joint family, like sons and wives, in that he could not enter into a contract which would be binding on the master. Even here there were exceptions. A contract entered into by a slave for family necessity, when the master was away, was binding on the master.[52]

E. *Humanitarian Law*[53]

Although wars were not uncommon in ancient India, they were to be undertaken as a last resort, for according to Manu, 'kings should aspire for more glorious victories than those of war; victories by battles were not spoken of highly by the wise'.[54] Similarly, Arthasastra declared that 'even when the advantages of peace and war are equal one should prefer peace for war causes loss of power and wealth and is troublesome and sinful'.[55] As one commentator observes:

> Generally speaking, kings in ancient India did not engage in war unless they were forced to it; military expeditions were begun, not on sudden provocation or on small causes but only after great deliberation and on weighty issues. So at least declare the works on Polity – Arthasastras and Dharmasastras alike.[56]

A declaration of war preceded the outbreak of hostilities. Such declarations were generally made through the *dutas* (envoys) in the form of the delivery of *sasanas* (royal writs) of an ultimatum. As Kautilya explains: '[w]rits are of great importance, in as much as treaties and ultimata depend on writs'.[57] Wars in ancient India were to be fought according to *Dharma Yuddha*, the rules of righteousness in war. As *Manusmriti* declares, warfare was to be conducted in a fair way and by open means.[58] The military organization of the time is described in Kautilya.[59] Specifically, according to Megasthenes, the military department of the Mauryan administration comprised a board of 30, divided into six committees: (1) admiralty, (2) army service, transport and commissariat, (3) infantry, (4) cavalry, (5) war-chariots, and (6) elephants.[60]

Manusmriti reflects the customary practice of refraining from the use of weapons which caused unnecessary pain or more suffering than was necessary to overcome the enemy. Certain methods of destruction were forbidden. Manu recalls that when 'a king fights with his foes in battle, let him not strike with instruments concealed, with barbed or poisoned weapons the points of which are blazing with fire'.[61] He further states that 'an Aryan who is in a chariot should never strike an enemy who is on foot, nor should an Aryan strike a suppliant, one who surrenders at discretion, non-combatants or one who is already fighting with another adversary'.[62]

Limits on the permissible use of force logically extended to a ban on 'ruthless destruction and sweeping devastation ... as is clear from the accounts of Greek travellers as well as from indigenous works of literature. Machines which caused wholesale destruction were of the *asura* variety and were certainly not recommended for use by men in war.'[63] Arthasastra lays down detailed rules regarding the time and region of fighting, the functions of the various divisions of the army, and the methods and uses of different kinds of battle arrays.[64]

A distinction between combatants and non-combatants was customary for the protection of the latter. According to Megasthenes:

> Whereas among other nations, it is usual in contests of war, to ravage the soil, and then to reduce it to an uncultivated waste, among the Indians on the other hand by whom husbandmen are regarded as a class that is sacred and inviolable, the tillers of the soil even when battle is raging in their neighborhood are undisturbed by any sense of danger, for the combatants, on either side in waging the conflict make carnage of each other, but allow those engaged in husbandry to

> remain quite unmolested. Besides they neither ravage an enemy's land with fire nor cut down its trees.[65]

Even among combatants, various regulations afforded them protection. Thus, under certain conditions, combatants were not to be killed, including a warrior whose armour had fallen off, who had laid down his weapon, was mortally wounded, who was weak with wounds, or was fighting with another.[66] Similarly, according to Mahabharata, some non-combatants were not to be killed. These included mere travellers, those 'engaged in drinking and eating', or those skilled in some special art, and those 'admittedly following peaceful walks of life'.[67] Prisoners of war and the sick and the wounded were to be treated humanely.[68] Likewise, elaborate rules governed the use of enemy property, treatment of persons in conquered territory and the treatment of conquered property.[69]

As to conquered territories, Manu urges alliances rather than annexation: 'While acquiring gold and territory the king does not prosper as much as he would if he had made a faithful ally, who would become powerful in the future.'[70] According to him, the customs of the defeated people should be respected by the conqueror.[71]

IV. Conclusion

Although the ancient Hindu law does not form the basis for the modern law of India, as reflected in the Constitution of India and India's legislation and judicial decisions, over 80 per cent of India's population professes Hinduism; and hence the question of Hinduism and human rights continues to be of vital importance.

Today, the people of India claim and enjoy full civil and political rights under the current legal framework of rights in the Republic of India, which is a federal, parliamentary democracy. The Constitution defines civil and political rights in its elaborate provisions on 'Fundamental Rights', which enshrine the concept of equality in law and protect the rights in a fashion similar to the Anglo-American system by granting the right to freedom of speech and expression, freedom of assembly, freedom to practise any profession or business and freedom to form associations or unions. It also abolishes untouchability and provides for special treatment of socially and educationally backward classes of citizens and tribes.

The Constitution of India also encompasses socioeconomic goals and objectives in its provisions on the 'Directive Principles of State Policy', which obligate the state to promote justice, equality and welfare and which parallel the rights contained in the International Covenant on Social, Economic and Cultural Rights. Although these are not enforceable rights in courts, they oblige the state to comply with these principles. Article 37 of the Indian Constitution reads:

> Application of the principles contained in this part: The provisions contained in this Part [Part IV] shall not be enforced by any court, but the principles therein laid down are nevertheless fundamental in the governance of the country and it shall be the duty of the State to apply these principles in making laws.

Justice Ramajois explains that 'non-implementation or violation by the State of the provisions contained in Part IV could be questioned or challenged by any method other than legal action. Therefore, non-performance on the part of the government in implementing these directive principles, or any action on its part in contravention of them ... [can] be the subject matter of public criticism, both in the legislature and outside, resulting in adverse public opinion against the government', although it could not be enforced through the courts.[72]

In the light of the sketch presented in the discussion in the first three parts of this article, it is fair to conclude that Hinduism and the modern development of international human rights are not in conflict; rather, they reflect similar values and are aimed at promoting human dignity.

Notes

1 GA Res. 217 A, UN GAOR, 3d Sess., pt. 1, at 71, UN Doc. A/810 (1948).

2 On relativism and human rights, see generally Christina M. Cerna, 'Universality of Human Rights and Cultural Diversity: Implementation of Human Rights in Different Socio-Cultural Contexts', 16 *Human Rights Quarterly* (1994), 740; Fali S. Nariman, 'The Universality of Human Rights', *International Commission Jurists Review* (June 1993) at 8; Reza Afshari, 'An Essay on Islamic Cultural Relativism in the Discourse of Human Rights', 16 *Human Rights Quarterly* (1994), 335.

3 Official preparatory meetings were held for Africa, Latin America and the Caribbean, and Asia. The text of the Vienna Declaration and Program of Action (UN Doc. A/CONF. 157/24 (pt. 1) (1993) is reprinted in 32 ILM 1661 (1993).

4 For a report of the Asian meeting, see UN Doc. A/CONF. 157/ASRM/8-A/CONF. 157/PC/59 (1993). See especially idem at 4–5 for the challenge to the universality of international human rights.

5 See UN Doc. A/CONF. 157/24 (pt. 1), at 20–46 (1993). Idem, para. 5 reads: 'All human rights are universal, indivisible and interdependent and interrelated. The international community must treat human rights globally in a fair and equal manner, on the same footing, and with the same emphasis. While the significance of national and regional particularities and various historical, cultural and religious backgrounds must be borne in mind, it is the duty of States, regardless of their political, economic and cultural systems, to promote and protect all human rights and fundamental freedoms.' Reprinted in 32 ILM 1661, 1665 (1993). Para. 32 reads: 'The World Conference on Human Rights reaffirms the importance of ensuring the universality, objectivity, and non-selectivity of the consideration of human rights issues.' Idem at 1671.

6 P.V. Kane (1968), *History of Dharmasastra*, vol. I (rev. edn Poona) p. 1 [hereinafter Kane]. Kane's five-volume definitive work is one of the principal source books on Hindu *dharma*.

7 Kane, vol. II, pt. I, p. 2.

8 Ibid.

9 See generally Ludo Rocher (1978), 'Hindu Conceptions of Law', 29 *Hastings Law Journal*, 1283, 1285.

10 M. Ramajois (1984), *Legal and Constitutional History of India*, vol. I, Bombay: N.M. Tripathi, 4.

11 Ibid.

12 See translation by Georg Buhler, entitled *The Laws of Manu* (Sacred Books of the East, vol. 25, 1886). *Manusmriti* is divided into twelve books and has 2694 couplets or *slokas*. Citations to *Manusmriti* are to Books and Slokas. Thus, VII.3 refers to Book VII and Sloka 3.

13 *Manusmriti*, VIII.15.

14 Ramajois, *supra* note 10, at 8.

15 *Bhagvadgeeta*, ch. VI, verse 31; ch. VII, verse 19; ch. VIII, verse 61; ch. XI, verse 38.

16 *Isa Upanishad*, verse 1. See also *Bhagvadgeeta*, ch. IX, verse 4; ch. XIII, verse 16.

17 See generally Durga Das Basu (1990), *Essence of Hinduism*, New Delhi: Prentice Hall of India, 36–47.

18 *Bhagvadgeeta*, ch. XIII, verse 27–28.

19 *Isa Upanishad*, verses 5, 6.
20 See, for example, *Bhagvadgeeta*, ch. V, verse 19; ch. VI, verse 31; ch. XIII, verse 31.
21 *Bhagvadgeeta*, ch. IV, verse 11.
22 *Bhagvadgeeta*, ch. IX, verse 29.
23 See *supra* note 1.
24 International Covenant on Civil and Political Rights, done at New York, 16 December 1966, entered into force 23 March 1976. UN GA Res. 2200 (XXI). 21 UN GAOR, Supp. (No. 60) 52, UN Doc. A/6316 (1967).
25 Optional Protocol to the International Covenant on Civil and Political Rights, 21 UN GAOR Supp. (No. 16) 59, UN Doc. A/6316 (1967).
26 International Covenant on Economic, Cultural and Social Rights, done at New York, 16 December 1966, entered into force, 3 January 1976. UN GA Res. 2200 (XXI), UN GAOR, Supp. (No. 16) 49, UN Doc. A/6316 (1967).
27 Barnett R. Rubin (1987), 'India' in Jack Donnelly and Rhoda E. Howard (eds), *International Handbook of Human Rights*, New York: Greenwood Press.
28 Ibid. at 137. See also M.N. Srinivas (1962), *Caste in Modern India*, London: Asia Publishing House.
29 See for example Rubin, *supra* note 27, at 137.
30 See for example Kane, vol. II, part I, at 18–104.
31 See ibid. at 48.
32 Ibid.
33 *Rigveda* IX, 112.3, cited in ibid. at 31.
34 *Rigveda* III, 44.5, cited in ibid.
35 *Purusasukta* X, 90.12, cited in ibid. at 33.
36 See ibid. at 49–50.
37 See ibid. at 50.
38 See ibid. at 48.
39 Ramajois, *supra* note 10, at 583, citing *Atharvaveda*.
40 Ibid. at 584.
41 Ibid. at 584.
42 See art. 17 of the Constitution of India (1948).
43 See arts 14, 15 and 16 of the Constitution of India (1948).
44 See Kane, vol. II, pt. I, 365.
45 See ibid.
46 See ibid. at 366, 368.
47 See ibid at 265.
48 Rubin, *supra* note 27, at 137.
49 See Kane, vol. III, 40–41.
50 See Kane, vol. II, pt. I, 180–87.
51 *Manusmriti*, VII, 299–300.
52 Ramajois, *supra* note 10, at 313.
53 I have borrowed in this part from my earlier work on 'International Law in Ancient India'.
54 *Manusmriti*, VII.198.
55 *Arthasastra*, VII.12.
56 S. Viswanatha (1929), *International Law in Ancient India*, 120.
57 *Arthasastra*, II.10.
58 See Viswanatha, *supra* note 56, 104.
59 See *Arthasastra*, Books IX and X.
60 Megasthenes, Fragments 35 and 36, cited in Viswanatha, *supra* note 56, 140, n. 1.
61 *Manusmriti*, VII.90.
62 See ibid., VII.91–93.
63 Viswanatha, *supra* note 56, 149–50.
64 See ibid., 150, n.2 for a succinct summary.
65 Megasthenes, Frag. 1, cited in M. Bhatia (1977), *International Law and Practice in Ancient India*, 100–101.

6 See ibid.
7 Cited in Bhatia, *supra* note 65, at 100.
8 See for example, Viswanatha, *supra* note 56, 154–55.
9 See ibid., 158–84.
0 *Manusmriti*, VII.208.
1 Ibid., VII.203.
2 Ramajois, *supra* note 10, 585.

Part III
Modern Hindu Law

[11]

RECENT DEVELOPMENTS IN HINDU LAW

By

GÜNTHER-DIETZ SONTHEIMER *

THE enactment of the Hindu Marriage Act in 1955 followed by the enactment of the Hindu Succession Act, the Hindu Minority and Guardianship Act and the Hindu Adoption and Maintenance Act in 1956 has opened a new chapter in the history of Hindu Law. On the whole the new Acts are viewed with relief by modern, western-educated Hindus who generally believe that the study of the preceding Hindu law has become a merely academic subject. However, a thorough understanding of these modern codifications, the social problems and their legal solutions involved, requires a more than superficial knowledge of Anglo-Hindu law (which is moreover only partially superseded by the new Acts), customary law, and the *dharmaśāstra.* Much of the way of life of the majority of Hindus is still intelligible with reference to these parts of Hindu law and, though it is commonplace to say that one can only assess the present and shape the future by analysing the past, this aspect tends to be ignored in a country which wants to forge ahead.

But whatever the practical values of a study of the History of Hindu law may be, there is no doubt that we still know embarrassingly little of the wider contributions to comparative legal thought and jurisprudence. Here interpretations are far from complete or final and sometimes suffer from the fact that Indian authors were intent to demonstrate the respectability of the Hindu legal system in face of unjustified generalisations by some Western scholars. In fact, a systematic and unbiased study of the *dharmaśāstra* can reveal for instance that nowhere in the world has more thought been devoted on the philosophical concept of Property and its legal implications than in India.[1] But in India

* Of the School of Oriental and African Studies, University of London. This paper is a slightly enlarged version of the talk given by Mr. Sontheimer at Cumberland Lodge.

[1] J. D. M. Derrett, "The Development of the Concept of Property in India c. A.D. 800–1800," 64 *Zeitschrift für vergleichende Rechtswissenschaft* 15–130; see *ibid. An Indian Contribution to the Study of Property* (BSOAS, 1956), xviii/3, p. 36 *et seq.;* see also Yvonne Bongert (Lille), "La notion de propriété dans l'Inde," *Etudes de Droit Contemporain* (Paris, Ed. Cujas, 1962), pp. 149–162. Professor P. V. Kane has only a short paragraph on the nature of Property in his *History of Dharmaśāstra*, Vol. III, p. 547.

the analytical study of Indian legal History is on the wane in spite of Professor P. V. Kane's and Professor Ganganatha Jha's numerous works which give us the means to proceed further.

1. *The Situation before the Codifications of 1955 and 1956*

If we have a cursory glance at the background of modern Hindu law, we find that the part of the *dharmaśāstra* called *vyavahāra*, or court-law, was administered until the early British period. The British administration of justice [2] faced the problem of applying a system of law which by then had widely distintegrated and given way to customary law which was administered in caste and family councils, though the *śāstra* remained influential in the background. The traditional method according to the *dharmaśāstra* was initially carried on by a few Indian authors, like Jagannātha, whose *Vivādabhangārnava*, better known after its translator as *Colebrooke's Digest*, admirably interpreted ancient sources and their medieval annotations in the light of modern developments. But the traditional system was too flexible and slow and its technique was often not known to British judges, and as a consequence theoretically accessible sources of law were not developed. Especially in the beginning only a few works had been published and translated and the employment of court pandits did not prevent Hindu law eventually taking a different shape, because after a sufficient amount of case law had been built up the rule of *stare decisis* emerged as a predominant source of authority. The notion of arriving at general principles by means of judicial precedents was inherently opposed to the *dharmaśāstra* where broad principles were applied to individual cases as occasion arose. The *śāstric* law was not officially abrogated and as it thus remained in competition with the precedents of the case law, Anglo-Hindu law became at times a bewildering subject, unless the doctrine of *communis error facit jus* was resorted to in order to cut the Gordian knot. Conflicting decisions of nearly two dozen High Courts, where problems were viewed from different angles and the opportunity to dissent was frequently made use of, did anything but contribute to the unity and certainty of the law. Though it cannot be said with confidence that Hindu law *pro tanto* stagnated under the British administration of justice,[3] there was certainly a case for legislation in order to achieve unity and certainty of the law.

[2] For the best survey of the British administration of Hindu law, see J. D. M. Derrett, in *Comp. Studies in Soc. and Hist.*, Vol. IV, No. 1, November 1961, p. 10 *et seq.*

[3] One may point, *e.g.*, to the rule which was developed in Southern India in supplementation of the *śāstric* law that a male member of a joint family may sell or mortgage his undivided interest for valuable consideration

But more zeal for codification was voiced amongst the new western influenced classes who pressed for social legislation. Certain social abuses had already been removed by the British administration with the introduction of the Hindu Widow's Remarriage Act, 1856, and the Caste Disabilities Removal Act, 1850. The Special Marriage Act, 1872, attempted to enable Hindus to make use of reforming tendencies to remove restraints imposed by the old law, whilst still living recognisably Hindu lives. Then the Hindu Gains of Learning Act, 1930, enacted that earnings as a result of special education at the expense of the family should be deemed the separate property of the acquirer. In practice the effects of this Act, occasioned by the wish of the members of the India Civil Service to keep their earnings separate from the joint family property, did not really penetrate to the masses. The intention to remove restrictions and improve the rights of women in property led to enactments of which the most important was the Hindu Women's Rights to Property Act, 1937. But as a consequence of this Act, a new series of conflicting decisions arose and it became obvious that piecemeal legislation was not feasible and that a comprehensive Code was called for.

The meandering history of the Hindu Code Bill from the time when the Rau Committee was formed is well known and may be omitted here.[4] It may suffice to say that it was finally decided to split up the Bill and to enact it in stages, because the "Code" had met with much opposition in the Constitutional Assembly in 1951, when it appeared to be too revolutionary to many members and, as they thought, to strike at the root of the intrinsic values of Hindu religion, culture and tradition. It is possible that the attempt to reconcile the diverse expectations as to what the "Code" ought to be—orthodox circles wanted it to be traditional and *śāstric*, reformers wanted unity and certainty, but above all modernity, whereas representatives of customary law wanted proper recognition of their interests—have not added up to make a consistent piece of legislation. The technical aims of the codifications were to unify the law of the Hindus relating to marriage, succession, guardianship, minority, adoption, and maintenance. Certainty of the law was another object, then the equality of the sexes and the elimination of restrictive and antique rules.

It has been suggested that many features have been introduced which really suit westernised classes in an urban setting which are

and gave the alienee an equity to work out his rights. The history of this rule can be traced in the case of *Peramanayakam* v. *Sivaraman* (1952) 1 M.L.J. 308; I.L.R. (1952) Mad. 835.

[4] The history is excellently depicted in J. D. M. Derrett's *Hindu Law Past and Present* (Calcutta, 1957) Chap. III.

a minority of the Hindus, the majority still living in the rural areas and expected to adjust to the Code. The villager is told that these Acts will eventually lead to a classless and casteless society, and though one can hardly entertain doubts that social reform was necessary, the doubt persists whether the reformers, representing a minority of the population, have sufficiently acquainted themselves with the sentiments, customs and needs of communities from the point of view of anthropological and sociological research. The villager was attached for centuries to traditional culture and it is doubtful whether he can adjust to the changed concepts visualised in these Acts without a systematic explanation of their significance and without the active guidance of the Indian élite.

2. *The Hindu Marriage Act (XXV of 1955)*

The *dharmaśāstra* had established a high concept of marriage out of the various possibilities which led to " marriages " amongst lower communities, such as the sale of a bride, a custom still practised by a substantial proportion of the population, for instance in Maharashtra, a union through mutual attraction and without the consent of the parents, and so on. Marriage was and still is a family affair which involved questions of status and prestige and even today a marriage outside the caste or without the consent of the parents is resented except amongst very westernised families. Usually an orthodox marriage in the *Brāhma* form was final, the bride having entered her husband's family for good. She might be " superseded " by another wife on account of a few specified reasons, but divorce was impossible. Though amongst certain communities women did possess more freedom, and divorce and remarriage was not unknown at any time in Indian history, this was not the law according to brahmanical standards which attracted the other castes.

In modern times, perhaps because cases of hardship were more often heard of or because one was inclined to pay more attention to the consequences of indissoluble marriages, it was felt that the possibility of dissolving marriages had become a desideratum.

The Hindu Marriage Act took into account these aspirations, but before we refer to the relevant provisions, the requirements of a valid marriage as laid down in the Act should be mentioned. A marriage should take place according to the customary rites pertaining to either party. The rite of *saptapadī* (section 7 (2)) is part of the marriage ceremony and the marriage is complete and final with the seventh step. An obvious example of a concession to a time-honoured ingredient of a Hindu marriage ceremony amongst high-caste communities, it leaves us guessing at what moment the marriage is complete and final amongst communities where this rite does not exist. Monogamy is now compulsory (sections 15, 17). The bridegroom must be over eighteen and the bride over fifteen and the consent of the guardian is required for the marriage, if the bride has not reached the age of eighteen years (section 5 (iii) and (iv)). But apparently, if the person who procures a marriage of himself or herself to be solemnised in contravention of the above rules is ready to undergo imprisonment up to fifteen days or to pay up to Rs. 1,000 or both, the marriage itself is valid (section 18 (*a*) and (*c*)). A further requirement is that neither party should be an idiot or lunatic (section (5) (ii)). Further, the marriage should not be within the degrees of prohibited relationship, unless the custom or usage governing each of them permits of a marriage between the two (section 5 (iv); section (3) (*g*)). The marriage should not be within the prohibited degrees of sapindaship, which have been reduced to three where relationship is traced through the mother and five where relationship is traced through the father (section 5 (*v*) and section 3 (*f*) (i and ii)). Restrictions against intercaste-marriages and intercommunal marriages have been removed according to the intention to build up a casteless society. As in the other Acts the definition of " Hindu " has been extended and includes all communities, except Muslims, Christians, Parsis, Jews and the Schedule Tribes (section 2).

Divorce was first introduced in the states of Bombay and Madras in the years 1947 and 1949 respectively. Customary divorce was always widespread amongst lower classes—a freedom which was not shared by the upper castes, as we have indicated already. Amongst the upper castes, divorce was something too unthinkable to be envisaged, or as in, *e.g.*, Maharashtra, called *ghata-sphota*, a ceremony which was formerly associated with loss of caste for the offender, an enormous proposition, whereas amongst lower classes it is symbolised as *kādi-mod*—a stick was broken as a sign that husband and wife may separate. Customary divorce has been retained in the Act (section 23 (2)) whereas for the upper communities statutory divorce has been introduced now for the whole of India. (In *Kishenlal* v. *Mst. Prabhu*[5] it was held that a custom allowing a caste *panchayat* to grant divorce at their discretion, irrespective of mutual consent of parties, is not reasonable and is opposed to public policy. This decision seems to indicate a tendency to restrict latitude in customary law relating to divorce.)

Now the wife can obtain under the Hindu Adoption and Maintenance Act separate residence and maintenance, and under the

[5] A.I.R. 1963 Raj 95.

Hindu Marriage Act judicial separation (section 10), nullity (sections 11 and 12), and divorce (section 13). The right of the husband to remarry during the lifetime of his wife without previous dissolution is abrogated so that the second marriage will be void and the issue illegitimate (sections 11, 5 (i)). Whereas judicial separation is now available for a single act of adultery, living in adultery is a ground for divorce (section 10 (1) (*f*); section 13 (1) (*i*)).

Further reasons for divorce are (section 13): ceasing to be a Hindu by conversion, incurable unsoundness of mind, virulent and incurable forms of leprosy, venereal disease in a communicable form —for the last three grounds a period of three years has to precede the petition. Further causes are: having renounced the world by entering any religious order, not having been heard of as being alive for a period of seven years or more, not having resumed cohabitation for a space of two years or upwards after the passing of the decree for judicial separation against that party, or having failed to comply with a decree for restitution of conjugal rights for a period of two years or upwards after the passing of the decree.[6]

As a decree of divorce is consequently difficult to obtain, the way adopted is usually to obtain a decree of judicial separation. Judicial separation constitutes a convenient expedient in a society where the idea that a woman remarries after divorce is not favoured. It prevents the complete severance of the relations between the wife and the family of the husband and avoids the possible desolation of the wife after divorce, while serving the purpose as far as the relations between the spouses are concerned. The ties which often exist between families and not only between particular marriage partners, especially when families tend to be bound together by repeated marriage ties, can be preserved in this manner. The grounds for judicial separation are desertion and cruelty such as to cause a reasonable apprehension in the mind of the petitioner that it will be harmful or injurious for the petitioner to live with the other party. There is also the possibility to file a petition for a decree for restitution of conjugal rights. There is a number of cases where

[6] The Uttar Pradesh Legislative Assembly has recently widened the scope and added two more causes, namely, the petition may be granted (1) if the husband or wife has persistently or repeatedly treated the petitioner with such cruelty as to cause a reasonable apprehension in the mind of the petitioner that it will be harmful or injurious for the petitioner to live with the other party, and (2) if the other party has not resumed cohabitation after the passing of a decree of a judicial separation against that party and (a) the period of two years has elapsed or the case is of exceptional hardship to the petitioner and (b) that the case is of exceptional depravity on the part of the other party. (Publ. in Uttar Pradesh *Gazette Extraordinary*, November 7, 1962. U.P.Act No. XIII of 1962.)

there have been attempts to make use of the possibility of obtaining annulment of marriage.[7]

A decree for restitution of conjugal rights may be obtained according to section 9 (i) when either party has without reasonable cause withdrawn from the society of the other and the District Court is satisfied of the truth of the statement made in the petition and that there is no legal ground why the application should not be granted. The provision in sub-paragraph (ii) of section 9 where it is laid down that nothing shall be pleaded in answer to a petition for restitution of conjugal rights which shall not be a ground for judicial separation or for nullity of marriage or for divorce, was tested in cases in which usually the husband merely wanted to obviate maintenance claims of the wife who had left her husband not necessarily because of reasons amounting to a matrimonial offence. Has the wife to prove a matrimonial offence though joint life and consortium has become impossible otherwise? In the case of *Gurdev Kaur* v. *Sarwan Singh*,[8] Justice A. N. Grover held that the petitioner succeeds on the strength of his own case and not on any defect in the respondent's defence. The cruelty alleged by the wife was possibly invented or exaggerated, but the judge was satisfied with the fact that an order had been made under section 100 of the Code of Criminal Procedure, 1898, which allowed the wife to live with her mother, and he held that as there was misconduct approaching cruelty though falling short of it, there was a legal ground why the application should be granted.

As a result of this judgment the old case law relating to restitution remains alive alongside with the provisions of the Hindu Marriage Act, 1955, relating to judicial separation, and the part of the Hindu Adoption and Maintenance Act, which replaces the repealed Hindu Married Women's Rights to Separate Residence and Maintenance Act, 1946.[9] Thus if the husband regularly visits a concubine or has suffered from a venereal disease in a communicable form for less than three years, or has deserted her for less than two years, the petition will succeed.

Provisions for dissolution of marriages may still effect curious situations in Indian surroundings where family ties are strong, though they are said to have weakened in modern times. There is the possibility of pressure from various sides on one's marriage. For instance the son is still—as he always used to be—practically

[7] See, *e.g.*, *Sivaguru* v. *Saroja*, A.I.R. 1960 Mad. 216; *Arun Kumar Patra* v. *Sudhansee Bala Patra*, A.I.R. 1962 Ori 65.

[8] A.I.R. 1959 Punj. 162, foll. in *Teja Singh* v. *Sarjit*, A.I.R. 1962 Punj. 195.

[9] J. D. M. Derrett, 62 Bom.L.R. (J) 17 *et seq.* at p. 21.

asvatantra, *i.e.*, dependent in respect of his father, even if he is grown-up and the right of birth and entitlement to partition of joint family property seems to indicate differently. He is expected to show an absolute respect for his father, who conducts the family affairs. In the case of *Smt. Mango* v. *Prem Chand* [10] the moving force behind husband and wife was the father of the husband. The husband applied for a decree for restitution of conjugal rights under section 9 and the learned district judge overruled the defence and passed the decree. When the wife appealed it was found that the district judge had not given much weight to a statement by the husband contradictory to what he deposed now before High Court. The earlier statement clearly revealed that it was the father of the husband who wanted his daughter-in-law to return for various reasons and it moreover indicated the complete dependency of the husband on his father. It was evident that the son was not the actual author of the suit. This was alleged by the wife together with allegations of maltreatment and indecent behaviour on the part of the respondent as well as his father, and the judge was convinced that the grounds were sufficient to hold that the husband was not able to keep his wife, and to constitute a reasonable excuse for her living separately within the meaning of section 9 (1).

The most common objections levelled at the provisions for dissolution of marriages are that they open possibilities to give vent to difficulties and family disputes whereas previously the equilibrium had to be re-established within the family without such possibilities. The new provisions cannot be said to fit easily into the traditional pattern of the Indian high caste family which westernised classes are likely to discard whereas lower communities tend to adopt it even today. The standard set by a new western-imported set of rules may appeal as fashionable and more progressive, the institution of marriage as it exists in the West frequently being understood by its more negative aspects.

3. *The Hindu Succession Act* (*XXX of 1956*)

The Hindu Marriage Act was quickly followed by the Hindu Succession Act. One would have expected that for such an important piece of legislation special care would have been devoted to the drafting of rules in view of the confused state of some parts of Anglo-Hindu law. But the main object of the Act seemed to have been to raise the rights of women to an approximately

[10] A.I.R. 1962 All. 447.

equal level with men and it has been called the Magna Carta of the rights of women to property.[11]

New rules of succession are introduced in sections 8–18 of the Act. It would be going too far to go into details, but it is worth mentioning that considerable confusion had arisen on the question whether section 8 is retrospective so that the property of a male who dies intestate devolves according to the provisions of the Act with retrospective effect. This anomalous position was actually taken by the Patna High Court,[12] but has since been refuted by several High Courts, and dissented from by the Patna High Court itself.[13]

The scheme on which intestate succession to males is based is now propinquity and natural affection and wherever this test as between relations cannot give a clear answer both of them have been taken as simultaneous heirs. The heirs are divided into four classes: class I contains a selection of near relations, class II contains more distant relations headed by the father who has not been included in class I. Class III follows with agnates and class IV with cognates; if there are no cognates, the State takes by escheat (section 29).

Succession to males and succession to females have not been assimilated and we get different rules of succession to females in sections 15 and 16. Section 14 removes the limited legal estate of women with retrospective effect. An instance of faulty draftsmanship may be found in section 15 (2), which may give property belonging to a woman who dies without male issue to the heirs of a living person.

The crucial section 6 of the Act retains the Mitakshara joint family system with coparcenary and survivorship in a modified form. In pure Hindu law joint family property was not inherited by females when the propositus died leaving a son, son's son, or son's son's son, or unseparated from his agnatic relations.

[11] But seemingly *beneficial* provisions like s. 6 may effect occasionally the contrary, as has been shown by G. K. Dabke (1958) 60 Bom.L.R., Journal, 8. For a review of the Act see J. D. M. Derrett, "The Hindu Succession Act, 1956: an experiment in social legislation" (1959) 8 American J.Comp.L. 485–501 and "Statutory amendments of the personal laws of the Hindus since Indian Independence," *Rapports généraux au Ve Congrès international de droit comparé, Bruxelles, 1960*, 101 *et seq.* (with bibl.). The valuable rights of illegitimate sons (*dāsiputras*) of *śudras*, have been totally abolished in the Act, probably with the intention to remove any remnant of caste system. See also J. D. M. Derrett, "Illegitimates: A Test for Modern Hindu Family Law" (1961) 81 J.Amer.Or.Soc., No. 3, 251–261 (with further references).

[12] *Lateshwar* v. *Mst. Uma Ojhain*, A.I.R. 1958 Pat. 502.

[13] See, *e.g.*, *Appa Saheb* v. *Gurubasappa*, A.I.R. 1960 Mys. 79; *Renuka* v. *Aswani*, A.I.R. 1961 Pat. 498. *Lateshwar* v. *Mst. Uma Ojhain* was overruled in *Ram Gulam* v. *Palakdhari*, A.I.R. 1961 Pat. 60.

But joint family property had been already made accessible to women, together with the separate property the deceased might have left, subject to a limited estate under the Hindu Women's Rights to Property Act, 1937. Now (with retrospective effect) whatever property is held by a woman and of which she is in actual possession or to which she is entitled to possession,[14] whether acquired before or after the Act, becomes an absolute estate with the commencement of the Act, according to section 14 (1).[15] The interest the deceased may have had in the joint family property, *i.e.*, ancestral property with accretions, is now made to pass by testamentary succession or according to the rules for the distribution of separate property of a male dying intestate, provided any relation, found in class I of the Schedule is in existence, but not if only a son, or a son of a predeceased son, or a son of a predeceased son of a predeceased son exists. If there is only male issue, the proviso does not apply, and the rule of survivorship according to the Mitakshara is still in force. Section 30, which introduces the power to dispose of the interest in joint family property by will, was meant to dispel all doubts upon the new basic proposition of testamentary power over one's interest, but does not give testamentary power in the cases where there is only male issue of the father and the proviso of section 6 can consequently not apply.[16] Testamentary power over the interest in the joint family property still gives a coparcener a chance to exclude females and other heirs claiming through females as specified in Class I of the Schedule, confining them to claiming maintenance. According to section 7, the interest in the joint family property of a Malabar *tarwad* and *tavazhi* can pass *only* by testamentary or intestate succession which amounts to a virtual extinction of the *legal* foundation of the Malabar joint family.

The interest of the propositus which is to pass by testamentary or intestate succession is to be ascertained at a notional partition,

[14] The extension of the meaning to constructive possession has been added by judicial interpretation; the Act (s. 14 (1)) speaks of property "possessed" by a female. See *Gostha* v. *Haridas* A.I.R. 1957 Cal. 557 (559); *Kotturuswami* v. *Veeravva*, A.I.R. 1959 S.C. 577; (1959) S.C.J.(R) 437.

[15] On the question of claims between reversionary heirs and alienees from a widow who has alienated before the commencement of the Act for purposes not binding on the reversioners, see *Amar Singh* v. *Seva Ram*, A.I.R. 1960 Punj. 530; *Mt. Janku* v. *Kisan*, A.I.R. 1958 M.P. 160 (F.B.); *Ram Gulam* v. *Palakdhari*, A.I.R. 1961 Pat. 61, where it was correctly held that the Act does not intend to benefit alienees and that a reversioner's right to set aside alienations is not affected. But see *Hanuman Prasad* v. *Mst. Indrawati* A.I.R. 1958 All. 304, where it was held that reversioners are abolished for all purposes (a minority view).

[16] *e.g.*, if a coparcenary consists of a father and three sons. The contrary statements in Raghavachariar's *Hindu Law* (4th ed.), p. 784 *et seq.* at 858, and Mulla's *Principles of Hindu Law* (12th ed.), p. 931 are open to doubt.

a concept which is taken from the Estate Duty Act, 1953, which was introduced because owners of separate property used to merge it with joint family property shortly before death, thus leaving no " estates " to be taxed. To ascertain the interest for purposes of section 6, the old rules for partition of joint family property apply, which immediately raises the question whether we have to take into account the mother's share allotted to her at a partition according to the Bombay High Court, but not according to the Madras High Court. Thus the share one may get at a partition varies according to the High Court which is seized with the case. The Act does not enlighten us on this point.

The daughter has now an equal share in the joint family interest of her deceased father along with the son, widow, etc. The effect of this provision may be to break up the old custom of keeping landed property in the agnatic line, but still it is indecent for a daughter to ask for a share in the land and especially the ancestral land, especially as girls quite frequently marry outside the village. Often the demand by the daughter for her share might be instigated by her husband and his agnatic kindred. The Act contains a right to acquire the land in case the daughter or other heirs specified in class I of the Schedule proposes to transfer the interest in the land or business (section 22). But then there is the question of ready cash in rural communities. It is interesting to note that the Act contemplates a virtual auction amongst the family members, as the one who offers the highest consideration for the interest is preferred (section 22).

The Mitakshara joint family is said to be a dying institution. The complete abolition of the legal foundation of the joint family was abandoned, it being preferred that it should die a natural death. But there may be also other reasons why Parliament has consciously or unconsciously retained remnants of the institution. Sociologists mostly looked at the joint family as an extended family, several nuclear families living together under a " common roof " having food and worship in common, and sometimes two dozens of people sitting down at a dinner, not counting relatives and friends who may claim a moral right to be fed. One may still enter a train, *e.g.*, at Bangalore, and meet a fellow-passenger who by the time one leaves the train in Poona has introduced one to twenty-five of his relatives all returning to Indore from a pilgrimage to Cape Comorin. But these cases are getting rare. Moreover, the legal foundation of the joint family has been substantially affected by the introduction of the alienability of one's share in Southern India, estate duty, wealth tax, the Hindu Women's Rights to Property Act, 1937, the "pious obligation" of the son to pay antecedent debts of the father which are not tainted by immorality, and the present Hindu Succession Act. But there is one crucial aspect which may be beyond all momentary and accidental economical influences, at least for some time, namely the father-son relationship which is expressed by the idea that the father is reborn in the son, who pays the father's debts and continues his works. This is an ancient Indian concept preserved in juridical form by medieval legal authors and subsisting in Anglo-Hindu laws, retaining its importance in modern Hindu life and law. It centres on the idea that father and son have joint religious and social obligations, the son having a right by birth into the ancestral property. Here we find the backbone of the Hindu joint family which the other relatives and even the more distant kin may rely upon as a matter of course in all family affairs, and especially in times of need. "Mutual belonging, mutual responsibility, reinforced and expressed in terms of ancestral lands and privileges, ancestral rites and shrines, and the common and unquestioning obedience to the senior most prestige-worthy representative of the lineage, still to this day makes what the author of the Mitakshara would call 'unseparatedness' rather the rule than the exception."[17]

4. *The Hindu Adoption and Maintenance Act (LXXVIII of 1956) and the Hindu Minority and Guardianship Act (XXXII of 1956)*

The provisions of the short Hindu Minority and Guardianship Act, 1956, are rather an addition to the Guardian and Wards Act, 1890, to the extent that this Act is not superseded by the new provisions. The most important innovation is the abrogation of the powers of the *de facto* guardian with the commencement of the act.[18]

But it may be questionable whether the section affects the situation where a person deals with the property of a minor for legal necessity or benefit of the estate in the absence of a legal guardian so as to make the act more than voidable at the instance of the minor, if the act was not in fact for legal necessity or benefit

[17] J. D. M. Derrett in *Contributions to Indian Sociology*, No. VI, Dec. 1962, p. 47.

[18] s. 11; a *de facto* guardian, one who is not a natural guardian, testamentary guardian or a court guardian, but who being interested in the minor, though a stranger, takes charge of the management of the minor's property, had all the powers of a natural guardian in the matter of alienating the minor's property.

of the estate.[19] Now even a natural guardian or a testamentary guardian cannot mortgage, sell or otherwise alienate any immovable property of the minor or lease it beyond the time limits provided in the Act without the sanction of the court (sections 8, 9).

From a final glance at the Hindu Adoption and Maintenance Act, 1956, we learn that now a female can adopt to herself which she could do formerly only to her husband with his consent or after his death with his authority. The possibility that a widow may adopt a son to her husband posthumously so that the adoptee divests heirs, the famous "relation-back" doctrine, has been abolished, however not with retrospective effect. This doctrine was in practice often a powerful weapon in the hands of the widow against the agnatic relations of her husband. "Officially," *i.e.*, according to the *śāstra*, the posthumously adopted son was such for spiritual purposes, but the *śāstra* must have contemplated the creating of an heir for purposes of inheriting the property as well. The scope of the "relation-back" doctrine has now been settled by the Supreme Court for the cases which fall before the enactment of the Act.[20]

According to the new Act not only a boy may be adopted, but also a girl. An orphan can now be adopted, but strangely not an illegitimate child by his own mother. Recent amendments show that more attention is to be given to welfare than to questions of property.[21] Women who were generally free from obligations to maintain others have now been made liable nearly co-extensively with males (Chapter III of the Act). Dependants' claims to maintenance cannot be defeated by a will and the heirs are bound to maintain the dependants of the deceased out of the estate inherited

[19] See for the powers of a *de facto* guardian the important case of *Sriramulu* v. *Pundarikakshayya*, A.I.R. 1949 F.C. 218. The alienation is not valid because the person is a *de facto* "guardian" or "manager," but because there was an emergency, a necessity pressing upon the minor or his property.

[20] *Srinivas* v. *Narayan*, 1955 S.C.R. 1; *Krishnamurti* v. *Dhruvraj* (1961) 64 Bom.L.R. 165 S.C.

[21] Subs. (4) of s. 9 which deals with persons capable of giving in adoption has now been amended and reads as follows: (4) Where both the father and mother are dead or have completely and finally renounced the world or have abandoned the child or have been declared by a court of competent jurisdiction to be of unsound mind or where the parentage of the child is not known, the guardian of the child may give the child in adoption with the previous permission of the court to any person including the guardian himself. "Guardian" has been defined in an amendment (Explanation (ia)) for the purposes of this section: "guardian" means a person having the care of the person of a child or of both his person and property and includes:

(a) a guardian appointed by the will of the child's father or mother, and

(b) a guardian appointed or declared by a court.

See Indian Parliament Act No. 45 of 1962 (November 29, 1962), *i.e.*, Hindu Adoption and Maintenance (Amendment) Act, 1962, for further details.

by them from the deceased. A right of maintenance can be enforced against a transferee if he has notice of the right, or if the transfer is gratuitous.

Conclusions

The achievement of providing a simple unified legal system for a society with widely differing customs and laws, *e.g.*, succession laws which stretch from patriliny to pure matriliny, is indeed unique in the history of codification. Greater unity in law has been also achieved by the application of the enactments to communities like the Sikhs, Buddhist, Lingayats and so on, a step towards a general Civil Code visualised in Article 44 of the Indian Constitution. There is a definite trend in these Acts to assign more influence to the courts and the legal profession over family questions which were and are tackled by the traditional expedients of family, caste, and village.

Technically the Acts may create difficulties as occasionally there are ambiguities and flaws which possibly cannot be solved by the Supreme Court alone, but require legislative amendment. The paucity of decisions emanating from the Supreme Court on material points makes it difficult to judge even now—seven to eight years after the Acts came into force—the legal effect of some provisions of the Acts. The reaction of the general public to the Acts and the extent of their impact on the various communities cannot be conclusively judged from the decisions either of the Supreme Court or the High Courts.

[12]

Comments

STATUTORY AMENDMENTS OF THE PERSONAL LAW OF HINDUS SINCE INDIAN INDEPENDENCE

Hindu law in India was codified during the period between May, 1955, and December, 1956, in four statutes, namely the Hindu Marriage Act, (Act No. 25 of 1955), the Hindu Succession Act (Act No. 30 of 1956), the Hindu Minority and Guardianship Act (Act No. 32 of 1956), and finally the Hindu Adoptions and Maintenance Act (Act No. 78 of 1956). The process, which it is convenient to call "codification," lacks some of the characteristics of a conventional code, since there remain important parts of the Hindu law which are either entirely or substantially untouched by the legislation. But that portion of the system which has been affected has been so radically affected as to render the result almost unrecognizable for what it is: namely the culmination of a long process of modification and reform, both by way of judicial legislation and by statute, of the ancient legal system indigenous to India and known as the *dharmaśāstra*.[1] The story of the conflicts and heart-searchings which preceded the actual enactment of the statutes has been told elsewhere;[2] but a summary of the motives of the legislators, of the changes they have brought about, and of the results of their work—so far as they can be determined[3] or conjectured[4] from about two years' experience—is likely to interest those who use or study "family laws" in codified form. For it is certain that India's experiment is not less remarkable than the enactment of the Code Napoléon, while nothing comparable with it for width of scope or boldness of innovation has been seen in the Anglo-American systems. The Parliament which enacted the "Hindu Code" has deserved a wide reputation for its radical and even revolutionary legislation; but it is likely that its achievement in connection with the personal law of the Hindus will be amongst its more prominent memorials. The reader may need to be reminded that "Hindus" comprise communities of very widely differing customs and levels of culture, and that the total number of persons governed by the "Code" at the time of writing, though not known for certain, cannot be far short of 400 millions.

---

[1] The characteristics of this system, and its relationship to the Anglo-Hindu law, with adequate references to current literature, are explained in Derrett, "Hindu Law: the *Dharmashastra* and the Anglo-Hindu law—Scope for Further Comparative Study," 58 Z.f. vergleichende Rechtsw. (1956) 199–245.

[2] Derrett, Hindu Law Past and Present, Calcutta, 1957.

[3] It is curious that litigation on difficult parts of the "Code" has hardly begun to reach the division benches of the High Courts on appeals. We now know, however, that S.14 of the HSA does not confer rights upon alienees from widows who formerly owned property subject to a legal limited estate (see below): but the implications of the same section are hotly disputed between two groups of High Courts.

[4] Examples of such conjectures appear in Indian legal journals, e.g. (1957) 59 Bom. L. R. J. 33 and ff., *ibid.* 68 and ff., and the spate of editions of the various Acts contains quantities of conjecture as to the meaning of really obscure sections. See e.g. R. N. Sarkar, Hindu Marriage Act, Calcutta, 1956; N. D. Basu, Law of Succession, Calcutta, 1957; and D. H. Chaudhari, Hindu Adoptions and Maintenance Act, Calcutta, 1957.

Motives Leading to the "Code"

In the framing of the "Code," we see the uniting of several distinct programs of reform. The legislation was possible not because a majority of the electorate approved either the general proposition of codification or a substantial number of the major innovations, but because amongst the Members of the two Houses of Parliament there were large majorities combining those who believed respectively in the merits of one justification for the project, or perhaps more than one justification, whereas the same members were indifferent or even hostile towards others. It is no secret that the Acts were hastened through Parliament because the dominant party, the Congress Party, was pledged to secure reform of the Hindu law, and the event of the election could not be awaited with perfect confidence; it is equally well known that the educated and "enlightened" minority, which tends to occupy the majority of the seats in the central as well as state legislatures, did not, in passing these Acts, reflect the views of the vast bulk of the Indian public. The horror which is undisguisedly felt by many Hindus at the catastrophe which has befallen their system of family law may not be rationally capable of support, and it may well be true that the reforms were theoretically desirable or even inevitable; but the public accepts the statutes not because they have ardently desired them, but because they have been assured that they are essential if India is to proceed smoothly towards a socialist pattern of society, and, no doubt, because they are habituated to accepting the decisions of the above-mentioned minority as the best thing for them in the long run.

At first it will seem incredible that a "Code" of personal law should be framed and enacted in such circumstances;[5] and it may seem doubtful whether the product can survive. It is true that some amendments and adjustments will have to be made[6] if the "Code" is to work well, as will presently appear, but it is unlikely that any radical alterations will be made until eventually the Indian Civil Code which the Constitution promises us[7] supersedes it. For the motives which conspired to bring it to birth have been satisfied, and there is no longer any unexpended force which can prolong the process or redeem the rather obvious deficiencies in the work. The operative motives were these:

1. Features of the existing law which recognized the institution of caste were inconsistent with the democratization of the country and were therefore to be abolished.

2. For the same reason, rules of law which placed women at a disadvantage as compared with men were to be abolished.

3. For the same reason, customs or other rules permitting large properties to descend to a single heir were thought to be anachronistic.

4. Features of the existing law which tended to hamper free dealing with property were thought to be "backward," and ripe for removal.

5. Some other features were simply "old-fashioned" and quaint, and out

[5] See the comments of Professor A. Gledhill in Constitutional and Legislative Development in the Indian Republic, 20 B.S.O.A.S. (1957) 267 and ff., at pp. 274 and ff.

[6] The one legislative amendment which has already appeared is referred to below.

[7] See Art. 44.

of keeping with the spirit of the times. In particular, certain rules of a particularly religious color or derivation came under attack.

6. Certain topics of law suffered from uncertainty and a scandalous disharmony of decision between the various (and numerous) High Courts, and an opportunity to render certain that which was uncertain or anomalous would be welcomed.

7. Finally, any amendment which would tend to remove the many and striking distinctions between Hindus, and which would appear to render them a more homogeneous and unified people, if only on paper, would be of great political as well as psychological value, and would on that account have an independent justification.

A serious attempt to put all these programs into effect was made in the autumn of 1951, as soon after the inauguration of the Constitution as the pressure of business would permit. Nerve seems to have failed largely because the Constituent Assembly was not fully representative of the people: in other words, the serious doubts of lawyers and laymen alike joined in finding an obvious excuse for not coping with the problem. Pandit Nehru however persisted in his support of the projected code, and bills, brought in separately, were permitted to undergo quite radical amendment in committee and before the Lok Sabha, and the success of the Hindu Marriage Act (so named after objection had been taken to the quite accurate title "Hindu Marriage and Divorce Act") four years after the failure of 1951 at once promised the success, as a legislative venture, of the entire project.

What strikes the observer at once in the new "Code" is the absence of a positive driving force behind it. The Acts vary widely in quality of draftsmanship, and in the proportion of nontraditional matter which they embody. The motives of clearing away the dead wood have had a very full scope, but nothing vital has been put in its place. The justification for the retention of a "personal law" for Hindus in India seems to have been abandoned together with the Anglo-Hindu law which it substantially replaces there; for if the latter was cumbered with faults of every possible sort, it did purport to be an inheritance of the Hindus, and to be derived, if somewhat distantly in places, from the *dharmaśāstra,* which most Hindus were vaguely acquainted with and never failed to respect. The replacement is Hindu in name, and contains an occasional and embarrassing reminder of its predecessor, much as a ruinous but ancient building may be pulled down and replaced with a modern structure, which retains the same street-number, some panelling, a decorative window, or even a quaint chimney pot from the old house, alleging a continuity with the past which may appeal to sentiment, but does not deceive the eye. When readers notice that the Law Minister speaking or writing about one of these Acts claims either that it is really in close accord with the ancient Hindu law, or that it makes no important departure from the existing law, they will not suppose that these misleading statements are due to ignorance. Parliament and the public, whilst aware that something radical was being tampered with, were only too eager to be reassured as to the direction of the movement or the extent of the divergence. As so often with reforms, the desire to break with the immediate past was accompanied by a desire to claim authority from the remote past, and to pretend that innovations are really restorations of something that became corrupted in time. Unfortunately, such claims fail, on the whole, in this context. The "Hindu Code" has little in common with the *dharmaśāstra,* of however ancient a period, and if some resemblance can be discovered it is a coincidence. The advisors learned in the *dharmaśāstra* to whom the Hindu Law Committees turned at various times[8] made no determined effort to reintroduce traditional elements; and where the pre-codification law has been reproduced more or less faithfully, this was not because it was supported by any attractive arguments, but because it found no antagonist. Thus, portions of Anglo-Hindu law, of pre-Independence statutes and trifling scraps of *dharmaśāstra* learning are found cheek-by-jowl with slices of English law, of law which looks English but is not, and of rules which are unprecedented anywhere. Parliament knew that it must busy itself on this subject and must not lose time in so doing, but much of the work betrays an amateurish and improvised appearance. In any other country, this would by now have given rise to alarm and resentment. The authors of such provisions as gave estates to the heirs of living persons[9] would not escape ridicule. But India is a land where the incongruous and the inconsistent is not necessarily intolerable, where "bright ideas" tend to carry as much conviction as ponderous learning, and where the good intentions of the rulers more than compensate for unevenness in their performance. It is in this manner, then, that between 1955 and 1956 Indians, in fact predominantly Hindus, succeeded in removing forever the features of their law which attracted the contemptuous attention of the rationalist and evangelical groups in England; which the legislators of Macaulay's and Maine's days were eager to remove; which acquired a new lease of life as a result of the Mutiny; and which the timidity or indifference of the Imperial Government enabled to survive nearly a century thereafter. One of the first acts of independent India was to rid herself of a burden which the former rulers did not dare to disturb. It remains to be seen whether the public, thus relieved, will live under the "Code" in the spirit which is intended, or whether it will ignore the new facilities that are offered to it, and circumvent the hindrances that are now placed before those that wish to continue in the old (and in some cases apparently harmless) ways to which they were accustomed. We may now turn to the motives individually and see what results they have achieved.

Abolition of Caste

The chief sponsor of the "Hindu Code Bill" claimed that the project would break the supremacy of the "high castes." Whatever the accuracy of this prediction may be, it is certain that the "Code" eliminates most of the contexts in which caste will be referred to in litigation on matters of family law, and to that extent any protection which the Anglo-Hindu law used to afford to the concept of caste, and all that it involved, has ceased. The principal scope of caste-distinction was in the field of marriage. With the

[8] In particular Principal J. R. Gharpure and Dr. P. V. Kane were consulted, but neither attempted to increase the traditional element retained in the draft Bills.

[9] See HSA S.15(2).

very limited exception of Bombay State, there existed a general bar against marriages between persons of different castes, although the Anglo-Hindu law had somewhat mitigated the rigor of the *śāstra* by refusing to recognize more than four castes. This impediment was removed in a statute passed shortly after Independence (Act 21 of 1949), and the reform is re-enacted in the Hindu Marriage Act, 1955 (hereafter cited as *HMA*), sec. 5 and sec. 29 (1). Formerly the most numerous caste, the Śūdras, were entitled to be succeeded as heirs by their illegitimate sons, provided that these were born of concubines in the father's exclusive keeping at the time of conception. In competition with legitimate sons, these *dāsi-putras,* as they were known, were entitled to half the share which each would have had if he had been legitimate, and in competition with the widow, daughter, or daughter's son they were entitled to one half of the estate. This privilege is removed by implication in sec. 8 of the Hindu Succession Act, 1956 (hereafter cited as *HSA*). Whether or not a son was validly adopted might formerly have turned upon the performance or otherwise of certain ceremonies appropriate to adoption; in the case of Śūdra families these ceremonies were not required in every detail, and thus adoptions were in practice somewhat easier to prove. This anomaly is removed by virtue of the requirements prescribed in the Hindu Adoptions and Maintenance Act, 1956 (hereafter cited as *HAMA*), sec. 11. Formerly the adopted son of a Śūdra might share equally with a legitimate son according to certain High Courts, whereas adopted sons of the higher castes were confined to a one-fourth share in competition with a legitimate son of the body. This privilege has been abolished by HAMA sec. 12, so far as relates to adoptions made after the Act came into force. The very capacity to adopt a Hindu child belonging to another caste, unheard of formerly, has been created by the statute (sec. 10). In succession to the separate property of a woman, known as *strīd-hanam,* difference of caste was recognized to the extent that (according to the Bengal school of law) a Brahman co-wife's son would exclude a stepson by a wife of another caste: this rule in practice attracted little attention, for marriages between different castes, except where specially permitted by custom, were generally impossible before 1949, but between 1949 and 1956 a case of discrimination on the ground of caste alone could occur amongst those subject to that particular school. All such possibility is removed in the case of a proposita dying after the 17th June, 1956, by the terms of HSA, sec. 15.

There are two respects in which difference of caste may still be observed, and these have been left, in all probability, by oversight. Formerly, and probably still, no Śūdra could become a *sannyāsi,* that is to say, a religious ascetic, unless a legal custom permitted. Whether a person had validly become a *sannyāsi* is a matter of importance, since upon so becoming a man's property passes as if he had died, and should he accumulate property thereafter it passes to a special order of "spiritual" heirs. The terms of the "overriding effect" section of the HSA (sec. 4) would appear to leave the former law untouched, and the incompatibility of the former law with that set out in the vesting sections of the HSA suggests that, in the case of a member of the higher castes (the "twice-born"), a *sannyāsi* or his relations have a special privilege, for, *inter alia,* estate duty may be levied on the property of those who die, but not, it would appear, on that of those who have abandoned the world. Śūdras have not been relieved by any provision in the "Hindu Code." Further, a former rule that "twice-born" might be taken in marriage only before their initiation ceremony has been performed (a rule operative outside Bombay State), whereas Śūdras might adopt boys up to their marriages (but not thereafter), does not seem to have been abolished by the HAMA, for that Act provides, in sec. 10 (iv), that a boy above the age of 15 years may be adopted if a custom so permits. The alleged custom will have to be proved, and probably can only be proved (if at all), with reference to caste.

Equality of the Sexes

Formerly, the legal disabilities of women were very striking. The task of removing them commenced as far back as 1937 (a few years earlier in advanced princely states such as Baroda and Mysore), and certain Bombay statutes dealing with marriage and divorce which were roughly contemporary with Independence were followed by enactments in the States of Madras and Saurashtra at short intervals after Independence. The task is almost completed by the "Code," and certain advantages have in fact been left with the previously disabled sex. The principal grounds for attack upon the old law referred to marriage and property rights; the withholding of subordinate rights from women did not give rise to as great an outcry amongst the westernized minority as these, but they are academically at least as noteworthy. Except amongst certain communities of matrilineal history in Malabar, a male was entitled to have more than one wife at a time, whereas a woman was prohibited from having more than one husband. The demand for compulsory monogamy has been met throughout India by HMA, sec. 17. Divorce is available upon various grounds, including the previous marriage of the husband to a woman who is still living, renunciation of the world, living in adultery, and being converted from Hinduism. Judicial separation is now available upon various grounds, including desertion, cruelty, insanity, or a single act of adultery; and the wife may obtain separate residence and maintenance (a remedy introduced first in 1946) upon the grounds of desertion, cruelty, ceasing to be a Hindu, keeping a concubine, etc., and for *any other cause* justifying separate residence (for this last remedy see HAMA, sec. 18(2)). The Anglo-Hindu law had been kind to a wife so far as maintenance was concerned, but, except in the States mentioned above, divorce had not been available in most of the "twice-born" castes, and the grounds upon which a woman might resist a petition for restitution of conjugal rights were uncertain. Now either spouse may obtain an order for the payment of the costs of litigation, and for interim maintenance, out of the property of the other (HMA, sec. 24).

Formerly a mother was inhibited from acting as guardian of her minor child if the father had appointed another person as testamentary guardian, and similarly the mother's own power to appoint a guardian by testament was defective. These anomalies have been removed by the Hindu Minority and Guardianship Act, 1956 (hereafter cited as *HMGA*), sec. 9. The general priority of the father as guardian is however maintained.

Formerly, a female illegitimate child had no general rights of inheritance and no rights of maintenance at civil law. It appears that an illegitimate daughter may inherit as if legitimate from her mother and her mother's kin (*sed quaere?*), according to HSA, sec. 3(*1*)(*j*), and her rights of maintenance out of her living putative father's estate are established by HAMA, sec. 20(2), and, as a dependent, out of his estate when deceased by sec. 21 and 22 of the same statute.

Formerly, a female could neither adopt to herself, except in the very restricted *ḳritrima* form known in a portion of one State of northern India, nor be adopted by another. The spinster's, divorcee's, and widow's rights to adopt are established in HAMA, sec. 8, while the capacity of a girl to be adopted is introduced in the same statute, secs. 10 and 11. The adopted child, of whichever sex, is treated in law as equivalent to a legitimate child of the body, with trifling exceptions.

Succession, of all the chapters of the law, reveals the contrast between the present and the past most clearly. Formerly, sons excluded daughters in succession to their fathers, while daughters largely, but not uniformly, excluded sons in succession to their mothers. There were many customs excluding all female heirs, and the various schools of Hindu law varied in the number (it might be as low as five) and relationship of female relatives who might be permitted to inherit. In Madras, for example, until 1929, a sister was 466th in the order of succession, but after a statute of that year she was advanced to 13th in order, after the father's father. Prior to the same statute, she had not inherited in northern India at all, except where local or caste customs permitted it. The widow was often excluded by custom, and it was not until 1937 that, in British India, a widow was permitted to take a share in undivided joint family property, the most common and most important class of property in all India except Bengal and Assam. But even where females were allowed to inherit, they were always, with a few important exceptions in Bombay State, subjected to a limited estate, which seriously impaired their freedom of dealing with the inheritance (see below: Freedom of Disposition). Even where a woman inherited from another woman, who had enjoyed her property absolutely, she took subject to a limited estate. It had even been held by the Privy Council that where a woman who was married or widowed prescribed for a title in property, she prescribed for a limited estate and not an absolute estate; and an old decision of the same tribunal had held it a presumption of law that a legacy to a woman, without qualification in respect of title, would convey a limited and not an absolute estate.

In both respects, the new law is an improvement. Females are admitted as heirs equally with males of the same degree. All property inherited by a female is her absolute property, unless the will or a compromise or decree otherwise provides. And this revolution, perhaps one of the most fundamental in this series, is retrospective, so that the limited estate, which was once a fruitful source of litigation is very nearly a thing of the past. In one respect, females are still discriminated against. Heirs related to the propositus through females, if they are more remote than the mother's sister, will be postponed to heirs related through males, for a residuary patrilineal prejudice still remains. But the discrimination will apply equally to the cognatic males and cognatic females. Not so fair would appear to be the preference accorded to the father's father over the mother's father, or to the son's daughter's son over the daughter's daughter's son. Once again the female is at no disadvantage, but discrimination between the sex of the stocks remains, and appears to be irrational—for when once members of a family allied by marriage have been admitted there seems to be no justification for preferring a relation one family removed over another who is two or more families removed: see Schedule to HSA.

Formerly a Hindu who had no male issue might adopt a son without consulting his wife, and could give her son away in adoption without taking her consent; she, for her part, could not give or take without the husband's actual or implied consent (the rule depended upon the local interpretation of an ancient and ambiguous text), unless he were insane, in which case she could give away their son freely. A female heir, in the view of the Bengal school of law, was disqualified from the succession if she was 'unchaste' at the time when it opened; a similar disqualification did not apply to a male heir. The first group of rules is abolished, so far as discrimination between the sexes persisted, by HAMA, sec. 7 and 8; and the second disqualification has been removed by HSA, sec. 28. It is to be noted, however, that a husband is not entitled to be maintained out of the estate of his deceased wife (HAMA, sec. 21), and a husband who obtains alimony from his wife in matrimonial proceedings (HMA, sec. 25) may lose it for a single act of intercourse with a woman outside marriage. The latter rule observes parity between the sexes, the former does not.

Formerly women were not permitted to alienate a certain class of *strīd-hanam,* though it belonged to them absolutely, without the consent of their husbands, if alive. This rule would seem to have been abolished by sec. 14 of the HSA, as also the rule which enabled a husband to seize and utilize any *strīd-hanam* of his wife in an emergency, even one of his own making, without obligation to repay it unless it were possible and convenient for him to do so.

The freedom which these changes offer to women are likely to have widespread effects, some of which cannot be otherwise than unsettling amongst communities where women have led a sheltered, dependent, and submissive existence for so many millennia.

Impartible Estates

Students of the history of codification elsewhere will be aware that "modernization" has often meant the removal of features from a scheme of succession which smacked of feudalism, and which tended to keep property undivided in the hands of a succession of representatives of a family. India has until recently known numerous examples of hereditary chiefships of various degrees of importance with impartible estates attached to the dignity, and also impartible estates without connection with such official rank. The Congress Party, which always found the Rajas and Maharajas hostile to their programme, pledged itself to the liquidation of their privileges and estates. By various means, which need not be detailed here, the great estates, with a few exceptions in Madras State (where they were protected to some extent by a statute) have been dissolved, and, as a last stroke, the HSA has provided, in sec. 5, that all estates, except a negligible few, shall descend according to the normal law, and shall thus be partible. An important chapter of the Anglo-Hindu law is thus virtually deleted. Fragmentation, however, is recognized as a menace, and the HSA provides that local statutes impeding fragmentation of agricultural holdings remain unaffected by the reforms.

Freedom of Disposition

As with the English property legislation of 1925, so the "Hindu Code" aims at removing the obstacles which had formerly hindered free dealing with their property by persons who were entitled at law to its enjoyment, but not necessarily to its disposal. In former ages, when movement between classes and occupations was very limited, and large families lived communally upon an undivided corpus of property for several generations, the large number of instances in which an individual was authorized to utilize property for a limited number of purposes but was precluded from alienating it without necessity was not felt as a hindrance to well-being, but rather an advantage. Families are now smaller, the legal standard of freedom allowed to those invested with limited powers of alienation has risen in some cases, and the possibility that transfers of such property will be followed by litigation tends to depress its market value unduly. For all these reasons, the principal instances of limited owners, or persons vested with limited powers of alienation over property not their own or not wholly their own have been abolished or severely curtailed. The female heir who owned an estate subject to the limitation that she might burden it validly for her own maintenance for the payment of the previous male owner's debts, and the repose of his soul, but might not bind the reversioners except in such cases and in cases of pure necessity, such as for the preservation of the property itself, has become a feature of legal history, and the HSA has secured that in the vast majority of cases (at any rate in intestate succession) the property of a female shall be as freely alienable as that of a male. There remains the instance of the manager of joint family property, who was authorized to alienate the corpus of the property for the benefit of the family, for necessity, and, to a limited extent, for pious purposes. As long as the male members of the family were undivided in status, no one ordinarily possessed any right to dispose of the joint property except the managing member, and the limitations upon his power of disposition were embarrassing to alienees, who might be charged after several years with the whole or a part of the consideration, on the ground that the alienation was unauthorized by the law, and in extreme cases the alienation itself would be set aside at the instance of the nonalienating members of the family. The "Hindu Code" tackles this problem in the following way: as regards joint families in Malabar—that is to say joint families predominantly of a matrilineal character—the joint tenure has been prospectively abolished (HSA, sec. 7) and a tenancy in common (i.e. with defined shares) has been virtually substituted for it, for whenever a member of such family dies his interest passes as if it were separate property, and after a few deaths in the family its former constitution will be completely subverted. As regards the vastly more numerous joint families governed by the Mitāksharā school of Hindu law, the HSA provides (sec. 6) that if one of a large number of close relatives survive the deceased his interest will pass as if it were a defined share to the heirs by testamentary or intestate succession, and not by survivorship to joint members of the family as was formerly the case. As a result, accretions of interests to *Mitākshарā* joint families will henceforth be rare, and the institution will gradually die out, and with it the problem of the limited powers of alienation of the manager—for he too is a moribund institution.

A strange rule of Hindu law allowed a person, who was interested in looking after a child whose guardian he was not, to alienate the child's property validly, provided that the alienee took care to ascertain that the alienation was required for necessity or the child's benefit. The power of the *de facto* guardian was strictly limited, and transactions entered into by him have been impeached many years afterwards on the grounds that the alleged necessity did not exist and that the alienee did not take sufficient care to acquaint himself with the facts. The HMGA endeavors, perhaps unsuccessfully, to abolish the difficulty by abolishing the *de facto* guardian. In order to alienate the property of a minor, a guardian must be authorized by the statute, and it turns out that the powers even of natural and testamentary guardians have been somewhat reduced by its provisions (secs. 8, 11).

Modernity

The Anglo-Hindu law had in course of time eliminated many of the characteristic features of the *dharmaśāstra,* but numbers of archaic features survived. Advanced Hindus felt that the limited estate of women, and the legality of polygamy were such features, and these have been mentioned above. The rule enabling a concubine to live, if chaste, a life of ease at the expense of the joint family to which her lover belonged in his lifetime, seems to be old-fashioned, and, whatever merits the rule might have in the eyes of some Hindu communities, it has been abolished by the general provisions of the HAMA. An illegitimate son's right to be maintained for life out of joint family property is similarly abolished. Both these abolitions were to be expected in view of the intended disappearance of the legal joint family, but the motives to remove the rules were not simple. It was old-fashioned that a boy of 14–15 should be entitled to adopt a son, or that a young widow of the same age should be entitled to adopt a man older than herself, that a man should give a son in adoption or take a son in adoption without consulting his wife: all these rules disappear in view of the provisions of the HAMA. That orphans should be incapable of adoption, and that illegitimate children should be kept out of so useful an institution, were accidents derived from the complexion of the antique Hindu adoption law. The orphan, under the HAMA, sec. 9, can now be given in adoption with the consent of the court, and the illegitimate child can be given in adoption, but not received in adoption by its own mother. The rule that an illegitimate daughter cannot be maintained at the expense of the joint family, except with the consent of all interested parties, is a rule of an archaic (if mistaken) origin, and is properly abolished by the general provisions of the same statute.

Rules of a reputedly religious origin which prevented until 1928 any Hindu from inheriting, and since 1928 prevented any Hindu governed by the Bengal school of law from inheriting, or taking a share at a partition of family property, if he was blind from birth, deaf and dumb, an idiot, or suffered from virulent leprosy, have been abolished by the HSA, sec. 28, and will hardly be missed.

The well-known pious obligation, by which the sons, sons' sons, and sons' sons' sons of a man were obliged to pay his debts if they were not tainted by illegality or immorality, up to the extent of their interests in joint family property—an institution which led to plentiful litigation and which worked anomalously, allowing indirectly acts which the Hindu law itself reprobated directly,—was of a distinctly archaic character, and it was once proposed to abolish it distinctly. Now however the HSA has ensured that the volume of joint family property shall be progressively and rapidly diminished, and therefore the pious obligation is indirectly doomed to extinction. The absurd situations to which it often gave rise had, more than any other abuse, drawn unfavorable attention to the legal condition of the Hindu joint family.

Certainty

Ever since the first textbooks in an European language were written on Hindu law, the complaint has been aired that that system was filled with ambiguities and uncertainties. The earliest judges attempted to impose a certainty where none could be made out from the books then available by giving pragmatic judgments. The process has been mitigated by regard for precedent, and by the skilled investigations of the Privy Council, before whom decisions and texts from all available quarters were regularly cited; but the differences of opinion between the High Courts were astonishing, and the gaps that required to be filled were very numerous. There was even doubt on which sources of law should be referred to to determine how such gaps should be filled, and the interesting source of law called Justice, Equity & Good Conscience provided strange and sometimes conflicting answers. Whether an unchaste woman of the twice-born classes could validly give her son in adoption was never settled; nor whether a man could take in adoption if he were deaf and dumb but the complaint was curable; nor whether an alienation by gift by a manager of a joint family for an unjustified purpose was void or merely voidable; nor whether an alienation could be questioned by a person born several years after it took place, though prior to his birth there had lived two persons with rights to question the alienation, both of whom were now dead, and who had died successively, the latter himself having been born after the alienation; nor whether invincible repugnance was a ground for nullity of marriage; nor, finally, whether an alienation by a non-managing member of a *Mitākshară* joint family would carry away, in some parts of India, his share of the property calculated with, or without, reference to the female members who might be entitled to shares in the event of a physical partition. A host of unsolved problems remained, several of them stemming from the earliest days of British administration of Hindu law, and some created by legislation in and immediately after the end of the British period. The wide differences between the Hindu law as administered in British India and in French India point to the capacity for error which the system had come to possess by the commencement of the 19th century. The "Hindu Code" aims, somewhat precariously, at achieving certainty and unity, and it is to be hoped that after the Supreme Court has had an opportunity to pass opinion on topics which are left ambiguous in the Code that certainty will be much nearer than it has ever been before.

UNITY

Formerly, every part of the Hindu law might be abrogated in a specific case by proof of the applicability of a valid custom. The result was a patchwork of rules even in British India. Certain states had enacted codes of Hindu law of their own, and numerous states, small in area and poor in resources, apparently administered Hindu law, if at all, upon lines that had long been obsolete in British India. Some advanced states were well ahead along the road to reform, while others, such as the component States of Malabar had codified matrilineal or otherwise divergent systems in a series of irreconcilable statutes. In the Punjab customs have reigned supreme, whether they were applicable to Hindus, Muslims, or Christians, for they were recorded in respect of practices of agricultural peoples, whose way of life was one, irrespective of religion. The Congress Party, in its struggle for political domination, has always believed in the basic unity of all Hindus. The definition of "Hindu" has always been difficult, because Hinduism possesses no creed or hierarchy, and the law has always regarded individuals as Hindus for the purposes of application of the personal law provided they were not Muslims, Parsis, Christians, or Jews, on the one hand, or members of aboriginal or criminal tribes on the other, provided that the latter term is confined to tribes which have imitated some characteristically Hindu ways but have not adopted a Hindu way of life. The "Hindu Code" assumes that all that do not belong to another religion shall be governed by it, except for the exclusion of what are called Scheduled Tribes, such as the Bhils, Garos, Santals, Gonds, etc., for so long as the government thinks fit. The original intention to abolish all customs inconsistent with the central concepts of the "Code" has not been carried out completely. Malabar customs have been abolished to a very large extent, but a few deviations from the general order of descent and distribution of estates have been allowed to those who would have been governed by the peculiar Malabar systems. Marriage and adoption benefit to some extent by the maintaining of customs so far as will permit marriage within the various limits of prohibited relationship, and will permit the adoption of children above the age of 15 or the adoption of married persons. Nevertheless, many rights are now made available to those who did not enjoy them before, such as divorce, while those who previously enjoyed a right of divorce virtually by mutual consent have retained this right by a special concession (HMA, sec. 29(2)),[10] while a conformity which formerly did not exist has been introduced by way of experiment, the effects of which have yet to be detected. Both the giving and the withholding of rights are bound to have repercussions, especially amongst the less educated communities, who will adjust themselves to the changes more slowly, and the desire

[10] See also Special Marriage Act, 1954, S.15.

for unity, which is a political object, may not in fact be achieved so effectively by this legislation as was anticipated.

The Result

1. Some strangely archaic features remain. Adoption is not possible if the adopter already has a son, or grandson by a son, or, if a girl is to be adopted, has a daughter or even a son's daughter. The state cannot take property as *ultimus heres* until an infinite number of degrees of kindred is exhausted. All through the statutes an appeal to Hindu solidarity is seen, and is strangely inconsistent with the claim that India is a secular state. If a Hindu changes his or her religion, a number of disagreeable results appear. He is liable to be divorced by his wife, he or she may forfeit an existing claim to maintenance, he or she may lose the right to give a child in adoption or to consent to the giving of the child by the other parent, and he or she may lose the right to be the guardian of his or her own issue. The issue of such a person are deprived by his or her conversion of the prospective right of inheritance from his or her unconverted relations. Equally archaic, though much more easy to justify, are the rules enabling persons comparatively remotely connected with a *propositus* or *proposita,* such as a predeceased son's son's widow, to claim to be maintained out of the estate. The intention that individuals shall attempt to stand on their own feet more than was perhaps encouraged previously makes itself seen; but it was obviously too early to deny legal rights of maintenance to people who may be married very early in life, have no qualifications for earning their living, and are prevented by social prejudice from marrying again.

2. Together with these occasional archaic features appears an interesting reliance on foreign legal experience. Numerous rules have been introduced from English law, most strikingly in the HMA which however by no means slavishly copies the English Matrimonial Causes Act. Even in the HSA, numerous rules, such as that providing a *commorientes* presumption, are plainly drawn from England. In the interpretation of certain parts of the HAMA, notably those relating to the matters to which the court shall have regard in determining the rate of maintenance to be paid to claimants, it is likely that English and other Commonwealth decisions on family protection statutes will have to be consulted. The general intention of the HMGA is as far as possible to assimilate the state of Hindu minors to that of non-Hindu and non-Muslim minors in India, and, with a few, though striking, exceptions, the Hindu law of minority will tend to be merged in the Anglo-Indian law laid down in the Guardians and Wards Act, 1890.

3. Though parts of the modern Hindu law retain that independence of litigation which formerly characterized that system, e.g. in matters of adoption, succession, and (where permitted by custom) divorce, where the intervention of the state was far less frequently required than is the case in western countries, the general tendency of the new system is to bring more business to the court, and more work to the hands of lawyers. Though legal tangles over property promise to be less complicated and less hazardous, care will have to be taken in more contexts than was usual formerly to secure the sanction of the Court to a normal act of importance in family life. Even a

natural guardian will on occasions have to journey far to instruct counsel to obtain permission for him to deal with the minor's estate. Before a decedent's estate can be distributed a host of claimants will have to be satisfied, and complicated compromises will have to be worked out if undue fragmentation is not to reduce seriously the value of the estate. If, as is almost always the case, there are minors involved, the court must be approached for consent, and even uncontentious litigation costs time and money. This marked alteration in the character of the law by no means displeases the reforming section of the community, who feel that it is consonant with India's march towards modernity.

4. In the course of the drafting of the bills which subsequently became the "Hindu Code," and the passage of these bills through both Houses of Parliament, a process which took much time and involved the contribution at various stages of many minds, some of which seem to have been applied to the task rather hurriedly, numerous slips were intruded into the text. One of the problems set by the HSA has already been treated exhaustively but inharmoniously by most of the High Courts and another was corrected by Act 73 of 1956. It would serve no useful purpose to detail or even illustrate the mistakes here. Some of them are very obvious, while some may be capable of being counteracted by judicial interpretation. The topic has been dealt with elsewhere. Countries other than India which administer Hindu law, i.e. Pakistan, Burma, Malaya, and East Africa,[11] may have much to learn from both the successful and the less attractive features of India's "Hindu Code", but it will be some time yet before the new system emerges sufficiently clearly from judicial exposition and normal practice for its merits to be appreciated correctly.

J. DUNCAN M. DERRETT *

[11] See Hindu Law in Kenya, A.I.R. 1958 Journal 1–6.

* Reader in Oriental Laws in the University of London; M.A. (Oxon.); Ph.D. (Lond.); Barrister-at-law.

[13]

THE INFLUENCE OF COMMON LAW AND EQUITY ON HINDU LAW SINCE 1800

A. *Introduction*

Speaking generally, from the time when in the late eighteenth century the East India Company adopted the principle of direct rule and established *muffassal* courts,[1] the rule governing a case in which a Hindu is concerned is to be found in a statute, or, failing that, in matters of succession, religious usage, and institution, the Hindu law, except when excluded by custom, and, failing that, in "justice, equity and good conscience."

It was not until the middle of the nineteenth century that the enactment of codes, generally based on English law, commenced, so that, in their first century, the *muffassal* courts were very often obliged to have recourse to the rule of "justice, equity and good conscience," which involved the extension of the rules of Hindu law to matters besides those specifically mentioned above. Eventually the codes covered most of the undefined sphere formerly occupied by the rule of "justice, equity and good conscience," but that still provides the residuary law for India.

In this same period, however, the Hindu law was not a law known to the judges. They took the law governing a case to which the Hindu law applied from the *pandit*, a Hindu law officer of the court, who was sworn to give his opinion according to the *sastras*.

It is difficult to say with certainty how and to what extent Hindu law was applied during the preceding five hundred years of Muslim rule. One can only assume that it was mainly left to the castes and the *panchayats*, and that custom often dictated the rule applied. It would seem probable that, when the Anglo-Indian courts first began to take cognisance of questions of Hindu law, custom showed considerable differences from the rules of the *sastras*, and varied considerably in different parts of India.

In 1877, Nelson, a Madras judge, expressed the view that the Hindu law administered by the Anglo-Indian courts was a "phantom of the brain, imagined by Sanskritists without law, and lawyers without Sanskrit."[2] Even for Southern India, this is a

[1] From 1726 the courts in the Presidency towns were established by royal charter: those outside the Presidency towns, *i.e.*, in the *muffassal*, were established by the Company.

[2] Nelson, *View of the Hindu Law as administered by the High Court of Madras*, p. 2.

gross overstatement, but it may be conceded that the result of taking the rule of law from the *pandit* often involved the elimination from the horizon of the court's outlook of much customary law. When English officials and lawyers began to study the Hindu law, they turned to the *sastras*, and the Commentaries, the sources of the *pandits'* knowledge. When the post of *pandit* was abolished, and the judge was expected to know the law, he turned to the same sources, and the writings of English and Indian officials and lawyers. The *pandit* knew that the law of the Sanskrit texts was an ideal law, never susceptible of complete and identical application, but subject to modification by custom, which varied from time to time, place to place, family to family, and caste to caste, but the English lawyer and the judge of the Anglo-Indian court was too often disposed to regard the texts in the same light as an English statute. It was not that he did not realise that they combined rules of law with rules of religion and morality, but it was difficult to assign the rules to their proper category.

The paramountcy of customs was proclaimed and respected, but there were practical difficulties in establishing custom to the satisfaction of a court. The courts did not apply the English technical rule that a custom must have existed from time immemorial, but the collection and presentation of the necessary evidence seems to have involved such expense to a party and labour to his legal adviser as often to discourage a litigant from pleading it.

In the Island of Bombay, where a "Court of Judicature" had existed since 1672, it was the practice to refer cases in which Hindus were concerned either to a body of merchants or to the castes; in other words there was a compulsory reference to arbitrators, who doubtless frequently relied on their own knowledge of custom.[3]

The same practice was doubtless followed in the other courts established before 1778, and possibly, at first, sometimes in the *muffassal* courts established after that. The Land Revenue Settlements also established, within a limited sphere, several customs, but, in the civil courts, as the English rules of evidence were increasingly enforced, and were given statutory force in 1872,[4] the difficulty of proving custom increased.

In the Punjab, possibly owing to the delay in separating executive and judiciary, and in Bombay, which had a legacy from the old "Court of Judicature," custom seems to have been given more weight than elsewhere, but, speaking generally, the legal

[3] Fawcett, *First Century of British Justice in India*, p. 184.
[4] By the Indian Evidence Act.

system developed from 1778 imposed a degree of rigidity and uniformity upon the Hindu law which it had not known earlier, and applied its rules to many persons who had not been aware that it was binding on them.

If not earlier, at least after the amalgamation of the *muffassal* and presidency towns' systems of courts in 1861, the English rule of judicial precedent was established. The decisions of a High Court were binding on all subordinate courts within its territorial jurisdiction, and a full bench decision was binding on the court itself. The decisions of the Privy Council were binding on all courts in India, but it recognised different schools of law, so that a decision might have a limited territorial effect. The result is that, to an increasing extent, the rule governing a question of Hindu law is no longer to be sought in the texts of the Sanskrit writers, but, as in England, in the decisions of the courts. The application of the rule of *stare decisis*, and the principle *communis error facit jus* makes it more difficult for an Indian court to resile from an unfortunate position than for a French court to perform the same feat; a development of the law by the courts comparable to that which took place in China between the downfall of the Ts'ing dynasty in 1911, and the establishment of the code of 1931 was inconceivable. The courts' attitude soon made it clear that amendment of the law to reconcile it with the actual state of Hindu habits must come from the legislature. Until the legislatures became representative, British policy demanded that legislation directly affecting the personal law of Hindus should be avoided as far as possible, but, since that time, the stream of innovations, often influenced by English legal notions, has steadily increased.

In estimating the influence of English law and equity upon the Hindu law, the influence of Hindu notions upon Englishmen serving in India must not be forgotten. For ninety years after the establishment in 1778 of the East India Company's *muffassal* courts, the final court of appeal from such courts was not the Supreme Court, composed of English lawyers, but the *Sudder Diwani Adalat*, manned by the East India Company's servants. In 1861 the Supreme Courts and the *Sudder Adalats* were amalgamated to form the new High Courts, and the subordinate courts were presided over by English or Indian civil servants. The former absorbed many ideas from the Indian pleaders who practised before them. Those of them who, with Indian *muffassal* judges and pleaders, achieved promotion to the High Courts had, in many respects, a common approach to the problems presented to them, which sometimes differed from that of the judges appointed direct from the English

Bar. It was the former who were mainly concerned with appeals from the *muffassal* courts, where most of the questions of Hindu law arose, and it was their decisions which made the precedents. The mind of the judge appointed direct from England had been conditioned by experience in a different field. The promoted *muffassal* judge had naturally a knowledge of English law, but less extensive than that possessed by the other type of judge, and it was usually modified by his experience of the Indian codes, usually based on English law, but with important differences which in some cases extended beyond detail.

In India, therefore, the development of the Hindu law in the courts was conditioned by an approach to its problems which I would describe as Anglo-Indian. It is true that the Privy Council was the ultimate court of appeal, but it was not until 1868 that the practice of appointing retired judges of the Supreme Courts or High Courts to the Judicial Committee superseded the previous practice of using them as assessors. Many important decisions of the Board have been delivered by Hindu Privy Councillors, but, speaking generally, they, like the retired British judges of the Indian High Courts, have displayed this "Anglo-Indian" approach to the questions before them, and, even in cases in which the purely English approach has predominated, its characteristic features have been reluctance to depart from the *sastric* texts, except in cases of conflict, either internal, or with the statute law, or with proved custom, a disinclination to introduce rules of English substantive law, except to fill a gap, and only then in an assimilable form, careful study of the course of Indian decisions on a particular question, upholding them whenever possible, frequently indicating legal or equitable principles on which they might be based, and, whenever necessary, deciding between conflicting schools of thought. The fact that, in some of the early decisions we find language more appropriate to English law, for instance references to "equitable estates" of coparceners, must not blind us to the fact that the Board often did justice in questions of Hindu law, where the Indian courts had failed through taking too narrow a view of the problem; the Board never countenanced the introduction into India of the English distinction between legal and equitable estates.

As business in Indian courts was usually conducted in English, and as from 1864 the Hindu law was a law the courts were deemed to know, most judges had to rely on English translations of the writings of the Hindu jurists. These contained some mistakes, and sometimes failure to understand the original writers' method of exposition created misunderstandings. If occasionally the result was the introduction of innovations into the law, they are neither sufficiently numerous or serious for mention here.

Inevitably, English terms of art crept into the translations and into the language used in the courts. This gives rise to the danger that a term may carry with it associations which are out of place in the Hindu system. To describe a *Dayabhaga* coparcener as a "tenant-in-common" is in no way misleading, but a *Mitakshara* coparcener does not, as is sometimes said, hold in "joint-tenancy" as understood in English law. The word "coparcener" has a very different meaning in English law, but those sufficiently learned to know its meaning in English law will be in no danger of using it in the same sense in Hindu law. Unauthorised alienation by a widow, a manager, or a coparcener are sometimes described as "void" or "voidable," though, in the sense in which these words are used in English law, it is difficult to fit such transactions into either category. Yet, it may safely be said that the influence of words upon the Hindu law has been negligible; it is new ideas which have been absorbed.

The Hindu law is only applicable in British India in matters of succession, inheritance, the joint family, partition, maintenance, gifts, wills and religious usage and institution. In all other matters the Hindu is governed by the general law, now mainly statutory, and adapted from the law of England. The Hindu law has necessarily had to give way to statutory provisions, and, in particular, English procedural law, especially its rules for execution, which made the early Company's courts in Madras and Bombay popular with Indian litigants; these have made a profound impression upon the Hindu law. Though no attempt was made to introduce the English law of real property into India, the statute law relating to marriage, transfer of property *inter vivos*, and by will, and succession, originally introduced to meet the needs of persons not governed by the Hindu or Muhammadan law, have disseminated ideas which proved attractive to the Hindu. Whereas the Indian Muslim has tended to revert to the *Sharia*, the Hindu has been remarkably receptive of English principles of law, possibly because so many Hindus have displayed such remarkable ability in the field of Anglo-Indian law. Of this there can be no clearer evidence than the steady extension to Hindus of the rules of the Indian Succession Act, and the Transfer of Property Act, and the recent legislation in relation to marriage. Up to the present, Indian independence has produced no change in the direction of the evolution of the law; on the contrary, the development during the British period in India seems to have been accelerated.

B. *The law of the Joint Family*

In the sphere in which, in British India, the Hindu law supplied the rule governing a case, the law of the Joint Family is fundamental. All other chapters of the law have to serve its purposes. Starting from the patriarchal family, in which the patriarch alone had property rights recognised by an outside authority, it developed long before the British period into a corporation, the coparcenary, comprising broadly the *agnate males*, with interests in the joint family property fluctuating with births and deaths, and indefinable until partition occurred, for an agnate acquired an interest at birth, which, on his death, passed by survivorship to the other coparceners. The manager, no longer necessarily the senior agnate, still retained a very wide discretion in the management of the property, and the disposal of its income, but his powers of disposal of the *corpus* were considerably curtailed, and the rights of a coparcener to demand partition, and ascertainment and delivery of his share were recognised. Though this was a step in the direction of a wider recognition of the right to separate property, it involved the creation of a new coparcenary between the separated coparcener and his after-born sons.

This, at least, was the position in the greater part of India, as set out in the *Mitakshara*, but in Bengal, the *Dayabhaga* school denied the son any interest in his father's lifetime, and devolution followed the same rules as governed inheritance to separate property. There, though the manager's powers were generally the same as elsewhere in India, the coparcenary might include female heirs, and every coparcener had, not a fluctuating interest, but a share, defined by the law of inheritance, which he held in quasi-severalty. Partition made the male coparcener the absolute owner of his share, and only family loyalty could deter him from demanding it. Bengal had gone a step further than the rest of India in the direction of recognition of separate property.

It has been said that the influence of the Anglo-Indian legal system upon *Mitakshara* joint family law has been to leave it so different from the original that what is left of it were best swept away. Speaking broadly, the draft Hindu Code proposes to apply the rules of the *Dayabhaga* joint family all over India.

Not only does the Hindu law require a man to pay his debts; it threatens him who does not with dire punishment in the next life. The English law has, however, effective procedural measures to compel him to pay in this life, by seizure and sale of rights and interests capable of being realised. At an early stage in its development, the Anglo-Indian law held, without being over-assiduous to explain how or why, that a *Mitakshara* coparcener's undivided interest was liable to attachment and sale at the instance of a judgment-creditor to purge a separate and personal debt, resolving the conflict between the other coparceners' rights of survivorship and the creditor's right to be paid in favour of the latter. In 1877, a decision of the Privy Council made this law for the whole of British India.[5] Two years later, the same tribunal held that even an attachment by the creditor would defeat the other coparceners' rights of survivorship, if the judgment-debtor died before the execution sale.[6] In the latter case, the Privy Council, searching for a principle to explain the established practice, which it recognised as contrary to *Mitakshara* law, said it was " founded on the equity, which a purchaser for value has, to be allowed to stand in his vendor's shoes, and work out his rights by means of partition." In the former case, the Board drew an analogy between the position of a coparcener and that of a partner, but efforts to extend the analogy compelled the legislature to lay down in the Indian Partnership Act, of 1932 that coparceners are not partners.

Logically, if a judgment-creditor can attach and sell a coparcener's interest in the joint family property in execution for a separate private debt, there is no reason why the debtor should insist in being brought to court; he could save public time and money by making over his interest to his creditor. Conceding that, there is no reason why he should not dispose of his interest to raise funds to meet anticipated personal expenditure, and from that the recognition of the right of free alienation of his interest for value should follow. If the basis is that the purchaser acquires an equity to exercise his vendor's right to partition, that applies equally in the case of a voluntary alienation and in the case of an execution sale. In Bombay, Madras and Madhya Pradesh the courts have accepted this view, but elsewhere they have held that this inroad into the *Mitakshara* law can not be pushed further by deductive reasoning. Attempts to induce the Privy Council to extend the principle to the case of the alienee under a voluntary alienation for value in other parts of India have failed, as the Board refused to take it further than it had been taken by the Indian courts,[7] though the Board has suggested a distinction between an attachment in execution, and a voluntary conveyance, in that the former created a lien or charge in favour of the judgment-creditor.[8] It follows, of course, that the insolvency of a coparcener renders his interest liable to be partitioned and sold for the benefit of his creditors.

[5] *Deen Dayal* v. *Jugdeep*, 4 I.A. 247.
[6] *Suraj Bansi Koer* v. *Sheo Persad* (1879) 6 I.A. 88.
[7] *Balgobind* v. *Narain* (1893) 20 I.A. 116.
[8] *Suraj Bunsi Koer* v. *Sheo Persad* (1879) 6 I.A. 88.

It may still be open to argument whether the disposal by a coparcener of his interest for value, or its sale by legal process, if consummated by partition, effects his separation from the family, but there seems ample authority for saying that it does not.[9] It would seem to follow that, after partition has been effected for the benefit of his alienee or judgment-creditor, he retains his coparcenary interest in what remains, or at least in what is subsequently acquired, although the interest which passes to the alienee or judgment-creditor is the interest he had at the moment of alienation or attachment.[10] He could, presumably, make a fresh alienation, after the first alienee had been satisfied, and continue the process until the other coparceners were driven to separate from him. In any case, the law, as developed, is calculated to encourage partition.

Possibly the most curious perversion of *Mitakshara* joint family law is the change made in the doctrine of the pious obligation. The texts oblige the son to pay his father's debts to relieve him of punishment in the next world, but debts tainted with immorality are excluded from consideration in this connection. The obligation naturally did not arise until after the father's death, and was unlimited, and not dependent upon the receipt of assets from the father. One may doubt whether it should have been regarded as a rule of positive law at all; obviously it would be difficult for Anglo-Indian courts to enforce it in the form just stated; it conflicted with the English rules that payment of a legal debt may be enforced against any valuable asset of the debtor, and that no person should be obliged to discharge the debt of another beyond the extent of the assets devolving from him. The doctrine ceased to apply to separate property received by inheritance from the father, because it was, in any case, held liable to purge any legally enforceable debt of the father, whether tainted with immorality or not; it only applied to joint family property. The courts, however, deduced from the son's duty to pay his father's untainted debt a right of the father to alienate his son's interest to purge such a debt, and made this right available to a creditor of the father. Having made the rule operate in the father's lifetime, the courts required, however, not only that the debt should be untainted, but also "antecedent." A mortgage of the son's interest simultaneous with the debt would not bind the son's share, but a mortgage to secure a pre-existing debt would,

[9] *Aiyyagiri* v. *Aiyyagiri* (1902) 25 Mad. 690; *Gurlingappa* v. *Nandappa* (1890) 21 Bom. 798; *Patroo Lal* v. *Parbhavati* [1943] All. 205.

[10] *Peramanayakam* v. *Sivaraman*, A.I.R. [1952] Mad. 419.

provided that the two transactions were really independent.[11] Nevertheless, the courts professed assiduity in following the texts on the question whether a debt were tainted or not, and held debts due for liquor, lust or gambling, or incurred by criminal acts, tainted. Regarding debts arising from a civil liability the position is not very clear. Debts incurred by ill-advised litigation are not tainted, and regarding debts arising from tortious acts, it is impossible to lay down a principle. A debt untainted at its inception cannot subsequently become tainted. Obviously, the effect of the development of this doctrine is to encourage a demand for partition by sons against an extravagant or unwise father.

The manager of the joint family can alienate the *corpus* of the joint family property for legal necessity or the benefit of the estate.[12] "Legal necessity" has been explained to include any purpose which a reasonable Hindu would deem proper, but "benefit of the estate" is interpreted sometimes narrowly to imply protective measures only, and at other times more broadly to include any non-speculative act such as a prudent manager would perform. The courts have, however, given additional protection to the alienee from the manager by engrafting upon the *Mitakshara* rule an equitable extension. If the alienee honestly makes such inquiries as are possible to a reasonable man, and is satisfied of the necessity for the alienation, he is entitled to the benefit of his bargain, notwithstanding that there was, in fact, no necessity for it, or that the money paid by the alienee was misapplied.[13]

Many Hindu families carry on a business, and formerly a family business was normally hereditary. If the business is carried on solely by members of the family, generally the law of the Joint Family applies, though the alienee from the manager is then in a more favourable position, for his inquiries need go no further than whether the money is needed for the business. If a stranger is introduced into the management, his rights are governed by the Indian Partnership Act which is substantially English law; his partnership, however, is not with the family, but with such members of it as enter into contractual relations with him. This involves the inconvenience that the death of a member of the family dissolves the partnership, and its reconstruction of the enterprise is to continue,[14] whereas a death in the joint family firm has no such consequences.

[11] *Brij Narain* v. *Mangla Prasad* (1924) 51 I.A. 129; *Subramania* v. *Sabapathi* (1928) 51 Mad. 361.

[12] This is a paraphrase of *Mitakshara*, I.i. 27–29 in *Hanooman Persaud* v. *Mst Babooee* (1856) 6 M.I.A. 393.

[13] *Hanooman Persaud* (*supra*).

[14] *Pichappa* v. *Chokalingam*, A.I.R. [1934] P.C. 192.

During the British period, there was an increasing tendency for Hindu families to embark on new enterprises, but the Privy Council held that the *Mitakshara* gave a manager no power to impose on a minor coparcener the risk and liability of a new business. The courts in India were assiduous to find a way out of this restriction upon the adventurous, by maintaining that an alienation of joint family property to raise funds to start a new business might be upheld as a benefit to the estate, and by narrowing the conception of a new business.[15] The restriction puts the joint family business at a disadvantage in comparison with other forms of business association, and tends to encourage the break-up of the joint family.

A coparcener who decided to follow a learned profession or other avocation requiring an expensive training found himself faced with special difficulties. Anciently, when separate property was unknown, the earnings of every member were invariably the property of the family, but *Yajnavalkya* recognised separate property in what a coparcener acquired "without detriment to the father's estate," and the *Mitakshara* specifically stated that this was an essential condition to any acquisition becoming a coparcener's separate property, which did not include "what is earned by *science* at the expense of ancestral wealth."[16] Madras, at least, gave a literal interpretation to these texts. The *Dayabhaga*, however, more favourable to self-acquisitions, maintained that the acquisitions of a coparcener could not be regarded as joint family property merely because the family had supplied him with food and other necessaries.[17] It was only when joint family property was used for the express purpose of making the acquisition that it became joint family property. In 1877 the Privy Council approved the view held in Bengal that a coparcener who had received any education whatever at joint family expense did not thereby debar himself from ever acquiring separate property in his earnings, and said that it might be necessary to review the interpretation placed on the *Mitakshara* texts in Madras.[18] In 1882 the Bombay High Court held that an elementary education at the family expense would not deprive a subordinate judge's savings of its character as separate property, when the special skill which enabled their acquisition had been acquired while he was employed as a lawyer's clerk, and not at family expense.[19] In 1918 the Privy Council had to deal with a case from Scind of

[15] *Benares Bank* v. *Hari Narain* (1932) 59 I.A. 300.
[16] See *Mitakshara*, I.iv. 1 and 6.
[17] *Dayabhaga*, VI.i. 44–50.
[18] *Pauliem* v. *Pauliem* (1877) 4 I.A. 190.
[19] *Lakshman* v. *Jumnabai* (1822) 6 Bom. 242.

a coparcener who had been educated at family expense in the Government High School. He then became a pleader's clerk, and saved money out of his salary which was the basis of a large fortune made by him as a broker and moneylender.[20] The Board based its decision on the *Mitakshara* texts mentioned above, said that "learning" was a more accurate translation than "science," and that it meant a special training; it did not include the general elementary education suitable to the coparcener's station in life. His fortune was held to be his separate property.

With the progressive Indianisation of the public services, it was inevitable that, in 1920, two cases should come before the Privy Council in relation to the earnings of Indian civil servants who were coparceners in joint families, and who, to secure their appointments, had spent seven years in England at the expense of their families. The Board held that a coparcener's acquisitions remained the property of his family, if he was originally equipped for the calling in which they were made by a special training at the expense of the patrimony[21] and, while recognising the incongruity of applying them to persons following such an avocation, conceived it important to introduce no variations or uncertainties into established laws affecting family rights.[22] Though it would be difficult to find evidence of a desire on their Lordships' part to search for new interpretations of old texts, it is submitted, with great respect, that their decision in 1918 can more easily be based on the *Dayabhaga* texts than those in the *Mitakshara*. Their decision of 1920 created difficulties in practice. A Hindu member of the Indian Civil Service was obliged to adopt a mode of life similar to that followed by his European brethren, and he was not paid on a scale which left a great margin after essential expenses were covered. The inconvenience was felt by the individual as much as by the administration. Of course a member of a learned profession could protect himself by separating from his family, and these decisions were an encouragement to him to do so. However, by 1920, such Hindus were beginning to feel that the time had come for a change in the law. In 1901 a Bill to emancipate members of learned professions was passed by the Legislative Council in Madras, but popular indignation compelled the Governor to veto it. In 1930, the Hindu Gains of Learning Act was passed by the central legislature without a word of protest. By its provisions, all acquisitions of a member of a joint family, whether ordinary or extraordinary results of education or training of any

20 *Ramrakhiomal* v. *Rewachand* (1918) 45 I.A. 41.
21 *Amar Nath* v. *Hukam Chand*, A.I.R. [1921] P.C. 45.
22 *Gokal Chand* v. *Hukam Chand* (1921) 48 I.A. 162.

kind imparted by another member, or paid for out of joint family funds, became his own separate property. The professional man, the salary earner, and the wage earner now receive their earnings and hold their savings as separate property.

As already noticed, the right of a coparcener to demand partition, even against an agnate ascendant, was generally recognised before the British period, and it was well settled that it was sufficient for a coparcener to communicate an unequivocal intention to separate. This rule was naturally recognised by the courts, but they were faced with a difficulty when a coparcener instituted a partition suit, and then abandoned or withdrew it. The courts could do no more than regard it as "evidence that an intention to separate had been entertained."[23]

Whereas, at *Mitakshara* law "partition" means the ascertainment of the fractional shares of the coparceners, at *Dayabhaga* law it means physical division of the joint family property. The courts, therefore, proceeded to distinguish between severance of status and division of the family property.[24] The texts regard partition as possible once only, when it must be final and complete, though subject to rectification in cases of omission, mistake, and fraud. The courts, however, regarded separation of status as necessarily involving partition of the property, but held that division of property might be partial, and did not necessarily involve separation of status.[25]

Although the apostasy of a coparcener still, as under the old law, involves the separation of a coparcener from his family, the Caste Disabilities Removal Act of 1850 gives him the right to obtain the share to which he would have been entitled immediately before his apostasy. A coparcener who marries under the Special Marriage Act of 1872 is automatically separated from his family, but has the same rights in the family property as the apostate under the Act of 1850. The Act of 1872 makes his property no longer subject to the Hindu law of devolution, but to the Indian Succession Act, which is based on English law.

The Hindu Women's Rights to Property Act of 1937, which, like most of the legislation directly affecting the Hindu law, was not Government-inspired, gives a *Mitakshara* coparcener's widow the same interest in joint family property as he had at his death, with the right to partition. She takes, however, a widow's estate, *i.e.*, there are restrictions on her right to alienate the *corpus* similar to those imposed on a manager, and, on her death, it passes to her

[23] *Palani Ammal* v. *Muthuvenkatacharlu* (1925) 52 I.A. 83.
[24] *Girjabai* v. *Sadashiv* (1916) 43 I.A. 151 and 160.
[25] *Appovier* v. *Ramasubba* (1866) 11 M.I.A. 75 and 90.

husband's heirs. While this is a laudable attempt to improve the widow's position, it is incompatible with *Mitakshara* principles. It is interesting to note that this Act was called in aid, though, it is submitted, the logic is not obvious, by the Nagpur High Court recently to support a decision that a woman might be manager of a joint family,[26] but this decision caused the Madras High Court, with its traditional devotion to the *Mitakshara*, almost to throw up its hands in horror.[27] The Nagpur decision is, however, a straw which shows the way the wind is blowing.

To sum up, the influence of English law, directly and indirectly, has been to accelerate the process of extending the field of separate property, to make rights and interests in joint family property more freely transferable, and to encourage partition. The rules of joint family law have now only a limited application to the more intelligent, better-educated, and politically minded Hindus, and they seem disposed to limit the application of these rules still further. Though, at present, political leadership comes mainly from them, and political power lies mainly with them, they do not form a majority in India, and the possibility of a reaction against this policy or a reorientation of it, is not be ignored.

C. *Marriage*

According to the texts, marriage is a sacrament, complete and irrevocable at the conclusion of the rites; the wife was often married as a child, and remained with her parents until puberty. Its prescribed purpose was to ensure the perpetuation of the family name and the family worship; polygamy was therefore recognised. The wife, who must be of her husband's caste, but outside the prohibited degrees, passed from her own family into the family of her husband. Most texts deny the right of the widow to remarry, and for centuries her lot was unhappy. The wife and the widow had a right to maintenance in the family of the husband, but no right by survivorship in the joint family property, and no right of inheritance to the husband except in the absence of male issue; even then the widow took a limited estate, as explained earlier. She may, however, have peculiar property of her own, *stridhana*, governed by special rules of devolution, which generally favour females. Subject to the husband's right to take it in emergencies, a wife may deal as she pleases with gifts from her own blood relations, and gifts of movables from her husband. Her husband may, and she may not without his permission, in his lifetime, deal with

[26] *Commissioner of Income Tax* v. *Lakshminarayana*, A.I.R. [1949] Nag. 128.
[27] *Radha* v. *Income Tax Commissioner*, A.I.R. [1950] Mad. 538.

gifts from strangers, and her own earnings, but her powers over it are absolute on his death.

The case law has done little to change the position set out above, and it is the statute law which has accomplished the marked change in the position of women which has taken place during the British period. The British may claim to have initiated this process, and British example and education, and the early enactment of statutes with more generous provisions for women of other faiths have all helped, but the more sweeping changes have been effected by recent legislation either initiated, or actively supported by Hindus.

When the British first assumed political responsibility in India, cases of *sati*, *i.e.*, a widow immolating herself on her husband's funeral pyre, were not uncommon. After some reluctance, due to the policy of non-interference in religious and family matters, they decided to suppress the practice. Then, in 1856, the Hindu Widows' Remarriage Act legalised widow remarriage, but deprived the widow of her rights of inheritance to her deceased husband's property, and, on the petition of his relations, of the guardianship of his children.

The Indian Succession Act of 1856, which applied to all persons of Indian domicile other than Hindus, Muslims, and Parsees contained rules of intestate succession based broadly on English principles, which placed the widow in a more favourable position than she enjoyed under the Hindu law.

In 1872, the Christian Marriage Act provided for celebration of marriages, either by a religious ceremony before a minister or priest, or by a civil ceremony before a registrar, and no marriage to which one party is a Christian is valid, except when celebrated in accordance with the provisions of the Act.

In the same year the Special Marriage Act was passed. The noteworthy effect of the Special Marriage Act of 1872 was to introduce among a small but influential section of the Hindu community a system of marriage which required the consent of the contracting parties, which did not place the wife under the power of the husband, and which recognised divorce for grave matrimonial faults. The occasion for its enactment was the desire of the members of the *Arya Samaj*, a Hindu theistic sect which had absorbed many Western notions, to contract valid marriages without resort to the ancient Brahmanical rites. The British Indian Government, while anxious to meet this need, regarded the multiplication of marriage laws on a sectarian basis as undesirable, so its provisions provided for civil marriage before a registrar of persons who were prepared to declare themselves to be neither Christians, Jews, Hindus or Muslims. No person with a spouse living could marry under the Act, and neither party might be an ascendant or descendant, or brother or sister of an ascendant or descendant of the other, nor might they have a common ancestor nearer than great-great-grandparent. Advantage was taken of the Act, not only by *Aryas*, but other Hindus, including those of different castes and those within the prohibited degrees for Hindu sacramental marriage, which are, by Western standards, unnecessarily restrictive, and not susceptible of accurate exposition. The Act was amended in 1923 to permit marriages between Hindus without formal renunciation of their faith. Hindus who take advantage of it may, however, find it inconvenient that their property devolves, not according to the Hindu law, but in accordance with the rules in the Indian Succession Act. Marriages under this Act may be dissolved under the Indian Divorce Act of 1869, originally only applicable to Christians; a marriage may be annulled for physical incompetence; the husband may be granted a divorce for his wife's adultery, and the wife for her husband's adultery combined with cruelty or desertion, or for his apostasy coupled with remarriage. The Hindu Marriages Validating Act of 1949 validates inter-caste marriages, so that difference of caste no longer impels intending spouses to have recourse to a statute which changes their personal law so considerably.

The *Sharda* Act of 1929, while not invalidating child marriages among Hindus, imposes criminal penalties on those who bring them about.

The Hindu Married Women's Right to Separate Residence and Maintenance Act of 1946 entitles the wife to maintenance and a separate residence, if the husband takes a second wife or keeps a concubine, or apostatises, or is guilty of cruelty or desertion, or suffers from a loathsome disease. The Bombay Prevention of Bigamous Marriages Act of 1946, the Bombay Hindu Divorce Act of 1947, and the Madras Hindu (Bigamy Prevention and Divorce) Act, 1949 make a second marriage by the husband with a wife living void, and render him liable to criminal punishment. Either spouse may obtain a divorce for impotence, insanity, loathsome disease in, or desertion, or continuous infidelity by the other.

The Hindu Women's Rights to Property Act of 1937 has much improved the position of the widow, who, on intestacy, now receives a share in her husband's estate equal to that of a son.

The draft Hindu code of 1948 aimed at further progress in the direction taken by the legislation mentioned above. It proposed to make civil and sacramental marriage available to all Hindus, without any effect upon their personal law. The prohibited degrees for sacramental marriage were simplified, clarified and ameliorated. Child marriages would be voidable at the instance of either party. Monogamy would be compulsory throughout India, and divorce available to all on grounds similar to those in the recent legislation in Bombay and Madras.

Opposition to this proposed legislation seems to have convinced its supporters that the code of 1948 was too large a step in the direction of uniformity. The Hindu Marriage and Divorce Bill, 1952, which deals only with sacramental marriage, retains most of the provisions of the code of 1948, but it preserves the existing law on matters not dealt with in the Bill, and gives greater scope for custom. Civil marriage is to be dealt with in a separate Bill.

D. *Adoption*

The ancient law developed various devices for the perpetuation of the family name and worship, when marriage failed to achieve that object, but, of these, adoption alone survived at the commencement of the British period. Not only may a sonless man adopt, but his widow may, in most parts of India, adopt in his name, after his death, subject to conditions which vary in different parts of India.

The motive for adoption may, in part at least, be secular, and, when it is done by a widow, who cannot be compelled to adopt, it may even be to spite reversioners. The texts prescribe no circumstances in which the power is extinguished, but commencing in 1870,[28] the Privy Council elaborated the doctrine that, if a male Hindu F dies, leaving a widow M, and a son S, who dies later, leaving a son SS, or a widow W, M has lost the power to adopt, because the religious duty to continue the family line and worship which lay originally on F has passed through his son S either to SS or W. This rule has regard solely to the religious aspect of adoption, and so also has the rule that—apparently for all purposes—an adoption by a widow takes effect as from the death of her husband.[29] This latter rule, which is comparatively recent, devests estates acquired by survivorship or inheritance in the interim, though the widow herself is partially protected by the Hindu Women's rights to Property Act of 1937, and the adoption may take place many years after the death of her husband. This later rule has not been received with universal acclamation in India; in particular Bombay has expressed alarm at its possible consequences and has sought to limit its implications.

[28] *Bhoobun Moyee* v. *Ram Kishore* (1870) 10 M.I.A. 279.

[29] *Amarendra* v. *Sanatan* (1933) 60 I.A. 242; *Anant* v. *Shankar* (1943) 70 I.A. 232.

Viewed from the religious standpoint, rules that neither an orphan nor an only son may be given in adoption are reasonable, and the latter inevitable. There are texts to support both, but the courts have only enforced the former rule. The *Mitakshara* itself quotes the text prohibiting the latter,[30] but this was held to be only a religious injunction in the leading case decided in 1899.[31]

Another rule in the texts, and which naturally follows from the *Sastric* view of adoption, is that no boy may be adopted if he is the son of a woman who, before her marriage, was within the prohibited degrees for marriage with the adoptive father. In 1899 reversing a full bench decision of the Allahabad High Court, the Privy Council held that this was a rule of law,[32] but this decision evoked no applause from Hindus, many of whom, it would seem, felt it contrary to a custom which was, at least, in the course of formation. The Bombay High Court proceeded to limit its application to the relations of the adoptor specifically mentioned in the Privy Council judgment.

From what has been said, it would seem that the Privy Council's decisions have acted as a brake upon the development of the law of adoption, in some parts of India, on a secular basis. A glance at the Draft Hindu code, however, suggests that there is little to criticise in the policy of the courts. It is true that it is proposed to abolish the rule forbidding the adoption of the son of a woman whom the adoptor could not have married, and to remove the anomalies and uncertainties regarding the existence of the widow's power to adopt, but the rule regarding its extinction, and the rule that for all purposes adoption by a widow relates back to the adoptive father's death, which were developed in the courts, are to be retained.

What has been described as a somewhat incongruous but equitable graft upon the law of adoption is the rule of evidence known in English law as estoppel, the rule that, when one person has, by word or conduct, intentionally caused another to believe a thing to be true and act upon that belief, the former may not, in legal proceedings between them, deny the truth of that thing.

The rule has been applied in those parts of India where a widow cannot adopt without her husband's authority, in cases where, having purported to adopt a son, the widow subsequently sues for a declaration that it was invalid for want of authority. In one such case[33] the Privy Council held the widow estopped from pleading want of authority, because she had represented that she has such

30 Mit. I.xi. 11.
31 *Sri Balusu* v. *Sri Balusu* (1899) 26 I.A. 113.
32 *Bhagwan Singh* v. *Bhagwan Singh* (1899) 26 I.A. 153.
33 *Rani Dharam Kunwar* v. *Balwant* (1912) 39 I.A. 142.

authority, and thereby intentionally induced the boy to leave his natural family and to change his mode of life so as to make a return to it a hardship. The same rule has been applied to other relations in the adopting family, but it is of limited application. It is only applicable in special circumstances in an action. It cannot convert an invalid adoption into a valid one. The representation must be one of fact and is only available against the person or persons making it; it must be intended to involve and in fact involve the adoptee in an irrevocable transfer from his natural family.

E. *Inheritance*

The rules of inheritance in Hindu law developed with the recognition of separate property from the rules of survivorship, and, in *Mitakshara* law they apply only to separate property. In *Mitakshara* law, the main principle is that the nearest agnate succeeds. Though the texts give other reasons, the widow is recognised possibly because, at one time, she managed the estate of the *paterfamilias* after his death, and the daughter and her son possibly because, at one time, a sonless man might appoint a daughter whose sons would be deemed to be his. Other cognates do not succeed until the agnates to a remote degree have been exhausted.

Whereas in *Mitakshara* law, the heir has the duty to offer oblations for the spiritual benefit of the deceased, in *Dayabhaga* law the main principle is that the preferential heir is he who can confer most spiritual benefit upon the deceased by his oblations. The oblation to the maternal grandfather is recognised for this purpose, possibly because of the ancient practice of appointing a daughter, but it is less efficacious than an agnate's oblation. On these bases, the *Dayabhaga* law has evolved rules applicable also to joint family property, which are free from the uncertainties experienced in *Mitakshara* law, but which introduce cognates earlier than the other system. Until very recently, it has remained unaffected by statutes, partly because, on account of its operation on joint family property, there has been a more noticeable tendency of property to fall into the hands of women than elsewhere.

Despite the differences between the two systems, in the majority of cases the devolution of the property is the same, for, except that in *Dayabhaga* law the father takes before the mother, the nearest heirs in order of succession in both systems are :—(i–iii) the three immediate agnate male descendants, (iv) the widow, (v) the daughter, (vi) the daughter's son, (vii) the mother, (viii) the father, (ix) the brother, (x) the brother's son, (xi) the brother's son's son. Tradition and long practice had fixed the position of these heirs so firmly that neither juristic theory nor judicial decisions could interfere.

In *Mitakshara* law, when there is no agnate claimant, the texts give little assistance, and most of the rules for selecting the relation entitled to succeed are the work of the courts. It is true that the texts prefer the deceased's own cognate relations to his father's, and his father's to his mother's. The elaboration of that rule, and the evolution of the rules that the nearer line excludes the more remote, and then the individual nearer in degree the more remote are, no doubt, based on analogy and dialectic traceable to the *Mitakshara*, but the courts cannot agree as to the limits within which cognate relationship embraces a right of inheritance, and, after the rule that the nearer excludes the more remote, they have introduced the test of spiritual benefit.[34] Though this doctrine is not unrecognised among commentators of the *Mitakshara* school, its introduction at that stage into *Mitakshara* law is open to criticism.

The courts have deprived the murderer of the right to inherit from his victim on grounds of public policy.[35]

Non-interference in matters of personal law being a cardinal principle of British government in India, the influence of English law upon the Hindu law of inheritance has been necessarily mainly indirect. The possible heirs of a Hindu intestate include individuals in degres of relationship far more distant than any Western system of law would tolerate, but no attempt to narrow the field of heritable relationship was likely after experience of the operation of Lord Dalhousie's doctrine of lapse, whereby, on failure of natural heirs, a princely state lapsed to the British Government. Though a foreign government in the nineteenth century may have found it advisable not to press its claims against those of remote relations of a deceased person, an indigenous government of the twentieth century, obliged by the constitution to establish the welfare State, cannot be so tender, and the Hindu Code Bill proposes considerably to limit the degrees of relationship within which rights of inheritance are recognised.

The statutory amendments of the law of inheritance during the British period were not inspired by the British Government, but were promoted by Hindu legislators, influenced by English law through the medium of the Indian codes.

The texts disqualified persons suffering from mental and physical infirmities from rights of inheritance and survivorship;

[34] *Jatindra* v. *Nagendra* (1932) 58 I.A. 372.
[35] *Kenchava* v. *Girimallappa* (1924) 51 I.A. 368.

the origin of these rules is probably, in part, that such persons might be a liability to their families standing in arms against their enemies, or unable to assist in the management and enhancement of the family property, or unable to carry on the family name, or perform the rites of family worship. Though the texts protected persons so disqualified by giving them rights of maintenance, by comparison with the rules in the Indian Succession Act, these rules seemed too severe for the present age, and the Hindu Inheritance (Removal of Disabilities) Act of 1928 removed all such disqualifications except congenital insanity, but it did not apply to persons governed by *Dayabhaga* law.

The following year saw the first manifestation of the impulse to improve the rights of inheritance of women and cognates. The Hindu Inheritance (Amendment) Act inserted in the list of heirs at *Mitakshara* law, between the father's father and the father's brother,[34] the son's daughter, the daughter's daughter, the sister, and the sister's son. The Draft Hindu code proposes to give these newly recognised heirs still higher places in the order of succession.

The Hindu Women's Rights to Property Act of 1937, which applied to all schools, gives the widow the same share on inheritance as if she were a son, and the son's widow the share of a grandson or a son according as there is or is not a grandson surviving.

The obvious direction of this legislation is departure from the notion of the joint family towards the conception of a new social unit comprising the husband and wife and their children, with rules of inheritance based on the degree of affection, irrespective of sex, deemed to exist between the deceased and the heirs. The provisions of the Draft Hindu code suggest further steps in the same direction; the first class of preferential heirs, who take as a body, comprises the widow, the daughter, the three immediate agnate male descendants, and their widows. The next class take in the following order: (a) the parents, (b) grandchildren not included in the first class, (c) great-grandchildren who do not take in the first class, (d) brothers and sisters, (e) nephews and nieces, (f) the paternal grandparents, (g) the widows of the father and brothers, (h) paternal uncles and aunts, (i) the maternal grandparents, (j) maternal uncles and aunts. After these classes have been exhausted, the rule that agnates are preferred to cognates comes into operation, and then the preference of the male to the female line, but the doctrine of spiritual benefit seems likely to be discarded.

[34] After the brother's son's son (see above), come (xii) the father's mother, and then (xiii) the father's father.

F. *Impartible Estates*

An impartible estate is an estate which, by special law or custom, devolves on a single heir, usually selected according to lineal primogeniture.

The texts are silent regarding such estates, and the law applicable to them has been evolved by the courts. Whereas, in Bengal, there was a natural predisposition to look upon them as the separate property of the holder for the time being, where the *Mitakshara* prevailed, notwithstanding that the right of common enjoyment, and the right to demand partition was denied to junior members of the holder's family, it was held that their right to succeed by survivorship was sufficient to preserve the joint character of the estate. It was also held that the holder's right to alienate the *corpus* of the estate was limited in the same way as the right of the manager of a joint family.

Then, in 1888, the Privy Council repudiated the doctrine that an impartible estate was joint family property,[37] and recognised the unfettered right of the holder to dispose of the estate *inter vivos*. Eleven years later the right of disposal by will was recognised.[38] In 1932, however, the Board reverted to the theory that an impartible estate was joint family property,[39] but without reimposing restrictions on the holder's right to alienate. In the meantime Indian provincial legislatures had, to some extent, reimposed these restrictions in parts of India.[40]

The recognition of the alienable nature of an impartible estate, and the rule that the estate loses its impartible character in the hands of the alienee, combined with the impossibility of creating a new impartible estate,[41] except by Crown grant, is another instance of the tendency of Anglo-Indian law to make property in general more freely transferable.

The recent legislation which, throughout India, has generally deprived landowners of their rights in their estates, save in small demesne lands, suggests the early extinction of impartible estates.

G. *Wills*

The greater part of the modern Hindu law of wills is a modification of the English law on this subject. There are certain texts from which a testamentary power might have been developed, but these are no more cogent for this purpose than the texts in the Burmese

[37] *Rani Sartaj Kuari* v. *Deoraj* (1888) 15 I.A. 51.
[38] *1st Pittapur Case* (1899) 26 I.A. 83.
[39] *Shibaprasad* v. *Prayag* (1932) 59 I.A. 331.
[40] See, *e.g.*, the Madras Impartible Estates Act, 1904.
[41] See *Palaniammal* v. *Muthuvenkatacharlu* (1925) 52 I.A. 83.

Dhammathats. In Burma, however, the English courts decided against recognition of testamentary power in Burmese Buddhists, whereas in India they took the opposite course in relation to Hindus. Hindus, from contact with Muslims and Europeans, were familiar with the notion of testamentary power before the question arose in the Anglo-Indian courts, but the Burmese, for many centuries before the British conquest, were more isolated and less receptive of foreign notions. In both countries the answer to the problem seems to have been determined by consideration of its reception by those whom it would affect.

In 1724, the Court of Judicature at Bombay referred to " the castes " the question whether a Hindu had testamentary power, and opinions were divided. After hearing the parties, the court decided in the affirmative, but the grounds are not recorded.[42] The decision may have turned on the question whether the property affected was separate property or not, for the rule is and has always been that there is no testamentary power over *Mitakshara* joint family property or over any other property that cannot be transferred by gift *inter vivos.* When the *muffassal* courts were established in Bombay, they denied testamentary power to Hindus until they came under the control of the High Court. In 1866 recognition of testamentary power, which the Supreme Court had always assumed to exist in the City of Bombay, was extended to the whole of the Presidency.[43]

In Bengal, where the *Dayabhaga* school had long since abandoned the principle of devolution by survivorship, the practice of making wills had become sufficiently prevalent to be acceptable to the *pandits.* Reported cases in which testamentary power was recognised date back to 1792, and the *pandits* of the *Sudder Dewani Adalat* laid down in 1812 that the same rules applied to bequests as to gifts; every person who had authority, while in health, to transfer property, possessed the same authority in bequeathing it.

In Madras, the early development was uneven, though based on the principle that the validity of a will must be tested by the same rules as apply to gifts, but its application long denied testamentary power to a man with male issue, and even resulted in the setting aside of wills made to the prejudice of the testator's widow and daughters.

In 1870 the Hindu Wills Act was passed, but its provisions only applied to wills made in Bengal and the cities of Madras and Bombay, and to wills affecting immovables in the same territory. It forbade the creation of estates and interests in property not

[42] See Fawcett, *The First Century of British Justice in India*, p. 199.
[43] *Norottam* v. *Narsandas* (1866) 3 Bom.H.C. 8.

recognised before 1870, and, for the first time made the validity of a will dependent on observance of prescribed formalities, identical with those demanded of testators to whom the Indian Succession Act applied. These formalities are based on the provisions of the English Wills Act of 1837, but are less onerous. The will must be in writing, and the testator must sign or affix his mark. There must be two attesting witnesses, but it is sufficient that they have received an acknowledgment from the testator.

In 1872 there came before the Privy Council the question of the validity of the will of a wealthy and distinguished Bengali gentleman, whose only son had become a Christian.[44] The will, which disinherited the son, was drafted in language appropriate to letters patent creating a new peerage with a special mode of devolution. The bulk of the estate was left in trust for a succession of beneficiaries. Of these, the first was a relative J., who was to take for his life, and after him J.'s eldest son born in the testator's lifetime for his life, then came the first and other sons of sons of such eldest son successively in tail male (*i.e.*, male descendants of such eldest son should succeed each other, the holder for his life being selected by lineal primogeniture); then followed the other sons of J. born in the testator's lifetime in tail male, then the other sons of J. born after the testator's death in tail male. After failure or determination of the preceding interests, another relative S. was to take a life interest, and then followed limitations for his male descendants similar to those made in favour of J.'s. Upon failure of all these, a third and similar series of limitations in favour of the male issue of a relative L. followed.

This truly remarkable will was vastly different from the often ambiguously expressed letter to the collector with which the Anglo-Indian courts were mainly familiar. This did not, however, deter the sons from calling it in question.

The Board said that there was no objection to a devise of property on trust, provided that it was not an attempt to defeat the law, but held that a Hindu could not create by will an estate unknown to Hindu law, such as an estate in tail male. Furthermore, a disposition by will must comply with the rule of Hindu law of gifts that the donee must be in existence when the gift is to take effect.

The life interest in favour of J. was good, because such an interest could have been created by gift *inter vivos*, but as J. had no male issue, the subsequent limitations in their favour were bad in law. Though a benignant construction should be given to

[44] *Tagore* v. *Tagore* (1872) 1 I.A. (Supp.) 47.

a will, it must be such as to give effect to the testator's expressed wishes; the limitations in favour of S. and his issue could not take effect, because the testator's intention was, not that they should do so in the event of the preceding limitations being held invalid, but in the event of there being in fact a failure of J.'s issue. For similar reasons the dispositions in favour of L. and his issue failed.

This decision imposed on the Hindu testator restrictions more irksome than those to which the testator governed by the Indian Succession Act was subjected. Legislation to remove this distinction in relation to gifts *inter vivos* and by will, by bringing the rules applicable to a Hindu into line with the provisions of the Indian Succession Act and the Indian Transfer of Property Act, commenced in 1914 with the Madras Transfer and Bequests Act. This statute substituted, for the rule forbidding gifts to unborn persons, the perpetuity rule in the two statutes previously mentioned; a donor may control the devolution of his gift during the lifetime of persons living when his gift takes effect, and the subsequent minority of a person in existence at the end of the first period, provided that at the end of the second period the gift vests absolutely in the last-mentioned person. Where, however, a gift to an unborn person follows a prior disposition in favour of another, the gift to the unborn person must comprise the whole of the donor's remaining interest in the property. Two central Acts of 1916 and 1921 [45] extended these provisions to the whole of British India.

Between 1925 and 1929 the Indian Succession Act was repealed, re-enacted and amended, and the Transfer of Property Act amended so as to leave only minor differences between the law of gifts and wills applicable to Hindus and that applicable to persons of Indian domicile not governed by their personal law. All wills made after 1926 by Hindus must be in the form prescribed by the Act of 1870. In addition to the restrictions on testamentary power prescribed in the Act of 1914, a direction to accumulate income will not, with exceptions, be valid for more than eighteen years, and any restriction on enjoyment or the power to alienate, or any direction to postpone delivery imposed on a gift of an absolute interest is void.

In recognition of the improved standard of draftsmanship, these statutes in their ultimate form impose on Hindu testators what might be described as rules of construction, which, like the other rules discussed above, are derived from, but not necessarily identical with, the corresponding rules in English law; they are fewer, simpler and less technical. Except in so far as they apply, the

[45] The Hindu Disposition of Property Act, 1916, and the Transfer and Bequests (City of Madras) Act, 1921.

courts must endeavour to give effect to the intention of the testator, as ascertained primarily from the instrument, but having regard to the notions of the average Hindu.

In this connection, it is interesting to note the change in the rule of interpretation of a bequest to a Hindu female. In 1874 the Privy Council held that, unless the contrary appears from the will, the beneficiary would only take a limited estate,[46] but the Indian courts endeavoured to limit the scope of this rule to a devise of immovables by a husband in favour of his wife. Since 1929, the rule in the amended Succession Act that, when property is bequeathed to any person, he takes an absolute estate, unless it appears from the will that a restricted interest was intended, has applied to Hindu females.

H. *Religious and Charitable Endowments*

The texts impose upon the Hindu the duties of sacrifice and charity. The performance or attempted performance of these duties brings before the courts questions of supervision of institutions, and of the validity of gifts and bequests.

In England, after the Reformation, grants to "superstitious uses" (*e.g.*, a trust to say masses for the soul of a deceased person) became illegal, but a statute of Elizabeth I allowed trusts for charity, and the English courts construed that statute as permitting trusts for the relief of poverty, for the advancement of religion, for the advancement of education and for certain other purposes.[47] The Indian courts, in determining whether a gift is charitable, apply the same basic tests as the English courts, save that, under the head of "advancement of religion," they allow bequests for purposes which, even in the light of the more liberal modern construction of the statute, would be excluded from the category of permissible dispositions.

As in England, the perpetuity rule and the rule against accumulations do not apply to grants to charity.

The English rule that a trust must be such that its administration is susceptible of review by the court[48] and may therefore be void for uncertainty is also applied in India. Though these decisions are open to criticism, gifts to "*dharma*" and "for the spread of the Hindu religion"[49] have been held void.

[46] *Md. Shumsool* v. *Shewakram* (1874) 2 I.A. 7.
[47] *Morice* v. *Bp. of Durham* (1805) 10 Ves. 522; *Commissioners of Income Tax* v. *Pemsel* [1891] A.C. 581.
[48] *Morice* v. *Bp. of Durham* (*supra*).
[49] *Ranchordas* v. *Parvatibhai* (1899) 26 I.A. 71; *Venatanarasimha* v. *Subba* (1923) 46 Mad. 300.

If the mode of application of his gift prescribed by the donor of a gift to charity cannot be executed, the English *cy-près* doctrine may be invoked, and the court required to prescribe a mode as near as possible to that specified by the donor.

Regarding temples and *maths* (theological colleges), the courts accepted the position that the *shebait* and *mahant* stand in a position similar to that of the manager in a joint family; he combines with the duty of management a beneficial interest in the income of the institution, but he can be removed if he puts himself in a position which makes it impossible for him to discharge his functions without danger to the endowment; he is not liable as a trustee. The courts are mainly concerned with disputes as to the right to hold or continue in office, and as to the validity of alienations by the holders of these offices, to which rules similar to those governing a manager's alienations have been applied.

During the British period there has been an increasing tendency to vest the management of religious and charitable endowments in trustees. This may be done by the instrument of gift, and, in such cases, as well as in other cases in which a trust may be implied, the courts have statutory powers [50] adapted from English law, to remove or appoint trustees, to call for accounts, to give directions, and to settle a scheme of management. These powers do not extend to private trusts, nor to *maths*, and their abuse is prevented by the provision that the court may only be moved by or with the consent of the Advocate-General or the Collector.

Legislation has shown a growing tendency, accelerating with the passing of British rule, to reduce managers of religious institutions to the position of trustees. A striking example is the Madras Hindu Religious and Charitable Endowments Act of 1950, subjecting all such institutions to rigorous government control.

I. *Caste Questions*

If a Hindu is outcasted, or subjected to caste discipline, the consequences for him may be extremely serious, but the texts give no guide to the courts as to how they are to deal with questions between an individual and his caste, so they have adapted the English law relating to domestic tribunals, mainly the law of clubs.[51] The courts recognise the autonomy of castes, and their constitution, whether despotic, oligarchic, or democratic; they will only interfere when a civil right is involved, *i.e.*, where it is proved that a right to property (including a right to enter a temple or use a place of

[50] s. 92, Civil Procedure Code.
[51] In a series of cases beginning with *Dawkins* v. *Antrobus* (1879) 17 Ch.D. 615.

sepulture), or a right to office has been infringed, or the plaintiff has been defamed. A suit for a bare declaration that a person has been unjustly outcasted, or for an injunction to readmit him, will not lie. Even when a civil right is involved, the courts will not interfere unless the rules of the caste have been infringed, or the rule is unreasonable, or the rules of "natural justice" have been ignored.[52]

It would seem probable that the sphere to which the courts have confined themselves is narrower than that over which jurisdiction was exercised in the past under the rule of Hindu sovereigns, who would have given redress for grievances which the Anglo-Indian courts ignored as involving only social privileges.

"Natural justice" involves adequate notice to the person against whom the caste intends to proceed of the gravamen of the charge against him. He must be given the opportunity of being heard, though not necessarily in person, before the caste, or those members of it, who, by its constitution, are charged with the duty of dealing with the matter. There must be a genuine effort to examine all relevant material, and the decision must be bona fide. The plaintiff can not appeal on the facts to the court, nor get a rehearing there of the question.

A statement that a person has been outcasted is prima facie defamatory, but a bona fide decision of a caste is privileged, and the communication of such a decision to members of the caste enjoys qualified privilege. Where the plaintiff succeeds on a plea of defamation, it is usually on the ground of excessive publication.

In one case[53] it was pointed out that, in England, anyone was free to join a club, and, if he did so, he must be deemed to have agreed to be governed by its rules; further, if he were expelled from it, the consequences were less serious than those suffered by a Hindu excommunicated by his caste, of which he became a member at birth, being bound for life by its rules, without any volition on his part. It was suggested that the Hindu needed more protection from the courts than the Englishman required against his club. Neither in this, nor in any other case, was the law taken any further than it had been taken in the English law of clubs; any attempt to do so would run the risk of violating a cardinal principle of British policy, that of non-interference in religious matters. During the past 150 years the consequences of being outcasted have become less serious, while in England the rules outlined above have been extended to trade unions, and in England today expulsion from a trade union may have very serious consequences indeed.

[52] *Nathu* v. *Keshawji* (1902) 26 Bom. 171.
[53] *Jagganath* v. *Akali* (1893) 21 Cal. 463.

J. *Conclusion*

Regarded from the social angle, the main effects of English law upon Hindu law have been to set in motion a process, still incomplete, of substituting for the joint family as the social unit, the household, comprising the husband, wife, and their children, and of enhancing separate rights in property. This has been accompanied by the growing recognition of the right to choose one's partner in marriage, and the increasing emphasis on the necessity of placing women on a more equal footing with men. From being a law primarily designed to meet the needs of the wealthy territorial family, it is becoming a law primarily designed to suit the *intelligentsia*. The opposition to the draft code of 1948 has, however, made the politically dominant class more willing to meet the desires of the other classes, and to defer, at least, the imposition of complete uniformity.

From the standpoint of the legal practitioner, despite the recognition of schools of Hindu law, a large measure of uniformity has been achieved, and the Hindu law has become largely a matter of case-law. If and when the projected legislation referred to above is enacted, Hindu law, like most other chapters of Indian law, will be mainly based on codes, but the English rather than the Continental method of interpretation will be followed; the interpretation will be crystallised in binding precedents. The proximity of the Supreme Court will leave less room for conflicting decisions of High Courts; there will be fewer differences between different schools, and less room for custom. The degree of uniformity already achieved will be enhanced.

Ultimately, one may envisage this projected legislation, though no doubt with concessions and amendments, becoming the basis of a uniform personal law for India. One of the directive principles of the Indian Constitution is that "the State shall endeavour to secure for all citizens a uniform civil code throughout the territory of India.[54] One of the members of the Constituent Assembly, replying to criticisms of this principle on the ground that it infringed the fundamental right to freedom of religion, replied: "Religion must be confined to its proper sphere, and the rest of life regulated and unified so that we can become a strong and consolidated nation. Our first problem is national unity. We must be able to say 'By our way of life and our personal law, we are a strong and consolidated nation'."[55]

ALAN GLEDHILL.*

54 Art. 44.

55 Sri K. M. Munshi, member Drafting Committee of the Indian Constitution Constituent Assembly: Debates, pp. 547–8.

* Lecturer in Indian and Burmese law at the School of Oriental Studies, University of London.

[14]

Marriage and Divorce in India: Conflicting Laws*

INDIA—the cradle of the ancient Vedic Aryan (Hindu) civilization—is today a multi-religious, though officially secular state. During the last 2,500 years it has heroically faced Persian, Greek, Huna, Shaka and Kushana, Turkish, Mongol and English on-slaught and has still maintained its distinctive Hindu culture.[1]

Hindu law, which is a branch of Dharma,[2] is believed to be of

---

*By Ved Prakash Nanda, Candidate for LL.M., Northwestern Univ.; M.A. 1952, Punjab Univ.; LL.B. 1955, LL.M. 1957, Univ. of Delhi.

1. See WIGMORE, PANORAMA OF THE WORLD'S LEGAL SYSTEMS 213 (library ed. 1936), where, like all other Western scholars, he includes Indo-Aryans among the immigrant and conqueror alien races. Aryans, according to him, entered India at abount 2000 B.C. During the Nineteenth Century and the Twentieth Century Western scholars have been propounding one theory after another regarding the original habitation of the Aryans, shifting it from place to place. However, many of the modern Hindu scholars hold a strong opinion, based upon the internal evidence of the Rig-Veda (the most ancient grantha or sacred book of the Aryans), that the Aryans were indigenous to the Panjab in India, who were the original inhabitants of the Sapta Sindhu (the valley of the seven rivers—the Indus, the five Panjab Rivers and the Saraswati). See DAS, RIGVEDIC INDIA. On the controversial question of the exact age of the Vedic culture there is also a great diversity of opinion. While Muller in HISTORY OF ANCIENT SANSKRIT LITERATURE, views 1200 B.C. as the approximate origin of the Vedic hymns, Tilak, Jacobi, and Kane place it before 4000 B.C.; some of the modern noted scholars like Pt. Bhagwad Datt have, after their life-long research in the Vedic literature, placed it long before that period. Dr. Das places it at about 25000 B.C. For other Western scholars' opinions see WEBER, THE HISTORY OF INDIAN LITERATURE; MACDONELL, HISTORY OF SANSKRIT LITERATURE; KEITH & MACDONELL, PREFACE TO VEDIC INDEX; BARNETT, THE HEART OF INDIA, quoted in PAL, THE HISTORY OF HINDU LAW 38 (1958): in India "there is no twilight before dawn," which demonstrates one characteristic of ancient Hindu thought—an indifference to history. Pal further states that there is hardly any material for establishing the posteriority of the Vedic culture to those of Babylon and Egypt. *Id.* at 8.

2. It is difficult to translate the word "Dharma" into English. 2 Manu Smriti

Divine origin. It was originally contained in the Sruti (the ancient scriptures—the Vedas, the Brahmanas and the Upanishdas)[3] and the Smriti (works of sages of antiquity including the ancient "Dharam Sutras" which means strings or threads of rules of Dharma);[4] and subsequently in the commentaries and digests upon the Smriti,[5] and in custom judicial decisions and legislative enactments.

In the beginning Hindu law was territorial in character, but it seems that even in its early days it had started giving recognition to special legal systems for distinct legal classes and districts. We find that different schools of Hindu law had been set up as early as in the Sutra period itself. Vasishta's remarks in a later period that Manu has declared that the peculiar laws of countries, castes and families may be followed in the absence of rules of the Sruti is also quite significant.[6]

The early invasions had left the Indian life almost unaffected, but with the advent of the Muslim rule in the Twelfth Century, which broke the unity of the cultural life of the country, Mohammedan law came to be applied in those parts of the country which came under the Muslim domination. Thereafter came the English rule in the Eighteenth Century which left the Hindus, Muslims and other sections of the population mostly to their personal laws,[7]

---

defines it as, "What is followed by those learned in the Vedas and what is approved by the conscience of the virtuous who are exempt from hatred and inordinate affection." Medhatithi explains it as duty. This "eternal" word with its "eternal" meaning signifies an aggregation of duties and obligations—religious, moral, social, and legal.

3. Literally "Sruti" means "what was heard"—the utterances of the Creator. There is not much positive law (Vyavhara) in the Vedas which comprise (1) Rig-Veda, (2) Sama-Veda, (3) Yajur-Veda, and (4) Atharva-Veda.

4. Literally "Smriti" means "recollection," "that which was remembered." They are the Divine rules, the precepts of God in the words of the Rishis or Sages of antiquity who saw or received the revelations and handed down their recollections. These constitute the positive law or Vyavhara. Manu, the ancient law-giver, along with Narada, Brihaspati, Prashara, and Yajnavalkya, are some of the well-known Smritikars (who wrote Smritis or Codes), while Gautama, Baudhayana, Apastamba, Harita, Vasishtha, and Vishnu are accepted as the ancient Sutrakars (who wrote Sutras or aphorisms). Kautalya's Artha-shastra, written about 300 B.C., also contains positive law or Vyavhara. Manu's Code has been placed by Sir W. Jones at 1280 B.C. while MULLER, *op. cit. supra* note 1, places it at 200 B.C. The Smriti age continued until 300 A.D.

5. This period commences about 700 A.D. Of the Nobandha-karas, or the commentators on the Smritis, the best known are Vijnaneshwara, Medhatithi, Mitramishra, Kamlakara, Nilkantha Bhatta, and Devana Bhatta. Vijnaneshwara's commentary, Mitakshara, written in the Eleventh Century on Sage Yajnavalkya's Smriti, and Jimutvahna's digest of all the codes, called Dayabhaga, gave rise to the two famous schools of Hindu Law—Mitakshra and Dayabhaga, the latter prevalent in Bengal and the former in the rest of India.

6. 1 Vasishtha; 14 SACRED BOOKS OF THE EAST pt. 3 at 4 (1881).

7. The Bengal Regulations of 1772 (Hasting's Plan, Rule XXIII) provided that in all suits regarding inheritance, succession, marriage, castes, and other religious usages or institutions, Hindus and Muslims would be governed by their respective laws. This rule was in essence followed by subsequent regulations to the same effect, as illustrated by the High Courts Act of 1861, which provided that the

and introduced the concept of "Justice, Equity and Good Conscience."[8] The latter half of the Nineteenth Century was the era of codified territorial laws,[9] but personal laws were again left intact with only minor changes.

A queer result of the historical process of intermingling of races, influx of Parsees to India, and conversions to Islam and Christianity, is that along with territorial laws in the form of codes based more or less on English common law which govern and regulate the conduct of an individual in the society, personal laws based on religion still govern the status of an individual.[10] And as if to make matters more complicated, Hindus and Mohammedans are again divided into different schools and sub-schools with their different laws,[11] and in certain places custom over-rides the personal laws and reigns supreme in this field. Bishop Agobard's statement regarding Medieval Europe that none of five people meeting on the road or at table might be living under the same law applies with equal force to modern Indian conditions, at least in connection with the determination of questions of status.[12] It is beyond the scope of this paper to deal with the different laws prevalent in India in different fields of status, but it is proposed to discuss briefly the different laws of marriage and divorce in India and the question of mixed marriages.

Marriages Under Hindu Law, Old and New[13]

Even as far back as the Rig Vedic period, the institution of mar-

personal laws of the natives would govern in certain matters and in case of parties being subject to different personal laws, the law of the defendant would prevail.

8. Judges were asked to apply justice, equity, and good conscience in the absence of any rule of law to guide them in the pending disputes. After the High Courts Act of 1861 came into force, this concept was interpreted to mean the rules of English Law if found applicable to Indian society and circumstances.

9. In pursuance of the authority of the Charter Act of 1833 which had provided for the appointment of a Law Commission, the first Law Commission was appointed in 1834, the second in 1853, the third in 1861, and the fourth in 1879. In accordance with their recommendations various civil enactments, the Indian Penal Code and the Criminal Procedure Code were passed.

10. See Rao, *Private International Law in India,* 4 INDIAN YB. INT'L AFFAIRS 219 (1955), where the author explains how, after having adopted the English system of domicle in preference to the continental system of nationality as a basis for determination of questions of status (especially in the conflicts of law area), juristic thought in India adjusted itself to a law of domicile comprising a "composite system of personal law." *E.g.,* in the case of two people domiciled in India, the *lex domicilii* may differ according to their religious creed. Casdagli v. Casdagli, [1919] A.C. 45 (Indian), gave judicial approval to this innovation in the theory of domicile.

11. The codification of Hindu law in four acts in 1955 and 1956 has brought about radical changes in the old system governed by schools and sub-schools of Hindu law.

12. He talks of the diversity of law between the Franks, the Romans, the Lombards, the Goths, the Vikings, the Angles, and the Saxons. Similar is the diversity of the laws between and sometimes among the Hindus, the Muslims, the Christians, the Jews, and the Parsees in India.

13. Mayne in his classic treatise HINDU LAW AND USAGE (1878), states that

riage was well-established and marriage laws were fully recognized and observed. Rig Veda tells us about the place of a wife in her home in these words: "Over thy husband's father and thy husband's mother, over the sisters of thy lord and over his brothers, rule supreme."[14] The husband and the wife were called "Pati" and "Patni" respectively. A man was considered incomplete without a wife,[15] and the wife was considered half her husband.[16] Monogamy was the rule,[17] and marriage was indissoluble during the life-time of the husband.[18] Marriage in Vedic texts appears essentially as a union of two persons of full development. The girl herself chose her husband and she was not married before she exercised her judgment.[19] The conversation of Yama and Yami in the Rig Veda gives an indication that marriage between near relations was condemned in that period as sinful.[20] However, not much information is available regarding the legal relations between husband and wife after marriage. Skipping over the Brahmana and Sutra periods[21] which brought about only minor changes in the marriage law, we may briefly inquire into the Hindu law of marriage as the Smritikars (sages of antiquity who wrote Smritis) and later Nibandhakaras (commentators on Smritis) had left it to be applied during the Nineteenth and Twentieth Centuries, before their codification into the Hindu Marriage Act of 1955.

One of the fundamental differences in the Hindu system as compared with other systems is that it considers marriage not as a contract but a sacrament. It is one of the ten Samskaras or purificatory ceremonies required for the purpose of purifying the body from the inherited taint and for complete regeneration.[22] The Hindu ideal of marriage is that it is a holy union for the performance of religious duties.[23] Therefore, but for the Sanyasins

Hindu law has "the oldest pedigree of any known system of jurisprudence, and even now it shows no sign of decrepitude"; Freeman, *Hindu Jurisprudence,* 8 INDIAN YB. INT'L AFFAIRS 196, 213 (1959), quotes JAYASWAL, HINDU POLITY 366-67 (2d ed. 1943): "the great privilege of Hindu at the same time is that he is not yet a fossil; he is still living with a determination which a great historian has characterized as a tenacity which bends but does not break."

14. RIG VEDA, x. 85.46.

15. According to Shetapatha Brahmana.

16. She was called "ardhangini."

17. See MACDONNELL & KEITH, VEDIC INDEX 478-79; DERRETT, HINDU LAW PAST AND PRESENT 85 (1957): "The Aryans themselves were originally monogamous and their essential religious ceremonies required the participation of both husband and wife, sometimes the wife acted as her husband's deputy."

18. RIG VEDA x. 39.14.

19. RIG VEDA x. 27.12.

20. RIG VEDA x. 10.

21. For a history of these periods see PAL, *op. cit. supra* note 1, at 332-34, 344-48, 364-86.

22. Yajnavalkya 1.13.

23. Sage Apastamba states that from the time of marriage the husband and wife were united in the religious ceremonies and likewise in the rewards of acts of spiritual merit.

(monks) who are supposed not to marry, it was a duty urged by the Shastras (the sacred books) upon a man to marry for the purpose of procreating a son necessary for the continuation of the line of paternal ancestors and for the spiritual benefit of their and his souls. Furthermore, un-married men could not perform some of the most important religious ceremonies. Eight forms of marriage—four approved and four un-approved ones[24]—had come to be recognized during the Sutra period itself. Marriage ceremonies included "Kanyadan," the giving away of the girl by the father or the guardian;[25] "Panigrahna," by which the bridegroom accepted the bride by taking her hand; invocations before the sacred fire; and "Saptapadi" (walking seven steps) around the sacred fire together by the husband and the wife, the bride thereby signifying her consent. The marriage become irrevocable after the seventh step.[26] Minority was no bar to a valid marriage and physical or mental incapacity was not a material factor.[27] Polygamy — though not much in vogue — was permitted. Widow remarriage[28] was not looked upon with approval. The parties could not be within prohibited degrees of relationship,[29] and except as

24. The Brahma, Daiva, Arsha, and Prajapatya were the four approved forms of marriage, and Gandharva, Asura, Rakshasa, and Paischacha were not recognized. During the last two centuries, Brahma and Asura (and in some cases Gandharva) have been the only forms recognized by the courts, and all other forms have practically become obsolete. The main difference between the Brahma and the Asura forms is that the former is a gift of the girl, while in the latter consideration is received by the father or guardian for giving the girl in marriage. The importance of the distinction was that when a woman died leaving no issue, her stridhana (woman's property) devolved in one way if the marriage was in Brahma form and in another way if it was in the Asura form. However, marriage was always presumed to be in the approved form.

25. The hymns chanted at the marriage ceremony bring out the religious significance of marriage as a sort of sacrifice on the part of the girl with a purpose to continue Brahma's (God's) universe, which in secular language would be called perpetuation of the legitimate family. Hindu law does not contemplate marriage of males during minority; hence there are no rules regarding guardianship of males in marriage. Guardianship of a girl creates not a right but a duty to perform the marriage.

26. Even in Rig Veda after the completion of the seventh step, the bridegroom said, "with seven steps we have become friends [Sakha]. May I attain to friendship with thee. May I not be separated from thy friendship."

27. A minor bride's consent or lack of consent to a specific offer of marriage was immaterial; but the Child Marriage Restraint Act of 1929 prohibited marriages of infants and children. For justification of marriage without the express consent of the girl and that of early marriages of girls, see SARKAR SASTRI, HINDU LAW 89-92 (4th ed. 1910).

28. The Hindu Widow Remarriage Act of 1856 permitted such marriages. For justification of the rule against a widow's remarriage see SARKAR SASTRI, *op. cit. supra* note 27, at 116-17.

29. The Sages, Manu, Sumantu, Paithinasi, and Yajnavalkya, differ regarding the degrees of prohibited relationship; the maximum degrees laid down was seven on the side of the father and five on the side of the mother, while the minimum was five and three on the side of the father and the mother respectively. The joint family system which was the normal condition of the Hindu society accounted for more encompassing prohibitions covering more relatives than exist in other systems of jurisprudence. The purpose being that relatives who lived together in great intimacy from birth should never entertain the idea of marrying each other.

varied by custom (and later by enactments) parties could not belong to the same caste,[30] and could not be of the same family, that is, they could not both be Sapindas,[31] Sagotras,[32] or Samanpravaras.[33] Irregular marriages could be regularized by the Doctrine of Factum Valet.[34]

The legal effects of marriage were confined to religious purposes only and the concept of the unity of person by marriage did not extend to civil matters. The wife could hold separate property and, if not otherwise disqualified, she could enter into a contract with any person. She could sue or be sued in her own name. Broadly speaking, the spouses had no right in each other's property. How-

30. The observations of Northrop, *The Comparative Philosophy of Comparative Law,* 45 CORNELL L.Q. 617 (1960), regarding the caste structure of the Hindus (quoting some Hindu "scholars" and referring to the significance of the dual meaning of a sanskrit word), and his assertion regarding the efforts for the achievement of national unity in India on a "Law-of-Status" basis by the "Aryan Conquerors," cannot be taken as sound postulates. See note 1 *supra* for the controversial question of the original habitation of the Aryans who are no longer considered as conquerors by many notable scholars. So far as the caste structure of the Hindus is concerned, the bases lie much deeper than envisaged by Northrop. Lord Krishna in Bhagwad Gita says: the caste of an individual is determined not by birth, but by qualities and conduct due to his psychic state, as He says that He (the Creator) created four classes by the different distribution of qualities and actions (4, 13). Yudhishtra in Ajagara-parva of Mahabharta (ch. 180) states that the castes depend upon different characteristics of people and that they are not hereditary. They must have arisen out of differences of occupations and qualities, and looked at from that point of view every modern political society is divisible into four classes corresponding to the four casts of the Hindus: (1) The class of scholars, intellectuals, religious leaders, just as Brahmanas in Hindu society, (2) Warriors (in armed forces), administrative heads, courageous, and intelligent people as Kshatriyas in Hindu society, (3) Businessmen, industrialists and agriculturists as Vaishas, and (4) Laborers serving the preceeding classes or mechanics showing capacity only for physical labor as Sudras in Hindu society. The story of their origin (that He created the four classes from different limbs of his body) is simply an allegory representing society and its different classes as one human body and its limbs. This should be distinguished from the Marxist view which divides classes on purely economic ground; for Brahmanas, considered to be the highest class, were usually the poorest people in the Hindu society and the most respected ones. It is a remnant of a much later period, probably due to foreign domination, that the caste system in Hindus became inflexible and rigid. In early ages one could easily change one's occupation and move to another caste. The son of a Brahmana could become a Kashatriya, a Vaisha or a Sudra could become a Brahmana. Anuloma marriages, *i.e.,* marriages between a husband of higher caste and a wife of lower caste were permitted in certain cases, but not vice-versa.

31. According to the Mitakshra school, Sapindas are those persons who are connected to one another by the particles of the body of the same ancestor, while according to the Dayabhaga school, they are the persons connected to one another by the oblations or offerings of the funeral cake (pinda) to their ancestors. We have already noticed that the degrees of prohibition regarding marriage varied according to different writers.

32. Sagotras are those people who are descended from a common original sage who gave the descendants their gotra or family name.

33. Pravaras are those illustrious sages who contributed to the credit of a particular gotra.

34. Jimutvahna in Dayabhago enunciated this doctrine when he said, "A fact cannot be altered by a hundred texts," *i.e.,* when an act is done in contravention of certain texts, such an act will be deemed valid if the texts contravened are merely declaratory and not mandatory. It was applied in Sri Balasu v. Sri Balasu, 22 Mad. 398 (1899); Kshitish Chandra v. Emperor, 24 All India Rep. 214 (Calcutta) (1937).

ever, the husband could use his wife's property but he was liable to give back with interest, except when it was used in time of distress or for a religious purpose. The wife was not liable to pay her husband's debts except under certain conditions. The parties acquired mutual rights of inheritance, and were bound to live together. The husband acquired a right of guardianship over his minor wife, and she acquired the domicile of the husband.

But for customary divorce in certain states, or the provisions for divorce in Bombay, Madras and Saurashtra under enactments,[35] divorce was not permitted. The texts of some sages (including those of Devala and Katayana, cited in Ratnakara and Prashara Madhviya, and of Vasistha, which says a "Damsel at the death of her husband may marry again if the marriage had not been consummated," and of Narada which says that "If the husband be missing, or dead or retired from the world, or impotent, or degraded, in these five calamities a woman may take another husband") have been occasionally cited to show that there were provisions for remarriage and possibly for divorce too. Manu and Yajnavalkya were determinedly opposed to it, and the prevalent opinion was that marriage under Hindu law must be indissoluble even after the death of the husband. It was for the first time in 1952 that Tandolkar, J., could say, in the famous case of *A v. B*,[36] that Dharamshastra itself had recognized nullity of a marriage on certain grounds.[37] The courts also granted restitution of conjugal rights in certain cases.

On apostasy from Hinduism of one of the parties to the marriage, the marriage was not dissolved ipso facto and it was held by the courts that in such cases a wife could not, during her husband's lifetime, enter into any other valid marriage contract. This subject will be considered further under mixed marriages, but it may be pointed out here, that in cases of conversion to Christianity, the Native Christian Marriage Dissolution Act of 1866 provided that if the wife or husband of such a convert refused to cohabit with him or her on ground of such conversion, the marriage could be dissolved by taking proceedings under the act.

It was quite evident during the last one hundred years or so that Hindu law, which in the past had never been static and had always kept abreast of the needs of the times, had really fallen in

---

35. The Bombay Hindu Divorce Act of 1947 (Bomb. 22 of 1947); the Madras Hindu (Bigamy Prevention & Divorce) Act of 1949 (Mad. 6 of 1949); and the Sausashtra Hindu Divorce Act of 1952 (Saur. 30 of 1952).

36. 54 Bomb. L. Rep. 725 (1952).

37. See Derrett, *Nullity in the Hindu Law of Marriage,* 54 Bomb. L. Rep. 115 (1952); and for a subsequent discussion, see Thakor, *Sterility—A Ground of Nullity of Marriage,* 59 Bomb. L. Rep. J. 23 (1957); Derrett, *Nullity of Marriage,* 61 Bomb. L. Rep. J. 81 (1959).

a state of "arrested growth and progress." Different schools and sub-schools, conflicting interpretations of the texts, centuries of foreign domination and the resulting indifference and neglect, defeatism on the part of Hindus, the doctrine of "Justice, Equity and Good Conscience" and with it, the blending of the English element; all these and many more similar factors had the cumulative effect of creating confusion and chaos. Various inroads had already been made into Hindu law,[38] but they had hardly improved the matter. Since the beginning of the Twentieth Century there had been some occasional demands for a reform in the Hindu law and for its codification. But it was always considered a "delicate", "difficult" and even an "impossible" task. However, as piece-meal legislation had caused more uncertainty and confusion, in 1941 the government appointed the Rau Committee to study the question of codification of Hindu law and to make recommendations. Passing through various stages, the process of codification has culminated in the four enactments passed during 1955 and 1956.[39] With this codification Hindu law on various subjects has been radically changed. The relative advantages and disadvantages of codification in general and of Hindu law in particular cannot be discussed in this short paper, but it may be pointed out that there has been such a sharp cleavage of public opinion on this subject, that the Indian government was even compelled to forego the idea of having the "Hindu Code Bill" (as it was formerly called) passed by the Parliament, and had instead to get four separate acts enacted.

The critics of the acts are vehement in their charges that the new laws will eventually result in breaking the family life, social life, and religious life of the Hindus, and that instead of reforming, they will deform the society. They say that those responsible for the acts had only a shallow and one-sided knowledge and, therefore,

38. The important enactments, starting with the Abolition of Satti in 1829 were: Caste Disabilities Removal Act of 1850; the Hindu Widow's Remarriage Act of 1856; the Native Convert's Marriage Dissolution Act of 1866; the Special Marriage Act of 1872 (Amended, 1923); the Contract Act of 1872; the Indian Majority Act of 1875; the Guardian's and Ward's Act of 1875; the Transfer of Property Act of 1882 (Amended, 1929); the Anand Marriage Act of 1909; the Indian Succession Act of 1925; the Hindu Inheritance (Removal of Disabilities) Act of 1928; the Hindu Law of Inheritance (Amendment) Act of 1929; the Child Marriage Restraint Act of 1929; the Hindu Gains of Learning Act of 1930; the Hindu Women's Right to Property Act of 1937; the Arya Marriage Validation Act of 1937; the Hindu Woman's Right to Separate Residence and Maintenance Act of 1946; the Sagotra Marriage Act (the Hindu Marriage Disabilities Removal Act) of 1946; the Inter-Caste Marriage Act (the Hindu Marriages Validity Act) of 1949; the Special Marriage Act of 1954 (which repealed the Special Marriage Act of 1872); and various state acts permitting divorce and prohibiting bigamy.

39. In addition to the Hindu Marriage Act of 1955 the other three Acts are the Hindu Succession Act of 1956, the Hindu Minority and Guardianship Act of 1956, and the Hindu Adoptions and Maintenance Act of 1956.

they could not reach the deep and untrodden regions of the Sanskrit language to sympathetically understand the depth of the Hindu Dharma; and that not being intellectually sufficiently equipped for the task, they have only "Europeanized" the law, thereby trying to change the culture and civilization of Hindus. Notwithstanding the need for a change in the existing law, it must however be said that divesting the people of their ancient heritage and imposing upon them enactments alien to their culture and civilization can do little good for the society.[40]

The Hindu Marriage Act of 1955 (which governs marriages between Hindus)[41] amends and codifies the law relating to marriage. It has abrogated all the rules of the law of marriage hitherto applicable to Hindus (by virtue of any text, rule or interpretation

---

40. See, *e.g.*, Harkare, *Hindu Law and Its Codification,* 41 ALL INDIA REP. J. 2 (1954); Pusalkar, *Hindu Code—Is the Reform Imminent?* 37 ALL INDIA REP. J. 42 (1950); Hajela, *The Draft Hindu Code, Its Exposition, Comment and Criticism,* 36 ALL INDIA REP. J. 64-68 (1949), where, after criticizing the various provisions of the acts, Hajela concludes that the changes proposed are "not progressive in all cases, though . . . revolting in most cases"; Sarkar, *Aspects of Indian Law,* 2 INT'L & COMP. L.Q. 410, 415 (1953), where the author states that "the microscopic minority in a society has no right to impose its 'misguided opinions' on that society, as they do not understand the underlying spirit of the Hindu culture, nor do they understand how to accept and assimilate what is best in a foreign culture and civilization." He further states that such a legislation, being largely the product of the influence of certain Western concepts and institutions which are sometimes opposed to and often inconsistent with the original Hindu ideas, would lead to more chaos and confusion and lack of social discipline and order. See Supakar, *Some Aspects of the Draft Hindu Code,* 36 ALL INDIA REP. J. 76 (1949); SARKAR, EPOCHS IN HINDU LEGAL HISTORY 408 (1958); AIYANGAR, SOME ASPECTS OF THE HINDU VIEW OF LIFE ACCORDING TO THE DHARAMSHASTRA (1952). *But see* the opinions of those who advocated such a change: Justice Gajendragadkar's address to the Karnatak University, 53 BOMB. L. REP. 77 (1951); Ranade, *The Hindu Code Bill,* 51 BOMB. L. REP. 81 (1951); 36 ALL INDIA REP. J. 12 (1949); Divan, *Divorce Law of Hindus,* 40 ALL INDIA REP. J. 7-10, 14-15 (1953); and various articles by Derrett at 85 BOMB. L. REP. 97 (1956), 59 BOMB. L. REP. 178 (1957), 44 ALL INDIA REP. J. 86 (1957), and 41 ALL INDIA REP. J. 79 (1954), where he observes that no harm is done if the boundary between religion and law is allowed to become merely a "shadowy" one; see also 7 AM. J. COMP. L. 380 (1958), where Derrett states that this experiment (of codification and amendment of the personal laws of Hindus since Indian independence) is "not less remarkable than the 'Code Napoleon'" and that "nothing comparable with it for width of scope or boldness of innovation has been seen in the Anglo-American systems." However, in many articles he finds fault with the Indian legislature for not having completely secularized the said enactments. In *The Codification of Personal Law in India—Hindu Law,* 6 INDIAN YB. INT'L. AFFAIRS 189-211 (1957), Derrett provides a background of the codification in India and states that the acts which reveal "little formal connection with the Dharam Shastra . . . have released the Hindu population from many of the shackles of the past," and that "after a generation the connection with religion will have virtually disappeared, and such links as remain will have no moral, ethical or properly religious justification." One may question whether it is not too early to talk of the effects of the acts; whether this secularization of everything which had so far been inextricably connected with Hindu religion would do the society any good, and finally if the changes brought about by the acts are really "a release from the shackles of the past" and not merely an imitation of the West. To call everything related with the past "shackles" does not show a correct approach to the problem.

41. Section 2. The term "Hindu" includes Sikh, Jains, Buddhists, various sects and sub-sects of Hindus, and converts to Hinduism.

of Hindu law, or any custom or usage) with respect to all matters for which provision is made in the act.[42] It has repealed the existing forms of marriage and has introduced only the ceremonial form.[43] Marriage under the act is monogamous, as the first condition for a valid marriage is that neither party should have a spouse living at the time of marriage,[44] the other conditions being that the parties should not be debarred from marrying each other by reasons of prohibited degrees of relationship or Sapinda relationships,[45] and that as regards mental capacity and age, the parties must be competent to have a marriage solemnized between them.[46] Thus, the act permits inter-caste marriages, Sagotra and Sapravara marriages, and cuts down the degrees of Sapindaship.[47] Bigamy is punishable under sections 494 and 495 of the Indian Penal Code according to which an offender may be sentenced up to seven years' imprisonment and fine. Punishments for contravening other conditions laid down under section 5 of the act vary, but they are not so severe. In case of violation of the specified minimum age limits of eighteen years for the husband and fifteen for the wife, marriage does not become void or voidable, though the defaulters may be punishable with a fine which may extend to one thousand rupees.

The reliefs contemplated under the act are: (1) restitution of conjugal rights;[48] (2) judicial separation,[49] (3) divorce,[50] (4) decree of nullity of marriage in cases of (i) void marriages,[51] and (ii) voidable marriages.[52]

Provisions have been made for alimony and maintenance,[53] custody of children,[54] and for legitimation of children of void and voidable marriages.[55] Proceedings under the act may be held in camera and may not be printed or published.[56] The act does not apply to Scheduled Tribes without the notification of the Central Government, and they would, without such notification, be gov-

42. Section 4.
43. Sections 7 & 8. Section 7 provides that a Hindu marriage may be solemnized in accordance with the customary rites and ceremonies of either party thereto; and that when such rites and ceremonies include Saptapadi, the marriage would be complete and binding when the seventh step is taken. Section 8 makes provision for the registration of Hindu marriages.
44. Section 5(i).
45. Section 5(iv) & (v).
46. Section 5(ii), (iii) & (vi).
47. See notes 31-33 *supra* for the meaning of these Sanskrit terms.
48. Section 9.
49. Section 10.
50. Section 13.
51. Section 11.
52. Section 12.
53. Sections 24 & 25.
54. Section 26.
55. Section 16.
56. Section 22.

erned by their customs. It should also be pointed out that conversion to another religion is one of the grounds for divorce. The act has, to a considerable extent, followed the English Matrimonial Causes Act of 1950,[57] although with some changes to suit the Indian conditions.

While the act faces opposition from those who believe that such revolutionary changes were unwarranted,[58] it has not escaped criticism at the hands of those progressives who think that it should have gone still further in liberalizing the requirements for divorce and that it should have done away with the concept of judicial separation.

A Uniform Civil Code?

The preceding discussion brings one face to face with a pertinent question. In order to solve these problems on a juristic plane, should India not have a uniform Civil Code applicable to all the Indians alike irrespective of their differences of religions, creeds and customs? Would such juristic uniformity foster a sense of cohesion and oneness among the different communities by contributing to the social and political unity of the country? Article 44 of the Indian Constitution states in categorical terms that "the

111. 2 All E.R. 374 (1945) (P.D.A.).
112. See note 104 *supra.*
113. See note 104 *supra.* See also Kenward v. Kenward, 2 All E.R. 297 (1950), (C.A.) where Denning, L. J., said that when both parties were domiciled in the country where they were married and the marriage was valid there, "then, even if it lacks in our eyes some of the essentials of marriage, as, for instance, if it is potentially polygamous, we still regard it here, for many purposes, a valid marriage. . . ." *Id.* at 309.
114. See Lendrum v. Chakravari, [1929] S.L.T. 96.

state shall endeavor to secure for the citizens a uniform civil code throughout the territory of India." This principle is embedded in the Directive Principles of State Policy (Part IV of the Constitution of India), which many authorities on constitutional law have termed as nothing more than a "pious wish." Nevertheless, read with article 37[115] and article 25[116] of the constitution, it does indicate the significance being attached to this important but delicate matter, and shows the enthusiasm and intensity with which some of the modern Indian thinkers view it. However, mere wishes and enthusiasm alone can hardly break age-old barriers and prejudices, which may sometimes grow even more stubborn and insurmountable with the passage of time.

At the same time a realistic approach will bring out some other aspects of this thorny problem. First, but for Hindus, no other community in India has so far demanded a change in its personal law. Secondly, the strong appeal of religion and everything connected with religion (including laws)—especially in some of the communities of India—hardly needs any emphasis. The hypersensitivity of people to any tampering with their religious laws is easily understandable. Furthermore, legislation itself may not be an effective means to harmonize what are only superficially differences in law but which may be deep-rooted differences in racial backgrounds reflecting the differing value judgments of diverse communities; and which are perhaps the basis for peace and tranquility in individual families,[117] despite that some commentators have termed them "irrational," "ridiculous" and "absurd."

As two of India's foremost jurists have succinctly put it, unless and until the people are prepared for and are responsive to the laws, they cannot serve any useful purpose. Former Chief Justice Kania of the Supreme Court of India says, "Law must not be the will of the dictator but the organized will and the conscience of the people . . . it grows and changes . . . but . . . it is adapted to the conscience, will, and the needs of the people." Former Chief Justice Chagla of the Bombay High Court (presently Ambassador

115. Article 37: "The provisions contained in this Part, (Part IV) shall not be enforceable by any court, but the principles laid down are fundamental in the governance of the country and it shall be the duty of the state to apply these principles in making laws."

116. Article 25, 2(b) states that nothing contained in this article (regarding right to freedom of religion) shall prevent the state from providing social welfare reforms. Art. 25 forms a part of the fundamental rights guaranteed under the constitution.

117. As compared with western countries, marriages in India are much more stable and happy. For the magnitude of the problem of "broken homes" in the West, see Rheinstein's paper on *Marriage Stability and Laws on Divorce,* and other papers delivered at the International Association of Legal Sciences, Chicago Conference, Family Stability (1957). For a brief report of the Chicago Colloquia, see Comments, 6 AM. J. COMP. L. 523-25 (1957).

of India to the United States) has said, "The party in power must set a limitation to its own powers over legislative enactments and be neither ruthless nor dictatorial. . . . The law it passes should have the acquiescence of even the minority when it is placed on the statute book."

Viewed as above and taking into account the special conditions of India as they pertain today, the laws of marriage and divorce are perhaps bound to resist unification for a long time to come.[118] It is too much to say that "the day of the promised civil code is approaching demonstrably near"[119] and that the Hindu Marriage Act of 1955 is the first step in that direction. A word of caution should be sounded. A hasty action on the part of the legislature is not in the interest of the society. Until the time is really ripe for codification and unification, personal laws should be left alone, with minor changes wherever deemed necessary.[120]

In the end one may ask, Is it not wiser for the legislature to refrain from futile efforts to impose "unity"—which decidedly springs from within the society and cannot be imposed by a legislature—while permitting India to continue striving for unity in diversity?

118. See Notes, *Cambridge Colloquia on Comparative Law,* 8 INT'L & COMP. L.Q. 393 (1959).

119. See Derrett, *Development in Hindu Law,* 44 ALL INDIA REP. J. 86 (1957), who is of the opinion that the day of the promised civil code is approaching rapidly.

120. Even an ardent supporter of codification cannot help pointing out that the four acts on Hindu Law do not have an altogether salutory effect on the Hindu society. Various amendments proposed by different state legislatures and the mixed reception given by the public (with millions of people expressing the opinion that it has hurt their religious feelings) make it yet too early to pronounce that it was an unmixed blessing for the people. For the opinions of those who advocate a civil code, see, *e.g.,* Derrett, *The Codification of Personal Law in India, Hindu Law,* 6 INDIAN YB. INT'L AFFAIRS 189 (1957), *Developments in Hindu Law* 1955-56 44 ALL INDIA REP. J. 86 (1957); Kuppuswami, *Codification of the Law and the Constitution* 38 ALL INDIA REP. J. 60 (1951); Rao, *A Bharat Civil Code,* 55 BOMBAY L. REP. 47 (1953); Hussein, *A Unified Code for India,* 51 BOMBAY L. REP. 68, 71-72 (1949); Ranade, *The Special Marriage Bill, 1952,* 40 ALL INDIA REP. J. 6 (1953). But see Ramchandran, *A Uniform Civil Code for India,* 39 ALL INDIA REP. J. 12-14, 19-22 (1952).

[15]

ATEEQUE KHAN, LL. M.
Reader in Law, M.D. University, Rohtak

WOMEN'S DISABILITIES UNDER THE MODERN HINDU LAW OF PROPERTY : A CONSTITUTIONAL PERSPECTIVE

I. Introduction

Women's disability to own property seems to be a notable feature of the old Hindu law.[1] To a considerable extent that continues even after the enactment of the Hindu Succession Act of 1956.[2] Notably, this Act is a part of the Hindu Code which was enacted by the Indian Parliament over half a decade after the enforcement of the Constitution, among the basic objectives whereof, among others, are equality and socio-economic justice.[3]

The Hindu succession Act consists of only thirty sections—of which the last one (i.e., section 30) deals with, and is supplementary to, some other laws on the subject of testamentary succession.[4] The Act, in its preamble, envisages "to amend and codify the law relating to intestate succession among Hindus". The *Mitakshara* law of coparcenary is, therefore, outside the scope and objects of the Hindu Succession Act.[5] The Act, merely for reference sake, also takes note of agricultural properties succession to which is, substantially, governed by different post-independence local enactments pertaining to *zamindari* abolition and land reforms.[6]

In the context of a Hindu female's right to property, this paper briefly examines how far the statutory rules of inheritance, succession through survivorship and partition are in conformity with the constitutional objectives of equality and socio-economic justice. This will be done in the light of some judicial decisions and provincial legislations.

II. Pitfalls of coparcenary system

It has been said that:

> "The egalitarian principle in the matter of inheritance rights cannot be ignored for too long if equality between the sexes and respect for human dignity should inform family relations and property rights".[7]

Primogeniture

Following the constitutional objective of equality, the Hindu Succession Act has, impliedly, abolished the concept of "impartible estates" excepting those specifically saved by section 5 (ii) Consequently the archaic rule of primogeniture—an old custom that recognised a preferential right to succeed exclusively in favour of the eldest male and to the exclusion of all other descendants including females—has also gone. This implication of section 5 (ii) has been judicially confirmed in a case involving Nagaruntari Estate of Bihar.[9] Thus, the rule of primogeniture stands abolished and succession to the so-called impartible estates is now governed by the Hindu succession Act.

Survivorship

Anologous to primogeniture, the rule of survivorship in favour of men is, however, still retained by the statute. Section 6 of the Act provides a general rule to the effect that when a *Mitakshara* coparcener dies after the commencement of the Act, his undivided interest in the coparcenary property "shall devolve by survivorship upon the surviving (male) members of the coparcenary and not in accordance with this Act". Thus, the *Mitakshara* law of coparcenary continues to operate in the absence of specified heirs of class I, to the exclusion of new law of intestate succession envisaged by the Act[10].

It is a fact of common knowledge that a female can neither become a *karta* of the *Mitakshara* Hindu joint family, nor can she be a coparcener.[11] Emanating from the very concept of coparcenary, the discriminatory rule of survivorship is, however, still sustained even by the courts as they do not regard it as repugnant to the provisions of article 15 of the Constitution.[12] In our opinion, it is against the constitutional parameters of equality and socio-economic justice. Far back in 1929 Nehru had said:

> "Joint family system of Hindus, a rule of feudal age, utterly out of keeping with modern conditions, must go".[13]

What Nehru had so condemned as a "feudal relic" exists even today and perpetuates inequality in inheritance between sons and daughters.

Notional partition

To the aforesaid general rule that recognises survivorship an exception is, of course, provided by section 6 of the Act.[14] According to this exception, when a *Mitakshara* coparcener dies after the commencement of the Act and is survived by a female relative belonging to class I of heirs, or a male heir of class I claiming through a female heir of the same class,[15] the undivided interest of the deceased intestate coparcener in the coparcenary property shall be governed by the new law of intestate succession under the Act and not by the rule of survivorship. Accordingly, when an undivided *Mitakshara* coparcener dies leaving behind any of the nine class I heirs referred to in section 6 the law of intestate succession as laid down by the Act becomes applicable to his undivided share in the coparcenary property. The interest of the said coparcener shall be deemed, by an essential fiction of notional partition imposed by the law under Explanation I to section 6 of the Act,[16] to be the share in the property that would have been allotted to him if a partition of the property had taken place immediately before his death, irrespective of whether the deceased was entitled to claim partition or not.

Judicial interpretation

While interpreting this provision of the Hindu Succession Act, various High Courts gave divergent opinions till late seventies. Briefly, these interpretations were to the effect that:

(i) at the notional partition under section 6 no living person would actually get a share; only the share (so calculated) of the deceased coparcener would, by succession, go to his living class I heirs[17];

(ii) at the notional partition all living coparceners as well as the females entitled under the law of partition to a share would get the shares due to them; and in addition to this, share of the deceased coparcener would, by succession, go to his living class I heirs;[18] and

(iii) even at the notional partition (at which shares would be counted but not allotted) no shares would be counted for females, notional partition notwithstanding.[19]

Seemingly, setting the controversy at rest by upholding the extended view of statutory partition under section 6, the Supreme Court in *Gurupad's* case (1978),[20] gave a pragmatic ruling to the effect that the whole coparcenary will stand disrupted the moment one of the coparceners dies. To be more specific, where a coparcener dies leaving behind his widow, two sons and three daughters, the Supreme Court decided that:[21]

(a) at a notional partition the deceased as also his wife and two sons would be actually allotted 1/4 share each;

(b) the 1/4 share allotted to the deceased would, by succession, go equally to his widow, two sons and three daughters—each taking 1/4+1/6=1/24; and

(c) finally the widow and the two sons would get 7/24 (1/4+1/24) each and 1/24 would go to each of the three daughters.

The court held that partition for the purpose of section 6 was not a "processful step devised merely for the purpose of working out some other conclusions"; it was rather to be treated and accepted as a "concrete reality". In the words of Supreme Court (per Chandrachud, J.):

> "The fiction created by Explanation I has to be given its due and full effect. Once the assumption is made that there was a partition immediately before the death of the deceased, it must permeate the entire process of ascertainment of the ultimate share of the heirs through all its stages. All the consequences which flow from a real partition have to be logically worked out....The inevitable corollary of this position is that the heir will get his or her share in the interest which the deceased had in the coparcenary at the time of his death in addition to the share which he or she received or must be deemed to have received in the notional partition. The interpretation which we are placing upon the provisions of Section 6, its proviso and Explanation I thereto will further the legislative intent in regard to the enlargment of the share of female heirs qualitatively and quantitatively. ...By restricting the operation of the fiction created by Explanation I in the manner suggested by the appellant, we shall be taking a retrograde step, putting back as it were the clock of social reform which has enabled the Hindu women to acquire an equal status with males in matters of property. Even assuming that other interpretations of Explanation I are reasonably possible, we must prefer that interpretation which will further the intention of the legislature and remedy the injustice from which the Hindu women have suffered over the years".[22]

The Supreme Court, thus, made it possible for the main provision of section 6 to be subjected to a liberally extended view of its Explanation I. Undeniably, the judicial exposition reflects a progressive social trend. But to quote Professor Tahir Mahmood :

> "The question is whether this is what Parliament had intended while enacting section 6 in 1956"[23]

Recently, circumscribing the ambit of the extended view of notional partition in *Gurupad's* case and keeping in view the object of distributive justice behind the land ceiling laws, the Supreme Court (through Venkataramiah, J.) in *State of Maharashtra* v. *Narayan Rao*,[24] has significantly observed:

> "But it (the decision in *Gurupad's* case) cannot be an authority for the proposition that she ceases to be a member of the family on the death of a male member of the family whose interest in the family property devolves on her without her volition to separate herself from the family".[25]

In court's opinion the term "family" under the land ceiling laws is not confined to *Mitakshara* joint family but is wide enough to include *Dayabhaga* family as well, where despite unity of ownership members hold their property with definite shares. The Supreme Court emphasised that ownership of a definite share in the family property should not be considered a factor that militates against such a person being regarded as a member of the joint family for the purpose of land ceiling laws.[26]

III. Anti-women legal rules

Dwelling house—right to seek partition

The Hindu Succession Act does give shares to female heirs of class I in an intestate's property including the family dwelling house.[27] At the same time it denies them the right to claim partition, which it gives exclusively to their male co-heirs.[28] The share that goes to a female heir is regarded as her absolute property under section 14 of the Act. The statutory restriction imposed on her right to claim partition, however, negates the right. If the male heirs choose to partition the dwelling-house, no female heir (even their mother) can prevent them from doing so.[29] The Bombay and Orissa High Courts have held that where there is only one male heir he cannot refuse partition sought by the female heirs[30]; but Calcutta and Madras High Courts hold a contrary view.[31] Of late, the courts have even held that so long as there is a male heir no female heir can seek partition.[32]

Dwelling house—right of residence

Even more difficult to understand are the provisions made regarding the house of the father or mother. Daughters only have a right of residence, with no right to demand a partition till the brothers agree to partition their shares. Not all daughters have even the right of residence—to be entitled to it the daughter has to be unmarried, deserted separated or divorced. In other words, a daughter having normal life, as also one who is subject to harassment and cruelty in her husband's home, cannot claim the right of residence in the family dwelling house.[33]

IV. Conclusion

Whatever be the case, the existing rule of survivorship coupled with that of partition—both emanating from the age-old concept of *Mitakshara* coparcenary—are bound to cause hardship in practice, especially to the detriment of Hindu females. Sivaramayya rightly holds that the retention of *Mitakshara* coparcenary is a discrimination against daughters. The fact that such discrimination survived forty years of independence and is still entrenched, speaks volumes for discrimination against women in law and society.[34]

In order to remedy the situation, the Kerala state has already taken a lead and enacted the Kerala Joint Hindu Family System (Abolition) Act of 1976. On the other hand the Hindu Succession (Andhra Pradesh Amendment) Act of 1986 purports to confer on daughters rights in coparcenary properties.[35]

Looking to the constitutional mandate for equality and socio-economic justice, abolition of *Mitakshara* coparcenary should no longer be deferred.

References

* Paper presented at the National Seminar on "Law and Women" held at the Department of law, M.D. University, Rohtak on 26-28 March 1989.

1. The general rule relating to the incapacity of a woman to inherit was propounded by Baudhayana. In the presence of a son, son's and son's son's son, neither the widow nor the daughter of the deceased could inherit. The right of a restricted number of female heirs was recognised as an exception, but even when they inherited property, they took a "limited estate" and not an absolute estate like a male heir. By contrast, a son would acquire a right by birth in ancestral properties of the father according to the *Mitakshara* law. For further details see B. Sivaramayya, "Equality and Inequality: the Legal Framework", in *Equality and Inequality* ed. by Andre B'eteille, (Delhi 1984).
2. Justice Bhattacharjee finds it really surprising that the modern law-men with all their egalitarian philosophy and after declaring secularism and equality to be the pervading spirit of the National Charter have, almost with the zeal of a bigot, assigned to "religion" such a powerful and effective role in the Hindu Law Acts

of 1955-56. see his *Hindu Law and the Constitution,* 120 (Calcutta 1983).

3. S.P. Sathe points out that even Nehru's government could not abolish joint family property the source of discrimination against the daughter of a Hindu family. See his article in *Ineqality and the Law* by B. Sivaramayya in 30 *JILI* 507 (1988).
4. The Indian Sucession Act of 1925.
5. Kiran B. Jain, "A Review of the Hindu Sucession (Andhra Pradesh Amendment) Act 1986", VIII *Islamic CLQ* 225 (1988).
6. U.P., M.P., and Rajasthan have special rules for devolution of agricultural property. In U.P. *bhumidhari* rights devolve according to the special rules laid down in sec. 171 of the Zamindari Abolition and Land Reforms Act 1951, under which there is a clear and marked preference for males over females.
7. N.R. Madhava Menon, "Introduction", *Proceedings of National Convention on Uniform Civil Code for All Indians,* ix (New Delhi, 1986).
8. Section 5 (ii) of the Hindu Succession Act provides:

   > "This Act shall not apply to any estate which descends to a single heir-by the terms of any conenant or agreement entered into by the Ruler of any Indian State with the Government of India, or, by the terms of any enactment passed before the commencement of this Act".

9. *Bhaiya Ramanuj* v *Lalu Maheshanui,* AIR 1968 pat Pat 464.
10. *Raghunath* v *Rikhiya,* AIR 1985 Pat 29.
11. See Lotika Sarkar, "Empowering Women", *Seminar* 363 [November] 35-40.
12. *Nalini* v *State of Bihar,* AIR 1977 Pat 171; *Commissioner of Income Tax* v *Seth Govindan,* AIR 1966 SC 24, as cited in R(R.C. Nagpal, *Modern Hindu Law,* 635 (Lucknow, 1983).
13. Lotika Sarkar, op. cit., supra n. 11, at 39.
14. Proviso to section 6 of the Hindu Succession Act, reads:

   > "Provided that if the deceased has left him surviving a female relative specified in class I of the Schedule or a male relative specified in that class who claims through such female relative, the interest of the deceased in the Mitakshara coparcenary property shall devolve by testamentary or interstate succession, as the case may be under this Act and not by survivorship".

15. Class I heirs, as specified in the Schedule to the Act, are twelve in number. Of these twelve, those referred to in section 6 are all females and the daughter's son.

32 *Hindu Women's Rights*

16. *Explanation* I to section 6: "For the purpose of this section, the interest of a Hindu Mitakshara coparcener shall be deemed to be the share in the property that would have been allotted to him if a partition of the property had taken place immediately before his death, irrespective of whether he was entitled to claim partition or not".
17. *Controller of Estate v Anari Devi,* AIR 1972 All 179; *Shivaji Rao* v. *Rukminiya,* AIR 1973 Mys 113.; *P. Govinda v. Oblamma,* AIR 1971 AP 363; *Kethirajula v. M. Ramaswami,* AIR 1973 AP 58.
18. *Rangubai v. Lakshman* AIR 1966 Bom. 169; *Anand v. Haribandhu,* AIR 1967 Ori 194.
19. *Shrirambai v. Kalgonda,* AIR 1964 Bom. 263; *Mallava v. Paravatavva* (1970) 2 Mys LJ 571.
20. *Gurpad v. Hirabai,* AIR 1978 SC 1239, where the Supreme Court approved the decision of Bombay High Court in *Sushilabai v. Narayan Rao,* AIR 1975 Bom. 257
21. As analysed in Tahir Mahmood, *Hindu Law,* pp. 43-44 (Allahabad, 2nd. ed., 1986).
22. *Ibid.*
23. Ibid, p. 44.
24. AIR 1985 SC 716.
25. Ibid., at 721.
26. B. Sivaramayya, "Partition of Joint Hindu Family Property", 28 *JILI,* 226-28 (1986); B.N. Sampath, "Hindu Law", XVIII *ASIL* 245 (1982) and "Hindu Undivided Family in Taxation: A Saga of Conceptual Aberration," 20 *JILI,* 29-51 (1978); cf J.D.M. Derrett, "The Supreme Court and the H.U.F.: A Foot Note", 20 *JILI* 463-470 (1978); M.C. Bijawat, "The Law of Income Tax and Other Direct Taxes", XVIII *ASIL* 161 at 170 170 (1982); *Kaloomal (H.U.F.) v. C.I.T. Kanpur,* AIR 1982 SC 760; *Attorney General of Ceylon v. A.R. Arunachalam,* (1958) 34 ITR 42; *Commissioner of Income Tax v. Seth Govindram Sugal Mills,* (1965) 57 ITR 510 (SC); followed by the cases culminating in *Surjit Lal v. CIT Bombay* AIR 1976 SC 109; also S.R. Kharabanda & Prem Nath, HUF *Tax Planning and Assessment,* Ch. 15 (1985) and its review by D.C. Pandey, 28 *JILI,* 127 (1986).
27. *Putti Ramulu v. Kotha Gunnamma,* AIR 1975 Orissa 707.
28. Sec 23. *"Special provision respecting dwelling houses:* Where a Hindu intestate has left surviving him or her both male and female heirs specified in class I of the Schedule and his or her property includes a dwelling-house wholly occupied by members of his or her family then, notwithstanding anything

contained in this Act, the right of any such female heir to claim partition of the dwelling house shall not arise until the male heirs choose to divide their respective shares therein; but the female heir shall be entitled to a right of residence therein".

29. For a critique of the section see Paras Diwan, *Modern Hindu Law* 389 (Allahabad 1987)

30. *Anant Goparao* v *Janaki Bai,* AIR 1984 Bom. 319; *Hemlata v. Umasankari,* AIR 1975 Ori 208.

31. *Arun Kumar v. Janandra* AIR 1975 Cal. 232; *Surjya K. Das v Maya Dutta,* AIR 1982 Cal. 222; *Janabai v. T.A.S. Palani,* AIR 1981 Mad 62; *Vemavarapura v Chaturvedula* AIR 1981 AP 84.

32. *Patli v Kottia,* AIR 1985 Ori 70; *Punwasi v. Sukhadevi* AIR 1986 All 139.

33. Proviso to sec. 23 says: "Provided that where such female heir is a daughter, she shall be entitled to a right of residence in the dwelling house only if she is unmarried or has been deserted by or has separated from her husband or is a widow".

34. B. Sivaramayya, "The Hindu Succession (Andhra Pradesh Amendment) Act 1985; A move in the Wrong Direction," 30 *JILI* 167 (1988).

35. Since the Andhra Pradesh Amendment Act deals with the matter which is beyond the scope of the Hindu Succession Act, its constitutional validity has been questioned. See A.M.L. Narasimha Rao, "Hindu Succession (A.P. Amendment) Act, 1986: A Critical View". AIR 1988 *Journal* 85.

[16]

GENDER AND ECONOMIC INEQUALITY IN INDIA: THE LEGAL CONNECTION

DR. GITA GOPAL*

A woman is never fit for independence; her father protects her in childhood, her husband protects her in her youth, and her sons protect her in her old age.[1]

I. INTRODUCTION

The definition and institutionalization of equal rights at law is an important tool to combat the high degree of gender inequality in India. Gender equality is a constitutional mandate and many laws have been passed to improve the traditionally inferior social and

---

* M.A., 1976, L.L.B., 1980, Kerala University; L.L.M., 1981, S.J.D., 1988, Harvard University. Dr. Gopal is an Advocate in the Supreme Court of India and an attorney in Virginia. The author wishes to gratefully acknowledge the comments of Ms. Nena Manley on an earlier draft of this article.

[1] G. BUHLER, THE LAWS OF MANU 195 (F. Max Muller ed., 1990). Hindu law is based upon the Manusmritis or code of Man, of which Manu is the author. *Id.* According to the laws of Manu a woman must worship her husband as God even if he is a womanizer. NEERA DESAI & MAITHREYI KRISHNARAJ, WOMEN AND SOCIETY IN INDIA 28–29 (1987). A woman also should be kept dependent by her husband because she is passionate and disloyal by nature. *Id.* at 29.

economic status of women. Only a few privileged women benefit from this legal reform. Such legal reform includes the right to receive equal pay,[2] to receive maternity benefits,[3] to own or inherit property,[4] to terminate unwanted pregnancies,[5] and to be protected from cruelty at the hand of husbands through divorce or judicial separation.[6]

These legislative reforms have perpetuated a myth that Indian women occupy a high status in Indian society.[7] The reality is, however, that legislation has not improved everyday life for the majority of women. Seventy-one percent of Indian women are illiterate.[8] Ninety percent of the female labor force works in the underpaid and largely unregulated sectors of the economy.[9] A majority of women hold little or no property in their own names. Economically, socially, and politically, women remain at the lowest strata of society in India.

The inferior status of women in India is often attributed to the ineffective and inadequate implementation of existing laws.[10] While this is a problem, the key factor is the interrelation between legislation and the treatment of women: many gender biased legislative

---

[2] The Equal Renumeration Act, No. 25 (1976) (India), *reprinted in* P.L. MALIK, INDUSTRIAL LAW 821 (1990).

[3] The Maternity Benefits Act, No. 53 (1961) (India), *as amended by* Act Nos. 51 of 1970, 21 of 1972, 52 of 1973, 53 of 1976, and Act 61 of 1988, *reprinted in* MALIK, *supra* note 2, at 1309; The Employees' State Insurance Act, No. 34 (1948) (India) § 50, *reprinted in* MALIK, *supra* note 2, at 609.

[4] Hindu Succession Act, No. 30 (1956) (India), *reprinted in* ALLAHABAD LAW AGENCY, NEW ACTS OF HINDU LAW (1992).

[5] Medical Termination of Pregnancy Act of 1971 § 3 (wife does not need husband's consent to terminate pregnancy).

[6] Hindu Marriage Act, No. 25 (1955) (India), *reprinted in* ALLAHABAD LAW AGENCY, NEW ACTS OF HINDU LAW (1992); INDIA PEN. CODE § 498-A. Cruelty is any willful conduct by a husband, or a relative of the husband, which is likely to drive the woman to commit suicide or to cause grave injury or danger to her life, limb, or health. *Id.*

[7] DESAI & KRISHNARAJ, *supra* note 1, at 46.

[8] GOVERNMENT OF INDIA, MINISTRY OF INFORMATION AND BROADCASTING, RESEARCH AND REFERENCE DIVISION, INDIA 1991, A REFERENCE ANNUAL 13 (1992) [hereinafter INDIA 1991]. This figure refers to the 1981 census.

[9] GOVERNMENT OF INDIA, SHRAMSAKTHI, REPORT OF THE NATIONAL COMMISSION ON SELF-EMPLOYED WOMEN 28 (1988) [hereinafter SHRAMSAKTHI REPORT]. The female labor force also has little occupational diversification. According to a 1981 census, approximately 79.4% of female workers are engaged in agricultural activities, mainly as laborers. *Id.* The large female representation in the agricultural sector can be misleading, as this type of employment is not an adequate substitute for challenging employment by which women can become financially independent.

[10] *See* Meredith Sherman Fahn, *Noncompliance with India's Dowry Prohibition Act of 1961: A Society's Reactions to Imposed Law,* 4 TEMPLE INT'L & COMP. L.J. 101, 120–129 (1990).

provisions, despite the constitutional guarantee of equality, continue to reiterate traditional feudal attitudes about women's property rights and fail to provide women with equal access to economic resources. The focus must be shifted towards the basis of discriminatory legislative provisions to understand why legislation perpetuates the economic dependency of women on men.

To illustrate this economic dependence of women, this article analyzes the role of modern legislation in defining property rights of Hindu women in India.[11] It examines the interrelations between law and women's economic status within the family. This article submits that while law technically confers an equal social status on women, it also constrains the potential development of women by sustaining patriarchal norms, thereby denying women the access to economic resources outside the family, and providing an inequitable distribution of property within the family.[12] Part II provides a brief overview of the Indian legal system in order to provide background necessary to understand the impact of the courts on women's property rights. Part III discusses women's property rights related to marriage. Part IV explores women's property rights upon divorce. Part V explains gender and property rights upon death: it begins with the devolution of property through testamentary powers and then focuses upon gender inequalities in the intestacy context. Part VI discusses the institutionalized discrimination that prevents equal opportunities to own land. This article concludes that legal reform must be approached with the goal of eliminating underlying patriarchal beliefs that exist in many of India's modern laws concerning the economic rights of women.

II. The Indian Legal System

A. *The Indian Legal System*[13]

The Constitution of India, adopted by the Constituent Assembly on November 26, 1949, came into force on January 26, 1950.

---

[11] Hindu law only applies to Hindus. *See infra* text accompanying note 24. India's population consists of Hindus (82.6%), Muslims (11.4%), Christians (2.4%), and Sikhs, Buddhists, Jains and other minorities (3.6%). India 1991, *supra* note 8, at 18.

[12] This article confines itself to an examination of economic rights of Hindu women within the family structure. For an examination of women within the workplace, see Desai & Krishnaraj, *supra* note 1, at 50–136. For a detailed analysis of Indian women's political progress, see Leslie J. Calman, Toward Empowerment: Women and Movement Politics in India (1992).

[13] *See* India 1991, *supra* note 8, at 25, 32, 52, 784–89; Marc Galanter, Law and Society

The Constitution guarantees fundamental rights—certain basic freedoms—to all citizens individually and collectively.[14] These include the right to equality before the law,[15] prohibition of discrimination by the State on grounds of religion, race, caste, sex, or place of birth,[16] and equality of opportunity in matters concerning public employment.[17]

The Constitution divides legislative powers between the Union and twenty-five states. The Indian Constitution is quasi-federal in that it is applicable to all states.[18] The Union government has exclusive powers to legislate on matters enumerated in List I of the seventh schedule of the Constitution.[19] The state governments have exclusive jurisdiction over matters enumerated in List II of the seventh schedule.[20] The Union and the states have concurrent powers over matters in List III of the seventh schedule.[21] Personal or customary laws in List III govern matters such as marriage, divorce, intestacy, succession, joint family and partition, and adoption.[22] Consequently, personal laws applicable to Hindus in one state need not necessarily be applicable to Hindus in other states.

There is an integrated system of courts to administer both Union and state laws. At the apex of the judicial system is the Supreme Court of India (Supreme Court). There is a High Court in each state or group of states. The Supreme Court has original, appellate, and advisory jurisdictions. Appellate jurisdiction can be invoked in matters involving a constitutional question or questions of law of general importance, or if a High Court is of the opinion that a question needs to be decided by the Supreme Court. Under each High Court there is a hierarchy of subordinate courts with the High Court having supervisory powers over all courts within its jurisdiction.

IN MODERN INDIA (Rajeev Dhavan ed., 1989); THE INDIAN LAW INSTITUTE, THE INDIAN LEGAL SYSTEM (Joseph Minattur ed., 1978).

[14] INDIA CONST. pt. III.

[15] *Id.* art. 14.

[16] *Id.* art. 15(1).

[17] *Id.* art. 16.

[18] *See* DR. DURGA DAS BASU, INTRODUCTION TO THE CONSTITUTION OF INDIA 30 (1976).

[19] DURGA DAS BASU, CONSTITUTIONAL LAW OF INDIA 496 (1977).

[20] *Id.* at 507.

[21] *Id.* at 515.

[22] *See* Paras Diwan, *Family Law*, *in* THE INDIAN LEGAL SYSTEM 633 (Joseph Minattur ed., 1978).

B. *The Constitution and Personal Laws*

Article 44 of the Constitution makes it a directive policy of the states "to endeavor to secure for the citizens a uniform civil code throughout the territory of India."[23] This has not been achieved: each religious group in India is governed by separate personal laws.[24] Hindu personal laws have been codified by the federal and state governments.[25] Many provisions in such laws, however, reflect gender biases prevalent in traditional Hindu law, which clearly contravene the constitutional guarantees of gender equality.[26] According to Article 13(1), the courts have the power to declare that all "laws in force" before the Constitution are void if they conflict with these fundamental rights.[27] State legislation that abridges fundamental rights is also void.[28]

The courts, however, have been reluctant to hold that gender bias in personal laws rises to the level of a constitutional violation. In *State of Bombay v. Narasu Appa Mali*,[29] for example, the court had to decide the validity of the Bombay Prevention of Hindu Bigamous Marriage Act of 1946 which did not apply to polygamous Muslims. The petitioner argued that Article 13 of the Constitution rendered personal Muslim law permitting polygamy void because the Muslim law violated Article 15(1)'s prohibition of sex discrimination.[30] The court rejected this argument and upheld the validity of the Hindu statute on two grounds. First, the court held that the Constitution excludes personal law from the purview of Article 13.[31] Second, even if the term "laws in force" included personal laws, the practice of polygamy would not violate Article 15(1) because the article is based on "vital and compelling" social, economic, and religious grounds, and not on grounds of gender.[32]

---

[23] INDIA CONST. art. 44.

[24] Diwan, *supra* note 22, at 633–34.

[25] Hindu Marriage Act, *supra* note 6; Hindu Succession Act, *supra* note 4; Hindu Adoption and Maintenance Act, No. 78 (1956) (India), *reprinted in* ALLAHABAD LAW AGENCY, NEW ACTS OF HINDU LAW (1992); Hindu Minority and Guardianship Act, No. 32 (1956) (India), *reprinted in* ALLAHABAD LAW AGENCY, NEW ACTS OF HINDU LAW (1992).

[26] *See infra* parts III & IV (Hindu Marriage Act); part IV (Hindu Adoption and Maintenance Act); part V.B (Hindu Succession Act); part VI (land reform laws).

[27] INDIA CONST. art. 13(1). For an in-depth discussion on the scope of Article 13, see DR. DURGA DAS BASU, SHORTER CONSTITUTION OF INDIA 63–65 (1989).

[28] INDIA CONST. art. 13(2).

[29] 1952 A.I.R. 84 (Bom.).

[30] *Id.* at 88.

[31] *Id.* at 89.

[32] *Id. But see* Krishna Singh v. Mathura Ahir, 1980 A.I.R. 707 (S.C.) (Supreme Court indicated in dicta that part III of the Constitution does not affect personal law).

Courts have also been reluctant to apply constitutional principles to statutory provisions affecting the domestic domain. For instance, in *Kaur v. Chaudhary*[33] the issue was whether the statutory remedy of the restitution of conjugal rights violated the constitutional right of "personal liberty" in Article 21.[34] The Delhi High Court held that "in the privacy of the home and the married life neither Article 21 nor Article 14 have any place."[35] Upon review, the Supreme Court affirmed the decision, but did not address the question of whether constitutional principles apply to the home.

A recent ray of hope was seen in *In re Amina*,[36] a decision by a single judge bench of the Bombay High Court. The *Amina* judge held that the *Narasu Appa Mali* decision was erroneous and that personal laws must also be subject to fundamental rights.[37] The judge requested that this matter of public importance be heard by a larger bench.[38] While the matter appears straightforward, the religious and political underpinnings may prevent it from being taken up for further discussion. Nevertheless, it remains a matter of crucial importance for Indian women and requires resolution in order to achieve gender equality.

C. *The Challenge for Women: Social vs. Economic Laws*

Despite this existing confusion over whether constitutional principles are applicable to personal laws, the concept of gender equality has found significant legislative acceptance in redefining the social status of Hindu women, even in the realm of personal law. For example, the concept of equality prevails within the home, as the law refuses to accord men higher social status over women.[39]

---

[33] 1984 A.I.R. 66 (Del.).

[34] Article 21 protects life and personal liberty. INDIA CONST.

[35] *Kaur*, 1984 A.I.R. at 75. The court further stated:

> Introduction of constitutional law in the home is most inappropriate. . . . In a sensitive sphere which is at once intimate and delicate the introduction of cold principles of constitutional law will have the effect of weakening the marriage bond.

Id.

[36] 1992 A.I.R. 215 (Bom.).

[37] *Id.* at 219.

[38] *Id.* at 222.

[39] *See, e.g.*, Hindu Succession Act, *supra* note 4, § 14 (both spouses may hold and alienate property), § 30 (both spouses have full testamentary powers over their property); Hindu Marriage Act, *supra* note 6, § 13(1) (both spouses may sue for divorce on identical grounds), § 25(1) (both spouses may sue for maintenance), and § 9 (both spouses may sue for judicial restitution of conjugal rights); The Suppression of Immoral Traffic in Women and Girls Act, No. 104 (1956) (India) (prohibits immoral trafficking of women and protects the victims of prostitution); INDIA PEN. CODE § 498-A (cruelty by husband is a criminal offense); The Dowry

The constitutional guarantee of equality is therefore partially fulfilled. Indian women enjoy a social status of equality under the law that is enviable when compared with the position of women in other developing countries, and in some aspects, in developed countries. To enjoy such social status it is important that women have access to economic resources. Legislation regulating such access, however, is not based on standards of equality. Legal reform has sustained patriarchal norms and has fostered the dependence of women through their economic marginalization. Equality is sometimes overtly rejected, as legislative provisions may express a clear preference for males. In other cases, equality is covertly rejected by imposing gender blind norms upon an inherently unequal socio-economic relationship, which strengthens the powerful male interest. Parts III–VI illustrate the inequitable relationship between women and access to property within the family structure.

III. Women's Property Rights Upon Marriage

A. *Dowry and* Stridhan*: The Introduction to Property*

Traditionally, a woman had access to, and control over, any *stridhan* she received upon marriage.[40] *Stridhan* is movable property voluntarily presented to the bride from her family and friends. It consists mainly of jewelry, money, and clothing.[41] While a woman does not have a legal right to receive *stridhan,* customary rules place an obligation on her family to provide her with some property upon marriage. The practice of *stridhan* has changed over the years and has been replaced by the concept of dowry: a price paid to the bridegroom's family in connection with the marriage. The size and nature of the dowry often controls the bargaining and finalization of the marriage plans. The custom of dowry places women in situations of unconscionable stress and violence. Young women some-

---

Prohibition Act, No. 28 of 1961 (India) § 4, *reprinted in* Justice B.P. Beri, Commentaries on The Dowry Prohibition Act, 1961 127–35 (1988) (asking for a dowry is a punishable offense); Medical Termination of Pregnancy Act, *supra* note 5, § 3 (husband's consent not required for medical termination of pregnancy); The Maternity Benefits Act, *supra* note 3 (provides maternity leave); The Factories Act, No. 63 (1948) (India), *reprinted in* Malik, *supra* note 2, at 856 (provides maternity leave); The Mines Act, No. 35 (1952) (India), *reprinted in* Malik, *supra* note 2, at 1339 (provides maternity leave); The Plantation Act (1951), *reprinted in* Malik, *supra* note 2, at 1709 (provides creches).

[40] For a detailed discussion on the nature of *stridhan,* see Beri, *supra* note 39, at 289–473; A.S. Altekar, The Position of Women in Hindu Civilization 217–33 (2d ed. 1987).

[41] *See* Fahn, *supra* note 10, at 119.

times commit suicide to release their parents from the burden of dowry or to escape the emotional pressure from their inlaws' request for additional dowry.[42] Another far-reaching effect of dowry abuse is the rise in female infanticide.[43]

In 1961, the Parliament responded to these increasing atrocities by enacting the Dowry Prohibition Act,[44] which prohibits the giving or taking of any dowry in connection with marriage.[45] Merely demanding a dowry is a punishable offense.[46] Any person other than the woman who receives a dowry holds it in trust for the benefit of the woman.[47] A judicial magistrate may act upon a complaint registered by a recognized welfare institution or organization.[48] One accused of taking or demanding a dowry has the burden of proof.[49] The judge has the discretion to grant bail and set the amount.[50] If a woman dies an unnatural death within seven years of her marriage, any dowry received by her or on her behalf will be transferred to her children, if any, or to her parents.[51] Further, the Indian Penal Code has codified the offense of dowry death—a woman dying of unnatural causes under harassment by her husband or any relative.[52] The Evidence Act also has been amended so that the person accused of committing a dowry death is presumed guilty when it is

---

[42] *Id.* at 113.

[43] *Female Infanticide in Rajasthan*, INDIA SPEAKS, Oct. 8, 1992, at 21, provides a chilling story:

> The Rajput families have only one daughter each. Only the eldest daughter is allowed to survive as it is difficult to get a daughter married. The women admit that almost every family in the village is guilty of murdering their second daughter.

See generally John Van Willigen & V.C. Channa, *Law, Custom, and Crimes Against Women: The Problem of Dowry Death in India*, 50 HUM. ORGANIZATION 369, 370 (1991).

[44] Dowry Prohibition Act, *supra* note 39.

[45] *Id.* § 4. Dowry is:

> [A]ny property or valuable security given or agreed to be given either directly or indirectly (a) by one party to a marriage to another party to the marriage or (b) by the parents of either party to a marriage or by any other person, to either party to the marriage or to any other person at or before or any time after the marriage.

Id. § 2. There are certain exceptions. For example, gifts voluntarily given at the time of marriage, entered on a list made for this purpose, granted by relatives of the bride, and having values that are not excessive with respect to the financial status of the donor are of a "customary nature." *Id.* § 3.

[46] *Id.* § 4.

[47] *Id.* § 6.

[48] *Id.* § 7(c).

[49] *Id.* § 8-A.

[50] *See id.* § 8(2).

[51] *Id.* § 6(3).

[52] INDIA PEN. CODE § 304-B (1986).

shown that a woman has been subjected to cruelty or harassment for, or in connection with, a demand for dowry.[53]

The significant and well-intentioned legal reforms, however, have not been effective.[54] Dowry remains an increasing problem. Bride burning—often reported as kitchen accidents—is the most common form of violence against women. In 1986 alone there were 1,319 reported cases of bride burning nationally.[55]

The fault lies with the nature of the legislative intervention. *Stridhan* traditionally provided a woman with socially acceptable access to a share of her family's property upon marriage when she moved into her husband's family. Any remaining property was reserved for her brothers or, in other words, kept within her parents' family. Once legislation gave women access to family property through inheritance, irrespective of their marital status,[56] the belief was that the practice of giving *stridhan* would be redundant. Dowry could then be restricted, provided that there were exceptions for legitimate gifts upon marriage. While the reasoning behind the Dowry Prohibition Act appeared technically logical, the reality was that, given patriarchal traditions and attitudes, women do not normally inherit family property. For example, there are no prohibitions on a person's testamentary power to will exclusively family property to the sons.[57] In this situation, the prohibition of dowry weakens the socially accepted access to property by women.

If prohibiting dowry was the only solution, such legislation should have included complimentary measures to provide women with meaningful access to alternative property. For example, "jointly-owned matrimonial property" remains a foreign concept in India.[58] If women were allowed to jointly own their *stridhan* and

---

[53] INDIA EVIDENCE ACT § 113-A, No. 1 (1872) (India). The India Evidence Act is analogous to the United States Federal Rules of Evidence.

[54] *See* Fahn, *supra* note 10, at 120–29 (arguing that the Dowry Prohibition Act is a failure because of lack of enforcement, legal loopholes, judicial bias against women, women's lack of financial resources, and lack of support from the Indian people).

[55] Van Willigen & Channa, *supra* note 43, at 369. "Police records do not match hospital records for third degree burn cases among younger married women; far more violence occurs than crime reports indicate." *Id.*

[56] *See infra* part V.B (intestacy).

[57] *See infra* part V.A (wills).

[58] By contrast, United States law provides a surviving spouse with rights to property regardless of gender. There are two prevailing views in the United States. First, separate property states have "elective share" statutes that allow a "surviving spouse to take a fee interest in property against a will only in property which the decedent owned at death." WILLIAM M. MCGOVERN ET AL., WILLS, TRUSTS & ESTATES INCLUDING TAXATION AND FUTURE

any marital property, a woman would be entitled to a more equitable distribution of resources within the family. Section 6 of the Dowry Prohibition Act currently provides that, in cases of dowry death, the dowry devolves upon a woman's children or her parents. This provision only affects property falling within the definition of the term "dowry." Although Section 6 is a positive provision, it should be modified to apply to any property belonging to the woman including her share of the newly provided marital property. A husband and his family would then run the risk of losing far more than just dowry upon committing a dowry offense which leads either to the woman's death or termination of the marriage. If the husband were forced to weigh his need for a greater dowry against losing half of the marital property, there may be fewer instances of wife harassment or wife burning. Without such precautions, however, it is not surprising that legislation such as the Dowry Prohibition Act has been highly ineffective and has had a significantly adverse effect on women's property rights, social welfare, and personal safety.

B. *A Wife's Economic Rights*

In patriarchal societies in India, although it is customarily accepted that a woman belongs to her husband's family upon marriage, a woman's rights to property within her husband's family are meager. Marriage in India is considered in terms of *obligations*, not *rights*. The law offers little help to a wife who seeks to be economically independent.

As a wife, a woman has little or no control over her husband's property. She has no right over any property legally belonging to her husband during his lifetime, even if it may have been acquired during the pendency of their marriage. The husband may will, gift, or waste the entirety of his property as he pleases. In *Vinod Kumar v. State*,[59] for example, the Punjab High Court held that a husband cannot be charged with criminal breach of trust for failure to return the wife's *stridhan* because "the matrimonial home connotes a jointness of possession and custody by the spouses even with regard to

---

INTERESTS § 3.8, at 117 (1st ed. 1988). The amount of the elective share varies from state to state. Second, community property states (there are only eight) view marriage as a partnership and recognize contributions made by a non-wage earning spouse such as a housewife. *Id.* § 3.10, at 136. Therefore, a surviving spouse receives half of the couple's community property—everything earned during the marriage. *Id.* § 3.10, at 133.

[59] 1982 A.I.R. 372 (P&H).

the moveable property exclusively owned by each of them."[60] The Supreme Court overruled *Vinod Kumar's* "jointness" concept in *Pratibha Rani v. Suraj Kumar,* holding that *stridhan* is the wife's absolute property.[61] Thus, the husband or his relatives would have no rights over the *stridhan* and they would be deemed trustees if the *stridhan* was ever placed in their hands.[62]

The *Pratibha Rani* holding is very short-sighted and does not promote a women's meaningful access to property.[63] A stronger statement would have been to accept and expand the "joint possession" theory articulated in *Vinod Kumar*[64] and to expand it so as to provide that, if a husband acquires an equal right to the wife's *stridhan,* the wife acquires an equal right to the husband's separate property. Furthermore, by restricting its holding to gifts which were for the wife's sole use, the *Pratibha Rani* court may have encouraged the taking of dowry or gifts in forms that could be used only by husbands. For example, the husband could argue that the gift of a television is not *stridhan* because the wife does not exclusively use the item. While an opportunity to introduce the concept of matrimonial property at a national level was lost in these cases, it will hopefully be raised again.

A woman is also entitled to acquire economic resources through employment. Even in such situations, however, the access remains limited by legal hurdles. The remedy of restitution of conjugal rights[65] poses such a problem. One may apply for restitution of conjugal rights when either spouse has "withdrawn from the society of another" without a reasonable excuse.[66] Courts have permitted husbands to use this legal remedy to prevent women from working in places away from the matrimonial home if a husband does not agree with a woman's desire.[67] The reasoning behind these decisions

---

[60] *Id.* at 376.

[61] 1985 A.I.R. 628 (S.C.).

[62] *Id.* at 633–36.

[63] For a contrary view on *Pratibha Rani v. Suraj Kaur,* see P.S. Jaeswal & Nishtha Jaeswal, *Anti-Dowry Legislation in India: An Appraisal,* 30 J. OF INDIAN LAW INST. 78 (1988).

[64] 1982 A.I.R. 372 (P&H).

[65] Hindu Marriage Act, *supra* note 6, § 9. In 1983 the High Court of Andhra Pradesh held that the restitution of conjugal rights violated the fundamental right of privacy and human dignity guaranteed by Article 21 of the Constitution. Sareetha v. Venkata Subbaiah, 1983 A.I.R. 356 (A.P.). The Supreme Court, however, later overruled this decision. Saroj Rani v. Sudarshan Kumar, 1984 A.I.R. 1562 (S.C.).

[66] Hindu Marriage Act, *supra* note 6, § 9.

[67] Surrinder Kaur v. Gurdeep Singh, 1973 A.I.R. 134 (P&H); Gaya Prasad v. Bhagwati, 1966 A.I.R. 212 (M.P.); Pothuraju v. Radha, 1965 A.I.R. 407 (A.P.); Tirath Kaur v. Kirpal Singh, 1964 A.I.R. 28 (Punj.). *But see* Radhakrishnan v. Dhanalakshmi, 1975 A.I.R. 331, 332

is that, because it is the husband's prerogative to choose the site of the matrimonial home, it therefore is the wife's obligation to live with the husband.

In *Garg v. Garg*,[68] however, the Delhi High Court held that it would be unconstitutional to give the husband the exclusive right to select the matrimonial home.[69] The court indicated that where the husband has a less renumerative position than the wife, and where the husband's conduct has been reproachable, the wife has a valid reason to live separately.[70] *Garg* does not actually provide a significant advancement for women because the court also held that, where a husband and wife cannot agree on the matrimonial home, the husband must have the final say.[71] For example, the law does not support a wife's desire to work in a distant place if the husband has the financial ability to look after her. In such a case it would be possible for the husband to obtain a decree of restitution of conjugal rights. Furthermore, the husband may obtain a decree of divorce one year after a decree of restitution of conjugal rights.[72]

Similarly, in the absence of a matrimonial proceeding for divorce or maintenance, the wife has no right to be maintained if she chooses to live separately, except upon proof of specific conditions.[73] By failing to place an obligation on the husband to support an economically dependent wife who chooses to live separately, the law does not provide the woman with an alternative remedy if there are inadequate grounds for divorce or judicial separation. Courts have both legitimized spousal abuse and shown a willingness to define narrowly stringent conditions by holding that beating a wife "once or twice" during a span of three years is not an adequate ground for living separately.[74]

Consequently, during the course of the marriage, the wife remains under the economic control of her husband. In light of the strong social and traditional attitudes that perpetuate such control,

---

(Mad.) (holding there is no unqualified rule that the wife must remain with her husband where separation results from financial needs or an implied arrangement between the couple); Pravinaben v. S.T. Arya, 1975 A.I.R. 69 (Guj.) (same).

[68] 1978 A.I.R. 296 (Del.).

[69] *Id.* at 301.

[70] *Id.* at 302.

[71] *Id.*

[72] Hindu Marriage Act, *supra* note 6, § 13 (1-A)(ii).

[73] Such exceptions occur when the husband: deserts the wife, acts with cruelty causing apprehension that she will be harmed or injured, suffers from virulent leprosy, has another living wife, keeps a concubine in the house, ceases to be a Hindu, or any other cause that justifies her living separately. Hindu Adoption and Maintenance Act, *supra* note 25, § 18(2).

[74] Shobha v. Manohar, 2 Divorce and Matrimonial Cases 169, 170 (1989).

it is disheartening that legal reform not only fails to attempt to break the economic dependence of women within the relationship of marriage, but even perpetuates it through existing archaic legal provisions.

IV. Women's Property Rights Upon Divorce

Before the Hindu Marriage Act of 1955, divorce was not permitted.[75] The Hindu Marriage Act provides both the husband and the wife the right to file a petition for a divorce decree.[76] Aside from its social unacceptability, divorce is usually not a realistic option for most women who have little or no financial independence or education.[77]

The legal system is inherently unfair to women seeking a divorce. As mentioned previously, a woman is the legal owner of her *stridhan*.[78] Under Section 27 of the Hindu Marriage Act, a divorce court may only adjudicate rights regarding property "presented, at or about the time of the marriage, which may belong jointly" to the couple.[79] Because *stridhan* is not joint property, a woman must endure two lawsuits. She must first participate in the divorce proceedings. The woman must then bring another suit in a civil court against her ex-husband to recover her *stridhan*. The additional legal expenses and stress from prolonged litigation deter women from trying to recover their property.[80] Another unpleasant alternative is that the wife can initiate an action against her husband for a criminal breach of trust if she can prove that the disputed property is part of a dowry which is illegal.[81] Section 27 of the Hindu Marriage Act therefore operates against a woman's economic interests.

Upon separation or divorce, both spouses have the right to ask for maintenance, although many women do not even know of this

---

[75] Vinaya Saijwani, *The Personal Laws of Divorce in India with a Comment on* Chaudry v. Chaudry, 11 Women's Rts. L. Rep. 41, 50 (1989) (provides comparison between Hindu and Muslim personal laws of divorce).

[76] *See supra* note 6, § 13(1). The grounds for divorce include: adultery, cruelty, desertion, apostasy, mental disorder, leprosy, sexually transmitted diseases, entrance into a religious order, or absence. *Id.*

[77] Terree McGovern, *Modern Matrimonial Matters in India*, 70 Women Law. J. 18, 19 (1984).

[78] Pratibha Rani v. Suraj Kumar, 1985 A.I.R. 628, 636 (P&H).

[79] *See supra* note 6, § 27.

[80] *See* Maharajan v. Sarojini, 1988 A.I.R. 175, 178 (Or.). The court further stated that "the consequence is not an enviable one, particularly in view of the weaker status of women in our society and thus there is urgent need of a remedial measure through appropriate legislation." *Id.*

[81] *Pratibha Rani*, 1985 A.I.R. at 643.

right.[82] Although maintenance orders are case-specific, courts have been relatively sympathetic towards women. Thus, in *Radhakumari v. Nair*,[83] the court held that a husband could not claim immunity from liability to pay maintenance even if the wife was supported by her parents.[84] There is no statutory definition of maintenance. Courts therefore consider factors such as social status, age, education, and the needs of the children.[85] In *Urmila Devi v. Hari Prakash Bansal*,[86] for instance, the court held that an able-bodied husband is capable of working, and, thus, should maintain and support his wife despite the fact that neither spouse had an income.[87] Furthermore, in *Waghmare v. Waghmare*,[88] the court held that the wife's right to *pendente lite* maintenance and to litigation expenses should be available without reference to conduct because the wife's claim to maintenance is an incident of the status of matrimony.[89]

A woman must face many hurdles in her fight to obtain maintenance. For example, in *Guredev Kaur v. Channo*,[90] the Punjab and Haryana High Court held that because it is a personal obligation, the payment of maintenance must cease with the death of the husband.[91] The widow would then have to file an application for maintenance against her husband's estate pursuant to Section 22 of the Hindu Adoption and Maintenance Act.[92] Another court has held that an agreement in which a husband waives his right to child custody in exchange for the wife's relinquishment of her right to maintenance does not violate public policy.[93]

Courts traditionally have not been generous regarding the amount of a maintenance order granted to a wife. In *Rambu Sharma v. State*,[94] the court held that *pendente lite* maintenance is one-fifth of the husband's average net income for the past three years minus the wife's income.[95] If a person who has sufficient means refuses to

[82] Hindu Marriage Act, *supra* note 6, §§ 24, 25; Hindu Adoption and Maintenance Act, *supra* note 25, § 18; INDIA CODE CRIM. PROC. § 125; *see* McGovern, *supra* note 77, at 19.

[83] 1983 A.I.R. 139 (Ker.).

[84] *Id.* at 143.

[85] *Id.* at 145.

[86] 1988 A.I.R. 84 (P&H).

[87] *Id.* at 86.

[88] 1979 A.I.R. 264 (Bom.).

[89] *Id.* at 266. *Pendente lite* maintenance provides support during the proceedings.

[90] 1986 A.I.R. 251 (P&H).

[91] *Id.* at 252.

[92] *Id.*

[93] Manjit Singh v. Savita Kiran, 1983 A.I.R. 281 (P&H).

[94] 1989 A.I.R. 261 (M.P.).

[95] *Id.*

provide maintenance, the Code of Criminal Procedure requires such person to make a monthly maintenance allowance that cannot exceed 500 rupees ($18.00 per month).[96] Moreover, the Code does not require the magistrate to consider the husband's financial strength. Positive movement in the area of maintenance amounts, however, was seen in *Hema v. Lakshmana Bhat.*[97]

In *Hema,* the court rejected the contention that the "one-fifth of the husband's income" ceiling in the Indian Divorce Act applies to Section 24 of the Hindu Marriage Act.[98] After considering the parties' affluent background and length of marriage, the court held that 1,000 rupees per month, and not 800 rupees per month as the lower court had ordered, was a reasonable amount.[99] Hopefully courts will follow *Hema*'s lead and grant financially realistic amounts after consideration of factors such as the length of the marriage and the woman's contribution to the marriage.

The standard for modifying or rescinding maintenance orders varies between husbands and wives. The concept of "chastity," an archaic provision that survived legal reform, also deters a woman from litigating her right to maintenance. Before granting a maintenance order against her husband, a court must inquire into the wife's chastity.[100] Courts can manipulate easily the concept of "chastity," as there is no statutory definition. If the husband's matrimonial petition is granted on the basis of the wife's adultery, the wife cannot claim maintenance.[101] Courts have held, however, that a wife may receive a subsistence maintenance even if the divorce was granted on the grounds of the wife's adultery.[102] One court has held that while a claim regarding a wife's chastity is relevant to determine the quantum of maintenance, it cannot be the basis to refuse mainte-

---

[96] INDIA CODE CRIM. PROC. § 125(1).

[97] 1986 A.I.R. 130 (Ker.).

[98] *Id.* at 132. The court further stated that "the [c]oncept of equality between the spouses has gained recognition. That is why [Section] 24 of the Act enables either spouse to make a claim. [The] [s]tatus of the wife as an equal partner in marriage is now generally accepted." *Id.*

[99] *Id.* at 133.

[100] Hindu Marriage Act, *supra* note 6, § 25(3); Hindu Adoption and Maintenance Act, *supra* note 25, § 18(3); INDIA CODE CRIM. PROC. § 125(4) (1973).

[101] Hindu Marriage Act, *supra* note 6, § 25(3); Sardari Lal v. Vishano, 1970 A.I.R. 150 (J&K); Sachindra Nath v. Banamala, 1960 A.I.R. 575 (Cal.) (a wife divorced on the grounds of proven unchastity should be left to the resources of her immorality). See PARAS DIWAN, MODERN HINDU LAW 224–26 (1981) for a more detailed discussion of the preceding cases.

[102] Gulab Jagdusa Kakwane v. Kamal Gulab Kakwane, 1985 A.I.R. 88 (Bom.); Yogeshwar Prasad v. Jyotei Rani, 1981 A.I.R. 99 (Del.); Nathulal v. Mana Devi, 1971 A.I.R. 208 (Raj.).

nance.[103] Existing maintenance orders may be modified or cancelled if the woman can be characterized later as "unchaste."[104]

By contrast, if the husband's adultery is the grounds for divorce, a grant of maintenance in favor of a husband may be modified or rescinded only if "he has sexual intercourse with any woman outside wedlock."[105] The "chastity" standard for women and the "intercourse outside wedlock" standard for men creates the situation where a husband's maintenance order will not be disturbed. It is impossible for a husband to have a relationship "out of wedlock" because the divorce and order of maintenance dissolve the "wedlock."

Even if the court grants a maintenance order to a woman, she still faces difficulties in collecting the money.[106] Thus, while the area of maintenance has been more favorable to women, the fight to enjoy these benefits is tedious because of archaic legal provisions and a costly legal process. There has been substantial legal progress in that both a husband and wife have the right to seek maintenance.[107] Legal reform, however, will not be complete until the elimination of many archaic provisions can be achieved. The law must recognize that the concept of maintenance is in itself obsolete. A woman seeking maintenance is merely asking for the return of her own property—a share of the joint marital property which she has helped amass during the marriage. Rules of chastity[108] and one-fifth share[109] have no place in such a proceeding.

V. Gender and Property Rights Upon Death

A. *Right to Inherit Property by Will*

Under Indian law, a will always takes priority over the devolution of property through an intestacy statute.[110] Both a husband

[103] *Yogeshwar Prasad,* 1981 A.I.R. at 99.

[104] Hindu Marriage Act, *supra* note 6, § 25(3); Hindu Adoption and Maintenance Act, *supra* note 25, § 25.

[105] Hindu Marriage Act, *supra* note 6, § 25(3).

[106] In *Pankajakshan v. Challamma,* the court stated:

> Even after fighting many courts for establishing a meager sum by way of maintenance, [the woman] is driven to a second set of legal proceedings to effectively get the money in hand.

2 Divorce and Matrimonial Cases 135, 138 (1987).

[107] Hindu Marriage Act, *supra* note 6, §§ 24, 25.

[108] *Id.* § 25(3).

[109] *See* Rambu Sharma v. State, 1989 A.I.R. 261 (M.P.).

[110] Hindu Succession Act, *supra* note 4, § 30. The India Succession Act governs all questions regarding the validity of a will.

and a wife have full testamentary powers over their property.[111] Although there is no prima facie discrimination, such unrestricted testamentary power is detrimental to women in a patrilineal and patriarchal society. Because property normally passes to male heirs, female heirs often lose all rights to property, except the right to be maintained in some cases. The propounder of the will has the burden to remove all reasonable doubt surrounding suspicious circumstances regarding the execution of the will, such as a shaky signature, a feeble mind, or *unfair and unjust disposition of property.*[112] In *Khusbir Singh v. The State,*[113] the Delhi High Court did not consider the total disinheritance of the wife and daughter by will in favor of a son as an *unfair or unjust disposition of property.*[114] The *Singh* court highlighted the fact that the father "could have well thought that he will solemnize the marriage of his daughter during his lifetime and that may have led him to disinherit her."[115] The court further stated that "it is not unknown of Indian parents to deprive their daughters of any share in their estate."[116] This reasoning illustrates the traditional belief that a father's obligation consists of conducting his daughter's marriage and transferring his own remaining property to his male progeny.

B. *Right to Inherit Property Upon Intestacy*

Access to productive resources or other family property through inheritance may be the only source of economic power for seventy-one percent of illiterate and unskilled women.[117] The Hindu Succession Act, which governs all issues concerning intestacy, provides significant changes to women's traditional property rights.[118] This statute eliminates traditional distinctions between married or unmarried daughters and women who have or do not have children.[119] Under the Hindu Succession Act, daughters, sons,

---

[111] *Id.*

[112] Venkatarama Aiyar v. Thimmajamma, 1959 A.I.R. 443, 444 (S.C.) (emphasis added).

[113] 1990 A.I.R. 59 (Del.).

[114] *Id.*

[115] *Id.* at 64.

[116] *Id.*

[117] *See* INDIA 1991, *supra* note 8, at 13.

[118] An intestate is one who does not dispose of property through a will. *See* Hindu Succession Act, *supra* note 4, § 3(g).

[119] *See* Chando Mahtain v. Khublal Mahto, 1983 A.I.R. 33 (Pat.) (holding the Hindu Succession Act abrogates the divestiture of property upon marriage provision in the now repealed Hindu Widows Remarriage Act of 1937).

widows, and widowers have equal rights to inherit their parents' or deceased spouse's self-acquired and intestate property.[120] A widowed daughter-in-law also has a right to her father-in-law's intestate property[121] if she does not remarry before her father-in-law's death.[122] Women are the absolute owners of any property acquired through intestacy.[123] The Hindu Succession Act, however, only represents partial reform of women's rights, as many discriminatory traditions have been codified.

1. Women's Right to Inherit Joint Family Property

The joint family, or "coparcenary" is the typical Indian family where three generations of patrilineal kinship live in the same household.[124] In such a patrilineal family, the son is the natural successor, a good investment, and insurance for the family.[125] The joint family continues as long as there is a male member, even by adoption. Coparceners control property in a joint family. A coparcener is a lineal male descendant (up to the third generation) who acquires the right of ownership by birth;[126] however, women cannot be coparceners.[127] Each coparcener has ownership over the entire property until partition,[128] and may ask for such a partition.[129] Furthermore, possession and enjoyment of property is common.[130]

---

[120] *See supra* note 4, § 8 (lists those entitled to property of male Hindu intestate) and § 15(1) (lists those entitled to property of female Hindu intestate). Self-acquired property is individually acquired and can be distinguished from inherited or joint family property.

[121] *Id.* § 8.

[122] *Id.* § 24.

[123] *Id.* § 4.

[124] Desai & Krishnaraj, *supra* note 1, at 186–87. Hindu law comprises the branches of Mitakshara and Dayabhaga. This part analyzes the Mitakshara coparcenary in which the three generations of males are "related to the male ego as grandfather and his brothers, father and his brothers, cousins, sons and nephews, and their wives, unmarried daughters and sisters." *Id.* at 187; *see* Sunderlal T. Desai, Mulla Principles of Hindu Law 238–317 (1990); Gurupad v. Hirabhai, 1978 A.I.R. 1239 (S.C.) (defining coparcenary). Unlike the Mitakshara coparcenary, which is applied in the majority of India, the Dayabhaga coparcenary is confined to Bengal and Assam. Lucy Carroll, *Daughter's Right of Inheritance in India: A Perspective on the Problem of Dowry*, 25 Modern Asian Studies 791, 793 (1991). For a detailed explanation of the Dayabhaga coparcenary, see *id.* at 802–05.

[125] Desai & Krishnaraj, *supra* note 1, at 187–88.

[126] Carroll, *supra* note 124, at 793.

[127] *See* Raghunath Tiwary v. Rikhiya, 1985 A.I.R. 29, 30 (Pat.) (daughter does not have right to joint property upon birth).

[128] *See* Carroll, *supra* note 124, at 793.

[129] *Id.* at 794. A partition increases the number of joint family estates; it does not create separate estates. *Id.*

[130] *See* Carroll, *supra* note 124, at 793.

Property may be alienated for legal necessity only upon concurrence of other coparceners.[131] A deceased member's interest lapses upon his death and merges into the coparcenary property; however, his interest does not devolve upon his natural heirs.[132] Other dependent females have the right to be maintained by joint family property. A widow obtains an equal share upon partition, but does not have the right to ask for a partition of family property.[133] The law recognizes this inequitable customary arrangement and even encourages the formation of such units by treating these joint families as separate taxable entities.[134]

Traditionally, the joint family system excluded the Hindu daughter from succession to her father's property if there was a son, son's son, or a widow.[135] The Hindu Succession Act, however, does not significantly alter the inequitable distribution of joint family property to women.[136] The statute only partially amends the customary property rules, allowing a coparcener's interest to devolve through a will or through the Hindu Succession Act to a surviving female relative specified in Class I or to a male relative in Class I who claims through such female relative.[137] Therefore, while Hindu males own a share of the family rights at birth, females must inherit it.[138]

---

[131] Gurupad v. Hirabhai, 1978 A.I.R. 1239 (S.C.).

[132] Carroll, *supra* note 124, at 793.

[133] Hindu Succession Act, *supra* note 4, § 23.

[134] Income Tax Act §§ 2(31), 10(2), *as amended by* Finance Act, 1989 and Direct Tax Laws (Amendment) Act, No. 3 (1989) (India), *reprinted in* M.C. BHANDARI, THE INCOME-TAX ACT/RULES WITH REFERENCER (1989–90); *See* Maureen A. Maloney, *An Analysis of Direct Taxes in India: A Feminist Perspective*, 30 J. INDIAN L. INST. 397, 404 (1988).

[135] Carroll, *supra* note 124, at 791–92.

[136] The Hindu Succession Act addresses only the Mitakshara system. *See supra* note 4, § 6; *supra* note 124 and accompanying text (definition of a Mitakshara coparcenary).

[137] *See supra* note 4, § 6; *see infra* note 147 (list of persons in Class I of the Schedule). Raj Rani v. The Chief Settlement Commissioner, 1984 A.I.R. 1234 (S.C.), provides an example of property succession:

> Where a Hindu died after the enforcement of the Act leaving behind him his widow, three sons and three daughters, the devolution of his Mitakshara coparcenary property would be as follows: . . . [H]e would have [received] one-fifth interest on partition between him and his wife and three sons. If once his interest was determined to be one-fifth before his death, his interest would devolve upon his widow, three sons and three daughters equally and thus the share of each one of them would be one-fifth [multiplied by] one-seventh that is one thirty-fifth each and because the widow had inherited her husband's interest after his death her share would be augmented by one-fifth that is one thirty-fifth [plus] one-fifth [which] equals eight thirty-fifths.

Id. at 1235.

[138] Van Willigen & Channa, *supra* note 43, at 374.

Because inheritance is an area where the state and national government can legislate concurrently,[139] a few states have provided women more equality in the joint family system. For example, the states of Andhra Pradesh and Tamil Nadu have improved significantly a woman's status under the joint family system by permitting women to assume the status of a coparcener.[140] The state of Kerala has even abolished the joint family system altogether.[141] Hopefully, other states will follow these leads and recognize the social and economic value of women.

2. Women's Right to the Dwelling House

Female heirs to a male Hindu intestate's property cannot ask for a partition of the intestate's dwelling house in which the intestate's family lives *until* the male heirs choose to divide their respective shares.[142] This is so even if the house is part of the intestate's separate property. A female heir who is a daughter has the right of residence in the dwelling house only if she is single, has been deserted by or is separated from her husband, or is a widow.[143] A widowed daughter loses her right to residence upon remarriage.[144] Thus, the law in this area reiterates traditional patriarchal concepts towards women.

3. Property Succession of Male and Female Intestates

Under the Hindu Succession Act, the property of male and female intestates devolves differently. There is a clear preference for agnates[145] over cognates.[146] Living children and the widow share a male's intestacy property with relatives listed in Class I of the schedule.[147] In the absence of these heirs, the property devolves

---

[139] BASU, *supra* note 19, at 515.

[140] Van Willigen & Channa, *supra* note 43, at 375.

[141] *Id.*

[142] Hindu Succession Act, *supra* note 4, § 23; *see* Punwasi v. Sukha Devi, 1986 A.I.R. 139, 140 (All.) (male intestate's married daughter may not ask for a partition of the dwelling house).

[143] Hindu Succession Act, *supra* note 4, § 23.

[144] *Id.*

[145] A person is an agnate of another if the two people are related by blood or adoption wholly through males. *Id.* § 3(a).

[146] A person is a cognate of another if the two are related by blood or adoption, but not wholly through males. *Id.* § 3(c).

[147] Class I includes the son, daughter, widow, mother, son of a pre-deceased son, daughter of a pre-deceased son, son of a pre-deceased daughter, daughter of a pre-deceased daughter, widow of a pre-deceased son, son of a pre-deceased son of a pre-deceased son, daughter of

upon relatives listed in Class II of the schedule, which gives priority to the male intestate's father and does not make any provisions for the intestate's wife's relatives.[148]

By contrast, succession to a female intestate's property depends on the type of property. In the absence of children, property inherited from the female intestate's parents devolves upon her father's heirs.[149] Property inherited from her husband or father-in-law would go to the husband's heirs in the absence of children by the husband.[150] A female intestate's self-acquired property, a gift, or property received under a valid will first devolves upon her children and her husband.[151] Absent the preceding heirs, the property devolves upon her husband's heirs[152] and then upon her parents.[153] Once again, concepts of gender equality give way to patriarchal considerations that treat women as extensions of their husbands by favoring their husbands' heirs.

C. *Widows' Property Rights*

As previously mentioned, a widow has the right to inherit property from her husband's estate, but she cannot prevent her husband from transferring his property to a third person through a will.[154] Her father-in-law has a legal obligation to maintain her only if he has coparcenary property and only if she cannot maintain herself through her husband, parents, children, or their estates.[155] A widowed daughter-in-law ceases to receive maintenance upon her remarriage.[156] Patriarchy is abandoned, as the father-in-law's obligation does not attach unless the widow's parents are financially unable to maintain their daughter.

---

a pre-deceased son of a pre-deceased son, and widow of a pre-deceased son of a pre-deceased son. *Id.* § 8(a). "The Schedule," which is listed as an appendix, is read in conjunction with Section 8 of the Hindu Succession Act.

[148] *Id.* § 8(b).

[149] *Id.* § 15(2)(a); *see* Raghuwar v. Janki Prasad, 1981 A.I.R. 39 (M.P.) ("inheritance" in Hindu Succession Act § 15(2)(a) refers to intestacy property, not property passed under a will).

[150] Hindu Succession Act, *supra* note 4, § 15(2)(b); *see* Jayantilal v. Chhanalal, 1968 A.I.R. 212 (Guj.).

[151] Hindu Succession Act, *supra* note 4, § 15(a)(1)(a).

[152] *Id.* § 15(1)(b).

[153] *Id.* § 15(1)(c).

[154] *Id.* § 30.

[155] Hindu Adoption and Maintenance Act, *supra* note 25, § 19.

[156] *Id.*

An illustration may help to clarify this concept. Consider an uneducated woman living in a nuclear family without any source of independent earnings. This woman has been married for fifteen years. Her husband dies, transferring his property to a third party by will. The wife cannot prevent this transfer nor can she sue her husband's estate for maintenance under the Hindu Marriage Act or the Criminal Procedure Code. Her father-in-law does not have the obligation to maintain her because there is no coparcenary property.[157] Her parents are not legally bound to maintain her because she is not a minor[158] and is married.[159] The law casts an obligation on the husband's heirs (the third party) to maintain the widow.[160] A better resolution would be to restrict the husband's testamentary powers so that he would be obligated to leave a specific percentage of his property for his dependents.

VI. Women's Ability to Own Agricultural Land

Hindu women traditionally have had few opportunities to be landholding members of their families. This injustice remains true in modern India and elevates the level of economic disparity between men and women because land is an important source of economic and social power in this predominantly agricultural society. Legislative reform has institutionalized the gender bias by giving male family members more access to land ownership and land resources than female family members. For example, in Uttar Pradesh, a state which comprises one-sixth of the population, the interest in land passes first "to the male descendants in the male line of descent."[161] The land passes to the widow or widowed mother of the pre-deceased male descendant only if there are no such males available and only if the widow has not remarried.[162]

Agricultural land comprises the bulk of real property in India.[163] The Hindu Succession Act, however, does not govern the devolution of tenancies of agricultural land.[164] Agricultural land

[157] Hindu Succession Act, *supra* note 4, § 4.

[158] Hindu Adoption and Maintenance Act, *supra* note 25, § 21(v).

[159] *Id.* § 20.

[160] *Id.* §§ 21, 22.

[161] Government of India, Department of Social Welfare, New Dehli, Towards Equality, Report of the Committee of the Status of Women in India 137 (1975) [hereinafter Towards Equality].

[162] *Id.*

[163] *Id.*

[164] *See supra* note 4, § 4(2).

devolves according to the legislation of individual states.[165] Land reform laws cannot be challenged on grounds of violating a fundamental right because they fall within the Indian Constitution's ninth schedule.[166] Furthermore, the lack of statutory definitions in the Hindu Succession Act or the General Clauses Act of 1897 for terms such as "tenancy rights" has given the states a great amount of discretion. The result has been the enactment of many state laws that restrict a woman's interest in agricultural land even though women constitute the majority of the labor force in agricultural industries—a key sector of India's economy.[167]

Land reform laws and procedures restrict the size of land holdings. Surplus land is distributed to landless persons or used for developmental purposes.[168] These laws also discriminate on the basis of gender. For example, when determining the ceiling on land that a family may hold in Maharashtra, land held by a daughter comprises part of the total amount of land held by the family, while a son holds land separately.[169] Government regulations regarding development projects also reflect the bias against the concept of women owning land. In the Sardar Sarovar Project, a power project in Gujarat, the state resettlement policy provides separate agricultural and residential land for adult male sons of those families affected by the project.[170] The project considers adult daughters as members of their primary families instead of providing them with separate property.[171]

Land is a scarce but very important economic resource in India. Admittedly, dividing land between sons and daughters may split the size of the holding which may diminish the land's economic value.[172] This economic disadvantage, however, does not justify depriving women of land, the means to empowerment. Gender-neutral efforts must be formulated to maintain land holdings at a productive economic level, especially in a country that claims to uphold the constitutional principle of gender equality.

---

[165] BASU, *supra* note 19, at 507.

[166] INDIA CONST. art. 31-B.

[167] *See* TOWARDS EQUALITY, *supra* note 161, at 137.

[168] The ninth schedule of the Indian Constitution lists various Land Reform and Land Ceiling Acts for the states.

[169] Maharashtra Agricultural Land (Ceiling on Holdings) Act, No. 26 (1961) (India) § 3.

[170] Government of Gujarat, Government Resolution No. RHB-1085-D (Nov. 1, 1985), at 5.

[171] *Id.*

[172] *See* ALTEKAR, *supra* note 40, at 246.

VII. Conclusion

Gender analysis of Hindu law relating to a woman's access to property within the home reveals a consistent pattern of subordination of women's economic interests. The combination of high levels of illiteracy, lack of outside training, and discriminatory social traditions further prevents a woman from gaining access to economic resources. While enjoying the formal status of equality at law, in essence, a woman remains economically dependent on her parents, husband, or children from birth until death. Manu lives with a vengeance![173]

Law can be an important tool for social transformation. In India, however, law often perpetuates the economic subordination of women through the lack of an equitable framework. The primary task remains to amend all legislative provisions that institutionalize economic distributions based on gender differences and those that increase a woman's economic dependency. Such legislative reforms must be accomplished in a sensitive manner, recognizing that the implementation of gender-neutral legislation will not be accepted automatically into the hierarchical and male-dominated society. The present impact of legislation on Indian society admittedly has been very limited. Patriarchy, age-old social traditions, unequal economic relationships, lack of enforcement, and lack of means for women to become more independent, all play a significant role in creating and sustaining the inequality of women. Examination of women's status in the family and society is incomplete without the discussion of problems in a holistic manner.

Removal of legal constraints and legitimization of reform of property rights is an important and catalytic first step for women. Equal access to productive resources will provide women with an enabling environment in which they can break down gender-based traditional barriers that currently seem impenetrable. An equitable share of family property, however little at first, will give women relative strength within the family to resist oppressive relationships. Women will be taken seriously only when they have these economic rights. Until then, the emergence of women as equal players in the mainstream of Indian life will remain as it has for the last four decades—a slow, tedious, and sometimes regressive process.

[173] *See supra* note 1 and accompanying text.

Name Index

www.ingramcontent.com/pod-product-compliance
Lightning Source LLC
LaVergne TN
LVHW102105300926
849161LV00014B/3054